America's Freedom Trail

Massachusetts

New York

New Jersey

Pennsylvania

*A Tour Guide to Historical
Sites of the Colonial and
Revolutionary War Period*
BY M. VICTOR ALPER

COLLIER BOOKS

A Division of Macmillan Publishing Co., Inc.

New York

COLLIER MACMILLAN PUBLISHERS

London

America's Freedom Trail

Macmillan Publishing Co., Inc.
866 Third Avenue, New York, N. Y. 10022
Collier Macmillan Canada, Ltd.

Library of Congress Cataloging in Publication Data

Alper, M   Victor.
  America's freedom trail.

  Includes index.
    1.   Massachusetts—Description and travel—
1951–   —Guide-books.   2.   New York (State)—
Description and travel—1951–   —Guide-books.
3.   New Jersey—Description and travel—1951–
—Guide-books.   4.   Pennsylvania—Description and
travel—1951–   —Guide-books.   I.   Title.
F62.3.A46   1976b   974   75–44415
ISBN 0–02–097150–8

First Collier Books Edition 1976

America's Freedom Trail is also published in a hardcover
edition by Macmillan Publishing Co., Inc.

Designed by Jack Meserole

Maps by Clarice Borio, New York City, New York

Printed in the United States of America

For Hannah and Sam

Contents

New York

New Jersey

Pennsylvania

Useful Facts

List of Maps

Acknowledgments

I am grateful for the courteous assistance of the staffs of the Boston Public Library, New York Public Library, Free Library of Philadelphia, Library of Congress, Albany Public Library, Morristown Public Library, and Princeton Public Library. The following institutions also have been most helpful: the Society for the Preservation of New England Antiquities, Quincy Historical Society, New York State Historic Trust, Westchester County Historical Society, Monmouth County Historical Association, Salem County Historical Society, Historical Society of York County, Pennsylvania Historical and Museum Commission, and the National Park Service of the United States Department of the Interior.

I am indebted to the following people, who have been generous in their aid: Gail Rotegard, Boston 200 Corporation; J. Leopold Romero, Boston; Lawrence Whipple, Director, Lexington Historical Society; Gregory Farmer and David Proper, Old Deerfield; Mrs. Hall Carpenter, Quincy; Geraldine Bell, Saratoga National Historical Park; Michael Catoggio, Albany; Colonel Charles Briggs, Johnstown; Jean Graff, Rockingham; Mrs. Newlin Watson, Greenwich; Milicent Feltus, Freehold; E. Wilmer Fisher, Superintendent, Washington Crossing State Park; Allen Montgomery, Curator, Valley Forge State Park; and Robert A. Aylward, Washington, D.C. Thanks is due to J. Sokol for many stimulating discussions and to F. Roffman for an astute reading of sections of the manuscript.

I also wish to acknowledge my debt to these excellent books: Mark M. Boatner, *Encyclopedia of the American Revolution* (New York, 1966); Beverly Da Costa, ed., *Historic Houses of America* (New York, 1971); Marshall

Davidson, *Colonial Antiques* (New York, 1967); *Historical Handbook* Series, National Park Service (Washington, D.C., dates vary); John C. Miller, *Triumph of Freedom* (Boston, 1948); Frank Sarles and Charles Shedd, *Colonials and Patriots* (Washington, D.C., 1964); George Scheer and Hugh Rankin, *Rebels and Redcoats* (New York, 1957); and Christopher Ward, *The War of the Revolution* (New York, 1952).

To the Reader

This book describes major events and battles of the American Revolution and presents practical information for travelers who wish to explore America's Freedom Trail. Although Colonial and Revolutionary War Sites are emphasized in the text, subordinate sections—Non-Revolutionary Sites of Interest and Recommended Side Trips—are included to permit travelers to experience other aspects of a region's history. The suggested Walking and Driving Tours list the individual sites in the order encountered by sightseers. Afterward, these sites, arranged *alphabetically* according to category, are described in detail.

The narrative begins at Lexington and Concord—where the first shots of the Revolutionary War were fired—and ends at York, Pennsylvania, with the adoption of the Articles of Confederation, America's first constitution. The reader proceeds southward: from Massachusetts, through New York and New Jersey, and then into Pennsylvania. Since the narrative units are self-contained, however, one may start at any point.

Visitors to sites are advised to verify schedules and admission fees, which are subject to change. Because many historic houses are being restored for the Bicentennial, their contents may differ slightly from the descriptions herein. If recommended roads are under construction, alternate routes may be followed with the aid of a good road map. Every effort has been made to print the most recent data, but the author and the publisher cannot be responsible for any changes of information or omissions.

As you read these pages, it is hoped that the fascinating drama of the American Revolution may excite your imagination and stir your spirit.

Chronology of the American Revolution

1773

MAY 10
To save the mismanaged East India Company from bankruptcy, Parliament partially refunds taxes the company had paid and permits shipment of tea directly to retailers in the American colonies. Established importers and citizens protest.

DECEMBER 16
Boston Tea Party: Men disguised as Indians board three ships in Boston Harbor and heave 342 chests of tea into the water.

1774

MAY–JUNE
The Coercive Acts ("Intolerable Acts") passed by Parliament go into effect. The Massachusetts Government Act (May 20) modifies the provincial government by providing a new council under a military governor, who also has authority over town meetings. The Administration of Justice Act (May 20) protects officials of the Crown accused of capital offenses by permitting them to be tried elsewhere. The Boston Port Bill (June 1) closes Boston to commerce. The extension of the Quartering Act (June 2) provides for the housing of British troops in America.

JUNE 22
The Quebec Act grants the territory between the Ohio and Mississippi Rivers to the province of Quebec, thereby estab-

lishing Roman Catholicism and French civil law in the area.

SEPTEMBER 5   The First Continental Congress (fifty-six delegates from twelve colonies) meets in Philadelphia.

SEPTEMBER 9   Delegates from towns in Suffolk County, Massachusetts, adopt the Suffolk Resolves, which denounce the Coercive Acts as unconstitutional and recommend economic sanctions against England.

OCTOBER 25   Angry women of Edenton, North Carolina, sign a resolution protesting the tax on tea and the harsh policies of the British government.

1775

MARCH 23   Patrick Henry delivers his "Give me Liberty or give me Death" speech in Richmond, Virginia.

APRIL 19   At Lexington, Massachusetts, British soldiers fire on the Patriots, then march to Concord where the Redcoats are forced to retreat.

APRIL 19   The siege of Boston begins: Patriot forces surround the British garrisoned in the city.

APRIL 20   Royal Governor Dunmore of Virginia orders powder and munitions secretly removed from the Williamsburg Magazine, causing Patriots to march on the town.

MAY 10   The Second Continental Congress con-
              venes in Philadelphia.

MAY 10   Fort Ticonderoga, New York, is captured
              by a detachment of Green Mountain
              Boys under Ethan Allen and troops com-
              manded by Benedict Arnold.

MAY 24   John Hancock is elected president of
              the Continental Congress.

JUNE 11–12   The first naval battle of the American
              Revolution occurs near Machias, Maine,
              resulting in the capture of two British
              ships, the *Margaretta* and the *Unity*.

JUNE 15   The Second Continental Congress elects
              George Washington Commander-in-Chief
              of the Continental Army.

JUNE 17   At the Battle of Bunker Hill (Breed's
              Hill) the British rout the Patriots but
              sustain high casualties.

JULY 3   In Cambridge, Massachusetts, Washing-
              ton assumes command of the army.

DECEMBER 22   Esek Hopkins is appointed Commander-
              in-Chief of the Continental Navy.

1776

JANUARY 1   The American assault on Quebec fails.

JANUARY 9   Thomas Paine publishes *Common Sense*,
              urging Americans to declare their in-
              dependence of Great Britain.

FEBRUARY 27   The Patriots are victorious at the Battle
              of Moore's Creek, North Carolina.

MARCH 17 — The British evacuate Boston.

APRIL 17 — John Barry is the first commissioned officer of the American Navy to capture a British warship, the *Edward*.

JUNE 28 — Patriot forces on Sullivan's Island, South Carolina, repulse the British fleet, preventing its entry into Charleston Harbor.

JULY 4 — The Continental Congress adopts the Declaration of Independence.

AUGUST 27 — The British overpower the Americans during the Battle of Long Island.

AUGUST 29 — Washington's defeated troops retreat to Manhattan.

SEPTEMBER 15 — British warships move into the East River and force the Americans to withdraw from mid-Manhattan.

SEPTEMBER 16 — At Harlem Heights, New York, the Americans prove their ability to drive back the enemy.

SEPTEMBER 21 — Nathan Hale is captured.

SEPTEMBER 26 — Congress appoints Benjamin Franklin a Commissioner to Paris.

OCTOBER 28 — The Patriots are defeated at White Plains, New York.

NOVEMBER 16 — Fort Washington on Manhattan is captured by British and German troops.

NOVEMBER 20 — Americans abandon Fort Lee, New Jersey.

DECEMBER 8   The British occupy Newport, Rhode Island.

DECEMBER 26   After crossing the Delaware River, Washington and his men surprise the Hessians quartered at Trenton.

1777

JANUARY 3   At the Battle of Princeton Washington's counteroffensive compels the British to withdraw.

JANUARY 6   Washington establishes his winter headquarters at Morristown, New Jersey.

JUNE 13   The Marquis de Lafayette arrives in America to join the Patriot cause.

JUNE 14   The Continental Congress passes a resolution authorizing the design of the American flag.

AUGUST 16   Americans overpower their enemy during the Battle of Bennington.

SEPTEMBER 11   General William Howe's troops defeat Washington's army at the Battle of Brandywine, Pennsylvania.

SEPTEMBER 18   The Continental Congress flees Philadelphia.

SEPTEMBER 19   Patriots clash with General John Burgoyne's soldiers at Freeman's Farm (Saratoga Campaign).

SEPTEMBER 20   General Anthony Wayne's men are caught in a surprise attack, the "Paoli Massacre."

SEPTEMBER 26   General Howe occupies Philadelphia.

OCTOBER 4   American strategy fails at the Battle of Germantown.

OCTOBER 7   Americans defeat Burgoyne's troops at Bemis Heights (Saratoga Campaign).

OCTOBER 17   General Burgoyne surrenders his army at Saratoga, a serious defeat for the British.

NOVEMBER 15   Congress adopts the Articles of Confederation.

NOVEMBER 16   Fort Mifflin, Pennsylvania, is abandoned by the Patriots.

DECEMBER 19   The Continental Army establishes its camp at Valley Forge (until June 18–19, 1778).

1778

FEBRUARY 6   France signs a Treaty of Alliance with America.

MAY 18   General Howe turns over command of British forces in America to Henry Clinton.

JUNE 18   Clinton evacuates Philadelphia and marches toward New York City.

JUNE 28   A series of confused assaults occurs at Monmouth, New Jersey.

JULY 3–5   Indians and Loyalists destroy houses and massacre residents of Wyoming Valley, Pennsylvania.

DECEMBER 29   The British capture Savannah, Georgia.

1779

JUNE 16	Spain declares war on Great Britain.
JULY 5	New Haven, Connecticut, is attacked by a British expedition.
JULY 16	General Anthony Wayne's men capture the British-held fortification at Stony Point, New York.
SEPTEMBER 23	In an important naval battle John Paul Jones forces the surrender of the British ship *Serapis*.
SEPTEMBER 27	John Jay is named Minister to Spain.
OCTOBER 9	A Franco-American attempt to retake Savannah fails.
OCTOBER 25	The British evacuate Newport, Rhode Island.

1780

MARCH 15	Congress devalues American currency.
MAY 12	Charleston, South Carolina, is occupied by the British.
JULY 10	French troops under Rochambeau arrive at Newport.
AUGUST 16	Americans suffer a serious defeat at Camden, South Carolina.
SEPTEMBER 23	Benedict Arnold's treachery is discovered.
OCTOBER 2	Major John André, a British spy who negotiated with Arnold for the betrayal of West Point, is executed.

OCTOBER 7   Patriot forces crush their adversary at King's Mountain, South Carolina.

OCTOBER 14   General Nathanael Greene assumes command of the American forces in the South.

1781

JANUARY 5–7   British forces plunder Richmond, Virginia.

JANUARY 17   The Patriots are victorious at Cowpens, South Carolina.

FEBRUARY 20   Henry ("Light-Horse Harry") Lee routs a detachment of Loyalists marching to join Cornwallis' army at Hillsborough, North Carolina.

FEBRUARY 20   Congress appoints Robert Morris Superintendent of Finance.

MARCH 1   The last state formally ratifies the Articles of Confederation.

MARCH 15   Cornwallis wins the Battle of Guilford Courthouse, North Carolina, but approximately a quarter of his soldiers are casualties.

APRIL 23   Americans capture Fort Watson, South Carolina.

APRIL 25   The Americans are defeated at Hobkirk's Hill, South Carolina.

JULY 6   Cornwallis repulses Lafayette near Jamestown, Virginia.

AUGUST 22 — Cornwallis garrisons his troops at York-town, Virginia.

SEPTEMBER 5 — In a naval engagement off Virginia the French fleet inflicts heavy damage on British vessels.

SEPTEMBER 8 — At Eutaw Springs, South Carolina, the British take control of the battlefield after Patriot troops are thrown into disorder.

SEPTEMBER 28 — The American and French siege of Yorktown begins.

OCTOBER 19 — Cornwallis surrenders his army.

1782

MARCH 20 — England's Prime Minister, Lord North, resigns.

NOVEMBER 30 — American and English Commissioners sign the Preliminary Articles of Peace.

DECEMBER 14 — British troops evacuate Charleston.

1783

JUNE 24 — Congress flees Philadelphia after troops in the city revolt.

SEPTEMBER 3 — The Treaty of Paris officially ending the war and acknowledging America's independence is signed.

NOVEMBER 25 — The British evacuate New York City.

DECEMBER 23 — Washington resigns his commission as Commander-in-Chief of the Continental Army and returns to Mount Vernon.

Massachusetts

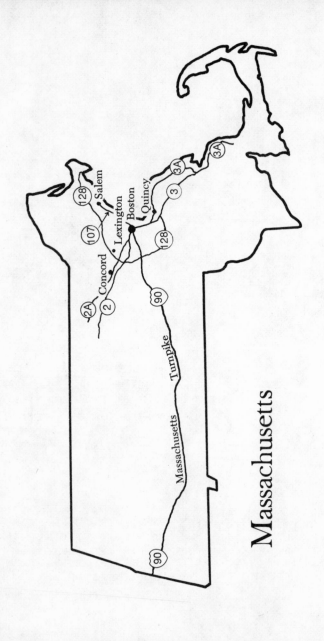

Massachusetts

Lexington

Revolutionary War History

Anticipating an outbreak of hostilities with the Royal Colonial government's army in the spring of 1775, the dissident Massachusetts colonists (calling themselves the "Patriots") began to collect military stores at secret locations. The military governor, General Thomas Gage, compelled to maintain the authority of the Crown, decided to send an expeditionary force to seize and destroy the supplies which Loyalist informers reported were concealed at Concord.

This was the objective that fateful evening of April 18, 1775, when Lieutenant Colonel Francis Smith began assembling about 700 men—elite grenadiers and light infantry—from the 3,500 British troops quartered in Boston. Second in command was Major John Pitcairn, an able and enterprising officer, who was highly respected by both the Patriots and the Loyalists. Their route for the march: through Cambridge, Somerville, the town of Menotomy (now Arlington), and then along the road toward Lexington and Concord.

At ten o'clock soldiers scurried to boats at the foot of the Common, on the banks of the old tidal basin of the Charles River, where the fat, slow-witted Smith kept them waiting for two hours. Finally, the boats were ordered to cross; two trips were required to transport all the troops and provisions. After being forced to disembark in a knee-deep backwater near the Cambridge shore, the men were kept standing idly about in the damp cold until almost two

Portrait of Paul
Revere. *Painting
by John Singleton
Copley.* (COURTESY
MUSEUM OF FINE
ARTS, BOSTON)

o'clock in the morning, and they became increasingly demoralized.

The march began along the Charlestown Lane (today
called Somerville Avenue), later veering onto the road that
is now Massachusetts Avenue. Under the moonlight the
scarlet-and-white column of eleven companies of grenadiers
and ten of light infantry plodded through the countryside,
which, near Lexington, began to reverberate with the
sounds of gunshots and bells. As a precaution, Smith sent a
courier back to Boston for reinforcements, though he little
realized the full significance of these disturbances—a relay-
ing of the call to self-defense brought by Paul Revere and
William Dawes.

Before stealing away on his dangerous mission, Paul
Revere instructed the young sexton of the North Church,
Robert Newman, to hang two lanterns in the steeple, thus
informing Colonel Conant and the Charlestown Committee
of Safety that the British were moving by water, across the
Charles River, and not over the Boston Neck. (At that time

Boston was connected to the mainland only by a thin isthmus, the "Boston Neck.")

Revere was then rowed across the Charles River, under the shadow of the British man-of-war *Somerset*. When he arrived in Charlestown, Colonel Conant and several Patriots met him and gave him a swift horse. Riding straight for Lexington and Concord, as he crossed the marshland known as Charlestown Common, he glimpsed the vague forms of two British officers crouched among the trees. Before they could lunge out of the blackness, he turned his horse sharply, retracing his path and taking the route to Medford, where he contacted the captain of the Minutemen and afterward awakened many households.

Close to midnight Revere arrived at the Lexington home of the Reverend Jonas Clarke, where John Hancock and Samuel Adams—who had been attending sessions of the Provincial Congress in Concord—were staying as guests. Breathlessly, he warned them of the imminent approach of the British Regulars. Soon afterward, William Dawes, who, like Paul Revere, had been spreading the alarm, appeared at the Clarke house.

Posing as a produce peddler during the preceding months, Dawes had befriended many road guards throughout Massachusetts. On the night of April 18 he devised a scheme beginning with a chat with an acquaintance on guard duty at the Boston Neck. When the gate was routinely opened for a squad of soldiers on patrol, he passed through unnoticed, as any curious spectator might. Once out of sight, he raced through Roxbury and Brookline, then north to Cambridge and Menotomy, and finally along the road to Lexington.

When the two couriers had refreshed themselves at the Clarke house, they set out for Concord, encountering on the way Samuel Prescott, a young Concord doctor, who was returning from courting his sweetheart, Lydia Mulliken. Prescott convinced Revere and Dawes that since he knew almost everybody in the area, his aid would be invaluable. Thus the trio galloped toward Concord alerting the inhabitants of approaching danger.

But soon they spotted British soldiers. Revere was taken prisoner, interrogated, then permitted to go free—on foot, for his horse was given to a sergeant of the grenadiers. The weary Boston silversmith trudged back to Jonas Clarke's house.

Dawes, having escaped, hurried his horse to a nearby farmhouse, where he decided it would be safer to return to Lexington on foot. Prescott, by jumping his horse over a low stone wall and disappearing into thickets near the Hartwell Tavern, eluded the Redcoats and eventually reached Concord. Receiving news of the British march from him, the Concord Patriots were able to finish hiding most of their arms and ammunition before morning.

By this time Lexington had armed itself. After Revere's arrival, Captain John Parker—who had served with Rogers' Rangers in the French and Indian Wars—had assembled the Minutemen on the Common to consider a course of action, but since the hour of the British arrival was uncertain, he dismissed the men. It was almost four o'clock in the morning when a scout from down the road toward Menotomy reported that the Redcoats were near. Captain Parker shouted to William Diamond, one of the company's drummer boys, to beat the call to arms. In the pale morning light seventy-seven Minutemen came running. Orderly Sergeant William Munroe formed them into two uneven lines stretched across the triangular Common as the townspeople milled around in their yards and behind stone walls.

To the ominous rhythm of snare drums the scarlet column entered the town, marching past Buckman Tavern and moving onto the Common. The Lexington men realized at once the weakness of their position, yet Parker issued the command: "Stand your ground; don't fire unless fired upon; but if they mean to have a war, let it begin here." Major John Pitcairn—ordering his soldiers not to fire but to sur-

The Fight on Lexington Common. *Painting by Howard Pyle.*
(DELAWARE ART MUSEUM, WILMINGTON)

round and disarm Parker's men—swung the Redcoats from
a column into a line extending far out to his right to get
around the Patriots' flank. Parker, not wishing to invite
wanton slaughter, ordered his men to scatter and, above all,
not to fire.

Suddenly a shot echoed across the Common; just who
fired first will probably never be known. Then pandemonium: a succession of shots, men clamoring, British
bayonets on the charge, militiamen darting in panic! Spur-
ring his horse into the ranks, Major Pitcairn—his sword
flashing downward as a ceasefire signal—futilely tried to
bully his men back into formation. When the firing ceased
and the coils of smoke cleared, the Common was strewn
with bodies. Parker's company, with eight dead and ten
wounded, was in a shambles. The British—with only one
man wounded—regrouped and, to the sound of fife and
drum, resumed their march toward Concord.

VISITORS' CENTER Information, maps, and booklets are available at the Visitors' Bureau located at the corner of Massachusetts Avenue and Meriam Street (across from the Minuteman Statue). Additional information about the region may be obtained from the Lexington Historical Society, 1 Bedford Street, phone 861–0928, or from the Chamber of Commerce, 1875 Massachusetts Avenue, phone 862–1450.

GUIDED TOURS **Gray Line Tours,** phone 427–8650, and **Copley Motor Tours,** phone 266–3500, both offer tours of the area. Buses leave from downtown Boston.

PUBLIC TRANSPORTATION The Massachusetts Bay Transit Authority operates buses throughout the area. For schedules and information, phone 722–5691 (Arlington).

TAXI SERVICE Airport Cab Service, phone 862–4600; Corrigan's Taxi, phone 259–9420; Lexington Taxi, phone 861–0500.

Colonial and Revolutionary War Sites

THE BELFRY *Off Clarke Street near the Lexington Common* In June 1761 a new bell was presented to Lexington by Isaac Stone, and a wooden belfry to house it was erected on a hill (now called "Belfry Hill") near the Jonas Munroe home. Seven years later the structure was moved near the meeting house on the Common. (A tablet marks the site.) It remained on this spot for thirty years, summoning the townspeople to worship and announcing the death of a neighbor. On April 19, 1775, the frenzied chime warned of the British advance.

When the third meeting house was constructed in 1794 with a bell steeple, the belfry was sold to a son of Captain John Parker, who moved it to his property to be used as a wheelwright's shop. Almost a century later it was presented to the Lexington Historical Society and was returned to Belfry Hill, not far from its original location. The old wooden tower, weakened by the ravages of time, was destroyed by a gale in 1909. The following year a replica was constructed on the site. Although the bell has long since disappeared, the tongue is displayed at the Hancock-Clarke House.

BUCKMAN TAVERN   *1 Bedford Street, opposite the Minuteman   Statue. Open April 19 to November 1, Monday through Saturday 10 A.M. to 5 P.M., Sunday 1 P.M. to 5 P.M. Adults 50¢, children 15¢.*   The original structure, built in 1709–1710 by John Muzzey, was a modest two-story saltbox house with a central chimney. In the 1760s, after several additions, a hip roof was constructed, providing three additional attic bedrooms and a garret. Except for the southeast ell, the building is substantially as it was in 1775 when John Buckman, a member of Captain Parker's company, was the proprietor.

Here, huddled near the taproom's great fireplace, on the morning of April 19, 1775, the Lexington Patriots assembled to await definite news of British troop movements. That afternoon, during the British retreat; two wounded Redcoats were carried into the tavern, one of whom died and was buried in the cemetery across the Common.

This tavern was not only a resting point for drovers and other travelers, but was also a center of activity for the townspeople. Posted on the Buckman taproom walls were notices of town meetings, elections, and auctions, as well as information about missing slaves and stray livestock.

During the evenings local farmers could be found in the large, beamed **Taproom** partaking of convivial companionship and a tankard of flip. Since guests were not permitted to stand at the bar, they clustered around the small tables. An early custom of the tavern is interesting: when a lad became tall enough to set his chin on the bar shelf without cheating by standing on tiptoe, he was then considered mature and would be served.

Above the large fireplace is a "smoke hole" into which guests deposited their clay pipes before bedtime to prevent fires. Nearby are displayed several fine Colonial flintlock muskets; one closely resembles the famous "Brown Bess" British musket. Hanging from the ceiling are leather buckets bearing the owner's name. Town ordinances required each family to provide these containers for the bucket brigades organized to fight local fires. Failure to comply resulted in a fine.

Almost every important household activity was performed in the **Kitchen**: cooking, baking, candlemaking, soapmaking, spinning, weaving, dyeing, and churning. On display here are many eighteenth-century tools and instruments. One unusual device used for winding yarn into skeins was referred to as a "Niddy Noddy," taking its name, some local historians believe, from a song that women sang while attending to this chore.

In early New England meat was usually hung (with dripping pan beneath) to cook in front of a blazing fire or roasted in a "tin kitchen" whose spit was kept revolving by means of a crank-handle. From the brick "bake oven" to the side of the fireplace came desserts—such appetizing dishes, as cookies, pies, and rice and Indian puddings.

The china in the cabinet is mostly Staffordshire from England. But china was a luxury in the eighteenth century; servingware of wood and pewter (an alloy primarily of tin and lead) was commonplace. Reports exist during

Colonial times describing a kind of lead poisoning, which was called the "pewter sickness."

By the door of the **Landlord's Bedroom** hangs a portrait of the convivial John Buckman. Members of the family snuggled in the trundle bed—with its sliding drawerlike compartment underneath for the children. Nearby is a chest holding a British government-issue blanket left by Redcoats who were once quartered in a Boston home.

Over the chest hangs a "courter's mirror," which a Colonial gentleman would present when proposing to his sweetheart. If the mirror was hung conspicuously during his next visit, he would know that his proposal had been accepted; however, if the mirror was placed face down on a table, he saw that he, like his gift, had been "turned down."

The comfortable **Ladies' Parlor** was the special province of the ladies, who, barred from the taproom, would rest, eat, drink, and gossip here. Each Sunday, after the morning service, women and children filled this room, having their lunch and replenishing the supply of hot coals for their footwarmers before returning to the unheated meeting house for afternoon worship.

The rosewood melodeon, built in France, was used in the meeting house on Sundays but was kept in the tavern the rest of the week so that the cold would not damage it. The legs of the delicate instrument folded to permit easy conveyance from one building to the other.

Standing in a corner is a handsome mahogany pendulum clock built for Dr. Joseph Fiske, the physician who attended the wounded at the Battle of Lexington. It was made by Benjamin Willard, a member of a distinguished clock-making family.

The small **Post Office** room was added in 1813; Rufus Merriam, the owner of the house at that time, was appointed postmaster. The only original furniture remaining is the postmaster's desk, where records were kept, some of which are still preserved here. The hostess' table is an old school desk from the first Normal School in America, which was located on the site where the Lexington Masonic Temple now stands. On the walls hang various prints, including one of Major Pitcairn and one depicting the Battle of Lexington.

Buckman Tavern is administered by the Lexington Historical Society.

HANCOCK-CLARKE HOUSE   *35 Hancock Street, ¼ mile north of the Lexington Common. Open April 19 to November 1, Monday through Saturday 10 A.M. to 5 P.M., Sunday 1 P.M. to 5 P.M. Adults 50¢, children 15¢.*   Built in 1698 by Reverend John Hancock (the second pastor of Lexington), the earliest section of this house consisted of a gambrel-roofed ell that contained a living room, a study, and two small chambers upstairs. Here, on an annual salary of £60, the pastor raised his five children (three sons and two daughters).

The oldest son, John, became the minister of Braintree (now Quincy), where the third John Hancock—the conspicuous signer of the Declaration of Independence—was born in 1737. The second son, Thomas, went into business for himself, becoming one of the wealthiest and most influential merchants in New England. He built the two-story addition to his parents' Lexington home, expanding it to eight rooms. The third son, Ebenezer, graduated from Harvard and later assisted his father in his pastoral duties.

Reverend Jonas Clarke, the third minister of Lexington, bought the house and property in the 1760s and lived here with his wife, Lucy Bowes (a granddaughter of Reverend John Hancock), and their thirteen children. On April 18, 1775, John Hancock and Samuel Adams, who had both been attending sessions of the Provincial Congress in Concord, were guests of the Clarke family.

After Paul Revere's capture on the Concord road and his subsequent return to the Clarke house, Hancock and

Adams were convinced of the need to flee before the arrival of British troops. Earlier, the stubborn Hancock, polishing a gun, had insisted on joining the fight; at one point he even went down to the Common to observe the activities of the Minutemen. But Adams finally protested: "It [fighting] is not our business. We belong to the Cabinet." The two men were then escorted by Sergeant Munroe to a hideout in the woods, and afterward escaped to the Thomas Jones house in Woburn Precinct (now Burlington). There Hancock sent for his Aunt Lydia and his fiancée, Dorothy Quincy, who were also guests of the Clarkes, and ordered them "to bring the fine salmon" they had for dinner. Still threatened, they all fled again—this time to Amos Wyman's home in Bellerica, where they found safety.

At the time of the battle the ground was open between Reverend Clarke's house and the Common, and the firing could be plainly seen from the windows. As Mrs. Clarke and her children were leaving the yard for a safer place, bullets whizzed by, barely missing them.

On the night of Tuesday, April 18, John Hancock and Samuel Adams were sleeping in a four-poster bed in the south chamber on the first floor—today referred to as the **Hancock-Adams Room**. Hancock is said to have concealed some of his papers in the Jacobean four-drawer chest now standing near the tall-case clock made in the 1830s by Burr and Chittenden of Lexington. The bedroom directly above the two Patriots was occupied by Hancock's fiancée and his aunt. Several fine period pieces as well as clothes and military uniforms of the Revolutionary period are exhibited here.

In the **Keeping Room** (sitting room) hang portraits of Reverend John Hancock and his wife by the well-known artist John Smibert (1688–1751), a Scot who settled in Boston. Revolutionary relics here include a musket used by Hammond Reed during the Battle of Lexington and a cane owned by Caleb Harrington, killed that morning on Lexington Common. The tiles framing the fireplace are not the originals, which were blue-and-white squares portraying scenes from *Aesop's Fables*. A section of the wallpaper that adorned these walls near the end of the eighteenth century is preserved under glass.

Before Thomas Hancock enlarged the house, the **Kitchen** functioned as a cooking–dining area as well as a sitting room. The original fireplace, much larger than the present one, had a beam (called the "lug pole") from which pots and kettles were suspended by chains or trammels, allowing for a variation in height. The large copper kettle nearby was useful for boiling clothes, preparing apple butter, and making soap.

Of unusual interest is the rocking churn with a cross rod that permitted a busy mother to churn butter and rock her baby at the same time. Other objects familiar in the Colonial household, such as a sausage filler, a butter scale, an herb still, and a candle mould, are displayed.

In the second-floor front bedroom—today called the **Dorothy Quincy Room**—Dorothy Quincy (John Hancock's fiancée) and Lydia Hancock (his aunt) slept on the eve of the Lexington battle. There are several period pieces here now, although the handsome four-poster bed is a later addition. Clothes and military uniforms of the Revolutionary period are displayed in the cases.

On view in **Jonas Clarke's Study**—near the simple pine desk on which he wrote his weekly sermons—are several interesting photographs and letters, including a copy of a dispatch relating news of the Battles of Lexington and Concord to the Committee of Safety in Philadelphia.

The **Museum Room** houses a varied collection, including one of the stamps issued under the Stamp Act of 1765, manuscripts of sermons by Hancock and Clarke, Jonas Clarke's diary, Amos Doolittle's engravings of the Battles of Lexington and Concord, the drum on which

William Diamond beat the call to arms, Major Pitcairn's pistols, and the bill of Dr. Joseph Fiske for treating wounded soldiers.

The property is maintained by the Lexington Historical Society.

LEXINGTON COMMON   *Bounded by Harrington Road, Bedford Street, and Massachusetts Avenue*   In 1707 a committee was chosen at a public meeting to negotiate with "Nibour Muzzey" about the purchase of this triangular plot of land that lay north of the meeting house, but the transactions to secure the one and a half acres for £16 were not completed until four years later. An additional acre was bought in 1722 for £25 to enlarge the Common toward the north, an area later reduced by cutting Bedford Street through the eastern side. Lexington Common, the first battleground of the American Revolution, is now the site of monuments marking points of historic interest: the Line of Battle Boulder, the Meeting House Rock, the Minuteman Statue, and the Revolutionary Monument.

LINE OF BATTLE BOULDER   The musket and powder-horn carved on this boulder point in the direction of the Minutemen's battle line. Inscribed is the famous command of Captain Parker to his men: "Stand your ground; don't fire unless fired upon; but if they mean to have a war, let it begin here." A team of ten horses was required to haul the twelve-ton stone from its original resting place two miles away.

MEETING HOUSE ROCK   Behind the Minuteman Statue stands a square granite stone marking the site of the first three Lexington meeting houses. The meeting house standing at the time of the Revolution was erected in 1713 adjacent to the location of the previous building. As represented in a print by Amos Doolittle, it was a plain, peaked-roof, barnlike structure. Measuring fifty by forty feet and twenty-eight feet high, it had two tiers of galleries and a main floor with high-walled pews sold according to the desirability of their location. From the tall pulpit Reverends John Hancock (1698–1752) and Jonas Clarke (1755–1805) dispensed theology to generations of Lexingtonians. A third meeting house, topped by a steeple, was completed in 1794, but it burned to the ground while being remodeled in 1846.

On one face of the stone is inscribed the names of the first seven pastors of the local parish and the dates of their tenure. The planting of the elm tree shading the stone was presided over by President Grant in 1875 as part of the town's Centennial celebration.

MINUTEMAN STATUE (HAYES MEMORIAL FOUNTAIN AND STATUE) This statue, considered an idealized figure of Captain John Parker, commander of the Lexington Minutemen, was created by the renowned Boston sculptor Henry Hudson Kitson (1863–1947). He spent years casting the bronze statue after a committee approved an eighteen-inch model of the work. Kitson searched throughout New England for an appropriate fieldstone for the fountain base, which was intended to

Line of Battle Boulder, Lexington Common (ALPER)

Minuteman Statue, Lexington Common (ALPER)

serve as a place for watering animals. Near Lexington he discovered an eight-foot-wide stone with a natural depression.

On April 19, 1900, a crowd of almost 40,000 attended the dedication ceremonies. The fountain and statue—made possible by a bequest of $10,000 from the will of Francis B. Hayes—were unveiled by a great-grandson of Captain Parker, Charles W. Parker. During the ceremony the fountain was turned on, and, as one reporter noted, "the worshipful spray leaped up to the feet of the Captain on the rocks."

MONUMENT TO THE REVOLUTION   On the west side of Lexington Common stands the Revolutionary Monument —now in a mantle of ivy—which the state erected in 1799. The elaborate inscription by the Patriot minister

Reverend Jonas Clarke includes the names of the heroes who fell in the Battle of Lexington, "the first Victims of the Sword of British Tyranny and Oppression."

In the rear of this monument is a stone vault containing the bodies of the men slain that day in April of 1775. Originally they were buried in a common grave in the old cemetery, but in 1835 their remains were exhumed, placed in a sarcophagus, and borne to the meeting house, where an eloquent eulogy was delivered by the popular orator and statesman Edward Everett. In the presence of a large crowd (including Josiah Quincy, president of Harvard College, and Daniel Webster) these freedom fighters were laid to their final resting place.

Many distinguished visitors have been received in front of the monument: Washington, Lafayette, Kossuth, and famous Civil War generals. After World War I the citizens gathered here to honor Lexington's returning soldiers.

The knoll upon which this monument stands, known as "Schoolhouse Hill," was the location of the town's first two schoolhouses.

MUNROE TAVERN *Located ½ mile east of Lexington Center on Route 225 (1332 Massachusetts Avenue). Open April 19 to November 1, Monday through Saturday 10 A.M. to 5 P.M., Sunday 1 P.M. to 5 P.M. Adults 50¢, children 15¢.* Built in 1695, this historic house is all that remains of the inn of Revolutionary days; an ell on the northwest side that contained a ballroom and a general store was torn down in 1860.

The proprietor of the tavern at the time of the American Revolution was William Munroe, an officer in the local militia and one of the men who stood guard the night of April 18, 1775 (after Paul Revere's warning) outside the house of Reverend Jonas Clarke, where John Hancock and Samuel Adams were staying.

On the afternoon of April 19, 1775, reinforcements under the command of Earl Percy, answering the summons dispatched on the previous night by Lieutenant Colonel Francis Smith, temporarily halted the chaotic British retreat from Concord. They held back the Minutemen long enough to convey the wounded soldiers into Munroe Tavern, where medical treatment was haphazardly administered in the dining room (now called the Percy Room).

As the British approached, Mrs. Munroe and her three children ran from the house to hide in the nearby forest, where she remained until her husband returned. The taproom was bustling with British soldiers guzzling all that the lame old barman, John Raymond, could find to slake their thirst. Before resuming their retreat, the soldiers maliciously killed the old man as he tried to escape, then sacked the house and set it on fire.

During the eighteenth century Munroe's was a popular resting place for New England cattle and sheep drovers en route to the Brighton stockyards; it also was frequented by farmers hauling their produce, wool, and dairy products to the Boston markets. While some of the drovers slept in the huge barn with the animals, others preferred the straw mattresses or cord beds placed in rows on the ballroom floor. When the tavern was crowded, guests were forced to share their mattresses. Drovers and farmers ate their meals in the taproom; some of the thriftier travelers who brought their own meat were allowed to cook on a "tin kitchen" set in front of the fireplace. Wealthy guests, arriving by carriage, were served their meals in the dining room and slept in upper-story rooms on comfortable feather beds under warm patchwork quilts.

In the **Taproom** the tired drovers and other guests exchanged stories and enjoyed a tankard of flip—a mixture of home-brewed beer, brown sugar, and rum into which a red-hot loggerhead was dipped until the drink foamed. The hand-hewn center beam in the room is the original, still showing the marks of the adze (an axlike tool with

Munroe Tavern, Lexington (ALPER)

arched blade). A pine tavern sign—bearing an image of a punch bowl and the word "Entertainment"—which once swung freely from a tree on the front lawn is now nailed firmly to a wall above the small tables and old Windsor chairs. Near the entrance hangs a wooden rack, once filled with clay pipes for use by the guests. Before returning a pipe to the rack, a smoker was required to break off the tip of the long mouthpiece, thereby making it clean for the next user.

The bulging plastered section in the ceiling hides a hole made, deliberately or accidentally, by a Redcoat's musket as he was leaving with his comrades on their retreat to Boston on April 19. Above the fireplace is an old flintlock gun whose owner, a young participant in the Battle of Lexington, had become so excited that he forgot to measure his powder and blew off the musket's end with an overcharge!

The **Percy Room** was used as a dining room in Colonial days. Visitors can still see the old floor with its wide boards and handmade nails, but the bricks of the fireplace have been relaid so that it lacks the depth of the original.

The inlaid Sheraton desk (*c.* 1770), with the original brasses, belonged to Colonel Munroe. The small travel trunk was owned by Munroe's youngest daughter, Lucinda, who used it for packing belongings which might have been crushed in a carpetbag. One of the small chairs, in the French style, was made by a boarder, who began building furniture to pay his debts.

The cabinet holds a wedding slipper of Colonel Munroe's first wife; her wedding ring with the inscription, "Hearts united live contented"; and a bonnet, which was often dyed or fitted with fresh bows to the delight of Mrs. Munroe's friends. Colonel Munroe's uniform on display—knee-length buckskin breeches and linen waistcoat—was made during Shays' Rebellion (1786–1787, an armed insurrection of Massachusetts farmers), but the uprising was suppressed before his militia unit could take an active part.

In the second-floor **Bedroom** stands a majestic four-poster canopy bed built in the early 1800s. The cabinet to the right of the bed displays baby clothes. Spinning the linen thread on a flax wheel (like one near the fireplace), weaving the cloth, and working the delicate needlepoint for these garments were all done by Colonel Munroe's wife and servants. A small white rocking chair, made by Jonathan Harrington (a local fifer of Revolutionary days), rests in a corner below a memorial picture of a pallid woman languishing near an austere funeral monument.

Although Lexingtonians cannot boast that George Washington slept at Munroe's, they do commemorate his visit and dinner here (in the room now bearing his name) on November 5, 1789, during a tour of New England.

After meeting the important citizens of Lexington, the first President was escorted upstairs to a sumptuous dinner—roasted beef, shoulder of pork, young pigeons, pies, and puddings. As he was relating a favorite anecdote, a hideous screech was heard from outside the tavern. Rushing to the window, the bewildered guests saw thirteen-year-old Lucinda Munroe dangling from a tree, which she had climbed to secretly observe the distinguished visitor. Fortunately, one of Washington's servants was nearby to assist the frightened child, and the incident was treated as a delightful joke to be added to the President's store of anecdotes.

The mahogany Sheraton card table, now standing in the center of the green-and-white-papered **Washington Room,** had been carried upstairs for that special occasion. Along the far wall are cases of the Munroes' silver and china and an interesting collection of inventory lists and letters, including one in which Washington complains about his false teeth. The ladder-back armchair in which the President sat while dining and pieces of the Leeds china on which the dinner was served are still a source of great pride to the Munroe family.

The site is administered by the Lexington Historical Society.

OLD BURYING GROUND *At the fork of Harrington Road and Massachusetts Avenue* Behind the First Parish Church (built 1847) is a cemetery with stones bearing dates as early as 1690. A long, narrow headstone near the entrance records the deaths of six children of one family within a twelve-day period. At the left of the entrance is an enclosure containing the graves of many members of the Merriam and Parker families.

A monument to Captain John Parker, commander of the Minutemen, was erected by the town in 1884 over the site of his grave. It is a single block of granite, pyramidal in form, set on a square base. Near it is the tomb of Reverend Benjamin Estabrook, the first pastor of

Lexington (1692–1697), and the grave of his brother Joseph, the first schoolmaster. An obelisk of white marble marks the burial place of William Eustis (1753–1825), a distinguished surgeon in the Revolutionary Army and one of the early governors of Massachusetts (1823–1825). The Hancock-Clarke tomb, covered by a rectangular stone slab set on six pillars, holds the remains of many members of these two distinguished families.

Concord

When, on the morning of April 19, 1775, reports of the bloodshed in Lexington reached the commander of the Concord Militia, Colonel James Barrett, he assembled the local Minutemen and sent messengers to summon militia from neighboring towns. The Concord company and their newly-arrived companions began to proceed toward Lexington along a ridge paralleling the road, but they soon caught sight of the advancing British. Reversing their direction, the militiamen countermarched toward Concord, acting almost as an escort for the Redcoats.

At 7 A.M. the British troops reached the center of the town and halted on the Common opposite Wright's Tavern. Colonel Barrett hastily called a council of war: young Reverend William Emerson of the Manse favored confronting the foe, but most other townsmen insisted on waiting until more reinforcements answered their call.

So the militia took to the road, passing Elisha Jones' house, then moving down the bend until it crossed the North Bridge over the Concord River and headed for Punkatasset Hill, the high ground overlooking the river.

Meanwhile Lieutenant Colonel Smith and Major Pitcairn surveyed the terrain from the town cemetery. After setting up headquarters in Wright's Tavern, Smith sent the light infantry outside the village limits, one company (twenty-eight men) to guard the South Bridge and seven companies to follow the retreating Patriots. Three of the seven companies were ordered to hold the North Bridge, while the other four, under Captain Lawrence Parsons, pushed toward Colonel Barrett's farm, where a large store of arms was reportedly cached. (However, Barrett earlier had returned home to reassure himself that the supplies were in no danger of being discovered.)

The grenadiers began conducting a door-to-door search—with remarkable restraint. One indignant old lady, with a mop whirling through the air, chased a Redcoat out of her sitting room. Nearby, several gentlemanly soldiers offered to pay the women of Amos Wood's family for inconveniencing them. And in another home an officer, informed that a room was occupied by an indisposed lady, refrained from entering and missed finding hidden munitions.

But some arms and supplies were uncovered. At Ebenezer Hubbard's house the soldiers found barrels of flour, which they smashed, and then, with an excess of enthusiasm, heaved other casks into the mill pond. (These containers were later salvaged, however, as the flour near the outer edges swelled and caulked the seams.) At the jail, where the stubborn jailkeeper, Ephraim Jones, Jr., had bolted the doors, the grenadiers—on Pitcairn's order—forced them open and found three cannon. Jones, who was also proprietor of the nearby inn, was later released so that he could prepare the major's breakfast!

Some dismantled gun carriages, together with barrels containing wooden trenchers and spoons, were piled in the street and a bonfire was started—the fire that was to kindle the Battle of Concord.

Meanwhile, Captain Parsons had marched his light infantry over the North Bridge and down the dirt road to the Barrett farm. At the bridge remained three companies (eighty-four men) under Captain Walter Laurie. He positioned the 43rd Oxfordshires at the western end of the bridge and the 10th Lincolnshires and the 4th Royal North Lancashires along a nearby ridge of low hills. Not far away, more than 400 militiamen stood poised, their ranks still being swelled by arrivals from towns such as Carlisle, Bedford, Chelmsford, and Acton.

The Redcoats and Patriots waited and watched each other impassively. Suddenly one of the militiamen noticed dark smoke from the bonfire billowing above the green-tipped trees. "Will you let them burn the town down?" yelped Lieutenant Joseph Hosmer of the Concord Minutemen. The answer was a hearty "No!" With fife and drum playing the lively tune "The White Cockade," the companies marched double file down the slope toward the bridge. Leading them were Major John Buttrick, second-in-command of the Concord forces, and Captain Isaac Davis, with recruits from Acton. Colonel Barrett, observing the columns on horseback from high ground in the rear, continued to shout orders not to fire. The indecisive Captain Laurie finally ordered his bewildered soldiers to cross the bridge and to regroup on the opposite bank. The Patriots almost upon them, several Redcoats frantically began tearing up the bridge's planking. Taking up formation, they fired three warning shots—followed by the crash of a full volley, which killed Captain Davis and several of his men. Major Buttrick screamed desperately: "Fire, fellow soldiers! For God's sake, fire!"

A fusillade of musket balls whizzed through the air and into the British lines, killing three men. After scattered return fire, the frightened Redcoats bolted toward Concord center. Halfway there they were joined by Lieutenant Colonel Smith and relief troops, but, as usual, his action was too late to be of value. Smith's soldiers, along with the bridge survivors, returned to the town, as the Patriots carried their dead and wounded to the John Buttrick house.

During the futile search of the Barrett farm Captain Parsons and his four companies heard gunfire and, growing panicky, raced back to Concord. They did not encounter any militiamen on the way.

At noon Lieutenant Colonel Smith gave the command: Return to Boston.

No incident marred their debilitated but orderly retreat until Meriam's Corner, where the road narrowed to a small bridge (replaced today by a culvert) spanning Mill Brook. As the Redcoats slowly crowded across the bridge, the militia—from behind barns, boulders, and walls—opened fire. Unable to see their attackers, who had been following them, the British soldiers became a hysterical, fleeing mob that ran for miles through a gauntlet of musket balls. Dead and wounded slumped to the earth. Smith was wounded in the leg and Pitcairn was thrown by his horse, which charged through fields and was later captured by the Minutemen.

By the time they neared Lexington, the remnants of the British troops seemed on the verge of surrender. Suddenly, bright scarlet-and-white uniforms glimmered on the crest of a hill near Munroe Tavern. Lord Percy, with melodramatic timing, had answered Lieutenant Colonel Smith's early-morning plea for reinforcements. After placing small cannon on nearby hills, Percy deployed his soldiers into a large square formation, offering Smith's exhausted men safety. The wounded were carried into Munroe Tavern, where they received medical aid.

But the respite was only temporary. Near 4 P.M. Percy gathered his forces, placed Smith's men at the head of his

The Retreat from Concord (NEW YORK PUBLIC LIBRARY PICTURE COLLECTION)

column (now almost 2,000 strong), and resumed the retreat to Boston. As they advanced along their route, the
militia (about 3,000 by this time) followed them, peppering
the conspicuous targets with shots. At Menotomy the battle
became more violent; there were heavier casualties on both
sides than in any other engagement that day. The British
pressed on toward Cambridge (through present-day Somerville), still looting, burning down houses, and killing inno-
cent bystanders. Because the Patriots blocked the approaches to Beech Street and the road to the Charles River,
Percy was forced to direct his men toward the narrow-
necked peninsula of Charlestown.

Daylight was beginning to fade as the Redcoats set up

VISITORS' CENTER   An audio-visual presentation of the
Battle of Concord is shown at the Minuteman National
Historic Park Visitors' Center, Liberty Street (North
Bridge Area), phone 369–6944. Books and tourist pamphlets are also available here. Information about Concord may also be obtained from the Chamber of Commerce, ½ Main Street, phone 369–3120. Serious students of the region's history may wish to consult the
Concord Antiquarian Society, 200 Lexington Road,
phone 369–9609.

GUIDED TOURS   **Gray Line Tours,** phone 427–8650, and
Copley Motor Tours, phone 266–3500, both offer tours of
the area. Buses leave from downtown Boston.

PUBLIC TRANSPORTATION The Massachusetts Bay
Transit Authority operates buses throughout the area.
For schedules and information, phone 722–5691 (Ar-
lington).

TAXI SERVICE   Concord Taxi, phone 369–5050; Colonial
Taxi, phone 369–3433.

a protective line near Bunker Hill. The militiamen wisely decided not to attempt an assault. Although hundreds of them remained on the opposite side of the Charlestown Neck, most of the weary farmer-soldiers plodded homeward.

In the darkness the British—under the protection of their warships in the river basin—embarked in small boats for Boston. The expedition to Concord had come to its bitter end: seventy-three British and forty-nine Patriots lay dead, and the Revolutionary War had begun.

Colonial and Revolutionary War Sites

FIRST PARISH MEETING HOUSE   *On Lexington Road, off Monument Square*   In the second decade of the eighteenth century the congregation of this parish moved into a meeting house on this site. The structure had a peaked roof surmounted by a high cupola, and the interior was simply furnished with plain wooden benches. (Pews were not installed until 1749.) The design of the building has been attributed to Charles Underhill.

In 1791 the church was enlarged by twelve feet, a front porch was added, and a spire was erected. Later, though, when the building was completely renovated in 1841, the spire and porch were removed and a fashionable Greek Revival portico crowned by a belfry was built to grace the facade. In addition, the interior was made more comfortable and ornate. Construction was supervised by Richard Bond, a Boston architect.

The church was ravaged by fire in 1900. The present structure—erected in the following year on the same site—is an enlarged reconstruction of its predecessor.

It was in the Colonial Meeting House that the First Provincial Congress of Massachusetts met in early October 1774. With John Hancock serving as president and Benjamin Lincoln as secretary, the delegates drafted a declaration protesting the building of British fortifications in the Boston area. When a committee presented the document to Thomas Gage, military governor of the colony, he reasserted his authority by declaring the Congress an illegal assembly. Ignoring his decree, the Second Provincial Congress met again in Concord on March 22, 1775, and remained in session until four days before the Battle at the North Bridge.

In the nineteenth century two famous literary figures— Ralph Waldo Emerson and Henry David Thoreau— worshipped regularly at the First Parish Meeting House.

NORTH BRIDGE AREA *At Monument Square in downtown Concord, turn right (at the Colonial Inn) onto Monument Street and proceed about ½ mile. A parking lot is located on the right side of the road at the North Bridge Area. (To reach the Visitors' Center, continue down the road about .3 of a mile, then take the first left turn onto Liberty Street.) Open daily 8 A.M. to 6 P.M. in July and August; 8 A.M. to 5 P.M. during the rest of the year. Free.* Since the mid-1960s the historic North Bridge Area has been administered by the National Park Service of the United States Department of the Interior. The major points of interest are described below.

BATTLE MONUMENT This monument marks the spot where the British soldiers fought and fell on April 19, 1775. The cornerstone was laid in 1825 in the presence of the surviving veterans of the battle, who listened to a stirring address delivered by Congressman Edward Everett. The granite obelisk was not completed until 1836. The inscription reads: "Here, on the 19th of April, 1775, was made the first forcible resistance to British Aggression." During the dedication ceremonies on July 4, 1837, printed leaflets containing Ralph Waldo Emerson's recently composed poem "Concord Hymn" were distributed to the spectators. (The first stanza of this poem was later inscribed on the pedestal of the Minuteman statue that stands on the opposite bank, across the North Bridge.)

GRAVE OF BRITISH SOLDIERS A plaque affixed to a low stone wall (located to the left of the Battle Monument) marks the graves of two British soldiers who lost their lives here during the Battle of Concord. Their names are unknown. The plaque bears a verse written by James Russell Lowell for the Centennial Celebration (1875): "They came three thousand miles and died / To keep the past upon its throne: / Unheard, beyond the ocean tide / Their English mother made her moan."

MINUTEMAN STATUE In 1870 Concord resident Ebby Hubbard bequeathed to the town $1,000 for the erection of a monument commemorating the Minutemen's stand on April 19, 1775. A committee was appointed in 1872, with John S. Keyes serving as chairman. The members agreed to commission Daniel Chester French (1850–1931), a young sculptor residing in the area, to design an appropriate work. French fashioned a small clay model nobly depicting a Minuteman grasping a musket in one hand while holding onto a plow with the other. It delighted the committee, and during the winter of 1873–1874 he made a seven-foot clay replica. In the spring of 1874 a plaster cast was done, and then the final bronze statue was cast at Ames Foundry (Chicopee, Massachusetts).

The statue was unveiled on April 19, 1875, on the eve of the Centennial of the Revolutionary War. Before the dedication ceremonies a procession of military units and prominent statesmen—including President Ulysses S. Grant and Vice President Henry Wilson (formerly a United States Senator from Massachusetts)—marched through the streets of Concord to the North Bridge site. There George William Curtis, a well-known writer and

Minuteman Statue, North Bridge (ALPER)

The North Bridge, Concord (ALPER)

an editor of *Harper's Weekly*, delivered the principal oration, reminding the large crowd that "Great events and a mightier struggle have absorbed our own generation; yet we who stand here today have a sympathy with the men at the Old North Bridge which those who preceded us here at earlier celebrations could not know." Later, Ralph Waldo Emerson spoke, referring metaphorically to the Battle of Concord as a "thunderbolt [that] falls on an inch of ground, but the light of it fills the horizon." A verse from his poem "Concord Hymn" (written in 1837) was inscribed on the pedestal of the Minuteman Statue.

NORTH BRIDGE   The wooden bridge that spanned the Concord River during Revolutionary days was constructed in 1760 by local residents. This, the "North Bridge," was the location of the skirmish between the Patriots and the Redcoats.

By 1791 the bridge had fallen into disrepair. It was torn down and another structure was erected on a site

nearer to the town. During the early 1870s—in preparation for the Centennial celebration of the Battle of Concord—a committee of townspeople determined to construct a commemorative bridge at the site where the
battle occurred. The replica was completed by the
autumn of 1874 and was officially dedicated the following year. It was destroyed by a flood in 1888.

Another bridge was erected in 1889, but within eighteen years it had so deteriorated that it created a safety
hazard. In 1909 the townspeople decided to replace it
with a Colonial-style bridge of cement. It resisted the
ravages of the elements—until 1955, when Hurricane
Diane caused serious structural damage.

The present North Bridge, which cost $48,000, was
erected in 1956 by the Massachusetts Department of
Public Works.

THE OLD MANSE *Monument Street, on the edge of the
North Bridge Area. Open April 19 through November
11, Monday through Saturday 10 A.M. to 4:30 P.M.,
Sunday 1 P.M. to 4:30 P.M. Adults 75¢, children 35¢.*
The Manse (Scottish term for "parsonage") was built in
1769 by the Reverend William Emerson, known by his
comrades as "the Chaplain of the Revolution." When the
First Provincial Congress met in Concord in October
1774, Emerson was chosen as its chaplain, and he opened
each meeting with a prayer. In a sermon at a regimental
muster on the Concord Green in March 1775 he gently
warned the local militia of the serious consequences of
violence, yet reminded them of their obligations to defend freedom.

When the hostility finally erupted between the
Patriots and the British, it did so on his doorstep. On
Wednesday morning, April 19, 1775, he and his wife
Phebe watched the fighting at the North Bridge from a
window at the Manse. Inspired by the cause of liberty,
Emerson joined in the defense of Bunker Hill in June
1775 and in September 1777 recruited soldiers to re-

inforce the garrison at Fort Ticonderoga. Soon afterward he was stricken with fever and died at the age of thirty-three.

In 1778 Dr. Ezra Ripley succeeded Emerson as minister in Concord and moved into the Manse. Two years later, against the protestations of his congregation, he took a wife—Emerson's widow.

During the second decade of the nineteeth century young Ralph Waldo Emerson (William Emerson's grandson and Ripley's step-grandson) visited his family here at various times. He lived at the Manse for one year (1834–1835) before moving into his own house (on Concord's Cambridge Turnpike).

After Ripley died, Nathaniel Hawthorne and his wife occupied the house from 1842 to 1846. Here Hawthorne wrote *Mosses from an Old Manse*. When the couple moved to Salem, the property was acquired by Ripley's son Samuel, and descendants of the Ripleys resided here until 1939, when the house was purchased by the Trustees of Public Reservations.

Today visitors to the house may view fine examples of eighteenth- and nineteenth-century furniture in addition to memorabilia of the ministers and writers who resided here. Among the furnishings original to the house are the two chairs in the small parlor, most of the furniture in the dining room, the green armchair in the large parlor, the day bed in Hawthorne's bedroom, and the desk in Dr. Ripley's study.

The small room at the rear of the second floor served as a study for both Ralph Waldo Emerson and Nathaniel Hawthorne during their respective occupancies. On one of the panes of the eastern windows the Hawthornes etched their names with a diamond. The window has remained as a memento of their tenure here.

WRIGHT'S TAVERN *Off Monument Square. Open Monday through Saturday 9* A.M. *to 5* P.M. This two-story frame house with hipped roof was built in 1747 by

Ephraim Jones, a town clerk and selectman. Four years later he sold it to Thomas Munroe, who converted the building into an inn which soon developed into a thriving business. After Munroe died in 1766, the property passed through several hands until 1775, when Amos Wright purchased it and became the innkeeper.

Here, on the early morning of April 19, 1775, the Concord Minutemen gathered to consider a course of action to repulse the approaching Redcoats. Later that morning the British officers, Lieutenant Colonel Smith and Major Pitcairn, set up headquarters in this dwelling while a detachment of their soldiers marched to the outskirts of the village, where they were confronted by the Patriots.

Legend has it that before the skirmish Major Pitcairn, while partaking of refreshment here, boasted that as easily as he stirred his toddy, so would his soldiers "stir the blood of the damn rebels before night."

After the Revolutionary War the building was purchased by the Kettell family and converted into a bakery. One of the Kettell daughters married John Thoreau, grandfather of author Henry David Thoreau.

Today a gift shop occupies the ground floor.

Important Colonial Houses

BARRETT HOUSE   *Two miles east of the North Bridge Visitors' Center. Follow Barnes Mill Road to the intersection of Lowell Road. Not open to the public.*   This two-story frame house (*c.* 1770) was owned by Colonel James Barrett at the time of the Battle of Concord. It was here that the Patriots had stored the arms and ammunition that the British had marched from Boston to seize. Soldiers searching the house did not discover the arms, which had been removed and hidden elsewhere on the grounds.

BUTTRICK HOUSE   *Liberty Street. Not open to the public.*   Some of the timbers in this house were taken from the structure which stood on this site in Revolutionary days—a small dwelling built in 1710 by William Buttrick. After the battle at the North Bridge, wounded Patriot soldiers were carried to the house, which was then owned by Major John Buttrick. The present structure was erected in 1848.

JONES HOUSE ("BULLET HOLE HOUSE")   *36 Monument Street. Not open to the public.*   The original section of this house was constructed in the late seventeenth century by John Smedley. At the time of the American Revolution the dwelling was occupied by Elisha Jones (a blacksmith), his wife Elizabeth, and their six children. As the British retreated from Concord on April 19, 1775, Jones watched from the doorway of this house and fired his musket at the fleeing enemy. One of the Redcoats interrupted his flight to return Jones' fire, but his shot was misdirected and the musket ball lodged about three feet to the left of the entrance doorway. The hole may still be seen today.

MERIAM HOUSE   *At the intersection of Bedford Road and Route 2A, about a mile outside of Concord. Not open to the public.*   This house—built in 1663 by John Meriam—was the home of his grandson Nathan and his wife Abigail in 1775. It was at Meriam's Corner (where the road to Lexington meets the Bedford Road) that the Patriot militiamen began to rout the retreating British after pursuing them from Concord.

Non-Revolutionary Sites of Interest

ANTIQUARIAN MUSEUM   *200 Lexington Road, ½ mile southeast on Route 2A. Open February through November, Monday through Saturday 10 A.M. to 4:30 P.M., Sunday 2 P.M. to 4:30 P.M. Adults $1.50, children 50¢.* The Concord Antiquarian Society was founded in 1886 to encourage the study of local history and to collect relics of the region's past. Since 1930 the Society's collection has been housed in this building, which was designed by Harry B. Little. The museum displays furniture dating from 1685 to 1870. Revolutionary War buffs will enjoy a diorama showing the skirmish at the North Bridge as well as exhibits of numerous Colonial weapons. One of the museum's cherished possessions is a lantern that was hung in the steeple of Boston's Old North Church (Christ Church) on the night of Paul Revere's ride.

EMERSON HOUSE   *Cambridge Turnpike and Route 2A. Open April 19 through November 30, Tuesday through Saturday 10 A.M. to 11:30 A.M. and 1:30 P.M. to 5:30 P.M., Sunday 2:30 P.M. to 5:30 P.M. Adults $1.00, students 50¢, children 25¢.* This fine house (which was built in 1828) was the residence of Ralph Waldo Emerson from 1835 until his death in 1882. He bought it upon his second marriage, to Lydia Jackson. In 1872 a fire partially destroyed the structure, and during the period of reconstruction the family traveled in Europe. The room to the right of the entrance hallway served as Emerson's study, where he completed his major works:

Nature (1837), *Essays*—including "Over-Soul" and "Self Reliance" (1841)—and *Representative Men* (1850).

ORCHARD HOUSE *Lexington Road near Hawthorne Lane. Open April 15 through October, Monday through Saturday 10 A.M. to 5 P.M., Sunday 2 P.M. to 6 P.M. Adults 75¢, youngsters (6–16) 25¢, children (under 6) free.* During the mid-seventeenth century a small frame house was built on this site by John Hoar. His descendants, who resided here for almost 100 years, enlarged the structure. In 1857 Bronson Alcott (Amos Bronson Alcott), educational reformer and philosopher, purchased the property and settled here with his family. Alcott became superintendent of the Concord public schools and later founded the Concord School of Philosophy (which met at the Hillside Chapel). His daughter, Louisa May Alcott, wrote her novels *Little Women* (1868–1869) and *Little Men* (1871) in this house. The Alcotts lived here until 1875.

SLEEPY HOLLOW CEMETERY *From Concord Square follow Bedford Street for a short distance* In this cemetery are buried Nathaniel Hawthorne (1804–1864), Henry David Thoreau (1817–1862), Ralph Waldo Emerson (1803–1882), and Bronson Alcott (1799–1888).

WALDEN POND RESERVATION *1½ miles south on Route 126* A cairn marks the site of the cabin built on the north shore of this pond in 1845 by Henry David Thoreau, who wrote an account of his experiences here in the well-known book *Walden* (1854). The pond and its environs are now a recreational area.

Boston

Revolutionary War History

In early September 1630 a group of Puritans led by John Winthrop began to build a settlement on the banks of the Charles River. On October 19 the legislature of the colony met in Boston, and two years later the town officially became the capital of Massachusetts.

With its excellent port, Boston soon developed into a thriving commercial center. Here in 1686 the first bank in America was chartered. A weekly newspaper established in 1704, *The Boston News-Letter,* was the first to be published regularly in the colonies.

In the 1760s in Boston were struck the first sparks of the growing anti-British discontent that later ignited the Revolutionary War. The passage of the Stamp Act in March of 1765—which legislated that all legal documents, licenses, contracts, newspapers, and pamphlets bear a tax stamp—caused protest meetings and riots. Tension mounted until August 14, when an effigy of the stamp officer Andrew Oliver (brother-in-law of Lieutenant Governor Thomas Hutchinson) was hung from a towering tree in South Boston. A large crowd stood watch over the figure until dusk, then they took down the effigy, laid it on a bier, and began to march through the streets chanting "Liberty for the Colonies—No Stamps!" When the procession reached the government building housing the stamp offices, the mob grew violent and stormed the structure. Afterward they surged forward to Fort Hill where the effigy was consumed in a roaring bonfire. Proceeding to Oliver's home nearby, the rioters smashed windows and looted property.

Twelve days later mobs roamed the streets, ruthlessly pillaging the houses of officials of the Crown. The house of Benjamin Hallowell, a commissioner of customs, was seriously damaged, and the residence of Lieutenant Governor Thomas Hutchinson was almost completely destroyed.

These acts of violence, along with others that occurred throughout the colonies, forced Parliament to repeal the Stamp Act the following March.

In June 1767, after Parliament passed the Townshend Acts—which imposed duties on glass, paper, lead, paints, and tea—the fury of the Massachusetts colonists increased. Boston was in turmoil with demonstrations and many outraged citizens advocated armed insurrection. At a protest meeting held in the fall a group of Bostonians formulated a resolution to boycott English luxury goods. Samuel Adams presented a formal document to the Massachusetts Assembly, which unanimously adopted the resolution in January 1768. A copy of the boycott agreement—along with a scathing denunciation of the British policy of taxation without representation—was subsequently sent to the legislatures of all other colonies.

Tension in Boston was rising and by spring the new royal governor, Sir Francis Bernard, petitioned to England for additional troops. On September 28, 1768, six transports carrying regiments of Redcoats sailed into Boston Harbor. When the municipal authorities refused to make arrangements for quarters, forcing the soldiers to bivouac on the Common, a cloud of antagonism settled over the city. Within a month several Loyalist merchants offered their warehouses for use as barracks, and the problem was resolved.

During the next year and a half the British soldiers encountered sporadic harassment from citizens: sentinels on duty were stoned and officers were jeered at. On March 2, 1770, when an off-duty soldier wishing to supplement his income requested a job at Grey's Ropewalk (where rope was made for ship rigging), the workmen ridiculed and beat him. Determined to seek revenge, he returned a short time later with a band of fellow soldiers but they, too, were overpowered and sent running. Word spread quickly, and during the following two days groups of resentful soldiers and spirited youths roamed the streets hoping to incite a brawl.

On the evening of March 5 violence again erupted, but this time blood was shed. A large, raucous crowd gathered in front of the Customs House (then located across the street from the Town House), where the citizens began to taunt a sentinel on guard duty, Private Hugh White. Within moments Captain Thomas Preston and a detachment of British soldiers marched into the area to maintain order. Preston urged his men to exercise restraint, but the mob began hurling rocks and sticks at White, and Preston realized that decisive action was necessary. He sent a detail of seven men, with bayonets fixed, through the hostile crowd to surround and protect White. Then the mob surged forward, baiting the soldiers with insults—daring them to shoot. Crispus Attucks, a husky black man, waved his club menacingly and struck Private Hugh Montgomery. Montgomery fell to the ground, but rose to one knee, raised his musket and fired at his assailant. At the sound of the musket, the unnerved soldiers began to shoot at random and the townspeople began scurrying away while Preston attempted to get his soldiers to cease firing and return to order. When the smoke cleared, three men lay dead (including Attucks) and two others, seriously wounded, lay dying. This event came to be known as the Boston Massacre.

In order to keep the citizens from breaking into open rioting, the Crown officers imprisoned Captain Preston and the eight soldiers involved in the incident and promised that justice would be served and the guilty punished. The soldiers were held in the Boston jail until October, when anti-British sentiment had subsided sufficiently for a fair trial to be held. John Adams and Josiah Quincy, Jr., although ardent Patriots, agreed to defend the accused. Because of the introduction of testimony proving that the soldiers had fired in self-defense, Preston and six of his men were acquitted. Two others were found guilty of manslaughter, punished, and discharged from the army.

Three years later, when Parliament passed the Tea Act of 1773, showing preferential treatment to the East India Company by giving them a monopoly on the selling of tea in the colonies, the clamor of protest once again arose in Boston. On November 3, five hundred townspeople converged on a warehouse on Clark's Wharf where agents of the East India Company had gathered. A delegation of Patriots entered and demanded the resignation of these officials, but they were met with obdurate refusal. When the mob heard of this, they began battering down the warehouse door, and the agents barely escaped with their lives.

On November 28, 1773, the merchant ship *Dartmouth* arrived laden with tea in Boston Harbor. The next day a group of Patriots called a meeting at Faneuil Hall, but the crowd grew so large that they were forced to move to the Old South Meeting House. There the townspeople enthusiastically agreed to Samuel Adams' plan that twenty-five armed Patriots guard the ship until the officials could be persuaded to permit the vessel to return to England. Within days two other tea ships, the *Beaver* and the *Eleanor,* arrived and docked at Griffin's Wharf. Although the Patriots threatened that serious action would be taken unless the ships left the port, the royal governor refused to submit to ultimatums.

On the evening of December 16 another public meeting was called at the Old South Meeting House. Only a small number of the 7,000 persons who had gathered there were able to enter to hear the speeches. When a message arrived that the royal governor had again refused to permit the ships to depart, Samuel Adams announced: "This meeting can do nothing more to save the country."

Adams' remark was a prearranged signal. Suddenly a group of men disguised as Indians appeared outside the meeting house. Followed by a throng of citizens, they marched to Griffin's Wharf, quickly boarded the three ships, and heaved the cargoes (342 chests valued at £10,000) into the water. This accomplished, the townspeople hurriedly returned to their homes.

In retaliation the British Parliament passed the Boston Port Bill, closing Boston Harbor to all commerce. On June 1, 1774, the day the bill went into effect, the harbor was blockaded by men-of-war and additional British troops filled the town. Sympathetic Patriots throughout the colonies set that day aside for prayer and fasting. During the following months provisions and armaments were smuggled into the Boston area.

Ammunition depots were set up by the Patriots in towns surrounding Boston. On the evening of April 18, 1775, General Thomas Gage (governor since May 1774) sent an expedition to Concord to destroy the military stores cached there. This action resulted in the Battles of Lexington and Concord—the beginning of the Revolutionary War.

The Patriots drove the British back to Boston and encamped on the hills surrounding the city, placing it under siege. The city became an armed camp, and the population was quickly swelled by hundreds of Loyalists from outlying towns who had fled with their belongings to seek the protection of the British army.

On June 12 Gage proclaimed martial law throughout Massachusetts, a decree somewhat weakened by the fact that his troops could not move outside the city to enforce it. His proclamation also offered pardon to the rebels if they would lay down their arms—but no pardon was offered to John Hancock and Samuel Adams. This overture was met with scorn.

By mid-June the 9,000 colonists who had traveled here to join the Patriot cause had taken up positions in a series of hastily erected fortifications. From his headquarters in

Samuel Adams.
*Painting by John
Singleton Copley.*
(COURTESY
MUSEUM OF FINE
ARTS, BOSTON)

Cambridge, General Artemas Ward supervised the operation of the militia units until July 3, 1775, when George Washington assumed command of the newly-commissioned Continental Army.

The Patriots gained the strategic advantage on March 4, 1776, with the arrival of cannon brought here from Fort Ticonderoga, New York, by Colonel Henry Knox. Under the cover of night the artillery pieces were secretly mounted on Dorchester Heights overlooking Boston, and the British awakened in the morning to see the muzzles of cannon trained on their garrison.

Howe issued orders for a night raid (March 5–6) on the positions, but a violent storm forced him to cancel the attack. Realizing that continued British occupation of Boston was untenable, Howe ordered an evacuation.

It took eleven days to load the ships with supplies. Then 11,000 British soldiers and 1,000 Loyalists boarded the vessels and set sail. On the evening of March 17, 1776, General Ward entered Boston with a force of 500 Patriots, and the city never again came under British domination.

VISITORS' CENTER   The Boston Information Center is located on the Tremont Street side of the Boston Common. Pamphlets and maps are available here. The Boston 200 Corporation is operating a Visitors' Hospitality Center in City Hall, Government Center. On the fourth level of the courtyard are found an information booth and special facilities for children, including a child drop-off service (for children between the ages of three and six). Other Visitors' Centers are being established for the Bicentennial. The central telephone exchange number is 338–1976.

Information about the city can also be obtained from the Chamber of Commerce, 125 High Street, phone 426–1250, and from the Boston 200 Corporation, 1 Beacon Street, phone 338–1775. Serious students of historic houses may wish to contact the Society for the Preservation of New England Antiquities, 141 Cambridge Street, phone 227–3956.

GUIDED TOURS   **Gray Line Tours,** phone 427–8650. The most popular tour offered is the "Boston Go-Around," a two–and–one–half–hour excursion that departs daily at 9:30 A.M. and every hour (on the half–hour) until 1:30 A.M. from mid–May until mid–November. During the rest of the year fewer tours are available. The cost is $5.00 for adults. "The Greater Boston Tour" takes in the historic sites of Boston, Cambridge, and Charlestown. It is a three-hour trip costing $6.50 for adults. Tours to Lexington and Concord are also available. Buses pick up passengers at the Copley Plaza, Statler Hilton, and Sheraton Boston.

Copley Motor Tours, phone 266–3500. A three-hour tour of the Boston-Cambridge area departs at 9 A.M., noon, and 2 P.M. from April to October. Fewer tours are scheduled during the rest of the year. The price for adults is $7.00. Tours of Lexington and Concord are also available. Buses pick up passengers at major Boston hotels.

Hub Bus Lines, phone 445–3770. Inquire about special sightseeing tours.

Children's fares are approximately one-half the price of an adult ticket. All the above tours, schedules, and fees are subject to change.

PUBLIC TRANSPORTATION The Massachusetts Bay Transit Authority operates subway and bus service in the area (including Cambridge and Charlestown). For information and schedules, phone 722–5657 or 722–5700. The Boston 200 Corporation plans to offer shuttle bus service to historic sites during the Bicentennial. Their Freedom Trail Bus will cost $2.00 for adults and $1.00 for children. For information, phone 338–1775.

TAXI SERVICE Boston Cab, phone 536–5010; Checker Cab, phone 536–7000; Town Taxi, phone 536–5000; Yellow Cab, phone 522–3000; Cambridge Taxi, phone 547–3000; Charlestown Taxi, phone 242–1200.

ENTERTAINMENT Consult Boston's two leading newspapers; the *Globe* Friday edition and the *Herald American* Sunday edition both have listings of the coming week's events. Also see *Boston After Dark*.

USEFUL TELEPHONE NUMBERS Time, 637–1234; Weather 936–1234; Boston Police, 338–1212; Boston Fire Department, 232–4646; Emergency Physicians Service, 482–5252; the Day's Events, 338–1975.

WALKING TOURS If your time is limited, the two walking tours below—of the Freedom Trail and the Back Bay area—will cover most of Boston's major sites. Try also to visit the Beacon Hill Historic District (see listing under Non-Revolutionary Sites) and the museums along the Fenway (the Gardner Museum and the Boston Museum of Fine Arts). NR signifies an important *Non-Revolutionary site.*

Tour A

THE FREEDOM TRAIL

Area bounded roughly by Commercial Street on the north, Boston Common/ Park Street on the south, Congress and North Streets on the east, and Tremont and Salem Streets on the west.

Start at the Boston Common, Tremont Street side (follow the marked walk):

Boston Common

State House

Park Street Church (NR)

Granary Burying Ground

King's Chapel

Statue of Benjamin Franklin

Old Corner Book Store

Old South Meeting House

Old State House

Boston Massacre Site

Faneuil Hall

Customs House Tower (NR)

Paul Revere House/ North End

Old North Church

End at Salem Street near Charter Street.

Tour B

THE BACK BAY

Area bounded roughly by Arlington Street on the north, Massachusetts Avenue on the south, Huntington Avenue on the east, and Beacon Street on the northwest.

Start at Clarendon Street, Copley Square area:

Trinity Church (NR)

Boston Public Library (NR)

Prudential Center (NR)

Christian Science Complex (NR)

End at Massachusetts and Huntington Avenues.

Colonial and Revolutionary War Sites

BOSTON COMMON   *Bounded by Park Street, Tremont Street, Charles Street, and Beacon Street*   In the seventeenth century this site was used as a common grazing area for cattle. Here the stern Puritans erected stocks and pillories for the punishment of citizens who violated the strict laws of the community. On the edge of the Frog Pond was installed a "ducking stool"—a chair mounted at the end of a long, levered pole—which was used to punish shrewish women.

When British soldiers arrived in Boston in 1768, they temporarily encamped on the Common and used the grounds for a muster field.

On the north side of the Common, on a lot adjacent to the present-day State House, once stood the elegant mansion of John Hancock, president of the Continental Congress (1775–1777) and the first governor of the Commonwealth of Massachusetts (1780). (The house had been built by his uncle Thomas Hancock in 1738.) In 1775 the building was commandeered by British General Henry Clinton for his residence and headquarters.

On the Tremont Street side of the Common stand two monuments associated with Revolutionary War events. The Boston Massacre Monument has a stone shaft with an allegorical female figure holding a flag in her left hand and a broken chain in her right hand. The names of the five Patriots killed during the Boston Massacre (Crispus Attucks, Samuel Maverick, James Caldwell, Samuel Gray, and Patrick Carr) are inscribed on the shaft. A bronze relief on the base depicts the scene of the hostile confrontation (March 5, 1770). The monument was erected in 1888 by the Commonwealth of Massachusetts.

The monument to John Barry (1745–1803) honors the "Father of the American Navy." Barry received a commission from the Continental Congress in 1775 to command the brig *Lexington* which, in April 1776, made the first capture of a British war vessel by a commissioned American ship. While commanding the *Alliance* (1781), he overpowered two British ships after a protracted battle. In 1794 he was appointed by President Washington to help plan the organization of the peacetime navy. This monument was erected by the city of Boston in 1949.

Today Boston Common provides an area for relaxation and recreation. The **Public Gardens**, located across Charles Street, contain fountains and formal flower beds. A popular attraction are the swan boats that glide gracefully across the man-made lake. The magnificent equestrian statue of George Washington was sculpted by Thomas Ball and was unveiled in 1869.

COPP'S HILL BURYING GROUND   *At the top of Hull Street (which is off Salem Street)*   In the early seventeenth century this land was the property of William Copp, who operated a windmill nearby. Copp and his family were buried here, and during the next century residents of Boston's North End were interred in the Copp's Hill Burying Ground. Among the important citizens laid to rest in this cemetery are the Reverend Increase Mather (1639–1723), a pastor of Christ Church (Old North Church) and later a president of Harvard, and his son, the Reverend Cotton Mather (1663–1728), who succeeeded him as pastor of Christ Church. Nearby are Edward Hartt, whose shipyard built the U.S.S. *Constitution*, and Robert Newman (1752–1804), sexton of

Statue of George Washington, Boston Common (ALPER)

Christ Church, who hung the lanterns in the belfry as a signal to Paul Revere.

During the Battle of Bunker Hill (June 17, 1775) British troops manned the artillery pieces located here and bombarded Charlestown.

FANEUIL HALL *At Dock Square, off Congress Street. Open Monday through Friday 9 A.M. to 5 P.M., Saturday 9 A.M. to noon, Sunday 1 P.M. to 5 P.M. Closed holidays. Free. The museum on the top floor is open weekdays 10 A.M. to 4 P.M.* In 1740 Boston merchant Peter Faneuil (1700–1743) offered to donate funds for the erection of a markethouse near Dock Square. The town's selectmen, delighted by his generosity, promised to name the building after its benefactor. John Smibert designed the two-story structure and Samuel Ruggles supervised the construction, which was completed in September 1742.

Faneuil Hall soon became a bustling center for merchants, townspeople, and visitors. The ground floor served as a market and the upper story was used as a town hall. A fire in 1763 destroyed the building, but it was rebuilt within a year.

From the patriotic meetings held here in pre-Revolutionary days Faneuil Hall has earned the affectionate title "The Cradle of Freedom." Samuel Adams and his cousin John Adams frequently spoke here, condemning the policies of the British government—legislation such as the Stamp Act, the Tea Act, and the Coercive Acts. The anger of the Patriots was vented at rallies held on the second floor throughout the late 1760s and early 1770s. At a meeting here on November 2, 1772, Samuel Adams organized the first Committee of Correspondence.

During the siege of Boston, British soldiers used Faneuil Hall as a barracks and a theater where satirical skits mocking the colonists were staged.

After the war, when the building returned to Patriot control, many elaborate receptions were held here honor-

Second floor of Faneuil Hall Boston (MASSACHUSETTS DEPARTMENT OF COMMERCE AND DEVELOPMENT, BOSTON)

ing prominent visitors such as President George Washington (1789) and the Marquis de Lafayette (1784).

In 1806 the floor space of Faneuil Hall was tripled by extending the width of the structure from forty to eighty feet and by adding a third floor. Architect Charles Bulfinch preserved the general appearance of the structure but moved the cupola (previously located in the center of the roof) to the east end. The Colonial weather vane—a four-foot metal grasshopper fashioned by Shem Drowne—still swings above the cupola.

Today the ground floor of Faneuil Hall houses private shops. The second-floor Meeting Hall, a popular tourist attraction, is dominated by a huge painting, *Liberty and Union Now and Forever*. Painted by Boston-born artist G. P. A. Healy in 1851, the work portrays the debate in the United States Senate between Daniel Webster (Massachusetts) and Robert Young Hayne (South Carolina) on January 26–27, 1830. The debate—precipitated by the Foot Resolution limiting public land sale—centered on states' rights and federal powers. The three busts under the painting are of John Quincy Adams (by J. C. King, 1865), John Adams (by M. J. Binon, 1818), and Daniel Webster (by J. C. King, 1850). Portraits by Patriot leaders George Washington, Samuel Adams, and Henry Knox also grace the walls.

Located on the third floor are the headquarters and useum of the Ancient and Honorable Artillery Com-, a volunteer military organization established in During the Revolutionary War many of its mem- active in securing supplies for the Patriot others served in the ranks of the Conti- including Generals William Heath, Ben- hn Brooks, and William Hull. A series ng battle scenes and a collection of here.

f Samuel Adams in front of

Faneuil Hall was sculpted in the late 1870s by Anne Whitney, a native of Massachusetts.

Behind Faneuil Hall stands **Quincy Hall,** built by Mayor Josiah Quincy in 1826. It is a two-story granite building, 535 feet long and 50 feet wide, covering 27,000 square feet of land. A multimedia presentation recreating scenes of eighteenth-century Boston has recently been installed here.

FRANKLIN STATUE/CITY HALL AREA   *School Street, off Tremont Street*   This bronze statue of Boston-born Benjamin Franklin (1706–1790) was placed here in 1856, during the sesquicentennial celebration of his birth. Paid for by public subscription, the statue was sculpted by Richard S. Greenough (the younger brother of the widely acclaimed artist Horatio Greenough), and it was cast by the Ames Foundry of Chicopee, Massachusetts. The bas-relief panels on the pedestal were designed by Richard Greenough and Thomas Ball. These scenes portray Franklin operating a printing press, signing the Declaration of Independence, experimenting with lightning, and signing the 1783 Treaty of Paris.

Nearby stands a statue of Josiah Quincy (1772–1864), mayor of Boston (1823–1828) and president of Harvard (1829–1845). The work was executed by local artist Thomas Ball in 1879 and paid for by a fund bequeathed to the city by Jonathan Phillips.

The Old City Hall was built in 1862 from the designs of Gridley Bryant and Arthur Gilman. It was used by the municipal government until it moved into new quarters (at the Government Center on Congress Street) in the late 1960s. Today this building houses private offices.

The site of Boston's first public schoolhouse is marked by a tablet near the Old City Hall. In 1635 Philemon Pormort was appointed the master of the modest here (which later evolved into the Boston Public School). Among its past students who, as adults, positions of leadership were the Reverend Cotton Mather, Samuel Adams, John Hancock, and Benjamin Franklin.

GRANARY BURYING GROUND *Adjacent to the Park Street Church on Tremont Street. Open daily 8 A.M. to 4 P.M. Free.* Named for the granary which occupied this site during Colonial times, this cemetery is famous because it holds the graves of many prominent Massachusetts citizens, including state governors Increase Sumner (1746–1799), James Sullivan (1744–1808), and Christopher Gore (1758–1827). The large monument in the center of the cemetery marks the final resting place of the parents of Benjamin Franklin—Josiah Franklin (1655–1744) and his second wife Abiah (née Folger, 1667–1752). At the rear of the cemetery, directly behind the Franklin monument, stands the gravestone of Paul Revere (1735–1818). Samuel Adams (1722–1803) is buried in a plot located to the right of the Tremont Street entrance. The remains of Peter Faneuil (1700–1743), James Otis (1725–1783), John Hancock (1737–1793), and victims of the Boston Massacre all lie in the Granary Burying Ground. Visitors are often told that Elizabeth Vergoose—believed by some to be "Mother Goose," the writer of children's tales—is also interred here. But the stone pointed out as the grave of "Mother Goose" is actually a memorial to Isaac Vergoose's first wife, Mary. Elizabeth was his second wife.

KING'S CHAPEL *Corner of Tremont and School Streets. Open Monday through Saturday 10 A.M. to 4 P.M., Sunday 12:30 P.M. to 4 P.M. Closed Thanksgiving, December 25, and January 1. Free.* With the erection of King's Chapel on this site in 1689, the Church of England was established in Boston. The Puritans, who had fled from the persecutions of that church, were openly hostile to the members of the congregation and did little to hide their contempt for the chaplain, the Reverend Robert Ratcliffe.

The building was a wooden structure with a bell

tower. The interior was plain, the only ornament being the escutcheons of the king displayed on the walls. The pulpit was sent by King James II; the communion silver and altar vestments were gifts of King William and Queen Mary; and the cushions were presented by Queen Anne.

By 1741 the Chapel had become so dilapidated that Peter Faneuil, a wealthy Boston merchant, began to raise funds for the construction of a new church. Peter Harrison, the noted architect of Newport, Rhode Island, was commissioned to design the structure. Royal Governor William Shirley laid the cornerstone on August 11, 1749, and construction continued until 1754. Huge blocks of granite (from the quarries in Quincy) were erected around the original walls of the old Chapel, and after the new stone exterior was completed, the wooden structure was torn down. (The portico was not added until the late 1780s.)

Early in the American Revolution, when Boston was a garrison for British troops, the royal governor and important military officers worshipped here. When the British forces evacuated the city in March 1776, the Reverend Henry Camer, a Loyalist, fled to Nova Scotia, taking with him the communion silver and the church records. Soon afterward, King's Chapel was renamed Stone Chapel.

The next minister was James Freeman, whose unconventional theology alienated the conservative members of the congregation but attracted freethinkers. He preached that the doctrine of the Trinity was fallacious and rewrote the Book of Common Prayer. In 1789 this congregation became the first avowedly Unitarian church in the United States.

In the adjacent cemetery are buried four royal governors of Massachusetts Bay Colony: John Winthrop (1588–1649), John Endecott (1588–1665), John Leverett (1616–1679), and William Shirley (1694–1771). The

King's Chapel,
Boston (ALPER)

rectangular stone marking the grave of William Dawes
(1745–1799)—the Patriot who rode to Concord on
April 19, 1775, to warn of the British advance—was
erected in 1899 by the Massachusetts Sons of the Society
of the Revolution.

OLD CORNER BOOKSTORE *Corner of School and
Washington Streets. Open Monday through Friday 8:30
A.M. to 6 P.M. Closed holidays. Free.* The present brick
structure standing on this site is a twentieth-century reconstruction of the building erected in 1718 by Dr.
Thomas Crease, who established his residence and
apothecary shop here. After his death the building passed
through the hands of many owners until 1828, when it
was leased to a firm of booksellers, Carter and Handee.
Several years later the property was acquired by a publisher, William D. Ticknor, whose young partner
James T. Fields championed writers such as Nathaniel
Hawthorne, Ralph Waldo Emerson, Henry Wadsworth

Longfellow, Henry David Thoreau, and John Greenleaf Whittier.

A popular meeting place for intellectuals, writers, and book lovers, the publishing house of Ticknor and Fields and its first-floor bookstore were affectionately called "Parnassus Corner" (after Mount Parnassus, mythical home of the Greek Muses).

Today the Old Corner Bookstore serves as the downtown office of the Boston *Globe*. On the ground floor visitors may view a collection of first editions published by Ticknor and Fields.

OLD NORTH CHURCH (CHRIST CHURCH) *189 Salem Street. Open daily June 1 to September 30, 9:30 A.M. to 4:30 P.M. During the rest of the year the church is open daily from 10 A.M. to 4 P.M. Sunday services are at 9:30 A.M. and 11 A.M.* Christ Church, known as the Old North Church, was completed in 1723. It was designed by William Price, and the builders supervising construction were Thomas Tippin and Thomas Bennett. Christ Church served as the principal Anglican Church of the North End during the eighteenth and early nineteenth centuries.

The original steeple, which was destroyed by a hurricane in 1804, was replaced in 1806 by a shorter spire designed by the noted Boston architect Charles Bulfinch (designer of the Massachusetts State House). In 1954 another hurricane damaged the slender spire, which was reconstructed the following year to resemble the original Colonial design. The original weather vane was the work of Deacon Shem Drowne, the eighteenth-century artisan who crafted the weather vane atop Faneuil Hall.

The eight bells hanging in the steeple were made in 1744 at the West of England Foundry of Abel Rudhall in Gloucester, England. The fifteen-year-old Paul Revere used to come to Christ Church to ring these bells.

The handsome interior is graced by two gleaming chandeliers, the gift of Captain William Maxwell in 1724.

The organ, built in 1759 by Thomas Johnston, is still in use today. The statues of the cherubim on the gallery supporting the organ were carved in Belgium in 1740 for a church in Canada, but they were captured by a Massachusetts privateer during King George's War. In a niche on the altar is a bust of George Washington, one of the earliest sculpted tributes to the first President.

Gifts from King George II to the congregation include the communion silver and the 1717 "Vinegar" Bible (so called because of the misspelling of "The Parable of the Vineyard," which reads "The Parable of the Vinegar").

The Old North Church has gained fame from the events of the evening of Tuesday, April 18, 1775, when the sexton, Robert Newman, hung two lanterns in the belfry as a signal to Paul Revere indicating the route of British troops marching toward Lexington and Concord.

During the siege of Boston British General Thomas Gage worshipped here in pew number 62. According to tradition, he witnessed the Battle of Bunker Hill (June 17, 1775) and the burning of Charlestown from the church steeple.

The body of Major John Pitcairn (1722–1775) is interred in the crypt beneath the church. Second in command of the British forces at Lexington and Concord, he was mortally wounded at the Battle of Bunker Hill. When, in the early nineteenth century, the British government requested that his remains be removed to England to be interred at Westminster Abbey, the sexton of Christ Church confused the location of the grave and by mistake sent the casket of another soldier. Thus, Major Pitcairn still lies at rest in Boston.

OLD SOUTH MEETING HOUSE   *Corner of Washington and Milk Streets. Open June through September, Monday through Friday 9 A.M. to 5 P.M., Saturday 9 A.M. to 4 P.M. During the rest of the year the building is open Monday through Friday 9 A.M. to 4 P.M. Closed Thanks-*

giving, December 25, and January 1. Adults 50¢, children free.   The first building on this site was erected in 1669 to serve as a place of worship and a meeting hall for members of the Congregational Church (which had broken with the Church of England). Throughout the winter months of 1689 local citizens gathered here to listen to the church's spiritual leader, the Reverend Samuel Willard, condemn the harsh policies of Royal Governor Edmund Andros, who attempted to force the congregation to adopt the rites of the Anglican Church. In April a mob seized the royal governor, made him prisoner, and hustled him aboard a ship bound for England.

Benjamin Franklin was baptized in the church here on

Old South Meeting House, Boston
(MASSACHUSETTS DEPARTMENT OF COMMERCE AND DEVELOPMENT, BOSTON)

January 17, 1706. The house of his parents was located nearby.

By 1729 the small cedar-board meeting house had fallen into disrepair and plans were laid for the construction of a new building, a brick structure with a tower. Dedication ceremonies were held on April 26, 1730.

In the period before the Revolutionary War many significant meetings were held here. In 1768 Bostonians assembled in the meeting house to demand that Royal Governor Bernard remove from the harbor the naval ships that had been sent to enforce the customs laws created by the Townshend Acts. In March 1770 somber crowds gathered here for a memorial service to the citizens slain in the Boston Massacre.

Old South is perhaps best remembered for its "Tea Party" meeting on the evening of December 16, 1773, in which Samuel Adams and irate townspeople awaited word from the intransigent royal governor as to whether ships carrying cargoes of tea (anchored in Boston Harbor) would be permitted to return to England. At a prearranged signal a group of Patriots disguised as Indians appeared in front of the meeting house, then marched to Griffin's Wharf where they dumped the chests of tea into the harbor.

Two years later, during the siege of Boston, because of the congregation's association with rebellion against the Crown, General John Burgoyne converted this building into a riding school for cavalrymen of the Queen's Light Dragoons. Pews were removed; dirt was spread across the floor; and the pulpit was destroyed. In the galleries the officers' ladies spent afternoons viewing the riding sessions. After the British departed, the building was restored for public worship.

In September 1778, when D'Estaing's French fleet was anchored in Boston Harbor, British warships were sighted off the coast. The bell of Old South rang out from the steeple signaling the French sailors to return to their ships and prepare to defend the port from attack. The British vessels, however, changed course and the danger to Boston quickly passed.

The meeting house survived the Great Fire of 1872, although almost all the buildings in the neighborhood were destroyed. The congregation then decided to move to Copley Square and build a new church. Soon afterward, the Old South Meeting House was renovated and the interior was refurbished. It has been preserved as a historic shrine and museum since 1876.

Today, in the museum, visitors may see prints depicting scenes of Revolutionary War events, a list of black men who fought in the Battle of Bunker Hill, Colonial weaponry, letters written by George Washington, and a large model of Boston as it appeared in 1775.

OLD STATE HOUSE (THE TOWN HOUSE) *206 Washington Street, at State Street. Open Monday through Saturday 9 A.M. to 4 P.M. Closed Thanksgiving, December 25, and January 1. Adults 50¢, children 25¢.* The first public building on this site, called the Town House, was built in 1658 from funds bequeathed to the city by Robert Keayne, a prosperous merchant and founder of the Ancient and Honorable Artillery Company. The wooden two-story structure, which measured sixty-six feet by thirty-six feet, provided chambers for the royal governor, the Governor's Council, the General Court, and the government library. The ground floor served as a marketplace for the town's merchants.

In 1711 a devastating conflagration completely destroyed the building. A new Town House was erected in 1713; it was 112 feet longer than its predecessor and was built of brick. The interior of this structure was gutted by fire in 1747. Reconstruction was undertaken and completed in three years.

This building is associated with many dramatic events

Old State House, Boston (MASSACHUSETTS DEPARTMENT OF
COMMERCE AND DEVELOPMENT, BOSTON)

of the American Revolution. Here, on February 24, 1761, James Otis delivered before the Massachusetts Court an impassioned oration against the Writs of Assistance, which had authorized the entry and search of private homes and businesses. As a result, he was elected to the Colonial Assembly in May, and there he continued to oppose the policies of the Crown.

After the passage of the Stamp Act in 1765, irate Bostonians gathered in front of the Town House to brazenly burn documents bearing the required stamps. It was here, on March 5, 1770, that the Boston Massacre occurred. A jeering crowd of townspeople clashed with British soldiers, resulting in the death of five persons. The British soldiers involved in the incident were placed on trial in this building in October. Six of them, and the commander, were acquitted; two were found guilty of manslaughter.

(The site of the Boston Massacre is marked by a **ring of cobblestones** outside the old State House at Congress and State Streets.)

In one of the chambers of the Town House, General Thomas Gage called a council of war to discuss strategy before the Battle of Bunker Hill (June 17, 1775).

On July 18, 1776, Colonel Thomas Crafts stood on the east balcony and read the Declaration of Independence to throngs of jubilant townspeople. That night the Patriots ripped the royal coat of arms off the building. Later, the Town House was renamed the State House and the second floor was turned into chambers for the legislature. It was here that the constitution of Massachusetts was drafted and adopted, and in September 1780 John Hancock was inaugurated in the Council Chamber as the first governor. When President George Washington visited the city in October 1789, he was escorted to the State House from where he reviewed a procession held in his honor.

The state government moved into new quarters on

Beacon Hill in 1798, and later this building was converted into a series of shops and offices. Not until 1881 was the venerable structure restored as a historic shrine.

Today, the building is maintained by the Bostonian Society. The Assembly Room and Council Chamber, both on the second floor, are filled with period furniture. On display are Colonial weapons, a coat that once belonged to John Hancock, pitchers made in Boston, and mementos of soldiers who fought at Bunker Hill.

PAUL REVERE HOUSE *19 North Square. Open Monday through Saturday 9 A.M. to 3:45 P.M. Closed holidays. Adults 50¢, children free.* Reverend Increase Mather, the pastor of Christ Church (Old North Church), owned the first house on this site. It was destroyed by fire in 1676, and the following year a two-and-a-half-story frame dwelling (designed by John Jeffs) was erected here. When Paul Revere acquired it in 1770, it had been enlarged to three full stories.

Revere (1735–1818) was born in Boston and as a youth learned the art of metalworking from his father. He became a leading New England silversmith and also turned to various other skills, such as engraving and printing. He designed the first seal for the United Colonies, and printed the first Continental bond issue. He also experimented with the manufacturing of gunpowder (and supervised the process at Canton, Massachusetts) and operated a foundry for the casting of cannon and bells. A man of multiple talents, Revere is still best remembered as the Patriot who rode to Lexington on the night of April 18, 1775, warning inhabitants of the approaching British troops.

In the early nineteenth century this building was converted into a tenement and store. It had fallen into disrepair and was rescued from demolition in 1908 by the Paul Revere Memorial Association. It was renovated under the supervision of architect Joseph Everett Chandler. Further restoration was undertaken in 1942.

The house consists of the main living quarters and an early kitchen ell at the rear. The section fronting on North Square has the characteristic seventeenth-century overhang and windows composed of leaded diamond-shaped panes. Today, the house is furnished with eighteenth-century period pieces. On display are several items once owned by Paul Revere, including a saddlebag, a pair of pistols, and a post from his bed.

REVERE MALL *The mall connects Hanover Street with Christ Church (Old North Church) on Salem Street.*   In 1646 Christopher Stanley bequeathed this land to the city with the stipulation that it be used for the construction of a free public school. In 1933 this area was converted into an enclosed mall.

The equestrian statue of Paul Revere which dominates this mall was designed by Cyrus E. Dallin, who made a model of the work in 1885. City officials, however, decided not to proceed with the project. In 1940 the statue, which was paid for from the George R. White Fund, was finally cast and placed here.

Bronze tablets describing important events in Boston's history are affixed to the walls surrounding the mall.

SITE OF COLONIAL TAVERN *Corner of State and Kilby Streets*   During Revolutionary times a popular tavern, the Bunch of Grapes, stood on this site. Paul Revere and other Patriots frequently gathered here to discuss political events. After the siege of Boston ended in March 1776, General George Washington and his officers were entertained at a lavish banquet in the tavern's dining room.

SITE OF BENJAMIN FRANKLIN'S BIRTHPLACE   *17 Milk Street*   It is believed that Benjamin Franklin was born (in January 1706) in his father's house which was located on this site. Benjamin was the fifteenth of seventeen children. His father was a tallow chandler and soapmaker. As a youth, Benjamin was apprenticed to his brother James, printer and publisher of the *New England Courant*. In 1723, at the age of seventeen, he left Boston for Philadelphia to work as a printer.

Marking the site is a plaque placed here in January 1961 by the Bostonian Society.

SITE OF THE LIBERTY TREE   *Washington and Essex Streets*   During the eighteenth century an inn stood here. In the late 1760s and early 1770s a large tree in front of the inn became known as the "Liberty Tree" because it was the rallying place for Boston citizens protesting the policies of the Crown. A plaque on a Washington Street building marks the approximate spot of the once famous elm.

STATE HOUSE   *Beacon and Park Streets. Open Monday through Friday 9 A.M. to 5 P.M. Closed holidays. Free guided tours are conducted from 10 A.M. to 2 P.M.* In 1798 the Massachusetts legislature moved from the Old State House (at present-day Washington and State Streets) into new quarters on this site. The new State House was designed by Charles Bulfinch, the architect who later participated in the design and construction of the United States Capitol. On July 4, 1795, large crowds assembled here to watch Samuel Adams lay the cornerstone of this building. Both he and Paul Revere delivered stirring speeches. The Massachusetts State House was completed in 1798 at a cost of $133,000.

By 1802 the huge wooden dome had begun to show the ravages of the elements, and Paul Revere was commissioned to fabricate copper sheathing to cover the spherical structure. The luminous gold leaf now covering the dome was applied in 1874. (During World War II the dome was painted gray as a precautionary measure so that it would not reflect light if the city were subjected to an air raid.) The building was enlarged by the addition of wings in the early twentieth century.

Today, the following rooms are open to the public.

The **Hall of Flags**—a circular room decorated in a variety of richly colored marble—contains flags of the Spanish-American War, World War I, and World War II. The elegant **Doric Hall** has rows of Doric columns and arched niches containing statues of American statesmen. The figure of George Washington was sculpted in 1826 by Francis Legatt Chantrey. The original Senate Chamber, now the **Senate Reception Room,** is distinguished by a balustrated gallery with slender Ionic columns and an extraordinary barrel-vaulted ceiling with Adam-style detail. The original Chamber of the House of Representatives, now the **Senate Chamber,** is dominated by the building's intricately decorated massive dome. The new **Chamber of the House of Representatives** is noted for its fine series of historical paintings by Albert Herter. Visitors are fascinated by the "Sacred Cod," the five-foot model of a fish symbolizing the state's early dependence on the fishing industry.

The **State Archives** (in the basement) display important letters and documents, including a copy of the Massachusetts Bay Company Charter brought to Boston in 1630 and an original printed copy of the Declaration of Independence. The **State Library** (at the rear of the third floor) was established in 1828 and today contains more than a million volumes dealing with law and history.

Two statues flank the State House steps. The figure of Daniel Webster (1782–1852), United States Senator from Massachusetts, was sculpted by Hiram Powers in 1859; the figure of Horace Mann (1796–1859), Massachusetts legislator and educator, was executed by Emma Stebbins in 1861.

At the top of the steps, to the left of the entrance, is a reproduction of the Liberty Bell presented to the people of Massachusetts in 1950 by John Snyder, Secretary of the Treasury, as a symbol of the United States Savings Bond Independence Drive held during the summer of

Tea Party ship, Boston (ALPER)

that year. The bell, cast in France in 1950, has dimensions and tone identical with those of the original bell located in Philadelphia's Independence Hall.

TEA PARTY SHIP AND MUSEUM *Congress Street Bridge, a short distance from South Station. If you are in the area of Boston Common, get onto Boylston Street and follow it into the shopping district. Cross over Washington Street onto Essex Street. Proceed along Essex Street until coming to Atlantic Avenue, then turn left and travel a short distance to Congress Street. Make a right turn and proceed to the bridge. Open during the winter from 9 A.M. to 5 P.M.; open during the summer from 9 A.M. to 7 P.M. Adults $1.50, children 75¢.* At the base of the Congress Street Bridge is moored a full-scale replica of the merchant brig *Beaver.* It was the smallest of the three British ships that brought East India tea to Boston in December 1773, precipitating the Boston Tea Party. Owned by Captain Rotches of Nantucket, it was built in Rhode Island and was active in trade between the northern colonies and England.

Construction of the *Beaver II* was begun in late 1972. Naval architect William Baker designed the vessel around the hull of an old training schooner that possessed dimensions similar to those of the original ship—an overall length of 112 feet and breadth on deck of 22 feet. The replica was built in a Danish shipyard: the new deck was laid, the gallery was erected, and the masts were set in place.

By the summer of 1973 the *Beaver II* was completed and set sail for the United States. With a crew of ten Americans and Danes, it crossed the North Sea to England where it stopped to load a cargo of tea. The arrival of the *Beaver II* to Boston Harbor was celebrated by the festive sprays of fireboats and the welcoming cheers of crowds. On the afternoon of December 16, 1973—the 200th anniversary of the Boston Tea Party—a reenactment of the historic event took place: a group of Bostonians wearing Colonial costumes and Indian disguises climbed aboard the ship and dumped ninety chests of tea into the water.

A museum on the pier adjacent to the ship contains copies of historical documents and informative audiovisual presentations describing the Boston Tea Party and the events leading to it.

Non-Revolutionary Sites of Interest

BEACON HILL HISTORIC DISTRICT *Bounded by Beacon Street, Charles Street, Revere Street, and Hancock Street* Beacon Hill was a fashionable residential area in the late eighteenth century and throughout the nineteenth century. The following houses—all private—are of historic significance.

29 Chestnut Street Edwin Booth (1833–1893), the famous actor, maintained a home here, although he spent most of his time in New York City and on tour in England.

50 Chestnut Street Historian Francis Parkman (1823–1893) took up residence here in 1864; he wrote his major works in this house.

49 Mt. Vernon Street Lemuel Shaw (1781–1861), Chief Justice of the Massachusetts Supreme Court from 1830 to 1860, resided here.

65 Mt. Vernon Street This was the home of Senator Henry Cabot Lodge (1850–1924).

76 Mt. Vernon Street Novelist Margaret Wade Deland (1857–1945) resided in this house, where she wrote *The Awakening of Helena Richie* and *The Iron Woman*.

85 Mt. Vernon Street This handsome dwelling was designed by the noted architect Charles Bulfinch for political leader Harrison Gray Otis (1765–1848), who moved here in 1800 from his house on Cambridge Street.

88 Mt. Vernon Street In the nineteenth century Enoch Train, an influential merchant and owner of a fleet of clipper ships, made his residence here.

10 **Louisburg Square**   This was the Boston home of Louisa May Alcott (1832–1888). Her father, Bronson Alcott, an educator and social reformer, died here in 1888.

20 **Louisburg Square**   In this house the famous Swedish soprano Jenny Lind (1820–1887), after a tour of the United States, was married to musician Otto Goldschmidt in 1852.

84 **Joy Street**   Here lived Thomas Bailey Aldrich (1836–1907), author and editor of *The Atlantic Monthly*.

131 **Charles Street**   Sarah Orne Jewett (1849–1909), author of the widely acclaimed novel *The Country of the Pointed Firs*, lived in this townhouse.

164 **Charles Street**   This house served as the Boston residence of Oliver Wendell Holmes (1841–1935), Justice of the Massachusetts Supreme Court (1882–1902) and Justice of the United States Supreme Court (1902–1935).

BOSTON PUBLIC LIBRARY   *West edge of Copley Square. Open Monday through Friday 9 A.M. to 9 P.M., Saturday 9 A.M. to 6 P.M., Sunday 2 P.M. to 6 P.M. Closed on holidays and on Sundays during the summer.* Designed by the prestigious New York architectural firm of McKim, Mead and White, this building was constructed between 1888 and 1895. It not only houses one of the largest collections of books in the United States but also contains a collection of fine paintings. The Puvis de Chavannes murals are highly prized because they are the only murals of this artist outside of France. On the upper-floor corridor is a series of murals by John Singer Sargent entitled *The Triumph of Religion*. The bronze entrance doors are the work of Daniel Chester French.

The annex (the "new building"), designed by Philip Johnson, opened in 1972.

CHRISTIAN SCIENCE COMPLEX   *Area at Huntington Avenue and Massachusetts Avenue*   The imposing structure of the Christian Science Publishing Company houses the presses and editorial offices of the highly acclaimed newspaper, *The Christian Science Monitor,* and publications of the Christian Science Church. The building also contains a remarkable exhibition, the Mapparium—an enormous, hollow globe of the world which visitors can enter to examine a representation of the earth's topography, the raised surfaces of continents and islands as well as the depths of the ocean basins.

The magnificent Mother Church consists of two structures connected by an interior passage. The smaller building of gray rough-faced granite with a square tower was completed in 1894. The large main church—an Italian Renaissance–style building with a central dome— was erected in 1904. Built of Indiana limestone and New Hampshire granite, it seats 5,000 people in its vast, open nave.

The other elements of the Christian Science Complex include landscaped malls, a 700-foot reflecting pool, a colonnade, and several concrete and glass office buildings. They were designed by I. M. Pei and Partners as a fitting setting for the Mother Church. The new section of the complex was completed in 1975 at a cost of $75 million.

CUSTOMS HOUSE TOWER   *India and State Streets. Open Monday through Friday 9 A.M. to 11:30 A.M. and 1:30 P.M. to 4 P.M. Closed holidays. Free.*   Designed by architect A. B. Young, the Customs House was completed in 1849 at a cost of $1 million. Here customs officials would record the taxes and duties levied on imports. The 500-foot tower, which was designed by Peabody and Stearns, was added in 1915. From the tower's observation deck, visitors are afforded a panoramic view of Boston.

GARDNER MUSEUM   *280 Fenway. Open September through June, Tuesday 1 P.M. TO 9:30 P.M.; Wednesday through Sunday 1 P.M. to 5:30 P.M. During July and*

August the museum is open Tuesday through Saturday 1 P.M. to 5:30 P.M. Closed holidays. Free. From September to June free concerts are held on Thursdays and Sundays at 4 P.M. Mrs. Isabella Stewart Gardner (1840–1924), wife of the wealthy businessman John Lowell Gardner, commissioned architect Edward H. Sears in 1902 to design this mansion in the style of a Venetian palazzo. With the aid of art scholar and connoisseur Bernard Berenson, she filled her home with masterpieces—paintings by Corot, Titian, Rembrandt, Tintoretto, Whistler, and Sargent. She bequeathed the house and her collection to the city of Boston for use as a public museum.

HARRISON GRAY OTIS HOUSE *141 Cambridge Street. Open weekdays 10 A.M. to 4 P.M. Closed holidays. Fee $1.00.* This elegant house was designed in 1795 by the distinguished architect Charles Bulfinch for Harrison Gray Otis (1765–1848), a Massachusetts legislator (1795–1797, 1802–1817), United States Senator (1817–1822), and mayor of Boston (1829–1831). Otis resided here until 1800, when he moved into his new home at 85 Mt. Vernon Street.

The exterior of this hipped-roof mansion is notable for the Palladian window above the entrance and the lunette window on the top floor. The interior has fine woodwork and delicate carving. The spacious rooms are furnished with exquisite period pieces.

Since 1916 the house has served as the headquarters of the Society for the Preservation of New England Antiquities.

JOHN KENNEDY BIRTHPLACE *83 Beals Street, Brookline. Open Tuesday through Saturday 9 A.M. to 5 P.M.; also on Sunday 1 P.M. to 5 P.M. from November through March. Closed Thanksgiving, Christmas, and January 1. Donations accepted.* John F. Kennedy (1917–1963), the thirty-fifth President of the United States, was born here and spent his boyhood days in this frame house. Now a National Historic Site, the building has been restored and furnished with pieces appropriate to the period of the Kennedys' occupancy.

MUSEUM OF AFRO-AMERICAN HISTORY *Smith Court, Beacon Hill. Open Monday through Friday 10 A.M. to 4 P.M. Adults $1.00, children 50¢.* This building, erected in 1805, was originally used as a meeting house for black people who refused to continue sitting in the segregated galleries of Boston's churches. Here, in 1832, William Lloyd Garrison held the first meeting of the New England Anti-Slavery Society. Today, visitors may see exhibitions relating to Afro-American culture. The museum also provides information and brochures about the Black Heritage Trail, a tour of Boston sites associated with black history.

MUSEUM OF FINE ARTS *465 Huntington Avenue. Open daily 10 A.M. to 6 P.M., Sunday 10 A.M. to 1 P.M. The museum remains open late—until 9 P.M.—on Tuesday and Thursday. Closed Thanksgiving, December 25, and January 1. Adults $1.50, children free. No admission fee on Sunday.* The main museum building, designed by Guy Lowell, was constructed between 1907 and 1909. The collection has grown over the decades to become one of the finest in the world. The museum is noted for its superb collection of Egyptian and Greek antiquities. Of particular interest are the gallery of American paintings and the collection of European paintings, which includes an exceptionally fine group of works of the Impressionist School. The period rooms present handsome decors and furnishings of the eighteenth and nineteenth centuries.

MUSEUM OF SCIENCE AND HAYDEN PLANETARIUM *Science Park overlooking the Charles River Basin. Open Monday through Saturday 10 A.M. to 5 P.M., Sunday 11 A.M. to 5 P.M. Late hours on Friday evening, until 10 P.M. Adults $2.00, youngsters (5–16) $1.00, children (under 5) free.* The museum features exhibitions on astronomy, natural history, and the physical sciences. The adjacent planetarium has shows Tuesday through Saturday at 11 A.M. and 2:45 P.M. (plus one at 8 P.M. on Friday), and on Sunday at 12:15 P.M. and 2:45 P.M., for which there is an additional 50¢ charge.

NEW ENGLAND AQUARIUM *Central Wharf, off Atlantic Avenue. Open Monday through Thursday 9 A.M. to 5 P.M., Friday 9 A.M. to 9 P.M., Saturday, Sunday, and holidays 10 A.M. to 6 P.M. Adults $2.00, youngsters (5–14) $1.00, children (under 5) free.* The tanks of tropical fish and unusual marine life on display here fascinate visitors of all ages. Of special interest is the four-story 200,000-gallon ocean tank with an extraordinary array of fish and animals. Marine shows are presented in the amphitheater.

PARK STREET CHURCH *Park and Tremont Streets. Open Monday through Friday 9 A.M. to 4:30 P.M. (to 4 P.M. in July and August), Sunday 9 A.M. to 4 P.M. and 4:30 P.M. to 9 P.M. Sunday services at 10:30 A.M. and 7:30 P.M.* Built in 1809 for a group of Congregationalists, this graceful church building was designed by Peter Banner, whose architectural plan was influenced by Christopher Wren's design of St. Bride's Church (London). The first pastor to serve at the Park Street Church was Dr. Edward Dorr Griffin, who later became the president of Williams College.

During the War of 1812 the brimstone for gunpowder was stored in the church basement, giving the site the name "Brimstone Corner."

The church was the scene of two important events in the nineteenth century. On July 4, 1829, William Lloyd Garrison held the congregation spellbound as he delivered his first major public address against slavery. Here, on July 4, 1832, the hymn "America" ("My Country 'tis of Thee") was first sung in public at a holiday program sponsored by the Boston Sabbath School Union. The lyrics were written by Samuel Francis Smith and were set to an old German tune, which is also used for the British national anthem.

The interior of the church is characterized by a dignified simplicity.

PRUDENTIAL CENTER   *Between Huntington Avenue and Boylston Street*   Built in the mid-1960s, the fifty-two-story Prudential Tower dominates a complex of office buildings, businesses, shops, and restaurants. A panoramic view of Boston and Cambridge may be seen from the Prudential Tower Skywalk, which is located on the fiftieth floor. It is open Monday through Saturday 9 A.M. to midnight, Sunday 1 P.M. to 11 P.M. Adults 75¢, children 25¢.

TRINITY CHURCH   *Copley Square. Open daily 8 A.M. to 4 P.M.*   The first church building of this parish was built in the mid-eighteenth century at the corner of present-day Summer and Washington Streets. In 1871 a tract of land at Copley Square was purchased and architect Henry Hobson Richardson was commissioned to design a large sanctuary to accommodate the growing congregation. A splendid new Trinity Church soon arose —a cruciform-shaped structure in the French Romanesque style, constructed of yellow-brown granite stone with brown freestone embellishment. The decoration of the interior was entrusted to John La Farge, and some of the windows were by Sir Edward Burne-Jones.

The building was consecrated on February 9, 1877. At that time the rector was the Reverend Phillips Brooks (1835–1893), who in 1891 became Bishop of the Episcopal Church of Massachusetts. In 1971 Trinity Church was designated a National Historic Landmark.

Outside the north transept stands a memorial to the Reverend Brooks executed by Augustus Saint-Gaudens. When the sculpture was dedicated in 1910, it caused fierce controversy, for a figure of Christ is shown with his hand placed on Brooks' left shoulder.

Cambridge

Revolutionary War History

Although the Cambridge Patriots were outspoken in their defiance of the Crown, little violence occurred in the town until September 1774. When, on September 1, British troops raided the local powder magazine and seized artillery pieces, the citizens rose up in outrage. The next day a mob of armed Patriots stormed the houses of Lieutenant Governor Thomas Oliver and two other officials of the Crown, forcing them to flee to Boston where there was a strong British garrison. In the spring of 1775, at the beginning of the siege of Boston, many other Cambridge Loyalists fled across the Charles River.

On June 15, 1775, the Continental Congress appointed George Washington Commander-in-Chief of the Continental Army (the troops recruited from throughout the colonies). Washington immediately left Philadelphia for Cambridge, where the soldiers were assembling to lay siege to British-controlled Boston. He arrived on July 2, and the following day, on the Cambridge Common, assumed command of 9,000 Patriots. (Not all the troops were present on this occasion, however, since many of the soldiers were manning the military installations that were arranged in a crescent around the besieged Boston.)

Washington issued orders for the strengthening of fortifications in the area and made preparations for sheltering and training the army. Hundreds of tents were erected on and around the Cambridge Common, with some men quartered in the buildings of Harvard College and in the houses of Loyalists who had fled the town. (Later, crude bar-

Washington and a Committee of Congress at Cambridge (NEW
YORK PUBLIC LIBRARY PICTURE COLLECTION)

racks were erected.) Intensive drilling and inspection took
place on the Common under the stern guidance of Generals
Artemas Ward, Charles Lee, and Israel Putnam.

Since this was an irregular volunteer army without
standard uniforms, Washington devised a means of dif-
ferentiating the ranks. Major generals wore purple sashes
across their chests, while brigadier generals used pink and
aides-de-camp, green. Field officers placed red cockades in
their hats, sergeants wore knots of red cloth on their right
shoulders, and corporals wore knots of green.

From his headquarters in the Vassall house, Washington
met with his staff to organize his forces: six brigades of six
regiments and three divisions of two brigades were formed.
But problems of discipline remained to be solved. Many of
the backwoodsmen who had come from Pennsylvania,
Maryland, and Virginia were accustomed to acting inde-
pendently and their stubborn individualism resisted regi-
mentation. The slow pace of the siege, which seemed to
produce few tangible results, was demoralizing, and consequently many men deserted.

In October Congress sent to Cambridge a committee—Benjamin Franklin, Thomas Lynch, Sr., and Benjamin Harrison—to confer with Washington. They remained for five days to discuss arrangements for additional munitions and supplies.

After Patriot troops had occupied Dorchester Heights overlooking Boston and had placed cannon there (which had been brought from Fort Ticonderoga by Colonel Henry Knox), the British realized their position was untenable and evacuated the city on March 17, 1776. When the British fleet, which had been anchored off the coast, departed ten days later, Boston and Cambridge were securely under Patriot control. The Commander-in-Chief left the area on April 4, 1776, hastening toward New York City, which he considered to be the next strategic objective of the British army. Cambridge was spared the scars of war during the remaining years of the Revolution.

When news reached the town that British General John Burgoyne had surrendered his army at Saratoga, New York, on October 17, 1777, the jubilant residents built a bonfire on the Common and fired numerous cannon in celebration. But the arrival of the defeated British army (frequently referred to as the "Convention Army") in the area in early November was greatly resented by the populace. The Cambridge Council had formed a committee to search for houses to quarter the British officers, but when the prisoners of war arrived, no suitable accommodations had yet been found. General Burgoyne and several of his staff were at first placed in cramped quarters in a dingy Cambridge tavern. The officers' baggage was heaped onto the Common and was looted by bands of disgruntled townspeople. Finally, housing was arranged for the officers. The thousands of foot soldiers were quartered in the barracks which had been hastily erected by Patriot troops during the siege of Boston.

In April 1778 Burgoyne and several of his officers were permitted to return to England on parole. But the other prisoners of war remained here until January 1779 when, in violation of the terms of the surrender agreement, they were marched south to prison camps in Virginia. The removal of the British troops from the area ended Cambridge's direct involvement in the war.

Colonial and Revolutionary War Sites

Cambridge is located directly across the Charles River from Boston. For information about public transportation and guided tours, see the Boston section.

BRATTLE STREET ("TORY ROW") In pre-Revolutionary days this street—then called King's Highway— was lined with many fine houses owned by prominent citizens who were supporters of the Crown. These houses were confiscated by the Patriots during the Revolutionary War. Those which still survive are briefly described below.

42 Brattle Street This gambrel-roofed house was built in the late 1720s by William Brattle, one of the wealthiest men in Cambridge. In 1774 Brattle was securing vital information for General Thomas Gage in Boston. According to tradition, one day he lost a report he had intended to deliver to British headquarters. It was found and printed in a local broadside, enraging the Patriots. Their hostility toward Brattle continued to intensify until, finally, he was forced to seek refuge in Boston. Thomas Mifflin, General Washington's aide-de-camp and Commissary General, occupied the house in 1775–1776. (Not open to the public.)

94 Brattle Street   Constructed in the late seventeenth century, this dwelling was the property of John Vassall (father of the owner of the house at 105 Brattle) and later was acquired by his brother Henry. Wealthy merchants, the Vassalls were active in the town's political affairs. After the building was confiscated, it was used as the medical headquarters of the Continental Army. In September 1775 Dr. Benjamin Church, chief physician of Cambridge, was discovered sending intelligence reports to the British and he was confined to this house during his trial in October. Found guilty, he was sent to Connecticut for imprisonment. (Not open to the public.)

105 Brattle Street   See the Vassall-Craigie-Longfellow House. (Open to the public.)

149 Brattle Street   Richard Lechmere built this house in 1761. After British General Burgoyne's defeat at Saratoga (October 1777), when prisoners of war were sent to the Boston-Cambridge area, Baron von Riedesel (the Hessian general) and his wife were confined to this house. According to tradition, they held many gay parties here for the British officers during the winter of 1777–1778. The building has been extensively remodeled. (Not open to the public.)

159 Brattle Street (Lee-Nichols House)   The oldest section of this house was built in the 1680s. In 1760 Judge Joseph Lee enlarged and renovated the structure and added the projecting vestibule. Judge Lee was moderate in his views, and although a Loyalist, was respected by many local Patriots. (Open to the public.)

175 Brattle Street   This house was built in the mid-1760s by George Ruggles, a Jamaican planter. After the property was confiscated in 1775, Thomas Fayerweather purchased it. Some wounded Patriot soldiers who had fallen in the Battle of Bunker Hill were brought here for medical attention. (Not open to the public.)

33 Elmwood Avenue (off Brattle Street)   Lieutenant Governor Thomas Oliver built this fine mansion in 1767.

In September 1774 local Patriots stormed the house, forcing him to flee to Boston. After the Revolutionary War the property passed through several hands, and near the end of the eighteenth century it was acquired by Elbridge Gerry, who had served as a member of the Provincial Congress and the Committee of Safety. As a delegate to the Second Continental Congress, he signed the Declaration of Independence. Gerry served as governor of Massachusetts in 1811–1812. In the nineteenth century this was the residence of writer James Russell Lowell. (Not open to the public.)

CAMBRIDGE COMMON *Massachusetts Avenue and Garden Street* It was at this site, on the evening of June 16, 1775, that 1,200 soldiers gathered to depart for Charlestown, where they would take up defensive positions on Breed's Hill and Bunker Hill. The president of Harvard College, the Reverend Samuel Langdon, offered a prayer for the success of their mission.

Here, on July 3, 1775, General George Washington formally took command of the Continental Army.

Today, visitors may see three Revolutionary War cannon captured from the British in 1775 and placed here as a tribute to the Cambridge Patriots.

CHRIST CHURCH *Garden Street, opposite Cambridge Common* Designed by architect Peter Harrison, this church was completed in 1761 during the pastorate of the Reverend East Apthorp. The belfry was added in 1766. In late 1774 the rector and most of the Anglican congregation, who were Loyalists, fled to Boston. Patriot soldiers used the building as a barracks throughout the summer and fall of 1775. According to tradition, the organ pipes were melted and recast into musket balls. When Martha Washington came to Cambridge in December 1775 to join her husband, she insisted that the building be returned to use as a church, after which the Washingtons frequently worshipped here.

COOPER-FROST-AUSTIN HOUSE *21 Linnaean Street.*
Open June 1 through October 31 on Tuesday and Thursday from 2 P.M. to 4 P.M. From November 1 through May 31 the house is open only on Thursday from 7 P.M. to 9 P.M. Fee 50¢. The oldest house in Cambridge, this structure was built about 1690. The section to the left of the entrance was added in 1720. The dwelling is two and a half stories with a lean-to and a central chimney. Period furniture is on display. It is now administered by the Society for the Preservation of New England Antiquities.

HARVARD   COLLEGE   COLONIAL   LANDMARKS
Harvard Yard, off Massachusetts Avenue   Harvard College was founded in 1636 with a grant from the General Court of the Massachusetts Bay Colony. Two years later it was named for John Harvard (1607–1638), teaching elder of the First Church of Charlestown, who bequeathed £780 and his library of 320 volumes to the institution.

Three Colonial structures are still standing on the Harvard campus.

Harvard Hall   To escape the 1764 smallpox epidemic, members of the General Court fled Boston and reconvened in Cambridge in this building. One week later the structure (built in 1672) was razed by a great conflagration that also destroyed the college's 5,000-volume library. Harvard Hall was rebuilt in 1764; it was enlarged to include dining rooms and a chapel.

Massachusetts Hall   Built in 1720, this building was originally a dormitory with thirty-two chambers. During the siege of Boston, Patriot soldiers were billeted here.

Wadsworth House   This house was built in 1726 for the first president of Harvard College, Benjamin Wadsworth. In early July 1775 General Washington stayed here briefly while his quarters at present-day 105 Brattle Street (Vassall-Craigie-Longfellow House) were being prepared. Wadsworth House was used as the official residence of the presidents of Harvard until 1849. The building now contains offices of the Alumni Association.

VASSALL-CRAIGIE-LONGFELLOW HOUSE (LONG-FELLOW NATIONAL HISTORIC SITE) *105 Brattle Street. Open June through October Monday through Friday 10 A.M. to 5 P.M., Saturday noon to 5 P.M., Sunday 1 P.M. to 5 P.M. During the rest of the year the house is open Monday through Friday 10 A.M. to 4 P.M., Saturday and Sunday 2 P.M. to 4 P.M. Adults $1.00, youngsters (7–17) 50¢, children (under 7) free.* This splendid Georgian mansion was built in 1759 for John Vassall by his father, whose house was located diagonally across the street. Vassall, a major in the British Colonial Army, was a staunch supporter of the policies of the Crown. In September 1774, when a Patriot mob forced Lieutenant Governor Thomas Oliver to flee his Cambridge house, Vassall and his family sought refuge in Boston where British soldiers were garrisoned. When the British army evacuated Boston in March 1776, the Vassalls and other Loyalists accompanied them. Eventually they resettled in England.

On July 3, 1775, about two weeks after the Battle of Bunker Hill, General George Washington took command of Continental troops in Cambridge and commandeered this house as his headquarters. He established an office and a council room on the first floor, using a suite on the second floor for his private chambers. Benjamin Franklin, John Adams, and John Hancock, as well as other important Patriots, met here with the newly appointed Commander-in-Chief to discuss the disposition of Continental troops. During the Patriot siege of Boston, Washington resided in this house. Immediately after his departure in April 1776, the building was converted into a military hospital.

After the Revolutionary War, in the 1780s, the house passed through the hands of many owners, each of whom resided here for only a short time. In 1791

Vassall–Craigie–Longfellow House, Cambridge (ALPER)

Andrew Craigie acquired the property, enlarged the house, and constructed several outbuildings (including the first greenhouse in Cambridge). Craigie, who had served as Apothecary-General in the Continental Army, increased his wealth through land speculation.

He married Betsy Shaw, the daughter of a Nantucket minister. They entertained frequently and lavishly, and their guests included Talleyrand, Louis Philippe (later King of France), and the Duke of Kent.

The Craigie's dazzling social life was but a facade for an unhappy marriage. Mrs. Craigie, fifteen years younger than her husband, had married for money and was in love with another man whose love letters she hid in the attic. Andrew Craigie had numerous affairs with other women and sired an illegitimate daughter with whom he kept in close contact, storing her letters in the cellar.

The prodigality of the Craigies exhausted their fortune, and after his death in 1819 his widow was compelled to take in boarders. Among the young men who rented rooms here were Josiah Quincy and Edward Everett, both future Congressmen and presidents of Harvard. Henry Wadsworth Longfellow, at the age of thirty, came to live here in 1837 while serving as professor of modern languages at Harvard.

When Mrs. Craigie died in 1842 the property was put up for sale. The following year, when Longfellow married Frances Appleton, her father (industrialist Nathan Appleton) bought the house as a wedding present for the couple. Here they made their home for the rest of their lives. Longfellow wrote his major works in the study on the first floor: *Evangeline* (1847), *The Song of Hiawatha* (1855), *The Courtship of Miles Standish* (1858), and *Paul Revere's Ride* (1861).

After Frances' death in 1861, Longfellow sought solace by undertaking a new translation of Dante's *Divine Comedy*. Longfellow died in 1882, and he was the first American whose bust was placed in the Poet's Corner of Westminster Abbey, London.

After his death, his descendants continuously occupied the house until 1913, when it was opened to the public as a museum administered by the Longfellow Memorial Trust. The furnishings reflect the period of the poet's residence, and many pieces on display once belonged to the Longfellows.

OLD BURYING GROUND   *Corner of Church Street and Massachusetts Avenue*   Residents of Colonial Cambridge and many Revolutionary War soldiers (including Cambridge men killed at the Battle of Bunker Hill) are buried here. Members of the prominent early-eighteenth-century Vassall family were laid to rest beneath an impressive tomb in this cemetery. Several presidents of Harvard College are also interred here.

Charlestown

On June 13, 1775, the Patriot commanders who were laying siege to Boston received reports that British General Thomas Gage was planning to send troops to occupy Dorchester Heights and the high ground of Charlestown—strategic areas which held commanding positions overlooking Boston. Two days later Patriot leaders decided that Bunker Hill in Charlestown should be secured and held by militia units and that the hills of Dorchester Heights should be occupied as soon afterward as feasible.

Three hills rose on the Charlestown peninsula. Bunker Hill, located near the northern end of the peninsula close to the Charlestown Neck, stood 110 feet high and sloped on its east and west sides to the water. It was connected by a low ridge with Breed's Hill, which stood seventy-five feet high and was centrally located. The village of Charlestown lay below to the west of the hill. The third hill was Moulton's Hill, only thirty-five feet high, on the southeast edge of the peninsula.

On the night of June 16 Colonel William Prescott and a force of 1,200 men left Cambridge for Charlestown. En route they were joined by troops led by General Israel Putnam, who had also brought several wagons loaded with tools and supplies.

Soon after arriving at Charlestown, the men began building fortifications. Prescott's orders had been to fortify Bunker Hill (the highest of the three hills) but Putnam, who shared the command, persuaded him to choose Breed's Hill instead. In addition, secondary defenses were

erected on Bunker Hill in case a retreat became necessary.
Within four hours a redoubt, forty-five yards square, was
completed on Breed's Hill. Afterward, 100 yards of breastwork were built (to protect the Patriot east flank) as well
as several flèches (V-shaped outworks). A rail fence was
constructed toward the east, along the edge of a bluff
overlooking the beach.

Determined to prevent the Patriots from gaining the
advantage, General Gage ordered an attack. On June 17,
as British naval ships bombarded the peninsula, twenty-
eight barges bearing 1,500 Redcoats and twelve cannon
slipped out of Boston toward Charlestown. General William Howe, commander of the operation, landed his men
on the riverbank northeast of the village and quickly moved
to the protection of Moulton's Hill to await reinforcements
before launching an attack. Meanwhile, the battery on
Copp's Hill in Boston and the British men-of-war in the
bay fired incendiary projectiles and shells into Charlestown village, setting the buildings afire.

Attack on Bunker Hill, with the Burning of Charles Town
(NATIONAL GALLERY OF ART, WASHINGTON, D.C.)

When reinforcements arrived near 2 P.M., the battle commenced. General Robert Pigot began to lead his Redcoats up Breed's Hill while Howe's wing moved toward the rail fence that was manned by Patriot forces under Colonel John Stark and Captain Thomas Knowlton. Prescott issued orders: "Don't fire until you see the whites of their eyes!" Obeying this command, the marksmen were able to repel Pigot's advance; Howe's troops, after attempting an unsuccessful bayonet charge, were also driven back.

Twenty minutes later, under the blazing sun, General Howe organized a second attack. He and Pigot's forces combined for the main thrust up the hill toward the redoubt as a light infantry detachment cautiously approached the rail fence. The Patriots unleashed a barrage of fire from the redoubt, breastwork, and rail fence—and the enemy bolted in retreat, leaving behind their dead.

Having again failed, Howe regrouped his forces for a third assault. He ordered his men to remove their heavy knapsacks which had hindered their advance. This time the troops of Howe, Pigot, and Clinton joined for the principal attack on the Breed's Hill redoubt with only a diversionary maneuver directed at the fence. Heavy artillery pieces were aimed at the breastwork, sending the militiamen fleeing. Against the unrelenting fire of Patriot guns, the British infantry marched in their traditional column formation up the hill, then broke into a bayonet charge. By now the Patriots' supply of ammunition was virtually exhausted. Clambering over the redoubt walls, the British forced the defenders to engage in hand-to-hand combat. Thirty Patriots were killed before the fortification was abandoned. When the Patriots finally did fall back, their retreat was orderly.

The losses were high on both sides. The British reported 1,150 casualties (including 92 officers) out of a force of 2,500. Major John Pitcairn, who was second in command at Lexington and Concord, was killed. The Patriots lost

441 men out of 3,000. Dr. Joseph Warren, president of the Second Massachusetts Provincial Congress, was fatally wounded during the final assault.

Although technically a defeat, the defense of Breed's Hill (which has come to be known as the Battle of Bunker Hill) had a positive effect on the course of the Revolutionary War. It showed that poorly equipped and ill-trained Americans could fearlessly confront and vigorously fight British Regulars. Furthermore, it convinced the Continental Congress of the need for a strong military leader to train the army and direct its strategy. On July 3, 1775, George Washington, under commission of the Congress, arrived at Cambridge to assume command of the Continental Army.

Colonial and Revolutionary War Sites

To reach Charlestown from Boston, take Storrow Drive (along the Charles River) toward the Mystic River Bridge by following signs to Revere and Interstate 95 North. As you approach the bridge, take the off-ramp to Charlestown. For information about public transportation and guided tours, see the Boston section.

BUNKER HILL MONUMENT *Monument Square is bounded by High Street, Lexington Street, Bartlett Street, and Concord Street. Open daily 9 A.M. to 4 P.M. Closed December 25. Admission 10¢ to climb the 294-step spiral staircase.* The Bunker Hill Monument Association was organized in 1823 to plan an appropriate tribute to the Patriots who fought here on June 17, 1775.

After $54,000 had been raised, the Association commissioned architect Solomon Willard to design a monument. The cornerstone was laid on June 17, 1825—the fiftieth anniversary of the battle—by the Marquis de Lafayette, who had returned to the United States to visit his Revolutionary War comrades. Before the large crowds which had assembled for the occasion, Daniel Webster, then a member of the United States House of Representatives, delivered a moving oration in which he exhorted the people to "Let our object be our country, our whole country, and nothing but our country." He saluted the forty survivors of the battle who were present with these words: "Venerable men, you have come down to us from a former generation. Heaven has bounteously lengthened out your lives that you might behold this joyous day."

*Bunker Hill
Monument,
Charlestown*
(ALPER)

The monument, a 220-foot obelisk, was constructed of blocks of granite hauled here from the quarries of Quincy, Massachusetts. Work was interrupted in 1834 when the Association encountered financial difficulties. Several acres of the original site had to be sold and a successful campaign was organized to raise money. Work was then resumed, but at a very slow pace, and the monument was not completed until 1843. Daniel Webster returned for the dedication ceremonies that year, and again his dazzling oratory mesmerized a crowd of 100,000, whipping them to a patriotic frenzy as he shouted: "Thank God! I—I also—am an American!"

At the base of the obelisk stands a statue of Colonel William Prescott (1726–1795), commander of the Patriot troops on Breed's Hill. It was sculpted by William Westmore Story in 1881.

A small museum near the monument houses exhibits relating to the battle. The marble statue (1857) of Joseph Warren—the president of the Second Massachusetts Provincial Congress who had lost his life defending Breed's Hill—is the work of Henry Dexter.

DEXTER HOUSE *14 Green Street. Not open to the public.* Built in 1791, this house was the residence of Samuel Dexter (1761–1816), a United States Congressman, Senator, and Secretary of the Treasury and of War under President John Adams.

HARVARD MALL *Harvard Street* In 1629 settlers built a small fortification on this site for protection against Indian raids. The following year a small frame house was built within the walls for Royal Governor John Winthrop. Soon afterward, however, he moved to Boston and a large public building, the Great House, was then erected on the grounds. It housed the chambers of local officials, the Court of Assistants, and the First Church of Charlestown.

The site, which was the Town Square during the

Revolutionary War, is now a mall created with funds from an anonymous Harvard alumnus who wished to honor John Harvard, a seventeenth-century Charlestown resident and benefactor of Harvard College.

LARKIN HOUSE   *57 Main Street. Not open to the public.* This house was built in 1795 to replace an earlier structure burned by the British. The owner was Deacon John Larkin who, with other members of the Charlestown Committee of Safety, met Paul Revere on the night of April 18, 1775, after he had been rowed across the Charles River from Boston. Larkin gave Revere the horse used on his journey to spread the warning of the British advance on Lexington and Concord.

PHIPPS STREET BURYING GROUND   *Proceed northwest along Main Street, then turn left onto Phipps Street.* This cemetery contains hundreds of gravestones dating from the seventeenth and eighteenth centuries. These stones are arranged in groups that mark the perimeters of family plots.

Among the distinguished citizens buried here are Nathaniel Gorham (1738–1796), a president of Congress (1783, 1786–1787), and Oliver Holden (1765–1844), composer of hymns. Members of prominent local families—such as the Tufts, the Larkins, and the Frothinghams—are also interred here.

The monument to John Harvard (1607–1638), after whom Harvard College was named, was erected by Harvard students in 1828. A teaching elder of the First Church of Charlestown, he was buried in Charlestown in 1638, but the marker locating his grave was destroyed when British shells devastated the town during the Battle of Bunker Hill.

THOMPSON HOUSE   *119 Main Street. Not open to the public.*   After the Revolutionary War Timothy Thompson and his wife Mary returned to Charlestown to discover that their home had been destroyed by the fire caused by British shelling of the town in June 1775.

They constructed another dwelling—a residence that included a carpentry shop. A son, Benjamin, became a state senator and later a United States Congressman.

U.S.S. *CONSTITUTION   On Water Street, in the Boston Naval Shipyard. (Cross Charlestown Bridge, turn right on Chelsea to Wrapping Street, then turn right again.) Open daily 9:30* A.M. *to 4* P.M. *Free.*   This forty-four-gun frigate, which was designed by Joshua Humphrey and built in the shipyards of Boston's North End, was launched on October 21, 1797. She saw her first action in the undeclared naval war with the French.

During the War of 1812, serving as the flagship of Captain Isaac Hull, the *Constitution* engaged in battle and defeated the British warship *Guerrière* (August 19, 1812). The *Constitution* so successfully withstood the fire of the enemy cannon that the British sailors vowed her sides were made of iron. Since then she has carried the sobriquet "Old Ironsides."

The *Constitution's* superior firepower and maneuverability enabled her to overpower other enemy ships such as the *Java* (December 29, 1812) and the *Cyane* and the *Levant* (February 20, 1815).

In 1830 the *Constitution* was condemned as unseaworthy, but Oliver Wendell Holmes' poem "Old Ironsides" aroused public sympathy and funds were raised to repair her. Twenty-five years later she was commissioned for use as a training ship at the Portsmouth Navy Yard. Having fallen into disrepair in the 1920s, the ship was once again saved with funds raised through a public subscription. After being rebuilt, the *Constitution* was moored here in the Boston Navy Yard, her permanent home.

WARREN TAVERN   *105 Main Street. Open Monday through Saturday 11:30* A.M. *to 11* P.M., *Sunday 12:30* P.M. *to 10:30* P.M.   This structure, built by Eliphalet Newell, was one of the first buildings erected after the burning of Charlestown in 1775. The tavern was renamed in honor of the Patriot Joseph Warren (1741–1775) who was killed at the Battle of Bunker Hill.

The Masonic Lodge of Charlestown (King Solomon's Lodge) was founded here in 1784 and used one of the tavern's rooms for its meetings. Paul Revere was a charter member.

Today, the building—which has been restored to the appearance of a Colonial tavern—is a restaurant.

Recommended Side Trip

Salem

From the Boston area proceed along Storrow Drive to the Mystic River Bridge by following signs to Revere and Interstate 95 North. Soon after crossing the bridge, take Route 107 North—the highway to Lynn and Salem.

The first settlers arrived in Salem in the early 1620s. In 1628 John Endecott, acting as royal governor of the colony, established the seat of government here. (Two years later it moved to Charlestown.) Shipbuilding and sea transport became Salem's principal industries, and by the mid-seventeenth century a thriving trade had been established with the West Indies. As shipbuilders and merchants grew prosperous, the town rapidly expanded.

In 1692 a group of frenzied young women began accusing residents of the town of trafficking with the devil. Hysteria and suspicion grew, accusations and innuendos were widely circulated, and a series of witchcraft trials was held before Judges John Hathorne, Samuel Sewall, and Jonathan Corwin. One hundred seventy persons were accused and jailed, and twenty were executed: thirteen women and six men were hanged on Gallow's Hill, and one resident (Giles Corey), who refused to enter a plea in court, was crushed beneath heavy stones. In the spring of 1693, after months of terror, the townspeople began to question the testimony of the witnesses and one of the presiding judges resigned. The governor finally ordered the remaining accused to be released from jail, but the psychic scars on the town remained for generations.

Eighty-two years later a frenzy of a different sort gripped Salem—the frenzy for independence. After the Boston Port Bill closed Boston Harbor on June 1, 1774, the transaction of commerce shifted to Salem and nearby Marblehead. The General Assembly, which had fled Boston to convene in Salem on June 17, strongly protested the British action. When members of the Assembly met again on October 5, they decided to form a new body composed of representatives from throughout Massachusetts—the Provincial Congress—which would take action against the oppressive policies of the Crown. General Thomas Gage, the Commander-in-Chief of British forces in America who had unsuccessfully attempted to dissolve the legislative body, was further enraged.

Four months later Gage received reports that the Patriots at Salem were amassing munitions, including nineteen cannon. Determined to seize the materiel before the armaments could be used against forces of the Crown, he ordered Colonel Alexander Leslie and a detachment of 250 men to make a surprise raid. On the night of Saturday, February 25, 1775, the soldiers departed from Boston in ships. Early the next morning they disembarked at Marblehead and swiftly marched the five-mile route to Salem.

Major John Pedrick, a local resident, observed the British troop movements and immediately set off on horseback to warn the Salem Patriots. Arriving in Salem, he burst into the meeting house, where the Reverend Thomas Barnard was delivering his Sunday sermon. Interrupting,

Pedrick exhorted the parishioners to take up arms against the oncoming foe. Within moments the congregation, men and women alike, ran out of the meeting house and hurried to the North River Bridge to rescue the armaments and the forge concealed there. While the cannon were being removed, Captain David Mason, leader of the local Patriots, ordered the drawbridge raised, thereby cutting off British access to the Patriot cache.

By the time the Redcoats had entered Salem, the local militia had taken up positions around the far side of the bridge and a large crowd of hostile citizens had also assembled. At the river Colonel Leslie attempted to seize two nearby boats, but before his soldiers could reach them the Patriots had rendered them useless. Patriot Joseph Whicher arrogantly displayed his defiance and a British soldier thrust a bayonet into his shoulder.

The situation had now reached a breaking point, and Leslie was preparing to order his soldiers to open fire on the militia when the Reverend Barnard intervened. The two men conferred and a compromise was reached to preserve the honor of His Majesty's troops. The drawbridge was lowered; the British soldiers were permitted to cross over to a predetermined point unmolested by the Patriots. This accomplished, they then retraced their route and returned to Marblehead.

Had not the British and the Patriots restrained their enmity, the first shots of the Revolutionary War might have taken place here at Salem—not at Lexington two months later.

During the war years that followed, privateers (armed private vessels commissioned to capture enemy ships) were fitted at Salem. These ships seized valuable British cargoes, which were turned over to supply the Continental Army.

CROWNINSHIELD-BENTLEY HOUSE *126 Essex Street. Open June 1 through October 15, Tuesday through*

Saturday 10 A.M. to 4 P.M., Sunday 2 P.M. to 4:30 P.M. Closed holidays. Adults 75¢, children 25¢. The oldest section of this house, which dates from 1727, was built by John Crowninshield, owner of a small fleet of merchant ships. The structure was enlarged in 1794. The Reverend William Bentley, pastor of Salem's East Church and a noted scholar, was a boarder here from 1791 to 1819. In the twentieth century the house was moved here from its original site at 106 Essex Street.

ESSEX INSTITUTE *132 Essex Street. Open Tuesday through Saturday 9 A.M. to 4:30 P.M., Sunday and holidays 2 P.M. to 5 P.M. Free.* Founded in 1848, this museum houses an exceptionally fine collection of Colonial furniture, eighteenth-century American portraits, and Chinese *objets d'art.* The research library contains important volumes, diaries, and manuscripts associated with local history. The Essex Institute also administers several historic houses in the area. (Visitors may purchase a combination admission ticket here.)

GARDNER-PINGREE HOUSE *138 Federal Street. Open Tuesday through Saturday 10 A.M. to 4 P.M. Also open on Sunday during the summer from 2 P.M. to 4:30 P.M. Adults 75¢, children 25¢.* This elegant Federal house—built by Captain John Gardner in 1804—was designed by the distinguished Salem architect Samuel McIntire. The exquisite architectural detail makes this one of McIntire's finest achievements. The property was acquired by David Pingree in the 1830s and his descendants lived here until the early twentieth century.

HOUSE OF THE SEVEN GABLES *54 Turner Street. Open daily July 1 to Labor Day 9:30 A.M. to 7 P.M. From Labor Day to June 30 the house is open daily from 10 A.M. to 5 P.M. Closed Thanksgiving, Christmas, and January 1. Adults $1.25, children 35¢.* Built in 1668 by Captain John Turner, this house derives its fame from Nathaniel Hawthorne's novel, *The House of the Seven*

Gables (1851). Hawthorne, a native of Salem, frequently visited this dwelling while his cousin Susan Ingersoll was residing here in the 1840s. Located on the grounds also is the house in which Hawthorne was born in 1804. It was moved here in 1958 from its original site at 27 Union Street.

PEABODY MUSEUM *161 Essex Street. Open November through February, Monday through Saturday 9 A.M. to 4 P.M., Sunday and holidays 2 P.M. to 5 P.M. From March through October the museum is open Monday through Saturday 9 A.M. to 5 P.M., Sunday and holidays 2 P.M. to 5 P.M. Closed Thanksgiving, Christmas, and January 1. Adults $1.00, youngsters (6–15) 50¢, children (under 6) free.* This outstanding museum (built in 1824) displays numerous ship models, an ethnological collection from the Far East, exhibits describing the natural history of Essex County, and a collection of Chinese export porcelain.

PICKERING MANSION *18 Broad Street. Open by appointment. Adults $1.50, youngsters (13–18) 75¢, children (under 12) free.* The oldest house in Salem, this dwelling was constructed in 1660 by John Pickering and has been occupied by his descendants ever since. John Pickering, Jr., served as a member of the Colonial legislature. Timothy Pickering, Jr., who was born here in 1745, fought in the New York and New Jersey campaigns during the Revolutionary War and served as Adjutant General under George Washington.

PIERCE-NICHOLS HOUSE *80 Federal Street. Open Tuesday through Saturday 2 P.M. to 5 P.M. Closed holidays. Adults 75¢, children free.* Jerathmiel Pierce's house, built in 1782, is distinguished by its architectural design and handsome interior carving by Samuel McIntire. In 1801 Pierce's daughter Sally married George Nichols, and later they inherited the property.

PIONEER VILLAGE *Forest River Park, off Derby Street. Open daily June 1 through Labor Day, 9:30 A.M. to 6:30*

P.M. *Open Labor Day through October 12, 10 A.M. to 5 P.M. Adults 50¢, children 25¢.* This village is a recreation of an early-seventeenth-century New England community. It includes thatched cottages, bark-covered huts, a blacksmith's forge, a brick kiln, and stocks and pillories. The austerity of the surroundings reflects the rigorous conditions under which the Puritans labored to create a new world out of a wilderness.

ROPES MANSION *318 Essex Street. Open early May to October 31, Monday through Saturday 10 A.M. to 4:30 P.M. Closed holidays. Adults $1.00, children 50¢.* This mansion was built in 1719 by the Barnard brothers. The property was acquired in 1768 by Judge Nathaniel Ropes of the Superior Court. A staunch Loyalist, he infuriated local Patriots by his conservative views, and in March 1774 a mob of Patriots stormed his house, damaging the door and shattering the windows. Descendants of Judge Ropes resided here until 1913.

SALEM MARITIME NATIONAL HISTORIC SITE *Lower Derby Street area. Open daily except holidays.*

Custom House Constructed in 1819, this building was used for the collection of tariff duties. Writer Nathaniel Hawthorne worked here as surveyor of the port from 1846 to 1849. (Free.)

Derby House Captain Richard Derby built this house in 1761 as a wedding gift for his son, Elias Hasket Derby, who became one of Salem's most successful merchants. In the late 1770s Elias was the owner of privateers that preyed upon British vessels and captured valuable supplies used by the Patriots. (Adults 50¢, children free.)

Derby Wharf Extending 2,000 feet into Salem Harbor, Derby Wharf was built in 1762 and restored in 1938. During the Revolutionary War privateers were fitted here before sailing to engage British ships. In the first half of the nineteenth century the wharf was the center of activity of Salem's shipping district.

WARD HOUSE   *Behind the Essex Institute, 132 Essex Street. Open June 1 to October 15, Tuesday through Saturday 10 A.M. to 4 P.M., Sunday 2 P.M. to 4:30 P.M. Closed holidays. Adults 50¢, children 10¢.*   The oldest section of this house was constructed in 1684, and a large wing was added years later. Now, in the lean-to, visitors may see re-creations of an early apothecary's shop, a weaving room, and a nineteenth-century Salem store (or "cent" shop).

WITCH HOUSE   *310½ Essex Street. Open daily May 1 to November 25 from 10 A.M. to 6 P.M. Adults 50¢, children 25¢.*   In this house (built in 1692) Magistrate Jonathan Corwin, a judge of the Witchcraft Court (1692–1693), held preliminary examinations of persons accused of witchcraft. The house has been splendidly restored and furnished in a style typical of the late seventeenth century.

Quincy

Revolutionary War History

A trading post was established here in 1625 by Thomas Morton, a British trader and adventurer. The settlement gradually developed into a quiet farming community. In the late 1740s, when Joseph Palmer and Richard Cranch established a glass-manufacturing business here, the village (then called Braintree) began to assume an industrial appearance. By the end of the decade, however, their business had failed. Meanwhile, quarrying emerged as a principal industry because of the large deposits of granite in the area. After King's Chapel (1754) in Boston was constructed of Quincy stone, the quarries became famous and demand for the granite increased.

During the early phases of the American Revolution local Patriots were fiercely outspoken and held numerous meetings to protest the harsh policies of the British government. Rallying to aid their comrades in Boston after the city's port had been forcibly closed on June 1, 1774 (by the Boston Port Bill), they kept essential supplies flowing to the city.

John Adams (1735–1826), the most distinguished citizen of Quincy, was a member of the Massachusetts House of Representatives (1772), a delegate to the Continental Congress (1774–1778), a signer of the Declaration of Independence (1776), a Commissioner to France (1777–1779), and a member of the committee that drafted the Treaty of Paris (1781–1783), which formally ended the Revolutionary War. After the war he served as the first Vice President

Portrait of John Adams, *Painting after John Singleton Copley.* (COURTESY MUSEUM OF FINE ARTS, BOSTON)

of the United States (1789–1797) under George Washington and succeeded him as President (1797–1801).

His son, John Quincy Adams (1767–1848), also a resident of Quincy, served as Minister to the Netherlands (1794–1796), Minister to Prussia (1797–1800), Massachusetts senator (1801–1803), United States Senator (1803–1808), Minister to Great Britain (1815–1817), Secretary of State under President James Monroe (1817–1825), and was elected the sixth President of the United States (1825–1829).

John Hancock (1737–1793), who was the first signer of the Declaration of Independence, was also a native of this town. Highly respected by Patriot leaders throughout the colonies, he was chosen to serve as president of the Continental Congress from May 24, 1775, to October 29, 1777.

These distinguished sons of Quincy have earned for it the title "City of Presidents."

VISITORS' CENTER Information about Quincy's historical sites may be obtained from the Chamber of Commerce, 36 Miller Stile Road, phone 479–1111, or from the Quincy Historical Society, 8 Adams Street, phone 773–1144.

PUBLIC TRANSPORTATION Bus service in the area is provided by the Massachusetts Bay Transit Authority. For information and schedules, phone 472–2467.

TAXI SERVICE North Quincy Taxi, phone 328–3450; Yellow Cab, phone 773–6262.

Colonial and Revolutionary War Sites

ADAMS BIRTHPLACE COTTAGES *133 and 141 Franklin Street. Open mid-April through mid-October, Tuesday through Sunday 10 A.M. to 5 P.M. Admission to both houses—adults 75¢, children 25¢.*

JOHN ADAMS BIRTHPLACE *133 Franklin Street* The modest house on this site was constructed in 1681 by Joseph Penniman. Members of the Penniman family lived here until May 1720, when John Adams, deacon of the local church, acquired the property. Here he and his wife, Susanna Boylston (of the influential Boston family), lived and raised their three sons, John, Peter, and Elihu. The oldest son, John—who was destined to become the second President of the United States—was born in this house on October 30, 1735.

John Adams graduated from Harvard in 1755, and after teaching school in Worcester for a short time, began to study law. By 1758 he was a practicing attorney. Upon the death of his father in 1761, he inherited approximately thirty acres of land and the dwelling on the lot (now 141 Franklin Street) adjacent to his birthplace. His birthplace was bequeathed to his brother Peter, but acquired by John in 1774. It was then rented to tenants. During this time he also maintained a second residence in Boston because of his law practice, but this did not prevent him from farming and improving the land here.

In 1803 John Quincy Adams (John Adams' son) took possession of this dwelling and permitted his brother Thomas to reside here until 1818—the year of their mother Abigail's death, when Thomas went to live with his father (in the mansion on present-day Adams Street). The house was then rented to a series of tenants until 1896, at which time the Daughters of the Revolution restored the building and opened it to the public.

Today, the John Adams Birthplace Cottage is appointed with fine furnishings of the eighteenth century.

JOHN QUINCY ADAMS BIRTHPLACE   *141 Franklin Street*
The oldest section of this house was built by Gregory Belcher in 1663 and it was enlarged in 1716. The lean-to, which gives the structure its saltbox shape, was added about 1740. The property was purchased by Deacon John Adams in 1744.

John Adams inherited this house in 1761, and when he married Abigail Smith (daughter of the Reverend William Smith of Weymouth) three years later, the couple returned to live here. During the next twenty-four years Adams established his reputation as a great statesman.

Their three sons and three daughters were born here. John Quincy Adams, born on July 11, 1767, became the sixth President of the United States. In 1783 the house was leased to tenants who operated the farm while the family was in Europe. Upon returning in 1788, they moved into a larger residence (on present-day Adams Street).

John Adams birthplace, Quincy (ALPER)

In 1803 John Quincy Adams (then a United States Senator) purchased this house from his father. An Adams descendant donated the property in 1896 to the Quincy Historical Society, which undertook its restoration.

The interior is furnished with typical period pieces. On display are family possessions, including a nightcap of John Adams, one of Abigail's silk dresses (made in France), and John Quincy Adams' doeskin riding breeches.

Both houses were designated National Historic Landmarks in 1963.

ABIGAIL ADAMS CAIRN *Penn's Hill, South Quincy.* Erected in 1896, the cairn on this hill marks the spot where, according to tradition, Abigail Adams and her seven-year-old son John Quincy watched the smoke billowing from Charlestown as British shells set fire to the town during the Battle of Bunker Hill (June 17, 1775).

ADAMS NATIONAL HISTORIC SITE *135 Adams Street. Open daily mid-April to mid-November* 9 A.M.

to 5 P.M. (closed rest of year). Adults 50¢, children free.
The oldest section of this house was built in 1731 by
Major Leonard Vassall, a wealthy merchant who owned
sugar plantations in the West Indies. He had settled in
Boston in 1723 and shortly afterward had bought land
here on which to build a summer home. In September
1787 John Adams, then Minister to Great Britain, purchased the house from Vassall's grandson, Leonard Vassall Borland; Adams called the estate "Peace Fields."

Four generations of Adamses—from John and Abigail
Adams (who took up occupancy in 1788) to Brooks
Adams (who died here in 1927)—made this their home.
Two United States Presidents resided in the house:
John Adams and John Quincy Adams.

The house was enlarged by the succeeding generations
of occupants. In 1788 John Adams added the kitchen ell
and in 1800 the large gabled ell containing the east hall,
formal parlor, and study. In 1836 John Quincy Adams
built the passage along the north side of the house

Garden view of Adams National Historic Site, Quincy (ALPER)

which connects the two ells. In 1869 Charles Francis Adams (son of John Quincy Adams) attached servants' quarters to the kitchen wing.

The house was designated a National Historic Landmark in 1946, and since 1952 it has been administered by the National Park Service of the United States Department of the Interior.

Today, the dwelling has been restored to mirror the various periods of the Adamses' residence. The furniture —mostly eighteenth- and nineteenth-century pieces— belonged to members of the family. In the **Dining Room** may be seen a mahogany dining table and knife cases owned by John and Abigail. The portraits of George and Martha Washington were painted by Edward Savage in 1790, when John Adams was serving as Vice President under Washington. Over the fireplace hangs Gilbert Stuart's painting of John Adams, who posed for it here in this house at the age of eighty-eight.

The Louis XV furniture in the **Formal Parlor** was purchased by John Adams in France during the Revolutionary War, when he and Benjamin Franklin served as Commissioners to France in 1778. These pieces were later used in the White House during Adams' presidency. (John Adams was the first President to occupy the White House.) The two gold chairs were the property of President James Monroe and were used in the White House during his term of office, but were purchased at an auction by Charles Francis Adams in 1860.

Here, in the formal parlor, friends and relatives gathered to mark the celebration of three golden wedding anniversaries: John and Abigail, on October 25, 1814; John Quincy and Louisa Catherine Adams, on July 26, 1847; and Charles Francis and Abigail Brooks Adams, on September 5, 1879.

James Monroe was a guest here in 1817, just after his inauguration as fifth President of the United States. John Quincy Adams was chosen to serve as his Secretary of

State. Lafayette was honored by John Adams at a reception given here in 1824.

The **Study** contains John Adams' French secretary-desk, noted for its elaborate inlay, and the second President's reading glasses and candlesticks. A rocking chair and globes owned by John Quincy Adams are also on display. In the far right corner stands a large wing chair in which, according to family tradition, John Adams was sitting when he died on July 4, 1826. (Thomas Jefferson also died on the same day—the fiftieth anniversary of the signing of the Declaration of Independence.)

In the **Presidents' Bedroom** may be seen John and Abigail's Dutch four-poster canopied bed, where Abigail died of typhoid fever in 1818.

The splendid **Library Building,** about fifty feet behind the main house, was constructed in 1870 by Charles Francis Adams, a United States Congressman and later Minister to the British Court. The shelves are lined with approximately 12,000 volumes, three-quarters of them collected by John Quincy Adams. There are books on all subjects—ranging from classical literature to law—written in ten languages. Most of the furniture here dates from the nineteenth century. Foremost in interest is the desk used by John Quincy Adams while serving in the House of Representatives (1831–1848) following his term as President. Sitting at this desk, he suffered a fatal stroke in 1848 in the House Chamber.

Crowds of tourists and troops of schoolchildren continue to make pilgrimages here to share in the historic memories this house evokes.

FIRST PARISH CHURCH *1306 Hancock Street at Washington Street. Open daily 10 A.M. to 4 P.M. Closed certain days during the summer.*   This parish dedicated its first meeting house on this site in 1637. The minister, John Wheelwright, was a celebrated freethinker who continually challenged the oppressive strictures of the Puritan establishment. In 1732, to house the growing congregation, a larger structure was built here under the pastorate of John Hancock, the Patriot's father. (John Hancock—the first signer of the Declaration of Independence—was orphaned early in life and was adopted by his uncle, Thomas Hancock, a wealthy and powerful Boston merchant.)

The present edifice, which dates from 1828, was designed by architect Alexander Parrish of Boston and was constructed of Quincy granite.

Located in the basement of the church are the crypts of Presidents John Adams and John Quincy Adams, who were interred alongside their wives.

QUINCY HOMESTEAD (DOROTHY QUINCY HOUSE)

34 Butler Road (off Hancock Street). Open mid-April through October, Tuesday through Sunday 10 A.M. to 5 P.M. Closed holidays. Adults 50¢, children 15¢. The original section of this house is believed to have been built in 1680 by William Coddington. It passed into the possession of the Quincy family in the mid-seventeenth century and was enlarged by succeeding occupants. In 1706 it was extensively remodeled by Judge Edmund Quincy.

Son of the first mayor of Braintree (now Quincy), Edmund Quincy graduated from Harvard in 1699 and spent his life in public service. He served as judge of the Superior Court of Judicature, a member of the Board of Overseers of Harvard College, and a representative to the conference arbitrating the Massachusetts–New Hampshire border dispute. In 1701 he married Dorothy Flynt (daughter of the Reverend Josiah Flynt of Dorchester). His grandson's daughter, Dorothy Quincy, who spent her childhood in this house, married John Hancock in 1775.

According to local tradition, John Hancock and Dorothy Quincy were preparing to be married in the parlor here in the summer of 1775, but the skirmishes at Lexington and Concord (April 18–19, 1775) forced them to postpone their plans. Hancock and Dorothy were guests at Jonas Clarke's Lexington house on the eve of the British attack. The next month Hancock traveled to Philadelphia to attend the Second Continental Congress. He was elected president of the Congress on May 24, 1775, and served until October 29, 1777. But he took time from his duties to marry Dorothy on August 28, 1775, in Fairfield, Connecticut, at the home of Thaddeus Burr.

The Hancocks established their residence in Boston, and the Quincy Homestead passed to other owners. In 1906 it was restored by the Massachusetts Society of the Colonial Dames. Today, the house is furnished with fine period pieces.

COLONEL JOSIAH QUINCY HOUSE 20 *Muirhead Street in Wollaston. (Travel down Hancock Street to Beach Street, turn right, then go around the block to Muirhead Street.) Open June through September on Tuesday, Thursday, and Friday from 1 P.M. to 5 P.M. Fee 50¢.*   Colonel Josiah Quincy, a prominent merchant and a local political leader, built this impressive Georgian house in 1770. A fervent supporter of the Patriot cause, he influenced his son Josiah, Jr., who wrote a series of anonymous articles for the Boston *Gazette* opposing British policies in the colonies.

Josiah, Jr., an attorney, joined with John Adams in defending British soldiers at a trial following the Boston Massacre (1770). Although both men were outspoken Patriots, their commitment to legal ethics prompted them to assume this responsibility, and their successful defense led to the acquittal of the British captain, Thomas Preston, and six of his men. (Two others were found guilty of manslaughter.) In 1775 Josiah, Jr., traveled to England to seek support for the Patriot cause, and he died on the return trip.

The house is furnished with fine pieces of the eighteenth and nineteenth centuries.

New York

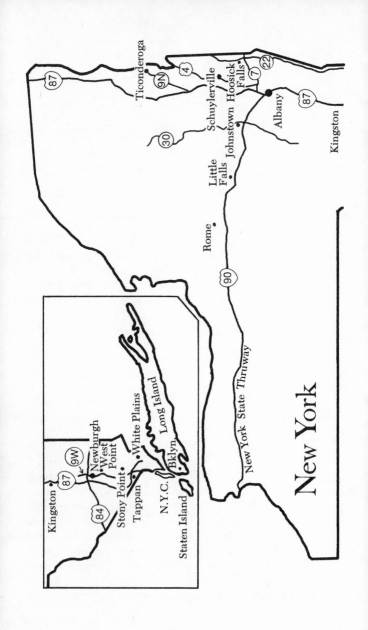

Ticonderoga

Revolutionary War History

Ticonderoga played an important role in American history because of its strategic location between Lake George and Lake Champlain.

In 1755, during the French and Indian Wars, French troops built a fortification here which they named Fort Carillon (because the water rippling in the lake sounded like "a chime of bells"). In July 1758 British General James Abercromby set out with a large expedition to attack Fort Carillon.

These movements were observed by French scouts, who sent reports to the fort's commander, the Marquis de Montcalm. Acting on this information, he ordered his men to erect a line of defense in the surrounding forest at the point where the British would have to cross. After three days of feverish activity, earthworks, an abatis, and a log wall (eight feet high and three-fourths of a mile long) were constructed.

The British reached the north end of Lake George on July 6. Recklessly confident of the ability of his 15,000 soldiers to overpower the French garrison of 3,500, Abercromby did not order the unloading of the large artillery pieces from the ships. On July 8 the British began their assault on the fort, but they were relentlessly driven back and never penetrated the French defenses. At the end of the day Abercromby's troops were forced to retreat to their ships. They had suffered 2,500 casualties while the French had successfully held the fort with casualties of only 377.

But the British had learned from this catastrophe: the

following year they launched a second, and successful, attack on Fort Carillon. Under the command of Sir Jeffrey Amherst, they positioned cannon in the hills surrounding the fort. For several hours they rained a steady hail of fire on the garrison below. When the French realized that annihilation was inevitable, they fled from the fort, blowing up the magazine and setting the barracks afire. The victors occupied the fortification and renamed it Fort Ticonderoga (a corruption of the Indian word "Cheronderoga" meaning "between two lakes").

After the French and Indian Wars the strategic importance of Fort Ticonderoga diminished and it was used merely for military storage. (Only fifty men were stationed here.) Not until the American Revolution did the fort again play a significant role.

Soon after the Battles of Lexington and Concord (April 19, 1775) New England Patriots decided to seize the powder and armaments stored at Ticonderoga. Two plans were developed simultaneously: the Massachusetts Committee of Safety authorized Colonel Benedict Arnold to recruit men for an assault, and the Connecticut Assembly commissioned Colonel Ethan Allen and his Green Mountain Boys to make a similar raid. Allen quickly organized an expedition, which started to march toward the fort. When Arnold learned of this action, he set out alone for the vicinity of Castelton, Vermont, where he joined the forces and reached an agreement with Allen to share the command (even though none of Arnold's men would participate).

A detachment of soldiers was sent to Skenesboro (present-day Whitehall) to secure boats to ferry the men across Lake Champlain. But when they had not returned by the early morning of May 10, 1775, Allen ordered the assault to begin without them. Eighty-three men crowded into several flat-bottomed boats and rowed across the lake. On the shore they drew up in three ranks and marched swiftly toward the garrison to surprise the still-sleeping British.

Entering a breach in the east wall, the Patriots encountered a sentry who took aim at the intruders, only to have his musket misfire. As he ran for cover, a second guard attempted to bayonet Colonel James Easton but Allen knocked him unconscious with the butt of his gun.

The Patriots rushed into the parade ground and took up formation while Allen and Arnold bounded up the steps of the west barracks. When a half-dressed, drowsy officer, Lieutenant Jocelyn Feltham, appeared at the entrance, Allen is said to have called for the surrender of the fort "in the name of the great Jehovah and the Continental Congress." Feltham scurried to the room of the commander of the garrison, Captain William Delaplace, who moments later appeared at the top of the inside staircase. Allen, with sword raised, mounted the stairs and demanded surrender. Realizing he had no alternative, Delaplace reluctantly submitted. The Green Mountain Boys then herded the captured soldiers onto the parade ground, where they were kept under heavy guard. (They were later transported to Hartford, Connecticut.) The spoils included 120 cannon, numerous artillery pieces, hundred of shells, 100 small arms, 10 casks of powder, and many barrels of food.

The Continental Congress decided that some of the cannon should be removed to Boston; on December 5, 1775, Colonel (later Major General) Henry Knox arrived at Fort Ticonderoga to supervise this undertaking. The next day, forty-three cannon and sixteen mortars were mounted on forty-two sledges yoked to oxen, and this "noble train of artillery" (as Knox called it) journeyed south to Albany. From there the convoy moved eastward across the Berkshire Mountains, over the snow-covered terrain of central Massachusetts, and finally reached Framingham (twenty miles from Boston). In March the cannon were placed on Dorchester Heights (overlooking Boston), where they

Major General
Henry Knox.
*Painting by Gilbert
Stuart.* (COURTESY
MUSEUM
OF FINE ARTS,
BOSTON)

were used in Washington's siege against the British troops who were occupying the city.

The Patriots held Fort Ticonderoga from May 10, 1775, until July 6, 1777. They were forced to surrender when British troops under General John Burgoyne erected a battery of cannon on nearby Mount Defiance. (The 800-foot hill overlooking the fort was thought by the Americans to be inaccessible.) At 3 A.M., under the cover of darkness, as the Patriot army was preparing to withdraw secretly, a French volunteer, Chevalier Matthias Alexis de Rochefermoy, accidentally set his quarters on fire. This blunder ended the Patriots' hopes of withdrawing unnoticed, and the British pursued them as they fled over a log bridge that stretched across the lake to Vermont. The British followed and overpowered the rear column at Hubberton, Vermont, on July 7. When King George received reports of the capture of Fort Ticonderoga, he prematurely exclaimed: "I have beat all the Americans!"

The fort became a critical supply depot in support of the operations of Burgoyne in New York State. In September 1777 Patriot Colonel John Brown (who had participated in the capture of Ticonderoga on May 10, 1775) organized a surprise raid on the fort. On September 18, 1777, with a detachment of New England militiamen, he seized the outworks of the garrison, capturing 300 enemy soldiers and liberating 100 American prisoners. But because he lacked the artillery to sustain a siege of the fort, he withdrew after four days.

After Burgoyne's surrender at Saratoga (October 17, 1777), the British abandoned Fort Ticonderoga and its importance once again diminished.

VISITORS' CENTER Located near the parking area for Fort Ticonderoga, the center sells pamphlets, books, and souvenirs. Phone 585–2821.

GUIDED TOURS During the summer months numerous tours of the fort are offered. Inquire at the Visitors' Center.

Colonial and Revolutionary War Sites

FORT TICONDEROGA *Two miles east of the town on Route 74. Open daily from 8 A.M. to 6 P.M. from mid-May to mid-October. During July and August the grounds remain open until 7 P.M. The fort is closed the rest of the year. Adults $2.00, youngsters (10–14) $1.00, children (under 10) free.*

MONUMENT ROAD   The monuments described below are located on the one-mile road leading from the entrance gate to the parking area near the fort.

Black Watch Monument   In 1925 the St. Andrew's Society of Glen Falls, New York, erected this monument to honor the heroic fighters of the 42nd Regiment—known as the Royal Highlanders or the Black Watch. During the battle of July 8, 1758, they suffered 600 casualties out of a force of 1,000.

British-American Soldiers Monument   This monument—a ten-foot-high stone crowned with an eagle—was erected by the Society of Colonial Wars in 1949. It honors the heroism of the troops serving under Major General James Abercromby in the attack of the French lines on July 8, 1758, and pays tribute to the soldiers under Sir Jeffrey Amherst who, on July 27 of the following year, captured Fort Carillon. Names of the British and American military units which served in these campaigns are listed on plaques attached to the monument.

Cross and Carillon Monument   After the Battle of Carillon in July 1758, Montcalm erected a large wooden cross here and conducted a ceremony of thanksgiving for his soldiers. The present-day cross and monument were erected in July 1958 (the Bicentennial of the battle) by the Committee of French-Americans to commemorate the French victory of Carillon.

French-Canadian Soldiers Monument   Near the parking area stands a commemorative stone from the city of Montreal to the French and Canadian soldiers who occupied and defended Fort Carillon. The monument was erected in 1939.

Howe Monument   This eight-foot slender stone column was erected in 1958 by the English Speaking Union of the United States to honor British General George Augustus Howe (1724–1758), who was killed

Cross and Carillon Monument, Fort Ticonderoga (ALPER)

on July 6, 1758, while leading his troops in Abercromby's inept attack on Fort Carillon.

Montcalm Memorial This stone pays tribute to Louis-Joseph de Montcalm (1712–1759), who defended Fort Carillon from the attack of the British and Colonial army under General James Abercromby. The monument was erected in 1927 by a committee of prominent citizens including Alfred C. Bossom, T. J. Oakley Rhinelander, Robert M. Thompson, and Howard Pell.

Nearby stands a reconstruction of a short section of the defenses that were erected by Montcalm's army in preparation for the battle.

War Monument The Society of the Colonial Wars in New York erected this monument in 1900 to commemorate the seventeenth- and eighteenth-century battles fought in this vicinity: Champlain with Hurons and Algonquins defeated the Iroquois July 30, 1609;

Montcalm defeated Abercromby July 8, 1758, at the assault of Fort Carillon; Amherst captured Fort Ticonderoga July 27, 1759.

ARCHWAY   A plaque on the archway to the parade ground lists the famous men who once passed through this entrance: George Washington, Benjamin Franklin, Benedict Arnold, Horatio Gates, Philip Schuyler, Henry Knox, Ethan Allen, Anthony Wayne, Seth Warner, John André, the Marquis de Montcalm, John Burgoyne, Jeffrey Amherst, and Thaddeus Kosciusko.

BARRACKS   Officers were quartered in the West Barracks; enlisted men were billeted in the East and South Barracks. In the summer troops were sometimes bivouacked in tents beyond the walls. It was in the West Barracks in May 1775 that the British commander, Captain William Delaplace, surrendered the fort to Colonel Ethan Allen and the Green Mountain Boys.

PARADE GROUND

Burgoyne Gun   *In front of the West Barracks*   This artillery piece, set on a gray cannon carriage, was brought into Fort Ticonderoga by General John Burgoyne's troops after they captured this fortification from Patriot General Arthur St. Clair (July 1777). The cannon was used in the campaign at Saratoga and was surrendered to the Americans in October 1777.

Demi-Lune   Two French cannon found during restoration may be seen on the demi-lune near the East Barracks. Through the floor grating visitors may see the original baking ovens built by the French in 1755.

Knox Gun   When, in December 1755, Patriot Colonel Henry Knox's train of oxcarts was hauling cannon across the frozen Mohawk River (north of Albany) en route from Fort Ticonderoga to Boston, this gun was lost when it broke through the ice. In 1800 it was recovered from the bottom of the river and placed in front of the Town Hall of a village in the Mohawk Valley. According to tradition, each time the en-

Parade ground, Fort Ticonderoga (ALPER)

trenched Federalist party won an election, they fired off the cannon in celebration. After twenty years, when the Democratic party finally gained control of local government, they took the cannon and dumped it back into the Mohawk River! Just prior to World War II the artillery piece was again retrieved from the river— this time to be salvaged for scrap iron. But a concerned citizen purchased it so that it might be returned to Fort Ticonderoga.

Knox Monument   *Near the Knox Gun*   The inscription on this monument reads: "From this fortress went General Henry Knox in the winter of 1775–76 to deliver to General George Washington at Cambridge the train of artillery from Fort Ticonderoga, used to force the British Army to evacuate Boston." The bronze plaque, executed by H. J. Albright, has a relief depicting ox-carts pulling cannon through the forests. The state of New York erected this monument during the Sesquicentennial of the American Revolution.

Montcalm Plaque   *On the wall behind the Knox Monument*   This plaque pays tribute to General Montcalm

Fort Mount Hope, Ticonderoga (ALPER)

and to the heroes of France and Canada who fought at the Battle of Carillon. The Council of France to America, with the cooperation of the Federation of the Society of St. Jean-Baptiste, erected this plaque in 1958, the 200th anniversary of the battle.

Split Mortar *Adjacent to the Knox Gun* In 1775, when Patriot soldiers were testing artillery on a boat on Lake Champlain, one of the mortars exploded and the top half was sent flying into the lake. The following year the remaining half was used as ballast in the U.S.S. *Trumbull*, one of the flotilla of small ships in the Continental Navy that had just been built under the supervision of Benedict Arnold at Skenesboro (now Whitehall). On October 11, 1776, off Valcour Island (near Plattsburgh) the fleet encountered British vessels. The British, by their superior seamanship, quickly gained the advantage and overpowered the Americans. Only four of the fifteen crippled American ships were able to make their way back to the Fort Ticonderoga area. One of them was the U.S.S. *Trumbull*.

RAMPART CANNON The cannon on the ramparts (facing the lake) saw action during the military campaigns of the eighteenth century. Crews of six to eight were required to load each cannon with powder, insert a ball, and set off the charge—a procedure that took nearly thirty seconds. The block-and-tackle system attached to each side of the carriage was used to limit the recoil of the cannon after it had been fired.

MUSEUM   Museum rooms in the South Barracks contain dioramas, paintings, maps, rifles, and utensils— all associated with Colonial life or events that occurred at Fort Ticonderoga. Of special interest are the Hampton Howell collection of miniature artillery pieces, a display of Colonial costumes, and a selection of George Washington memorabilia. Important works of art include paintings attributed to Thomas Cole, Asher Durand, John Trumbull, Charles Peale Polk, and William Dunlap.

Rampart cannon,
Fort Ticonderoga
(ALPER)

FORT MOUNT HOPE   *Heading east on Montcalm Street (toward Fort Ticonderoga), turn left onto Tower Avenue. Proceed one block, then make a left turn onto Burgoyne Road. Travel ⅜ mile to the site, which is located on the right side of the road. A 600-foot gravel road leads to the parking area. Open daily 8 A.M. until dusk from late May until mid-October. Donations accepted.*   An outpost of Fort Ticonderoga was first established here in 1755 by French troops under Montcalm. During 1758 and 1759 the post changed hands several times: it was first captured by the British under Abercromby, then re-captured by the French under Montcalm, and finally occupied by the British under Amherst.

In 1776 the Patriot army built fortifications here, but the following year General Burgoyne's troops seized the defenses. After the British defeat at Saratoga (October 1777), the Americans again occupied Mount Hope.

The blockhouse still standing here was built in 1776 by the Massachusetts State Regiment of Artificers. Several eighteenth-century cannon and the ruins of a Colonial gunboat are on display.

MOUNT DEFIANCE   *Heading east on Montcalm Street (toward Fort Ticonderoga), turn right onto Champlain Avenue. At the fork take the road to the left, The Portage. Then follow the signs to Mount Defiance. The Summit House on Mount Defiance is open daily from late May until mid-October. In summer the schedule is 8 A.M. to 8 P.M., in September and October 8 A.M. to 5 P.M. The charge on the toll road leading to Mount Defiance is $3.00.*   Early in July 1777 General John Burgoyne sent his commander of artillery, General William Phillips, and his chief engineer, Lieutenant William Twiss, to the summit of Mount Defiance (then called Sugar Loaf Hill). They were to ascertain whether it would be feasible to place a battery of cannon on this hill which overlooked the Patriot-held Fort Ticonderoga. Upon receiving an affirmative answer, Burgoyne ordered a roadway cut up the steep sides of the mountain, and by July 6 soldiers had placed four twelve-pound cannon in position. When General Arthur St. Clair, the Patriot commander, saw the British guns trained on the fort, he ordered his men to evacuate without firing a shot.

Although none of the original battery has survived, visitors to Mount Defiance are rewarded with a breathtaking view of the Lake Champlain Valley, the outlet of Lake George, and the ranges of the Green and Adirondack Mountains.

Recommended Side Trip

Crown Point Reservation (Fort St. Frederic and Fort Crown Point)

Directions from Fort Ticonderoga: After leaving Fort Ticonderoga, turn left, go about ½ mile to Routes 22/74, and turn right. Proceed a short distance, then turn right at the Crown Point sign onto a two-lane highway. After traveling several miles along this road (on which is located the International Paper Company), you will come to Routes 9N/22. Turn right and continue north to Crown Point. Travel about 3½ miles past the town until you come to a sign directing you to the toll bridge to Vermont. Here turn right and proceed about 4½ miles until you see the sign "French and English Forts: Museum and Beach," which is located on the left side of the road—just before

Fort Crown Point, Crown Point Reservation (ALPER)

the toll bridge. Follow the entrance road ½ mile back to the museum and parking lot. The road to the left leads to the ruins of Fort Crown Point; the road veering to the right leads to the foundations of Fort St. Frederic. (*Note:* From the intersection of Route 9N and Montcalm Street in downtown Ticonderoga, you can follow Route 9N North 12½ miles to the road leading to the Vermont toll bridge; turn right and proceed to the site of the two forts.)

The Crown Point Reservation includes picnicking facilities, a campsite, a playground, a small museum, and the ruins of two forts. The site is open daily from May through October. Free.

In 1731 the French built a fortification here, Fort St. Frederic, for use as a base from which to conduct raids on English settlements. The structure, which was enlarged in 1742, held more than 120 men. British attacks in 1755 and 1756 on the fort failed, but General Jeffrey Amherst's expedition in 1759 was successful. As the Redcoats approached, the French commander, Bourlamasque, ordered the defenses blown up and withdrew his troops into Canada.

The British then began to construct Fort Crown Point near the ruins of Fort St. Frederic. A fire in 1773 seriously damaged several of the buildings, some of which were never fully repaired. In May 1775 militiamen under Colonel Seth Warner captured this fort (soon after participating in the assault on Fort Ticonderoga), and took prisoner the small group of British soldiers stationed here.

Crown Point once again came under British control in October 1776, after the defeat of an American fleet near Valcour Island. Four ships of the battered flotilla—the *Trumbull, Enterprise, Revenge,* and *Liberty*—made their way to Crown Point. The Patriots hastily constructed a blockhouse for additional protection, but they were unable to repel their pursuers. Before withdrawing to Fort Ticonderoga, the fleeing Patriot sailors set part of the fort on fire.

Burgoyne's army bivouacked and replenished their provisions here in June 1777. Four months later, when his troops surrendered at Saratoga, Fort Crown Point reverted to American control.

Today, all that remains of Fort St. Frederic are earthworks and mounds of rubble that once had been the stone walls. But the walls of Fort Crown Point still stand, with well-defined areas that were barrack rooms. Of special interest are the two-story fireplaces. A narrow footpath leads around the top of the former ramparts.

Two small monument stones on the grounds were erected in 1928 by the New York State Education Department.

Albany

Revolutionary War History

While exploring the Hudson River for the Dutch East India Company, Henry Hudson anchored his ship, the *Half Moon,* in the shallows off the site of present-day Albany on September 19, 1609, and devoted several days to exploring the area. In 1630 Dutch merchant Kiliaen Van Rensselaer acquired huge tracts of land on both sides of the Hudson River and established the patroonship of Rensselaerswyck. Although he never came to America, he organized the settlement of the land under his jurisdiction. Within a short time houses, barns, and mills covered the countryside.

In 1685 (twenty-one years after the British took control of Manhattan) the Van Rensselaers relinquished their claim on the area and Albany came under British influence. By the beginning of the eighteenth century Albany had become an important fur-trading and commercial center.

In the summer of 1754 delegates from seven colonies met here to seek solutions to problems concerning their mutual welfare and defense. This congress also planned to formulate terms of peace to be presented to the Iroquois Confederacy (a league of major northeastern Indian tribes). A treaty with the Indians was successfully concluded, but more significant was the development of a proposal calling for a union of the colonies under a president general appointed by the Crown and a grand council with legislative powers. Referred to as the "Albany Plan," the proposal was drafted by Benjamin Franklin. However, the conflicting interests of the individual colonies and the apprehension of the British government prevented it from ever taking effect.

After the First Continental Congress met in Philadelphia in 1774, the Patriots of Albany organized a Committee of Correspondence with John Barclay as its chairman. The next year Philip Schuyler proposed a censure of King George III in the Provincial Assembly, and because Loyalists stormed out of the chamber, the resolution was easily passed. On June 4, 1776, when a group of citizens was gathered in the dining room of Cartwright's Inn in celebration of the king's birthday, a mob of Patriots broke down the door and assaulted the revelers. When the militia arrived to restore order, several of the defiant Loyalists were arrested and, according to local tradition, sang "God Save the King" as they were herded through the streets to the jail.

On July 19, 1776, a throng of citizens, along with several New York militia companies, was stirred to fever pitch when they assembled in front of the City Hall to hear the first public reading in Albany of the Declaration of Independence.

Throughout the Revolutionary War Albany was spared the scars of battle. The only real threat to the city occurred during the British campaign of 1777, when the capture of Albany was one of the major objectives. Burgoyne's surrender on October 17, 1777, at Saratoga (present-day Schuylerville) guaranteed Albany's safety for the remainder of the war. News of the surrender was celebrated by the firing of cannon and the ringing of bells. In the evening grateful citizens placed candles in their windows, and bonfires blazed on surrounding hills.

In January 1780 the New York legislature convened here for the first time. Since then Albany has served as the capital of New York State.

VISITORS' CENTER   Information about Albany is available from the Chamber of Commerce, 508 Broadway, phone 434–1214. Serious students of historic sites may also wish to contact the Historic Albany Foundation, 194 Elm Street, phone 463–0622.

PUBLIC TRANSPORTATION   The Capital District Transit System provides bus service in the metropolitan area. For information and schedules, phone 482–8822.

TAXI SERVICE   Albany Yellow Cab, phone 465–4757; Diamond Cab, phone 463–2126; Pine Hills Taxi, phone 463–4455.

Colonial and Revolutionary War Sites

CHERRY HILL   *South Pearl Street between First and McCarty Avenue. Open Tuesday through Saturday 10 A.M. to 4 P.M., Sunday 1 P.M. to 4 P.M. Closed Thanksgiving, December 25, and January 1. Adults 75¢, children and students 25¢.*   This handsome Georgian house was built in 1768 by Colonel Philip Van Rensselaer (1747–1798) of the influential Van Rensselaer family, which controlled large tracts of land along the Hudson River. Philip, a successful merchant, served as Commissary of Military Stores in New York during the Revolutionary War and was active in the political life of the young nation.

He resided at Cherry Hill with his wife Maria (daughter of Robert Sanders, a mayor of Albany) and their children. After his death in 1798 the mansion was continuously occupied by his descendants until 1963, when the Van Rensselaer Trust, which maintains the property, provided for the conversion of the estate into a historic shrine.

Visitors to the house may see the furnishings, silver, and works of art accumulated by generations of Van Rensselaers. The **South Parlor** contains several pieces of furniture that belonged to Philip: a Hepplewhite secretary-desk, a Boston-made Chippendale-style chair (one of a set of twenty-four once here), and a firescreen (with the original petit point embroidery done by one of his daughters).

Some of the **Dining Room** furniture—such as the sideboard, dining table, and Queen Anne chairs—also dates from the Colonial period. Lafayette and other distinguished visitors were entertained here and were often overnight guests in the second-floor **Guest Room,** which today is adorned with a series of James Eights prints of eighteenth-century Albany.

The **North Bedroom** boasts a fine four-poster canopied bed, a commode corner chair, and Maria Van Rensselaer's cradle (with her father's initials carved on it). In the **Doll Room** may be seen a large dollhouse containing miniature furniture and figures. Other items, such as antique games and a collection of dolls with china heads, are also on display here.

FIRST DUTCH REFORMED CHURCH *North Pearl Street at Clinton Square* The First Dutch Reformed Church, organized in 1642, is the second oldest Protestant congregation still active in the United States. Construction of the church building began in 1797 to the specifications of architect Philip Hooker's design, which called for a pedimented portico with four Doric columns. In 1858 the facade was modified and the portico was replaced by a projecting Romanesque block. The interior was enhanced by the addition of stained-glass windows and a grained-vault ceiling. The pulpit and the communion silver were imported from Holland and date from the mid-seventeenth century. A bronze plaque marks the pew box used by Theodore Roosevelt while he was governor of New York (1898–1900).

SCHUYLER MANSION ("THE PASTURES")   27 *Clinton Street, at the corner of Catherine Street. Open Monday through Saturday 9 A.M. to 5 P.M., Sunday 1 P.M. to 5 P.M. Free.*   This impressive brick Georgian house was built in 1762 by Philip Schuyler (1733–1804), a member of the New York Assembly (1768–1775), a general in the Continental Army (1775–1779), a delegate to the Continental Congress (1776, 1779–1781), and a United States Senator (1789–1791, 1797–1798).

During the Revolutionary War General Schuyler and his wife Catherine (a daughter of John Van Rensselaer) entertained here such guests as Benjamin Franklin, Baron von Steuben, Comte de Rochambeau, the Marquis de Lafayette, Aaron Burr, General Nathanael Greene, John Trumbull, and John Jay. After British General John Burgoyne's surrender at Saratoga (October 1777), he was confined to this house as a prisoner though he was extended all the courtesies of an honored guest.

Set on a hill, the Schuyler Mansion has a gambrel roof with square chimneys and pedimented dormers. The octagonal vestibule is an early-nineteenth-century addition. The floor arrangement is typical of houses of the Georgian period: a large central hallway with two rooms on each side. John Gaborial, master carpenter from Boston, supervised the carving of the interior panels and woodwork.

The building, which has been restored by the New York State Historic Trust, is furnished with appropriate eighteenth-century pieces, including many that were in the possession of the Schuylers. In the elegant **Drawing Room** ("Hamilton Room")—with its fine Hepplewhite furniture and French chandelier—Alexander Hamilton married Schuyler's daughter Elizabeth in December

1780. (The young couple spent the first weeks of their marriage here.) Among the rare pieces in the **Informal Parlor** are a handsome chest on chest (*c.* 1700) by Rhode Island cabinetmaker John Goddard and a stately block-front secretary-desk (*c.* 1750) made in Massachusetts.

General Schuyler's campaign chest, battle saber, and dispatch box are on display in the **Study**. The **Dining Room** contains china, wine glasses, and silver—all Schuyler possessions. A portrait of Alexander Hamilton hangs above the sideboard; the valuable Temple Prayer Rug dates from 1785.

Bedrooms are located on the second floor. The **Schuyler Bedroom** is furnished with a typical four-poster canopied bed, a handsome highboy with broken pediment and three finials, a Chippendale-style table, and blue-and-white porcelain garniture. The bedroom to the front of the house was used as a **Nursery** from 1762 to 1804, and it contains a cradle, a carriage, a rocking horse, and a collection of antique dolls and toys.

SCHUYLER MONUMENT   *At the traffic circle at Washington Avenue and Eagle Street*   This statue of Philip Schuyler (1733–1804), Revolutionary War general and member of the Continental Congress, was sculpted by J. Massey Rhind. The monument was presented to the city by George Hawley in 1925.

SITE OF CONTINENTAL ARMY HOSPITAL   *Lodge and Pine Streets*   The log structure that was erected here during the Revolutionary War served as a hospital for Patriot soldiers wounded in the Ticonderoga and Saratoga campaigns.

SITE OF COLONIAL COURTHOUSE   *Northeast corner of Hudson and Broadway*   This is the site of the courthouse where the New York State legislature held its first session in Albany from January 27 to March 14, 1780.

SITE OF KING'S ARMS TAVERN *At the end of Green Street* A popular hostelry, The King's Arms Tavern, was located on this site in Colonial times. At the outbreak of the Revolutionary War, irate local Patriots ripped down the sign and forced innkeeper Hugh Denniston to rename his tavern. George Washington was honored at a reception here in late 1782.

SITE OF LAFAYETTE HOUSE *East side of North Pearl Street above Maiden Lane* While in Albany in February 1778 as George Washington's envoy seeking support for the Continental Army in its winter encampment at Valley Forge, the Marquis de Lafayette resided in the house located on this site.

SITE OF "OLD ELM" *State and Pearl Streets* The sprawling elm tree that once stood on the corner of State and Pearl Streets became known as the "Freedom Tree"' because it was planted by Philip Livingston (1716–1778), a signer of the Declaration of Independence, who was born in a house near this site. The elm was cut down in the early twentieth century.

TEN BROECK MANSION *9 Ten Broeck Place. Usually open daily 3–4 P.M. Closed Thanksgiving, December 25, and January 1. Free.* This late-eighteenth-century house was built by Abraham Ten Broeck (1734–1810), member of the local Committee of Safety, brigadier general during the Revolutionary War, and later mayor of Albany (1779–1783, 1796–1799). The restored two-and-a-half-story dwelling has a fine collection of period furniture.

WASHINGTON STATUE *On Swan Street side of Capitol Park* This statue of George Washington (1732–1799) was erected by the New York State Commission in 1932 to commemorate the 200th anniversary of Washington's birth. A marker on the Washington Avenue side of the Capitol grounds states that he passed this site during his 1782–1783 tour of the Mohawk Valley.

Non-Revolutionary Sites of Interest

ALBANY INSTITUTE OF HISTORY AND ART   *125 Washington Avenue. Open Tuesday through Saturday 10 A.M. to 4:45 P.M., Sunday 2 P.M. to 5:45 P.M. Closed holidays. Free.*   The oldest museum in the state, the Institute has a fine collection of nineteenth-century American, English, and Dutch paintings.

ALL SAINTS' CATHEDRAL   *Swan Street near Elk. Open daily 7 A.M. to 5:30 P.M.*   Seat of the Episcopal Diocese of Albany, this cathedral was designed in the English Gothic style by Robert W. Gibson. The cornerstone was laid in 1884. The interior of the church is impressive: the chancel has elaborate stone carvings and the nave is accentuated by graceful arches. The oak stalls date from 1655 and were brought here from a church in Bruges, Belgium. Of special interest is the stained-glass window in the west end; it was designed by John La Farge, the well-known nineteenth-century American artist who was also responsible for the interior decorations of Trinity Church in Boston.

ST. PETER'S EPISCOPAL CHURCH   *State and Lodge Streets. Open Sunday through Friday 8 A.M. to 5 P.M., Saturday 8 A.M. to noon.*   The first church building of this parish was erected in 1715 about a block away. The rector, Reverend Thomas Barclay, served as chaplain to the British garrison in Albany in addition to attending to his pastoral duties at St. Peter's. In 1802 a second church was constructed on this site.

In 1859, to accommodate the growing congregation, the present building—designed in the Gothic Revival style by Richard Upjohn—was erected. The architect's son, Richard M. Upjohn, supervised the building of the square tower in 1876; he is also responsible for the design of St. Peter's altar and reredos (screen behind the altar). The second rear east window was designed by Sir Edward Burne-Jones, the famous English Pre-Raphaelite painter.

Residents of Albany claim that buried beneath the vestibule floor are the remains of British General George Augustus Howe (1724–1758, brother of William Howe, who was Commander-in-Chief of British forces in North America during the Revolutionary War). However, historians now contend that his grave is located in Ticonderoga, where he was killed in battle in 1758.

SMITH STATE OFFICE BUILDING *Behind the Capitol. An observation terrace on the thirty-first story is open Monday through Friday 9 A.M. to 4 P.M. Free.* This building was constructed in 1930 to house government offices. It is named for Alfred E. Smith (1873–1944), who was elected governor of New York four times (1918, 1922, 1924, and 1926).

STATE CAPITOL *State Street and Washington Avenue. Open Monday through Friday 9 A.M. to 4 P.M. Free guided tours available.* Construction of the Capitol building began in 1867, and the legislature occupied its chambers twelve years later. The massive structure, which covers three acres and cost $25 million, has rusticated stonework, arched windows flanked by columns, and pyramidal corner roofs. The building was designed by Thomas W. Fuller, although the architectural plans were modified by Leopold Eidlitz and H. H. Richardson. The ornate western staircase, lighted by a huge glazed dome, was designed by Richardson. The Assembly and Senate Chambers are located on the third floor.

STATE EDUCATION BUILDING *On Washington Avenue opposite the Capitol. Open daily 9 A.M. to 4:30 P.M.*

Free. Designed by Palmer, Hornbostel, and Jones and completed in 1912, this structure houses the State Library and the State Education Department. The building is distinguished by its colonnade of thirty-six Corinthian columns that extends along the entire front. Inside, a series of murals by W. H. Low on the theme of education adorn the walls adjacent to the rotunda. The main library and reading room are located on the second floor.

STATE EXECUTIVE MANSION *Eagle and Elm Streets. Not open to the public.* Thomas Olcott, an Albany businessman, built this mansion in the 1850s. When Samuel J. Tilden was elected governor of New York in 1874, he rented the house for $9,000 a year. His successor, Governor Lucius Robinson, persuaded the legislature to purchase the building for the governor's official residence. Since that time such notable statesmen as Grover Cleveland, Franklin D. Roosevelt, Alfred E. Smith, Herbert Lehman, Thomas E. Dewey, and Nelson Rockefeller have occupied the mansion. After the March 1961 fire, which destroyed most of the interior, it was extensively remodeled.

Recommended Side Trip

Schoharie

From Albany take Route 20 West to Duanesburg. Then travel southwest along Route 7 until you come to Route 30 South, which you should follow into the village of Schoharie.

On October 17, 1780, Sir John Johnson with a force of 1,500 British soldiers, Loyalists, and Indians besieged the small garrison located here. The attackers poured so intense a barrage of artillery fire on the Patriot fortification that Major Melanchthon Woolsey, the commander, believed defeat was certain and decided to surrender. A white flag was hastily tied to the end of a musket, and a militiaman was ordered to go out from the fort to offer the surrender. Before he could pass through the entrance gates Timothy Murphy, a hero of the Battle of Saratoga, turned his musket from the enemy outside and furiously shot the flag from its bearer's hand.

The militiaman attempted to retrieve the flag, but a second shot from Murphy's gun stopped him. Enraged, Major Woolsey shouted to the soldiers to overpower the mutinous Murphy, but his comrades rallied to his defense. Shouting his defiance, Murphy threatened to kill any man who dared to raise a flag of surrender.

While the Patriots confronted each other inside the fort, Johnson had concluded that his artillery would not be strong enough to batter down the walls. He therefore ordered his troops to withdraw, abandoning the siege.

Murphy's defiance of orders, which caused the delay of Woolsey's plan to surrender, resulted in the battle's turning in favor of the Patriots. Because of this outcome, and because of his heroic action at the Battle of Saratoga (October 1777) where he killed British General Simon Fraser, Murphy's breach of discipline brought him only a mild reprimand.

OLD STONE FORT MUSEUM   *Located just off Route 30 on the northern edge of the village of Schoharie. Open May 1 to October 31. The visiting schedule is 10 A.M. to 5 P.M. daily during June, July, and August. In May, September, and October the hours are Tuesday through Saturday from 10 A.M. to 5 P.M., Sunday noon* *to 5 P.M. Adults 50¢, children 25¢.* The Old Stone Fort was built in 1772 as a church by the Reformed Protestant High Dutch Church Society. Inhabitants of the Schoharie Valley decided to fortify the building so that it might serve as a refuge during attacks of Indian and Loyalist raiding parties. By 1778 a log stockade was constructed enclosing the church and a large tract of land. Soon afterward, small cabins and a tavern were built within the walls.

The stockade was built with a blockhouse at two of the corners. During an attack, while stalwart young men manned the cannon in the blockhouses, sharpshooters mounted the church's spire (demolished in 1830) to take aim at the enemy. This is the fortification that Sir John Johnson attacked on October 17, 1780.

Administered by the Schoharie County Historical Society, the Old Stone Fort is now a museum displaying Indian artifacts, Revolutionary War relics, and historical items of the region.

Beneath the floor of the church is the grave of the Reverend Johannes Schuyler, pastor here during the Revolutionary War. The remains of David Williams—one of the Patriots responsible for capturing Major John André (Benedict Arnold's coconspirator in the plans to surrender the garrison at West Point)—were brought here in 1805 and were interred in the cemetery adjacent to the church.

Hoosick Falls

Revolutionary War History

In early August 1777, after having captured Fort Ticonderoga (July 6), British General John Burgoyne moved
his troops southward toward Albany. When they reached
Fort Edward, Burgoyne became alarmed by the danger-
ously low level of provisions and ordered Lieutenant
Colonel Frederick Baum (of the German Brunswick
Dragoons) to take an expedition eastward to seize cattle,
horses, and wagons.

A force of German mercenaries, Loyalists, Indians, and
British Regulars was preparing to depart on August 11,
1777, when an informer arrived with reports that caused
Burgoyne to modify his strategy and choose another
objective—the garrison at Bennington, a Patriot supply
depot near the village of Hoosick Falls.

Meanwhile, Patriots in Vermont and New Hampshire
were monitoring Burgoyne's troop movements and were
preparing to meet the enemy threat. John Stark—who had
led New Hampshire regiments at Bunker Hill, Trenton,
and Princeton—was offered command of the American
force.

By Thursday, August 14, Baum's troops had reached
Van Schaick's Mill (about two miles west of the present-
day battlefield site). There a detachment of Patriots
under Colonel Gregg engaged the enemy's forces in a
brief skirmish and then retired. Stark's forces were deployed at a crossing of the Walloomsac River and then
withdrew two miles toward Bennington. Baum's troops
took up positions on a height above the river. By this

time Stark had sent word to Seth Warner in Manchester, Vermont, to have the Green Mountain Boys march to Bennington, and Baum had requested reinforcements from Burgoyne.

Early on Friday morning it began to rain and continued throughout the day. Despite the inclement weather, Baum deployed his men in small units and ordered the construction of fortifications. On the Bennington side of the river 150 Loyalists built a breastwork (which became known as the Tory Redoubt); on a hill overlooking the crossing 200 British soldiers erected a strong defense (referred to as the Dragoon Redoubt). Because of the storm no engagements were fought that day.

On the afternoon of Saturday, the 16th, the battle began. The Patriots devised a plan (the classic double envelopment maneuver) to divide the forces into three columns and then to surround and destroy the enemy. During the initial phase of the engagement, one column swung around to the left and attacked the Tory Redoubt as the second column marched to the right to hit enemy troops positioned there. Advancing down the road for a frontal assault, the third column captured the Dragoon Redoubt and attacked Baum's troops. The Patriots successfully encircled their adversary and closed in. During the fighting Lieutenant Colonel Baum fell mortally wounded.

As the Patriots were disarming their prisoners, word arrived that more than 600 well-equipped German reinforcements (under Lieutenant Colonel Heinrich von Breymann)—which had been sent by Burgoyne in response to Baum's request—were only two miles away. Patriot detachments immediately took up positions on the high ground overlooking the road and attempted to turn them back. But the Germans continued to advance. It was the propitious arrival of Seth Warner's Green Mountain Boys that finally gave the Patriots the advantage. They fired relentlessly, and soon Breymann's soldiers broke into a disorderly retreat and were routed. By dusk 30 Patriots and 200 enemy soldiers lay dead.

Stark captured hundreds of muskets, 4 cannon, 255 swords, and 4 ammunition wagons. In addition, 700 prisoners were taken. The victory at Bennington gave the Americans renewed confidence and volunteers rushed to join the army—recruits whose strength at Saratoga two months later led to the surrender of Burgoyne's army and the end of British control of upstate New York.

BENNINGTON BATTLEFIELD SITE *Located just east of Walloomsac on Route 67, about four miles northeast of Hoosick Falls. From the Albany area, take the Adirondack Northway to Exit 6 (Latham). Leaving the exit ramp, turn right onto Route 7 East (toward Troy). After traveling approximately 28 miles, take Route 22 North (through the town of Hoosick Falls) until you come to Route 67 East. Turn right onto 67 and proceed 2 miles to the Bennington Battlefield Site. A ½-mile road leads to the parking area. Open daily 9 A.M. to 9 P.M. Free.* New York acquired this battlefield site in 1915. It is now a state park used primarily for picnicking, hiking, and other outdoor activities. The following monuments commemorating the Battle of Bennington may be seen in the park.

BATTLEFIELD MONUMENT This monument marks the area (the exact spot is a mile west) where Colonel Heinrich von Breymann and his men (who had been sent to reinforce Colonel Baum's troops) were defeated during the second engagement on August 16, 1777. Colonel Seth Warner and his Vermont regiment distinguished themselves in this action. The monument was erected by New York State in 1927, the Sesquicentennial year of the battle.

RELIEF MAP A bronze relief map, located near the monuments, shows the local terrain and the important sites of the battle. It stands in the area where the Dragoon Redoubt was located.

SAN COICK BRIDGE MONUMENT   Erected in 1927 by the state of New York, this monument commemorates the skirmish at San Coick Bridge near Van Schaick's Mill on August 14, 1777. There a detachment of Colonel Frederich Baum's force confronted Patriot militiamen under Colonel Gregg. After destroying the bridge, the Patriots fired upon their enemy, who were helpless to cross over and pursue them.

STARK MEMORIAL   This memorial honors John Stark (1728–1822), commander of the Patriot troops during the Battle of Bennington. A veteran of the French and Indian Wars, Stark led a New Hampshire regiment at Bunker Hill and later participated in the Battles of Trenton, Princeton, and Saratoga. He was commissioned a major general in the Continental Army in September 1783. The stone was erected by the state of New Hampshire in 1927 to honor one of its heroic sons.

Recommended Side Trip

Bennington Battle Monument

Located 8 miles from the battlefield site—in Bennington, Vermont. From the battlefield site in New York, take Route 67 East to Bennington College, where you will come to two blinking lights. Turn right onto Silk Road and travel as far as you can. Then turn left and proceed to the end of the road, the monument site. Open daily March through November 9 A.M. to 5 P.M. Elevator fee 50¢.

When this 306-foot granite obelisk was completed in 1891, it was the highest battle monument in the world. A diorama of the Battle of Bennington is located on the ground level near the elevator door.

Near the Bennington Battle Monument—at the intersection of Monument Avenue and Route 9—stands a large bronze statue of a catamount. It marks the approximate site of the Green Mountain Tavern (later called the Catamount Tavern) where Ethan Allen and the Green Mountain Boys met to plan their attack on Fort Ticonderoga, New York, in May 1775.

Schuylerville Area

When Major General Horatio Gates assumed command of the Patriot army in the North on August 19, 1777, the spirits of Patriot soldiers were high—buoyed by their victory at Bennington on August 16 and by General Philip Schuyler's control of the territory just north of Albany. Morale was further boosted a week later when a British expeditionary force under Lieutenant Colonel Barry St. Leger was driven from the area surrounding Fort Stanwix in western New York.

With plans to reestablish British domination of New York State, General John Burgoyne's army of 6,000, which had been marching south from Canada, arrived near Saratoga (present-day Schuylerville) in early September.

First Battle of Saratoga— Freeman's Farm

On September 13, 1777, Burgoyne's forces began crossing the Hudson River from the east bank to Saratoga. Four days later he deployed his troops three miles from Bemis Heights.

Meanwhile, General Gates had ordered his soldiers to construct fortifications on Bemis Heights (a steep bluff rising 100 feet above the surrounding fields and woods) in preparation for halting the British advance. In addition,

147

redoubts were built to the west and east of this position. The Patriot forces were strengthened by reinforcements which continued to arrive daily, so that by September 18 American troop strength was estimated at almost 7,000.

Shortly after ten o'clock on the morning of September 19 General Burgoyne's soldiers began to organize their advance toward the American positions. The right column was led by Brigadier General Simon Fraser; the center column was under the command of Brigadier General James Hamilton (Burgoyne accompanied these forces); and the left column stationed near the river was commanded by Major General von Riedesel. Because of the rough terrain, it took nearly three hours for these columns to come into position to attack. At last the signal was given—three guns were fired—and the British lines surged forward.

During the British maneuvers Gates took no action. Finally succumbing to General Benedict Arnold's insistent demands, he sent Colonel Daniel Morgan's corps of riflemen to confront the enemy. Near the ravine south of Freeman's Farm, the Patriots initially repelled units of the British center, but then were driven back. As Morgan's men were regrouping, other troops (two New Hampshire regiments under Colonels Joseph Cilley and Alexander Scammell) came to their aid. While these Patriots took up positions along the south edge of Freeman's Farm, Burgoyne's soldiers formed a long line about a mile away.

Soon afterward, Arnold arrived with reinforcements and urged them to attack the British center in order to cut the formation in two. But the Patriots could not penetrate the line, and fierce hand-to-hand fighting ensued. Neither side could gain the advantage: the troops moved back and forth across the clearing in alternating patterns of advance and retreat.

Suddenly the tide of battle turned in favor of the British when Major General von Riedesel with three regiments of German soldiers and several pieces of heavy artillery moved into the fray. With a barrage of cannon fire, they swept the Americans from the field.

Although the British had pushed back the Americans, they had done so at a terrible cost: 640 soldiers had been killed, wounded, or captured. The Americans, too, had suffered high casualties—approximately 300.

The ineptitude of Gates, his inability to take decisive action, had lost the battle for the Americans. If only he had reinforced Arnold or had attacked Riedesel's isolated river posts (where supplies and provisions were stored), the outcome of the battle might have been very different that day.

Second Battle of Saratoga—
Bemis Heights

On September 20, 1777, the day after the Battle of Freeman's Farm, General Burgoyne determined to seize the advantage offered by the British victory. He accordingly informed his officers to prepare for an all-out attack against the Americans to be launched the following morning. But shortly before dawn on September 21, a courier arrived in the camp bearing a dispatch from General Henry Clinton (dated September 12) which stated that Clinton was marching northward into the Hudson Valley and would be reaching Saratoga soon. With the prospect of reinforcements at hand, Burgoyne ordered the attack postponed and decided to strengthen the defenses until the other forces could join him.

He ordered his soldiers to construct a series of redoubts. The two major redoubts were erected near the west end of the British line—the Balcarres Redoubt (near Freeman's Farm) and the Breymann Redoubt (a short distance to the north).

Meanwhile, the Patriot troops occupied and fortified the ground on and surrounding Bemis Heights. There disputes among the officers threatened to destroy unity. General Gates, in his report to Congress on the Battle of Freeman's Farm, failed to even mention Benedict Arnold's name. Then Gates gave orders to Colonel Morgan (who was under Arnold) to report directly to him. Outraged, Arnold confronted Gates and, railing at him for his indecisiveness in battle, demanded an explanation for his failing to give him the credit which he was due. A stormy argument ensued and Arnold was stripped of his command. He decided to leave camp to join General Washington, but was persuaded by his fellow officers to remain for the coming battle.

By the end of the first week of October thousands of Patriots had traveled here to join Gates, swelling his ranks to nearly 11,000. While the strength of the American army increased daily, the British began to weaken. Provisions were running low—rations had to be reduced, the men fell ill, and the horses starved to death.

On the morning of October 7 Burgoyne sent 1,500 soldiers on a reconnaissance and foraging mission. The right column was led by Lord Balcarres, the center was commanded by Riedesel, and the left column was under the command of Major Acland. A detachment from General Simon Fraser's company of Rangers and 600 auxiliaries marched in advance of the right flank. After pushing forward about a mile to the vicinity of the Barber Farm, the British soldiers formed a line (extending a thousand yards) in a wheat field while a group of their comrades reaped the wheat. Although most of these soldiers stood in the open field, the two flanks were positioned in dense forests.

The Americans seized the opportunity to attack. At 2:30 P.M. Colonel Daniel Morgan's men launched a surprise raid on the British from the west while General Enoch Poor's forces assailed the enemy from the east.

Morgan's soldiers swept through the woods and quickly routed the British. One of his riflemen, Timothy Murphy, mortally wounded General Simon Fraser. Poor's troops overwhelmed Acland's grenadiers, who withdrew in panic; Lord Acland was shot through both legs and was taken prisoner.

As General Ebenezer Learned's three brigades advanced on the British center, Benedict Arnold joined the fighting and rallied the Patriots. The enemy was pushed back to their redoubts. The Patriots then attacked the Balcarres Redoubt. Though the men crashed through the abatis and fought on bravely, they found the fortification impregnable. Undaunted, the impetuous Arnold rode through a barrage of fire and led his comrades toward the Breymann Redoubt, which they surrounded and overran. A bullet hit Arnold in the left leg, but he continued to inspire his men.

During the battles of October 7 the British losses included 600 wounded, killed, and captured; American casualties totaled 150.

As evening approached, Burgoyne, who realized his defenses were open to attack from the right and the rear, ordered a withdrawal to the north—away from Albany, one of his major objectives. That night the army encamped near the Great Ravine on the bluffs overlooking the Hudson River.

The next evening the weary British began to trudge toward Saratoga (present-day Schuylerville). Their progress was slow, impeded by rain, which turned the road into thick mud, and by the constant harassment of Patriot raiders at their rear. By October 11 the Americans had taken up positions near the British camp and had set up batteries. Two days later, when Burgoyne realized that any attempt to break through the Patriot lines would result in grievous losses, he consulted with his officers about the possibility of surrender. Then he sent an emissary to General Gates to propose a meeting to consider "matters of high importance to both armies."

On the morning of the 14th Major Kingston, Burgoyne's envoy, was conducted to Patriot headquarters where he was presented with Gates' terms for unconditional surrender. Finding these terms unacceptable, Burgoyne sent a counterproposal that his troops be returned to England on British transports with the promise "of not serving again in North America during the present contest," and that they be allowed to march out of camp to the honors of war and lay down their arms at the command of their own officers.

Burgoyne was amazed to find that Gates accepted his terms with only one addition, that the surrender take place the following afternoon. This led Burgoyne to believe that Gates had received news of Clinton's approach, and he therefore attempted to delay negotiations by requesting another concession—that the document of surrender be called a "convention" and not a "capitulation." Having agreed to this demand, Gates immediately sent his commissioners (Wilkinson and Whipple) to meet with the British commissioners (Craig and Sutherland) to draft the Articles of the Convention.

Burgoyne, however, incorrectly believing that Clinton was near, began to regret his offer to surrender. He asked his officers whether he might withdraw from negotiations, but they voted that the advantageous terms accepted by Gates could not honorably be refused.

Dressed in splendid uniforms, the British general and his officers rode to the American camp on the morning of October 17. As he presented himself to Gates, Burgoyne said, "The fortune of war . . . has made me your prisoner," to which Gates replied, "I shall always be ready to bear testimony that it has not been through any fault of your excellency." Later, the British soldiers laid down their arms. When Burgoyne formally presented his sword to

Surrender of General Burgoyne at Saratoga. *Painting by John Trumbull.* (OFFICE OF THE ARCHITECT OF THE CAPITOL, WASHINGTON, D.C.)

Gates, the American victory officially had been accomplished.

The surrender at Saratoga also forced the British to withdraw from Fort Ticonderoga and Crown Point, leaving northern New York under Patriot control. The victory at Saratoga—where 5,000 soldiers (including 300 officers) were captured—instilled new confidence in the Patriot army, and the positive effect on the morale of the American people was tremendous. The French government, which had been surreptitiously aiding the Patriots, openly recognized the war for American independence in a note signed by the king, which virtually made his country America's ally. On February 6, 1778, France and America formally signed a Treaty of Alliance. The Battle of Saratoga marked the turning point of the Revolutionary War.

VISITORS' CENTER   An audio-visual program at Saratoga National Historic Park describes the Battles of Saratoga. Books and pamphlets are offered for sale.

The park, which is administered by the National Park Service of the Department of the Interior, has a nine-mile tour road with the major points of interest clearly designated.

DRIVING TOUR

Start at Visitors' Center:

Freeman's Farm Overlook (Plaque)

Foot of Bemis Heights (American Soldiers Monument, Elm Marker)

Bemis Heights (Blockhouse, Hibernian Monument, Kosciusko Monument, Neilson House, New Hampshire Monument)

Site of American Fortifications (North Redan and Redoubt Sites)

Site of Chatfield Farm and Middle Ravine (Placard)

Site of Barber Wheat Field (Fraser Monument, Placard, Ten Broeck Monument)

Balcarres Redoubt Area (Balcarres Redoubt, Bidwell Monument, Bloody Knoll, Freeman's Cabin, Old Well)

Site of Breymann Redoubt (Plaque, Arnold Monument)

Site of Burgoyne's Headquarters (Plaque)

Site of the Great Redoubt (Plaques)

Take the exit road which leads to Route 4 (and the historic sites of Schuylerville).

Saratoga National Historic Park Sites

Saratoga National Historic Park is located 8 miles south of Schuylerville (off Route 4). From Albany take the Adirondack Northway, Route 87, to Exit 12. Travel several miles on Route 9, then turn right onto Route 9P and proceed until you come to Route 423 East. Traveling along 423, you will reach Route 32 North, which you should follow 2 miles to the battlefield site. (Another approach from the Albany area is to drive along Route 4 North and then proceed on Route 423 West for a short distance until you come to Route 32, which you should follow north to the site.) Tour roads are open daily from April through November. The hours are 9 A.M. to 7 P.M. during the summer, 9 A.M. to 5 P.M. the rest of the year. Free.

BALCARRES REDOUBT AREA

Balcarres Redoubt This position became the strongest point of the British defenses. The redoubt, which was 500 yards long and almost 14 feet high, was manned by 1,500 men. At least eight cannon were mounted on the log-and-earth walls. The redoubt was named for Alexander Lindsay, sixth Earl of Balcarres, who commanded the British Light Infantry at Saratoga. (White, red-tipped stakes mark the perimeter of this fortification.)

Bidwell Monument This rough stone monument honors Zebulon Bidwell, captain of the Fourth Company of the Connecticut Regiment. The Bidwell family erected

Freeman's cabin, Saratoga National Historic Park (ALPER)

the memorial in 1924 to honor their ancestor who died near this spot during the battle of September 19, 1777.

Bloody Knoll When the Patriots tried to capture the Balcarres Redoubt (October 7), they lost more men between this knoll and the redoubt than at any other place on the Saratoga battlefield. The small fortification here was built in the twentieth century.

Freeman's Cabin After the September 19 fighting, General Burgoyne ordered construction of fortifications at strategic areas. Here, on the Freeman property, the British erected a redoubt and included the farm buildings within the lines of defense.

James Freeman (who had emigrated here from Rhode Island) built on this tract of land a frame house, a barn, and several small log cabins. The family abandoned its homestead in 1777 when British troops moved into the area. None of the original structures has survived; the modest cabin now on this site is a twentieth-century reconstruction.

Old Well From this well British soldiers drew water during their occupation of Freeman's Farm.

(FOOT OF) BEMIS HEIGHTS

American Soldiers Monument This fifteen-foot monument honors the "Unknown American soldiers who perished in the Battles of Saratoga, September 19 and October 7, 1777, and were here buried in unmarked graves." The memorial was erected by the Daughters of the American Revolution of New York State in late 1931 to commemorate the Bicentennial of the birth of George Washington and to pay homage to the men who served the Patriot cause. Lieutenant Governor Herbert H. Lehman was the principal speaker at the dedication ceremonies. Afterward, an honor guard from the Clark Post of the American Legion fired a salute, and buglers from the Fort Orange Council, Boy Scouts of America, sounded taps.

American Soldiers Monument, Saratoga National Historic Park (ALPER)

Elm Marker   This small stone marker was presented by the Saratoga Chapter of the Daughters of the American Revolution who, in October 1931, planted elm trees on this site to honor both the Bicentennial of George Washington's birth and the chief officers of the Continental Army who participated in the Battles of Saratoga. A plaque lists the names of Horatio Gates, Benedict Arnold, Ebenezer Learned, Philip Schuyler, John Glover, John Paterson, Enoch Poor, and others. As part of the ceremony, representatives from the D.A.R. presented biographical sketches of each Patriot hero for whom a commemorative tree was being planted. That afternoon addresses were delivered by Mrs. Frank H. Parcells, State Regent of the Daughters of the American Revolution, and Mr. W. E. Howard, Superintendent of Lands and Forests of New York.

BEMIS HEIGHTS

This area takes its name from Jotham Bemis, who owned property at the foot of the hill. Here the core of the American defenses were concentrated. Nearby were encampment sites and a hospital.

Blockhouse   This blockhouse was erected by the Conservation Department of the state of New York in 1927. Since no such structure existed here in 1777, plans are under way to remove the blockhouse to another location. During the Saratoga campaign the barn of the Neilson farm—located near this site—was fortified with artillery pieces and protected by a breastwork of logs.

Hibernian Monument   The Ancient Order of Hibernians of Saratoga County erected this monument in 1913 to honor the heroic deeds of soldiers of Irish descent who fought here for the Patriot cause. The inscription cites the action of Timothy Murphy (1751–1818), the Pennsylvania sharpshooter who is credited with mortally wounding British General Simon Fraser during the battle on October 7. The Monument Committee organized to erect this stone was headed by the Reverend P. J. Donnelly and D. J. Falvey.

Kosciusko Monument Erected in 1936, this monument is a tribute to Thaddeus Kosciusko (1746–1817), the Polish-born engineer who came to America in 1776 to fight in the Patriot struggle for independence. Under the command of General Gates, he was consulted on strategy and supervised the building of fortifications on the Saratoga battlefields. From March 1778 to June 1780 Kosciusko was engaged in planning the defenses of West Point. In the final years of the Revolutionary War he served under General Nathanael Greene in the Southern campaigns.

Neilson House This red clapboard house is the original farmhouse of John Neilson who settled here with his wife in the early 1770s. Neilson was a member of the local militia and is known to have helped haul supplies to Fort Ticonderoga. The building, which has been restored, was used as temporary headquarters by Generals Enoch Poor and Benedict Arnold.

When Major John Dyke Acland of the British Grenadiers (and a former member of Parliament) was wounded and captured on October 7, he was carried to this house. According to tradition, his wife, Lady Harriet—who had accompanied him to the American Continent—traveled here to nurse him. With great tenacity, she convinced a ship's captain to sail through a storm down the Hudson River, and her persistence (along with a letter from Burgoyne) persuaded American sentries to let her pass through the lines. Lord Acland recovered and, after the surrender, was permitted to return to England on parole.

New Hampshire Monument This stone of New Hampshire granite was erected in 1929 by the state of New Hampshire to honor its sons who fought in the Battles of Saratoga. The inscription lists four officers:

Neilson House, Saratoga National Historic Park (ALPER)

Enoch Poor, brigadier general; Joseph Cilley, colonel of the First Regiment; Henry Dearborn, colonel of the Second Regiment; and Alexander Scammell, colonel of the Third Regiment.

FREEMAN'S FARM BATTLEFIELD OVERLOOK

Narrative Plaque In the fields to the east of this plaque occurred the first action of the Saratoga campaigns. On September 19, 1777, Patriot soldiers fired on the advance guard of the center column of Burgoyne's army. In the general fighting that followed, control of the field changed hands several times. Toward evening, when German troops under General von Riedesel arrived to reinforce the British, the Americans were compelled to withdraw to Bemis Heights.

SITE OF AMERICAN FORTIFICATIONS

Narrative Plaques Skillful military engineering converted this bluff into a stronghold. (Additional batteries were located on the river flats below.) The road paralleling the river was the route that Burgoyne had intended to follow to Albany. However, when he realized the strength of the Patriot positions here, he was forced to order his troops to swing around to the west of Bemis Heights—into the rough, wooded terrain—placing them at a strategic disadvantage.

North Redan A log breastwork similar to this one was used by the Patriots to control the road below (present-day Route 4). The cannon now seen here are not those used in the Battles of Saratoga.

SITE OF BARBER WHEAT FIELD

Placard On October 7 British soldiers were deployed in a battle line 1,000 yards across this field, the property of the Barber family. Patriot troops under General Enoch Poor attacked the Redcoats positioned to the right of the line, while Colonel Daniel Morgan's men struck the left flank and General Ebenezer Learned hurled his brigade at the center. Pushed back by the thrust of the Patriot charge, the British withdrew toward the Balcarres Redoubt.

North Redan, Saratoga National Historic Park (ALPER)

Fraser Monument A granite monument marks the spot where, on October 7, 1777, British General Simon Fraser (1726–1782) fell wounded, shot through the bowels by Timothy Murphy (one of Morgan's men). Fraser was carried back to the quarters of General von Riedesel, where the Baroness von Riedesel was preparing dinner for the officers. The dining table was converted into a makeshift bed, and the dying Fraser was placed upon it. When told of his condition, he wrote a farewell note to General Burgoyne asking that he be buried on the top of a nearby hill. After suffering through the night, he died eight o'clock the following morning. Only members of his personal staff were permitted to attend the funeral services.

Ten Broeck Monument This stone was erected in 1917 by the Livingston Chapter of the Sons of the Revolution to honor Brigadier General Abraham Ten Broeck (1734–1810), of the Albany militia, who participated in the October 7 battle. He later served as mayor of Albany (1779–1783, 1796–1799).

SITE OF BREYMANN REDOUBT

Narrative Plaque Constructed to protect the British right flank, this redoubt—a single line of log breastworks extending 200 yards—was defended by German troops under Lieutenant Colonel Heinrich von Breymann, who was mortally wounded during the Patriot attack on October 7.

Arnold Monument In the October 7 assault on the Breymann Redoubt, Patriot leader Benedict Arnold sustained a severe leg wound. This unusual monument depicts the lower part of a leg clad in a boot. Since it was felt inappropriate to fully portray such an infamous traitor, only his wounded leg was shown! Of white marble, the memorial was erected in 1887 by John Watts de Peyster, vice president of the Saratoga Monument Association.

SITE OF BURGOYNE'S HEADQUARTERS

Narrative Plaque A path leads to an area near a spring where General Burgoyne established his headquarters. From here he directed the building of fortifications and devised his battle strategies.

SITE OF CHATFIELD FARM AND MIDDLE RAVINE

Placard The farmhouse of Asa Chatfield, which once stood here, was used as an American observation post. On each side of the Middle Ravine British and American sentinels were posted during the period between the battles of September 19 and October 7.

SITE OF GREAT REDOUBT

Narrative Plaques The British built a system of fortifications along these hills to defend their artillery batteries, hospital, and supply depots. On the night of October 7 Bourgoyne withdrew his defeated army to this vicinity, and the next evening, pursued by the Americans, retreated northward to the village of Saratoga (Schuylerville).

Schuylerville Sites

FIELD OF GROUNDED ARMS *Traveling from the Saratoga Battlefield on Route 4 North, this site is about .3 mile before the Schuyler House, near Evans Street. The land is privately owned, but a historic marker has been placed here.* Here, on October 17, 1777, ceremonies took place which formally marked the surrender of General John Burgoyne's forces to those of General Horatio Gates. Early in the morning fifes and drums blared forth the strains of "Yankee Doodle" as the Patriot army formed into two lines. Then, at 10 A.M., the British marched out from their camp, with drums beating and with the honors of war, to the meadows near the river's edge. There they halted and, at the command of their own officers, piled their arms and emptied their cartridge boxes. They then filed back through the American lines until they reached a large tent where Generals Gates and Burgoyne were waiting. Burgoyne drew his sword, silently offering it to General Gates, who received it with a bow and then returned it to its owner. They then reentered the tent, where a dinner was hosted by the Americans for the defeated British officers. As the weary British soldiers began their long march to Boston (where they were to await transport to England), Generals Gates and Burgoyne were exchanging toasts. (In January 1779, in violation of the terms of the surrender agreement, the British prisoners of war were removed from the Boston–Cambridge area to Virginia. When the war ended, they were finally permitted to return home.)

SARATOGA BATTLE MONUMENT   *From the Schuyler House on Route 4, proceed a short distance until you pass Route 32. Then turn left onto Burgoyne Street and travel up the hill.*   The Saratoga Monument Association laid the cornerstone of this monument on October 17, 1877, to commemorate the 100th anniversary of the surrender of Burgoyne's troops. The gala occasion was attended by 30,000 people. A two-mile-long procession of military units, bands, and patriotic organizations marched through the streets of the village to the monument site. Orations were delivered by Horatio Seymour and George William Curtis, after which original poems recalling the Saratoga campaign were recited.

The 155-foot shaft was completed in 1883 at a cost of $105,000. Gables on each side rise to a height of forty feet over the entrances. Exterior niches contain statues of leading American military figures who fought in New York: General Philip Schuyler, General Horatio

Gates, and Colonel Daniel Morgan. A fourth niche is left empty to symbolize Benedict Arnold's betrayal of the American cause.

Jared C. Markham, architect of the monument, also designed the interior relief panels. The first-floor panels include *George III and His Ministers, Ladies of the British Court, Women of the Revolution, General Schuyler Trying to Obstruct the British Army, Wives of British Officers Accompanying the Army,* and *Mrs. Schuyler Setting Fire to the Wheat Field.*

The second-floor panels are *The Surrender, The Massacre of Jane McCrea, General Burgoyne Reprimanding Indians, General Schuyler Turning Over His Command to General Gates, The Fall of General Fraser,* and *The Wounding of General Arnold.*

Near the monument is a small stone to honor Major Nathan Goodale who, with his scouts, captured a large contingent of British soldiers and Loyalists during the interim between the major battles of September 19 and October 7.

SCHUYLER HOUSE *On Route 4 on the south edge of Schuylerville. Open from mid-June to early September Monday through Saturday 10 A.M. to 5 P.M., Sunday noon to 5 P.M. Adults 50¢, children 10¢.* On the night of October 9, 1777, General John Burgoyne rested in the house on this site—the summer residence of Philip Schuyler (1733–1804), general in the Continental Army and member of the Continental Congress. The next morning, after Redcoats pillaged the property, he had the house and nearby outbuildings set afire as a diversionary action during the British retreat.

With the aid of tenant farmers, prisoners of war, and Patriot soldiers, Schuyler was able to build a new dwelling on this site by the end of November 1777. Timber was procured from a nearby sawmill, and some of the hardware (nails, bolts, locks) was retrieved from the debris of the first house. The new structure—

Schuyler House, Schuylerville (ALPER)

a frame house measuring sixty feet long by twenty-one feet wide—had spacious rooms and a large central hallway.

After the death of General Schuyler and his wife the property passed to their grandson, Philip, who was forced to sell it in 1837 because of financial difficulties. The Strover family then purchased the estate, and their descendants lived here until 1950, when the United States Department of the Interior acquired the historic house.

The interior has been restored and furnished with fine eighteenth-century pieces. In the **Parlor** a portrait of General Philip Schuyler (a copy after Trumbull) is prominently displayed over the fireplace. The spinet (*c.* 1745) is similar to the one used by Schuyler's daughters. The wallpaper is a reproduction of the original eighteenth-century French paper, fragments of which were uncovered during the restoration.

The **Dining Room,** which has a large table of Hepplewhite design and a handsome sideboard, was the scene of elaborate dinners prepared for distinguished guests. Visitors included George Washington, Lafayette, George Clinton (a general in the Continental Army and a governor of New York), Alexander Hamilton (who married Schuyler's daughter Elizabeth), and the Chevalier de Chastellux (a French officer and writer). The drop-leaf table with ball-and-claw feet belonged to the Schuylers. The cupboard, now used as a china closet, has a trap door through which the servants passed food that was prepared in the basement kitchen. (The kitchen outbuilding was a later addition.) The portrait of the lovely woman who looks down serenely on the room is the general's wife, Catherine (of the Van Rensselaer family).

A rare odometer may be seen in the **Study**. The instrument was once pushed across the fields to measure rods (5½ yards), furlongs (220 yards), and miles. Other items here, such as a field desk and quill pens, re-create a Colonial ambiance.

Bedrooms are located on the second floor. The chest in the **Master Bedroom** was the property of the Schuylers. Draped across the bed is a gold gown worn by Mrs. Schuyler to a ball held in honor of Lafayette. The Bible near the blanket chest bears the date 1589.

The other two bedrooms were occupied by the Schuyler children.

Johnstown

Revolutionary War History

When settlers first arrived in this region in the 1750s, it was called by the Indians "Kalenka," which means "place for food and drink." A village founded here in 1760 by Sir William Johnson (1715–1774) was named Johnstown in his honor. One of the most influential men in New York, Johnson—Superintendent of Indian Affairs for the Northern Colonies and a major general in the British army—was a staunch supporter of the policies of the Crown, even in the 1770s when public opinion in the colonies was turning toward independence.

On October 25, 1781 (six days after Cornwallis' army surrendered at Yorktown), a minor battle occurred in Johnstown. A raiding party of approximately 700 Loyalists and Indians, which had been marauding in the upper Mohawk Valley, arrived in the town where they encountered a Patriot force commanded by Colonel Marinus Willett. In the late afternoon the Loyalist line, under Major John Ross, formed along present-day Hall Avenue. The Patriots, after establishing a base in the jailhouse, approached their foe from the southeast but were quickly driven back. The frightened militiamen were sent scurrying across Cayadutta Creek. They regrouped to attack, but Ross' men not only succeeded in repelling subsequent assaults but also captured a cannon and an ammunition cart. Only the approaching darkness saved the Patriots from annihilation.

The Loyalists and Indians withdrew from Johnstown, but three days later Willett's forces had increased their numbers and set out in pursuit. On October 30, 1781, they overtook their foe at Jerseyfield and there, at last, the Patriot forces were victorious.

VISITORS' CENTER Information about Johnstown's historical sites is available from the Chamber of Commerce, 132 West Main Street, phone 762–3417.

PUBLIC TRANSPORTATION Bus service in the area is limited.

TAXI SERVICE John's Taxi, phone 762–8280; ABC Taxi (Gloversville), phone 725–3127.

Most of the major Colonial sites may be seen by walking through the area bounded by West Green Street on the north, Montgomery Street on the south, Perry Street on the east, and Melcher Street on the west. (To visit Johnson Hall on Hall Avenue it will be necessary to drive there.)

WALKING TOUR

Start at North Market and Main Streets:

St. John's Church

County Courthouse

Colonial Cemetery

Burke's Tavern

County Jail

End at South Perry and Montgomery Streets.

Colonial and Revolutionary War Sites

BURKE'S TAVERN *West Montgomery and South William Streets. Not open to the public.* Built in 1765, this house was a Colonial tavern operated by innkeeper James Burke. In 1788 the structure was moved here from its original location near the corner of South William and Main Streets—on a lot formerly owned by Sir William Johnson. The inn was acquired in 1812 by Isaiah Younglove, a cousin of Burke, and descendants of the Youngloves resided here until 1926. That year the property was purchased by the Daughters of the American Revolution, who still use it as their chapter house.

COLONIAL CEMETERY *West Green Street* This cemetery is now on land once owned by Sir William Johnson. Several Revolutionary War Patriots are buried here. In 1907 the Daughters of the American Revolution erected a memorial arch at the cemetery's entrance.

COUNTY COURTHOUSE *North William Street near Main Street. Open weekdays 9 A.M. to 5 P.M.* In 1772, when Tryon County (present-day Fulton County) was created by an act of the Colonial Assembly, Johnstown was named the county seat. Construction of a courthouse began immediately. The first Court of General Quarter Session was held here September 8, 1772, with Sir Guy Johnson (Sir William's nephew) presiding.

During the Battle of Johnstown in October 1871 a Loyalist raiding party under the command of Captain Walter Butler laid siege to this building for a short time.

In 1812 Aaron Burr argued a case here, creating a sensation. His brilliant defense of his client, Solomon Southwich, against charges that he had attempted to bribe officials to favor incorporating the Bank of America resulted in an acquittal.

The only extant Colonial courthouse in New York, this building has been in continuous use for more than 200 years.

COUNTY JAIL *116 South Perry Street. Not open to the public.* This stone jail was built in 1772 on a hill overlooking the settlement.

Before the Revolution the building was used as a civil prison for the region west of Schenectady County. During the War of Independence the jail was fortified with palisades and two blockhouses, thus earning the name "Fort Johnson."

A unit of Loyalists unsuccessfully attempted to attack the defenses here prior to the major engagement of the Battle of Johnstown on October 25, 1781. Three days after the battle the Patriot forces assembled on the jailhouse lawn before embarking on their pursuit of the enemy.

In 1783 George Washington visited the site while touring the Mohawk Valley. In a brief speech he paid tribute to the local militiamen who served the cause of liberty.

After the peace treaty was signed with England (September 3, 1783), the jail again became a civil prison. Only minor repairs were made until the first decade of the twentieth century, when the interior was extensively renovated and the sheriff's residence was erected on the adjoining lot.

On Memorial Day 1900 the Johnstown Historical Society placed on the jailhouse lawn a cannon and cannon balls marking the site of the Colonial fort and honoring the memory of the Patriot heroes of the Battle of Johnstown.

JOHNSON HALL   *Located about .3 mile down Hall Avenue, northwest of the center of town. Follow Perry Street north to West Green Street. Turn left and proceed to West State Street, which you should follow to a fork in the road. Bear right onto Hall Avenue and travel .3 mile to Johnson Hall. Open Tuesday through Saturday 9 A.M. to 5 P.M., Sunday 1 P.M. to 5 P.M. Closed Thanksgiving, December 25, and January 1. Free.*   This splendid Georgian mansion was the residence of Sir William Johnson (1715–1774), the founder of Johnstown. As a young man, Johnson had come from Ireland to manage his uncle's estates in the Mohawk Valley, and within a short time he had acquired his own tracts of land.

During the French and Indian Wars it was Johnson's diplomacy that aligned the Six Nations—the Iroquois Confederacy composed of the Mohawk, Oneida, Onondaga, Cayuga, Seneca, and Tuscarora tribes—on the side of the British. (Johnson was a staunch Loyalist, and although he died in 1774, his influence remained

Johnson Hall, Johnstown (ALPER)

alive: the Iroquois Confederacy, with the exception of the Oneida tribe, chose to fight with the British during the Revolutionary War.)

In September 1755 he distinguished himself in military service by leading a force of Colonials and Indians in a victory over the French at Lake George. In recognition of his services to the Crown he was knighted, awarded a baronetcy, and appointed Superintendent of Indian Affairs for the Northern Colonies.

Johnson Hall was built in 1763. An overseer's cottage, a coachhouse, and a mill were constructed nearby. In the rear stood a long, narrow Council Building in which Sir William held his conferences with the Indians.

In 1764, when Pontiac, chief of the Ottawa Indians, led his tribe against the British, Johnson had two block-houses constructed at the sides of his mansion for protection in the event of an Indian raid. Two years later the uprising, known as "Pontiac's Rebellion," was brought to an end with a peace treaty concluded between Johnson (representing the British government) and the Ottawa chieftain.

In the summer of 1774 Sir William died suddenly at Johnson Hall after addressing a large Indian council. He was survived by three children, John, Ann, and Mary. He also had several illegitimate children by a young Indian woman, Mary ("Molly") Brant (sister of the Mohawk chieftain Joseph Brant), who had become housekeeper at Johnson Hall after the death of his wife Catherine Weisenburg Johnson.

Johnson's son, John, inherited his estates and his title. During the Revolutionary War Johnson Hall became a bastion of Loyalist support. In January 1776, after learning that Sir John Johnson was aiding Royal Governor Tryon, a Patriot force mobbed his house, forcing Johnson to disband a contingent of 200 armed Loyalists garrisoned on the estate. In May, after his life had been threatened, Sir John was forced to flee to

Canada without his family. Soon afterward, a band of Patriots pillaged Johnson Hall and made hostages of his wife Mary and their two children. They were transported to Albany and imprisoned. The harsh treatment they received resulted in the death of Mary's newborn infant.

Meanwhile, Sir John organized other Loyalists in Canada into the King's Royal Regiment (sometimes known as "Johnson's Greens" because of the color of their coats). They returned to New York State and staged many successful raids against Patriot strongholds.

In 1779 his properties in New York were confiscated by the state. After the Revolutionary War Johnson Hall was sold at auction to James Caldwell, an Albany merchant. In the nineteenth century the property was owned by the Aiken family and subsequently by the Wells family. New York purchased the house in 1906, and after restoring it, opened it to the public.

The interior of Johnson Hall follows the typical Georgian floor plan—two rooms arranged on each side of a wide central hallway. Rooms are furnished with eighteenth-century pieces, and several items on display once belonged to the Johnson family.

In the **White Parlor** Sir John Johnson's portrait by John Mare (1771) seems to keep watch over the Chippendale sofa, chairs, and gate-leg table. The **Study** is well appointed with a small desk, a chest, and a collection of books. **Molly Brant's Room** is dominated by a four-poster canopied bed, and a finely carved chest stands nearby. Downstairs a **Museum Room** exhibits maps, manuscripts, and historical items, and it also features a diorama of the Battle of Lake George.

The house is administered by the New York State Historic Trust.

JOHNSON STATUE *At the head of Hall Avenue, the road leading to Johnson Hall* This statue was erected in 1904 by the Aldine Society of Johnstown. The inscription on the base reads: "In memory of Sir William Johnson, Baronet, a man strong in character, a colossal pioneer, sole superintendent and faithful friend of the Six Nations . . . founder of Johnstown, he established here the first free school in the state."

ST. JOHN'S EPISCOPAL CHURCH AND JOHNSON'S GRAVE *North Market and Main Streets* Sir William Johnson, who was concerned about the religious training of the settlers of the area, founded this parish and supervised the building of a church on this site. Upon completion of the structure in 1771, he presented the congregation with a bell and an organ. The church had a cupola and a wide door on the western side that was opened during services so that Indians sitting on the lawn might listen to the sermon. When Johnson died in 1774, he was buried beneath the chancel floor.

During the Revolutionary War the Reverend John

*St John's
Episcopal Church,
Johnstown*
(ALPER)

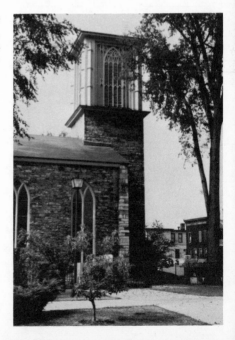

Stuart was rector of St. John's. A Loyalist, he incurred the wrath of many of the inhabitants of the area, and in 1780 he was forced to flee to Canada.

In November 1836 fire destroyed the church, and another structure was built on this site in 1840. The chancel was enlarged and a clergyman's vesting room was added to the new St. John's. In the 1860s the seats were reconstructed and beautiful memorial windows were placed in the casements. The parish house, which is connected to the church, was constructed in 1911.

The large stone memorial behind St. John's marks the grave of Sir William Johnson, which was removed from its original location under the chancel floor. In 1866 the local Masonic lodge dedicated the monument.

Recommended Side Trips

Little Falls

HERKIMER HOMESTEAD   *From Johnstown, take the New York State Thruway west (Interstate 90). Get off at Exit 29A and follow Route 169 North. Look for signs directing you to the site, which is located 3 miles east of Little Falls. Open daily mid-April through October 9 A.M. to 5 P.M., Sunday 1 P.M. to 5 P.M. Free.*   This house was the residence of Revolutionary War Patriot Nicholas Herkimer (1728–1777). Early in the Revolution he was chosen chairman of the county's Committee of Correspondence. When he received information in July 1775 that Guy Johnson (William Johnson's nephew) and a force of nearly 900 Indians were planning to attack the Little Falls region, Herkimer rallied the local Patriot leaders and called for a militia to meet the threat. The following month the danger abated, however, and no action was taken.

Herkimer was commissioned a brigadier general in the Tryon County Militia in September 1776. Throughout the turbulent years of 1776 and 1777 he supervised the capture of dangerous local Loyalists, including two of his own nephews (George Herkimer, Jr., and Thomas Bell).

On August 4, 1777, General Herkimer organized his Patriot militiamen to aid in the defense of Fort Stanwix (site of present-day Rome, New York) during the British attack led by Lieutenant Colonel Barry St. Leger. On August 6, while marching to the fort, Herkimer's men were ambushed in a ravine at Oriskany (five miles east of Rome), and he received a serious leg wound. After the battle he was carried to his house where, eleven days later, a surgeon had to amputate his leg. This grave operation caused his death.

The house was built in 1764, approximately ten years after Herkimer settled on this tract of land (which was a gift from his father). The architecture is credited to Samuel Fuller of Schenectady, who was also the builder of Johnson Hall in Johnstown. The structure is designed in the traditional Georgian style, with a modification of the typical floor plan. Pine paneling and fine carving enhance the interior.

After Nicholas Herkimer's death in 1777, the property passed to his brother George. In July 1782 a company of the Second New Hampshire Regiment was quartered for a short time in the house. In the 1830s, after construction of the Erie Canal, the dwelling was converted into a tavern which was operated by Daniel Connor. The interior was renovated and the facade was rebuilt in the fashionable Greek Revival style. As canal travel

declined, the building fell into disrepair. It was acquired
in 1913 by an agency of New York State, which arranged for the return of the dwelling to its eighteenth-
century appearance.

In the nearby cemetery members of the Herkimer
family—including Nicholas and George—are buried.

Rome Area

FORT STANWIX *Located in downtown Rome. The fort
is being reconstructed and may be completed by the Bi-
centennial. The site is bounded approximately by North
James, Liberty, Spring, and Dominick Streets. From
Johnstown or Little Falls, travel west along the New
York State Thruway (Interstate 90) to Rome.* A fortifi-
cation was constructed on this site by General John
Stanwix in 1758 during the French and Indian Wars.
In 1768 Sir William Johnson met here with 2,000
Indians to negotiate a treaty determining land titles in
areas of New York and Pennsylvania.

Early in the Revolutionary War General George Washington issued orders to reactivate the fort. In the summer of 1776 a detachment of troops commanded by
Colonel Elias Dayton began repairing the structure
under the direction of Nathaniel Hubbell. For a short
time the garrison was called Fort Schuyler in honor of
Patriot General Philip Schuyler.

On August 3, 1777, Patriot soldiers under Colonels
Peter Gansevoort and Marinus Willett defended the
fort against an attack of 2,000 British Regulars, Loyalists,
and Indians commanded by Lieutenant Colonel Barry
St. Leger. When news arrived that Benedict Arnold was
en route to the area with reinforcements, St. Leger
withdrew.

According to local tradition, the Stars and Stripes were flown in battle for the first time during the siege of Fort Stanwix. The successful defense of the fort prevented the Mohawk Valley from falling under enemy control.

ORISKANY BATTLEFIELD SITE *Located approximately 5 miles east of Rome on Route 69. Open weekdays 9 A.M. to 5 P.M., Sunday 1 P.M. to 5 P.M. Free.* On the morning of August 6, 1777, a force of Patriot militiamen commanded by Nicholas Herkimer, who were marching to relieve the besieged Fort Stanwix, were ambushed here by Loyalists and Indians. Although Herkimer was wounded, he was able to direct his men in battle and continued to inspire them. After almost six hours of vicious fighting, the Indians began to withdraw, forcing the Loyalists to give up the fight. Although the Patriots were able to hold their ground, they did so at a high cost—nearly 160 out of 800 soldiers were killed.

Today, the battlefield site, administered by the New York State Division of Parks and Recreation, offers facilities for picnicking. The small Visitors' Center has exhibits and dioramas explaining the battle. The following monuments are located on the grounds.

Battle Monument This eighty-four-foot shaft, placed here in 1884, honors the courageous Patriots who fought at Oriskany.

Herkimer Marker This granite stone marks the approximate spot where Nicholas Herkimer (1728–1777) received his wounds in battle on August 6, 1777.

Tryon County Militia Monument This monument pays tribute to the men from Tryon County who served the Patriot cause.

Newburgh Area

Revolutionary War History

The first settlement in this area was established in 1709 by a group of German Palatines led by a Lutheran preacher, Joshua Kocherthal. By the mid-eighteenth century large numbers of Dutch and Scottish families had settled here also.

Throughout the Revolutionary War the residents of Newburgh were subjected to brief attacks by Loyalist and Indian raiding parties. Many men of the community carried muskets in order to repel surprise forays and to ward off attempts at plundering.

In the fall of 1781, when Washington was leading the bulk of the Patriot forces in the Virginia campaign, he dispatched a contingent of 2,000 men under General William Heath to patrol the Hudson Highlands. When word arrived of Cornwallis' surrender at Yorktown, some of Heath's soldiers stationed near Newburgh celebrated the news with extra rum rations and the officers were feted at a formal dinner. Later in the evening an effigy of Benedict Arnold (the former Patriot general who had turned traitor just a year before at nearby West Point) was hauled out to be burned on a bonfire. Just as the effigy was about to be hung above the blazing logs, one of the officers shouted that the left leg should be spared since Arnold was wounded in that limb while bravely fighting for the Patriots at Saratoga. The assembled officers ceremoniously amputated the straw leg before the rest of the body was consigned to the flames.

Although Yorktown (October 1781) had been a major victory for the Patriots, a state of war still existed between England and America. The British army remained in control of New York City, Charleston, and Savannah as well as scattered areas throughout the South. General Washington decided to divide his troops: Rochambeau remained in the Yorktown vicinity, St. Clair was sent southward to aid General Greene, and the remaining troops, Washington's Continentals, were sent north to the Hudson Highlands.

Washington himself journeyed to Philadelphia to report to the Congress. He remained there fifteen weeks to confer with the delegates about his plans to reorganize the army, arguing and cajoling them into providing the necessary funds to properly clothe and feed his men.

On April 1, 1782, he rejoined his troops, who were encamped at the New Windsor Cantonment outside Newburgh, and established his headquarters at the house of Jonathan Hasbrouck. He remained here while the American and British governments negotiated the terms for the cessation of hostilities.

On April 19, 1783—exactly eight years after the skirmishes at Lexington and Concord—Washington announced that furloughs would soon be granted to the soldiers since England had agreed to the Preliminary Articles of Peace. By mid-August the army at New Windsor was reduced to a skeleton force and the Commander-in-Chief moved his headquarters to Rocky Hill, New Jersey, just outside Princeton, where the Congress was convening.

After the Treaty of Paris was signed on September 3, 1783, Washington was authorized to disband the army and permit the men to return to their homes. With the departure of the remaining troops, the signs of war were removed from Newburgh and its residents returned to plowing their fields, tending their shops, and exercising their newly won rights as citizens of an independent nation.

VISITORS' CENTER Information about the Newburgh area is available from the Chamber of Commerce, 72 Broadway, phone 562–5100.

PUBLIC TRANSPORTATION Local bus service (on weekdays) is provided by Gallagher Transportation Company, phone 565–7700.

TAXI SERVICE Ajax Taxi, phone 565–3020; Newburgh Taxi, phone 561–5000; Starlight Taxi, phone 565–2648.

Colonial and Revolutionary War Sites

HASBROUCK ESTATE — WASHINGTON'S HEAD-QUARTERS *84 Liberty Street. If you are traveling north or south on the New York State Thruway (Interstate 87), get off at Exit 17 and travel along Route 17K (Broadway) into downtown Newburgh, then turn right onto Route 9W South. (If you are traveling east or west on Interstate 84, get off at Exit 10 and follow Route 9W South into the town.) Approximately three blocks down the road, turn left onto Washington Street and proceed to the intersection of Liberty Street. Open Wednesday through Saturday 9 A.M. to 4:30 P.M., Sunday 1 P.M. to 4:30 P.M. Closed holidays. Free.*

HASBROUCK HOUSE Jonathan Hasbrouck, a prosperous farmer and merchant, built the main section of this house in 1750. The large western wing dates from 1770.

A Patriot, Hasbrouck placed his signature on a resolution at Newburgh (April 29, 1775) to oppose "the execution of the several arbitrary Acts of British Parliament, until a reconciliation between Great Britain and America on constitutional principles . . . can be obtained." In October 1775 he was appointed a colonel of the Ulster County Militia Regiment. In February 1776 Hasbrouck was elected to serve as a representative from Ulster County to the General Assembly of New York. He later saw action at Fort Constitution, New York, and at Sidman's Bridge (near the New Jersey border), but ill health compelled him to withdraw from military service in 1778. He continued to work for the Patriot cause by obtaining necessary supplies for the militia.

Baron von Riedesel and his wife, after being captured with Burgoyne's army at Saratoga (October 1777), spent a week in the Hasbrouck house. (They were later given their freedom as part of a prisoner exchange involving officers.) In 1779 Baron von Steuben visited here while traveling on official business for George Washington.

On July 30, 1780, Jonathan Hasbrouck became seriously ill. Doctors were summoned, but were unable to offer relief. He died the following morning and was buried near his home.

When the American army encamped at New Windsor (near Newburgh), this house was selected as the headquarters of George Washington. From January to April 1782 improvements were made to the dwelling; a small outbuilding was constructed to quarter the Commander-in-Chief's guard; and the storehouse was converted into a powder magazine. The widow Hasbrouck and her children went to live with relatives. In April Washington arrived, and soon afterward, Martha Washington, several servants, and aides-de-camp joined him. Of all the buildings used as headquarters by George Washington during the Revolutionary War, this is the one in which he resided for the longest period of time—from April 1, 1782 to August 19, 1783, sixteen and one-half months.

In May 1782 Lewis Nicola, an officer at the New Windsor Cantonment, sent Washington a letter expressing the popular opinion that America should become a monarchy with Washington as king. The Commander-in-Chief quickly and firmly responded: "I view [this proposal] with abhorrence and reprehend with severity." Once again he demonstrated the strength of his commitment to a republican form of government.

Visitors may see several pieces of furniture original to the house: a Dutch kas in the council room, an armchair in the sitting room, and a set of andirons in the study. The dining room furniture was brought here from a church rectory across the river, where the Washingtons worshipped. The desk in the study was used by the general in another house where he rested on his journey to Newburgh. The chest on chest in the parlor is believed to have been in the De Wint House (Tappan, New York) during Washington's occupancy in 1780.

In April 1850 the governor of New York signed into law an act preserving the Hasbrouck House, and soon afterward the structure was restored and opened to the public.

MILITIAMAN STATUE   *In front of the Hasbrouck House* David Barclay, a retired historian from the Newburgh area, bequeathed $5,000 to be used for a monument honoring local citizens who served as members of the Colonial militia. The statue was executed by Henry H. Kitson (sculptor of the famous Lexington Minuteman Statue) and was unveiled on Armistice Day 1924.

MUSEUM   *To the south of the Hasbrouck House* This museum, which opened in 1910, displays swords, pistols, costumes, maps, and prints associated with the Revolutionary War. Items relating to George Washington, the Marquis de Lafayette, and George Clinton (general in the Continental Army and first governor of New York) are prominent in the collection. Of unusual interest is a section of a log boom that extended across the Hudson River (north of the chain boom at West Point) to obstruct the passage of British ships. Also on display is a copy of the first printed edition of the Newburgh Addresses, issued in 1783 by dissident officers stationed at the New Windsor Cantonment to inform Congress of their grievances.

VICTORY MONUMENT   *Behind Hasbrouck House*   This large monument was erected to commemorate the end of the Revolutionary War and the American victory. In 1883, on the 100th anniversary of the signing of the Treaty of Paris, a group of prominent citizens from the Newburgh area formed a committee to organize a Centennial celebration and to formulate plans for a monument. Soon afterward, funds were appropriated by the United States Congress and the New York State legislature, and architect John H. Duncan was commissioned to design a tower to be placed on the grounds of the Hasbrouck House.

The fifty-three-foot-high monument—with four archways opening into an atrium—was completed and unveiled in 1886. The bronze figures which adorn the niches represent the various groups of soldiers who

Victory Monument, Newburgh
(ALPER)

fought in the Revolutionary War: cavalrymen, artillerymen, riflemen, and officers.

WASHINGTON STATUE　*In front of the Museum*　This statue by William Randolph O'Donovan is based on the well-known representation of George Washington by Jean Antoine Houdon that now stands in the Capitol in Richmond, Virginia. Originally this statue stood across the lawn inside the Victory Monument.

KNOX HEADQUARTERS　*On Route 94 in Vails Gate. From the Hasbrouck House return to Route 9W South. (Travel down Washington Street and turn left.) Continue until you come to Route 94 West. Turn right and proceed several miles to the Knox Headquarters, which is located on the left side of the highway. Open Tuesday through Saturday 9 A.M. to 4:30 P.M., Sunday 1 P.M. to 5 P.M. Closed holidays. Free.*　In 1734 the Ellison family built a one-story clapboard hunting lodge here. Twenty years later a two-story fieldstone addition (which became the main living quarters) was built for John Ellison by William Bull, a local stonemason. The house was enlarged in 1782.

During the American Revolution Ellison served in the local militia and supplied Patriot troops with flour from his gristmill, located on nearby Silver Stream.

This house was used as military headquarters regularly throughout the later years of the war. Its principal occupant was General Henry Knox (1750–1806), the artillery commander who was responsible for the transporting of cannon from Fort Ticonderoga to Boston (December 1775–January 1776), where they were placed to pose a serious threat to the British garrison. In June and July, and in the fall of 1779, he resided here along with General Nathanael Greene, then Quartermaster-General of the Continental Army. Knox returned in November 1780 and remained until July 1781. He departed to participate in the Virginia campaign and to prepare plans for the deployment of artillery for the siege of Yorktown.

From May to September 1782, while Washington was headquartered in Newburgh, he again occupied this house.

Knox had a distinguished military career. He fought bravely at Brandywine, Germantown, Monmouth, and Yorktown. A loyal advisor to Washington, he served as commander of West Point from the fall of 1782 until 1784. He was appointed Secretary of War in 1785, a post he retained for nine years.

After Knox left the area to become commander of West Point, the Ellison house was used as headquarters by General Horatio Gates (the victor of Saratoga), who commanded the New Windsor Cantonment, less than a mile away.

Today, fine eighteenth-century antiques grace the rooms. The lowboy in the living room, the Dutch kas in the office, and the chest in the second-floor bedroom are all rare pieces. The carved woodwork on the fireplace walls is exceptionally fine. The Knox House has been administered by the New York State Historic Trust since 1922.

NEW WINDSOR CANTONMENT *From downtown Newburgh follow Route 9W South to Route 94 West. Turn right and travel several miles. A short distance past the Knox Headquarters site, you will come to Temple Hill Road. Turn right and follow this road (crossing over Route 32) to its end. Then turn right and proceed about ½ mile to the New Windsor Cantonment. Open mid-April through October, Wednesday through Sunday 9:30 A.M. to 5 P.M. Free.* Near the end of the Revolutionary War, in the fall of 1782, General Washington chose this site for the encampment of the Continental Army. Approximately 7,000 soldiers were quartered in a city of 700 log huts, which had been built under the supervision of Baron von Steuben. Larger structures for the officers and an all-purpose assembly hall were also constructed.

It was here that George Washington faced several challenges to his leadership. Early in 1783 discontent grew rampant among the officers because of the failure of Congress to act on commitments made to the soldiers. Payment was in arrears, food and clothing accounts were outstanding, and retirement provisions were not confirmed. When word came that Congress planned to disband the army without resolving these demands, the officers at New Windsor—led by General Alexander McDougall and Colonel Walter Stewart—decided to take decisive action. On March 10 they sent Washington (who was residing at the Hasbrouck house) a document of protest claiming that the army would refuse to disband if the peace treaty were signed and would not fight if war should continue. Two days later a formal condemnation of Congress was issued by these angry soldiers. (These documents—probably written by General Gates' aide-de-camp, Major John Armstrong, Jr.—are referred to as the Newburgh Addresses.)

Shocked and dismayed, Washington summoned the officers to a meeting at the Temple (the New Windsor Assembly Hall) on March 15. In a tense atmosphere he denounced the conspiracy, entreated the officers to act reasonably, and argued that Congress was sympathetic to their grievances. As a result of his forceful words, all opposition crumbled: the mutineers once again became loyal comrades-in-arms.

In mid-June 1783 most of the soldiers began to return to their homes after Congress had granted the long-awaited furloughs. Three months later the treaty of peace was signed in Paris, and the war officially came to an end.

The New Windsor Cantonment is administered by the New York State Historic Trust in conjunction with the Palisades Interstate Park Commission. The major points of interest at the site are described below.

FARRIER SHOP   A building similar to this one served

as the shop of the army blacksmith. It contains tools of the Colonial period.

MUSEUM   This one-room museum displays eighteenth-century costumes, weapons, and tools. A diorama shows the Northern Army marching to the New Windsor Cantonment.

OFFICER'S HUT   This log hut is the only Cantonment building that has survived. A local inhabitant purchased the structure for $1.00 in 1783 (at a public auction held after the troops departed) and transported it to his property several miles away. In 1934 a civic-minded citizen bought the building and had it returned to the Cantonment.

SUTLER SHOP   A sutler (a civilian merchant who followed the army) established a shop here and sold to the soldiers provisions that he bought from neighboring farms.

THE TEMPLE   The Temple (or Public Building), used for religious services and meetings, was demolished soon after the troops left the New Windsor Cantonment. The present building is a reconstruction.

The Temple, New Windsor Cantonment (ALPER)

*Temple Hill
Monument,
New Windsor
Cantonment*
(ALPER)

An important event occurred here in August 1782, when Washington named the first American soldiers to receive the Badge of Military Merit (later called the Purple Heart) for bravery and heroism. (The decoration consisted of a purple, heart-shaped piece of silk, edged with a narrow binding of silver, and with the word "Merit" stitched across the face in silver.)

It was in the Temple, on March 15, 1783, that George Washington denounced the mutinous Newburgh Addresses and quelled conspiracy. He pleaded with his officers "not to take any measures which, viewed in the calm light of reason, will lesson the dignity and sully the glory you have hitherto maintained. . . . You will, by the dignity of your conduct, afford occasion for posterity to say, when speaking of the glorious example you have exhibited to mankind, 'had this day been wanting, the world would have never seen the last state of perfection to which human nature is capable of attaining.'"

TEMPLE HILL MONUMENT Erected in 1892 by the Newburgh Revolutionary Monument Association, this high fieldstone monument honors the American troops billeted here during the Revolutionary War. A plaque on one of the sides reads: "On this site the Society of the Cincinnati was born May 10, 1783." The Society—named for Lucius Quinctius Cincinnatus, a Roman patriot—was limited to Continental Army officers and their eldest male descendants. General Henry Knox drafted the organization's constitution, and George Washington served as the Society's first president.

Near the Temple Hill Monument is a small graveyard. Buried here are the remains of an unknown Revolutionary War soldier who was originally laid to rest at West Point but was reinterred at the Cantonment site in 1965. James Hall (1744–1813), who served in the campaigns of Trenton and Long Island, is also buried here.

Recommended Side Trip

Kingston

From Newburgh take Interstate 87 North for approximately 25 miles.

In mid-1776, when British troops threatened Manhattan (then the capital of New York), members of the New York legislature withdrew to White Plains. Later they were forced to seek refuge farther north in Fishkill.

Conditions in Fishkill proved inadequate and the delegates adjourned to Kingston in February 1777. The Assembly met in the Kingston Tavern, and the Senate convened in the house of Abraham van Gaasbeck.

On April 22, 1777, the bells of Kingston proclaimed the adoption of the state's first constitution. (John Jay, who later was to serve as the first Chief Justice of the United States, headed the committee which drafted the document.) In June the first elected governor of New York took his oath of office at the county courthouse here.

After reports reached Kingston in October 1777 indicating that British troops were approaching, the legislators fled. On October 16 Redcoats under Major General John Vaughan attacked the town, sacking and burning property.

DUTCH REFORMED CHURCH *Junction of Wall, Main, and Fair Streets*   The congregation of this church was organized in 1659. The first meeting house on this site (erected in the late seventeenth century) served the spiritual needs of the early Dutch settlers of Kingston. The present rectangular-shaped building with tower was constructed in 1852.

In the burial ground adjoining the church is the grave of George Clinton (1739–1812), a delegate to the Second Continental Congress and a general in the Continental Army. Under the new constitution of the state of New York, he was elected the first governor (June 1777). His energetic leadership as governor for six consecutive terms (1777–1795) earned him the title of "The Father of New York State." He also served as Vice President of the United States (two terms, 1804 and 1808) under Jefferson and Madison.

ELMENDORF TAVERN   *88 Maiden Lane. Not open to the public.*   This two-story limestone building was erected in 1725 by Conrad Elmendorf as a place where travelers could stop to refresh themselves and local citizens could gather for a tankard of ale. The Council of Safety chose this tavern for a series of meetings from October 11 to 15, 1777.

HOFFMAN HOUSE *Corner of Green and North Front streets. Not open to the public.* This house was built near the northwest corner of the stockade that had been constructed in 1658 to protect the settlement from Indian attacks. The dwelling survived the pillaging and burning of British troops (1777), sustaining only superficial damage. Members of the Hoffman family resided here for almost 200 years.

SENATE HOUSE *Clinton Avenue and North Front Street. Open Wednesday through Saturday 9 A.M. to 5 P.M., Sunday 1 P.M. to 5 P.M. Closed Thanksgiving, December 25, and January 1. Free.* The "Senate House" was built in 1676 by the Ten Broeck family. The property passed to Abraham van Gaasbeck in 1751. The room at the south end of the house (with a doorway opening directly onto the street) served as the meeting hall of the New York Senate in 1777. The state of New York, which acquired the building in 1887, has refurbished it and furnished the rooms with appropriate period pieces.

The adjacent museum, built in 1927, has a fine collection of twenty-eight paintings by the noted Kingston-born artist John Vanderlyn (1776–1852).

ULSTER COUNTY COURTHOUSE *Wall Street between Main and John Streets. Open weekdays 9 A.M. to 5 P.M.* It was in the former courthouse on this site that the first state constitution was adopted on April 20, 1777. Two days later the secretary of the New York Convention of Representatives stood in front of the building and read the constitution to the assembled citizens. On July 30, 1777, George Clinton took the oath as first governor of New York, and his induction into office was proclaimed by the sheriff of Ulster County from the courthouse steps.

The present building, which replaced the Colonial courthouse, was erected in 1818.

West Point

Revolutionary War History

When in early October 1777 British forces under General Henry Clinton captured Fort Montgomery and Fort Clinton (both located on the cliffs of the Hudson River in the Bear Mountain region), General Washington decided that the defenses at West Point should be further strengthened so that future British advances in the area would be checked. Consequently, early in 1778 Continental soldiers constructed a fortress (later called Fort Putnam) and a series of redoubts at West Point. In order to block British vessels from sailing up the Hudson, a huge wrought-iron, 180-ton chain was stretched across the river on May 1, 1778. (Attached to the links were pointed logs that floated on the surface of the river.)

On August 3, 1780, Major General Benedict Arnold assumed command of the fortifications at West Point. He had distinguished himself in numerous military campaigns (especially at Saratoga), but he had gradually become cynical about the Patriot cause and embittered by accusations of official misconduct which had led to a court-martial (April 1779–January 1780). When the British Commander-in-Chief, Sir Henry Clinton, offered him financial and political gain for the betrayal of West Point, Arnold seized the opportunity. In return for £20,000 he arranged to turn over to the enemy the garrison of 3,000 soldiers, the artillery, and the stores. The intermediary between the two men was Major John André, a young aide of Clinton's.

On the evening of Thursday, September 21, Major André slipped away from the British sloop *Vulture* (which had

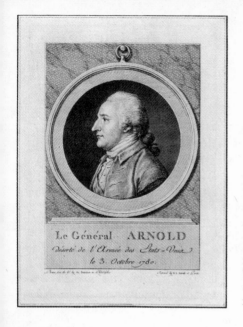

Portrait of
Benedict Arnold.
*Engraving by
Benoit Louis
Prevost.*
(METROPOLITAN
MUSEUM OF ART,
NEW YORK CITY.
GIFT OF WILLIAM
H. HUNTINGTON)

Le Général ARNOLD
*Deserté de l'Armée des États-Unis
le 3. Octobre 1780.*

anchored several miles south of West Point) and made his
way to a clandestine meeting with Arnold in the thickets
near the edge of the riverbank. When, at last, the conference ended at 4 A.M., it was too close to dawn for
André to return to the ship. He therefore was taken to the
Joshua Smith house four miles away, where he was to wait
until the following evening. This plan was upset, for during
the morning hours American forces had attacked the *Vulture*, forcing it to move downstream.

Realizing the gravity of the situation, Arnold quickly
arranged to have André pass through the American lines
positioned on the east side of the Hudson River, then
travel by overland route to return to British headquarters.
Concealing in his boot the incriminating documents which
Arnold had signed, André began his escape. But on the
morning of Saturday, September 23, he was captured near
Tarrytown by three Patriot militiamen—David Williams,
John Paulding, and Isaac Van Wart.

The papers were confiscated and immediately sent to General Washington. As soon as Arnold discovered that the Commander-in-Chief was aware of his scheme and was traveling to West Point, he escaped on the *Vulture* and sailed to take refuge with the British army. Arnold's accomplice, André, was taken to Tappan, New York, where he was tried and hanged on October 2, 1780.

After the Revolutionary War, when George Washington had become President, he urged the Congress to create an academy for the training of military officers, especially in the science of engineering. However, it was not until March 1802—during the administration of Thomas Jefferson—that the plan received Congressional approval. Later that year the first class of ten cadets was admitted to the new Academy.

The roll of distinguished graduates reads like a "Who's Who of Great Americans." At the head of the list are two United States Presidents, Ulysses S. Grant and Dwight David Eisenhower.

VISITORS' CENTER   An informative audio-visual program describing the history of West Point is shown frequently. Brochures and maps are also available at this center, which is located near South (Thayer) Gate. Phone 938–2638.

GUIDED TOURS   During the summer months **Bosch Transportation Company** offers guided tours. For information and schedules, phone 446–4588.

Visitors who do not have a car may also tour the Academy grounds by taxi. West Point Taxi is a local service; phone 446–4520.

Colonial and Revolutionary War Sites

FORT CLINTON AND KOSCIUSKO MONUMENT
Cullum Road, to the northeast of the Parade Ground
Originally this fortification was named for General
Benedict Arnold, but after he turned traitor it was renamed for George Clinton, who was serving as the first
governor of New York State. Little remains of the
square fort which originally held several hundred men
within its log-and-earth walls. The fort had triangular
bastions at each corner and was protected by an abatis
and by a battery located on the low ground near the
river. On October 6, 1777, these defenses as well as
Fort Montgomery (ten miles to the south) were captured
by British forces.

Near the remains of Fort Clinton stands a monument
to Thaddeus Kosciusko (1746–1817), the Polish soldier
and engineer who came to America to join the Patriot
cause and who later played an important role in building the defenses at West Point. The pedestal and shaft
were erected in 1828 by the Corps of Cadets of the
Military Academy; the statue, designed by West Pointer
John H. Latrobe, was presented in 1913 by the Polish
Clergy and Laity of the United States.

FORT PUTNAM   *Follow Mills Road to Michie Stadium.*
Continue around the curve, then turn right onto Dere-
field Road. Proceed along this narrow road for about ½
mile to a wide path, which you will see on the right-hand
side. Walk along this path, following it around to the
right, then climb the hill to the site of Fort Putnam.
On this site stands the remains of the walls of the
fortifications built in the spring of 1778 under the

Fort Putnam, West Point (ALPER)

supervision of Israel Putnam and his cousin Rufus Putnam. Thaddeus Kosciusko and Louis de la Radière were also instrumental in the formulation and execution of the plans of the fort. Erected on a rocky hill 451 feet above the Hudson River, the fort was built of stone and had parapets with fascines (sacks of earth and twigs

Iron chain links, West Point (ALPER)

bound together to form a protective covering to soften the impact of cannonballs). Fourteen artillery pieces were mounted on its walls, and approximately 170 soldiers were billeted within its barracks.

During the first decade of the twentieth century, steps were taken to halt further deterioration of this historic site and plans are now under way for partial reconstruction.

IRON CHAIN LINKS   *Trophy Point*   To prevent British ships from advancing up the Hudson River, the Patriots extended a 1700-foot, 180-ton chain from West Point to Constitution Island. The chain was forged in 1778 at the Sterling Iron Works, located twenty miles from West Point. A section of the chain—each link eighteen inches long and thirteen inches wide—has been preserved and may be seen stretched along stone posts arranged in a circle. Inside this circle of links is a Revolutionary War mortar surrendered by British troops at the Battle of Stony Point, New York (July 15–16, 1779).

WASHINGTON MONUMENT   *Parade Ground*   This equestrian statue of General George Washington is a replica of one by Henry Kirke Brown (1856) standing in Union Square, New York City. The West Point statue, the gift of an anonymous donor, was unveiled on May 19, 1916.

Non-Revolutionary Sites of Interest

CADET CHAPEL   *On hill overlooking the Academy buildings. Open daily 9 A.M. to 3:45 P.M.*   This neo-Gothic building was designed in 1910 by the architectural firm of Cram, Goodhue, and Ferguson. The design called for a long nave with short transepts and a high buttressed tower. One of the distinguished features of the building is its stained-glass windows. Particularly notable are the twenty-seven panels of the chancel window representing biblical figures. The organ comprises more than 15,000 pipes.

CIVIL WAR BATTLE MONUMENT *Trophy Point* Designed by Stanford White and executed by Frederick MacMonnies, this monument honors the soldiers who sacrificed their lives in the Civil War. A forty-six-foot-high Doric column, crowned by a winged statue of Fame, stands on a circular pedestal. The monument is flanked by cannon.

MICHIE STADIUM *Off Mills Road* This football stadium—which has a seating capacity of 26,000—was named in honor of Dennis Mahan Michie, captain of the first West Point football team. A member of the class of 1892, he was killed in action in 1898 at San Juan Hill, Cuba, during the Spanish-American War.

MUSEUM *Thayer Academic Hall; entrance on Cullum Road. Open daily 10:30 A.M. to 4:15 P.M. Closed December 25 and January 1. Free.* This museum, which opened in 1854, displays an exceptionally fine collection of weapons, flags, uniforms, and documents. Revolutionary War buffs will enjoy a diorama of the Battle of Saratoga (October 1777) as well as a series of paintings of Revolutionary War subjects, including *A French Regiment Marching through Philadelphia, The Battle of Bunker Hill,* and the *Capture of Major André.* Portraits of military leaders such as Francis Marion and George Washington are also on display.

Recommended Side Trip

Constitution Island

In early 1775 a Congressional Commission authorized Colonel Bernard Romans, an engineer, to draft plans for fortifications at Martelaer's Rock (now called Constitution Island). By September his proposal for blockhouses, batteries, and barracks was approved, and soon afterward men and supplies began arriving. In the meantime, Romans had quarreled with members of the Commission, and supervision of the project was subsequently granted to Captain William S. Smith.

By the spring of 1776 several buildings of the fort and the surrounding redoubts had been erected. The fortifications were not completed, however, because it was necessary to employ the men to reinforce the defenses at Fort Montgomery ten miles away.

When General Henry Clinton's forces attacked nearby Forts Montgomery and Clinton in October 1777, the thirty soldiers manning Fort Constitution destroyed their supplies and fled. On October 7 British troops occupied Constitution Island and destroyed its buildings and defenses.

The Continental Army returned to the area in January 1778. Although the major fortification was centered at West Point, two new redoubts and a large magazine were constructed on the island. In 1780 new barracks of stone were also built here.

After the signing of the Treaty of Paris in 1783, Fort Constitution was abandoned.

The major sites remaining on Constitution Island include: the Warner House, a Colonial structure that was purchased by the Warner family in the early nineteenth century; the stone wall (on the Warner property), believed to have been a section of a barracks which quartered American troops here from 1778 to 1783; and several redoubts (overlooking the river), including the Cliffside Redoubt and Romans' Redoubt.

GUIDED TOURS The Constitution Island Association conducts tours of selected sites on the island on Wednesday afternoons. Advance reservations in writing are required.

Stony Point

In late May 1779 General Henry Clinton embarked from King's Bridge (just north of New York City) with a force of 6,000 British, Hessian, and Loyalist soldiers in a flotilla of 70 ships and 150 flat-bottom boats. Their objective: to seize the Patriot fortifications along the Hudson River. For three years the British had occupied New York City but complete subjugation of the rest of the state had eluded them. Control of passage on the Hudson River was of prime importance. The first Patriot defenses to be taken, therefore, were the fort at Stony Point and the garrison across the river on Verplank's Point, Fort Lafayette.

On June 1 Clinton and his forces landed on Stony Point and captured the fortification without opposition. They then opened fire on Fort Lafayette, forcing the Americans to surrender.

During the month of June the British soldiers constructed two lines of abatis swinging around from one side of Stony Point to the other; these offered protection to the batteries that were erected near the fort.

The British gains at Stony Point and Verplank's Point alarmed General Washington. The enemy was now in a position to continue their advance and to impede commerce on the river. To regain control of the forts, General Anthony Wayne was ordered to lead 1,350 Patriots in a surprise attack on the area.

The Patriot soldiers arrived at Stony Point on the evening of July 15 and prepared to attack the enemy forces from two sides. At 11:30 P.M. one column, under Major John Stewart, approached from the north, while another column, under Lieutenant Colonel De Fleury, attacked from the south. Each column was preceded by a carefully selected twenty-man "forlorn hope" detachment (in modern parlance, a "suicide squad") which axed openings in the abatis so that the main body of the American force could pass through the defenses and move uphill to the fort. At the same time a third force, under Major Murfree, made a frontal assault on the abatis as a diversionary action. Without faltering, the Patriots advanced under the merciless fire of British guns.

De Fleury's column reached the fort first and clambered over the walls. The first to enter was Lieutenant Colonel De Fleury (a French nobleman who had joined the Patriot cause) who, brandishing a sword, slashed his way through the ranks and ripped down the enemy flag. Soon afterward, Stewart's column penetrated the second abatis and reached the fort. For fifteen minutes pandemonium reigned: the clash of bayonets and swords rang through the clear night air until, at last, the British were overpowered.

(Just minutes before, Lieutenant Colonel Henry Johnson, commander of the fort, had led almost half his garrison down the hill to fight Murfree's diversionary force. These British soldiers were cut off and later captured.)

During the short battle 63 British were killed, 70 wounded, and 543 captured. The Patriots reported 15 killed and 80 wounded.

After the defeat at Stony Point, General Clinton took swift action to fortify Verplank's Point. Washington, realizing it would take too many men to hold Stony Point indefinitely, ordered the evacuation of his troops. Before the soldiers departed, they removed the artillery pieces and provisions, then destroyed the fortifications.

This military success raised the spirits of the Patriot army and a grateful Congress awarded Wayne (who was wounded in the battle here) a gold medal and issued both De Fleury and Stewart silver medals for their heroism.

Revolutionary War Sites

STONY POINT BATTLEFIELD RESERVATION *Located on Route 9W just north of the village of Stony Point and several miles south of Bear Mountain State Park. Open daily May through October 9 A.M. to 5 P.M. Free.* Stony Point Battlefield Reservation is administered by the Palisades Interstate Parks Commission. Although the park is mainly a recreational area with hiking trails and picnic grounds, the original earthwork defenses of the fort may still be seen. Several plaques in the park describe details of the Battle of Stony Point.

ENTRANCE GATE *From Route 9W, turn onto Park Road and follow the winding road .7 mile to the Entrance Gate and Bridge* The Daughters of the American Revolution of New York raised funds for the construction of this impressive stone gate, which was dedicated and presented to the state in October 1909.

MONUMENTS Two monuments stand on the grounds (near the museum).

British Soldiers Monument This stone was erected in 1956 by the British War Veterans of America, New York Branch of the British Legion, to "perpetuate the memories of the men of the 17th British Regiment of Foot who died near this spot defending the Stony Point fortification."

Patriot Soldiers Monument   This monument honors the gallant American soldiers who fought here under the command of General Anthony Wayne on the night of July 15–16, 1779. The stone was erected in 1960 by the Jewish War Veterans of America, Veterans of Foreign Wars, Military Order of the Purple Heart, and American Legion of Rockland County.

MUSEUM   Among the interesting items in this two-room museum are letters from General Anthony Wayne to George Washington, fragments of Colonial bottles discovered during excavations, and a section of a gun platform. Several portraits of Continental officers—painted by the Cartographic Studio of New York University in 1935—are also on display. The museum was dedicated in 1936 under the auspices of the American Scenic and Historic Preservation Society.

Tappan

Revolutionary War History

Here, in the quiet town of Tappan, the British spy, Major John André—coconspirator with the traitor Benedict Arnold—met his inglorious end.

On September 23, 1780—two days after his secret meeting with General Benedict Arnold to set the terms for the betrayal of West Point to the British—Major André was captured at Tarrytown, New York. He was brought to Tappan and imprisoned in Mabie's Tavern on September 28. The next day he was interrogated before a military tribunal, which found him guilty of the charge of spying and ordered his execution.

Washington, from his headquarters in the house of the De Wint family, issued orders that André be hanged on the afternoon of October 1. After a communiqué arrived from British General Henry Clinton requesting a delay,

---

VISITORS' CENTER For information about Tappan's historic sites, contact the Historical Society of Rockland County, 20 Zukor Road in New City, phone 634–9629.

PUBLIC TRANSPORTATION Public transportation in the area is extremely limited.

TAXI SERVICE Jackson Cab, phone 359–0102; Pearl River Cab, phone 735–6050.

Washington agreed to postpone the execution for one day. Clinton's emissary was unable to convince the Commander-in-Chief to commute André's sentence, and the Patriots carried out the execution as planned.

Tappan was occupied by British soldiers for a short time in September 1778 and foraging parties occasionally passed through the town, but no major military action occurred here during the Revolutionary War.

Colonial and Revolutionary War Sites

DUTCH REFORMED CHURCH *Main Street at Old Tappan Road. Open Sunday morning.* The Dutch Reformed Church of Tappan was established in 1694. The first building on this site (*c.* 1700) was a crude meeting house of bark and mud. Since the congregation had no minister, Dirk Storm, a teacher and community leader, served as Voorlezer (public reader). In 1716–1717 a square stone church replaced the cabin, and soon the first resident pastor, Frederic Muzelius, arrived to undertake his duties.

When Tappan was occupied briefly by British troops in September 1778, the church was used as a military prison. Thirty-nine captured Patriot soldiers were held here after the "Baylor Massacre" (September 27, 1778) —an attack by British General Charles Grey on the Virginia Light Dragoons under Colonel George Baylor. (This bloody skirmish occurred in Old Tappan, several miles away in New Jersey.)

Here in the Dutch Reformed Church, on September 29, 1780, Major John André defended himself against charges of spying before a Patriot military tribunal of

fourteen generals (including Henry Knox, Baron von
Steuben, the Marquis de Lafayette, Arthur St. Clair,
James Clinton, and John Stark). Colonel John Laurance
served as the judge advocate. A letter of testimony
written by British General Henry Clinton was introduced, claiming that André had gone ashore to meet
Benedict Arnold under a flag of truce. But André, a
gentleman who adhered to a code of honor, denied this
fabrication—an act that led to his conviction.

The present church building was constructed in 1835
to accommodate the growing congregation. Reflecting
Federal–style architecture, it was modeled after the
Cedar Street Presbyterian Church of New York City
(demolished in the early twentieth century).

The earliest headstones in the adjacent graveyard
date from the 1740s. Lemuel Cushing, surgeon of the
23rd Regiment, was buried here. According to tradition,
100 Revolutionary War soldiers are buried in a common
grave in the northeast corner of the cemetery.

MABIE'S TAVERN (THE '76 HOUSE) *Main Street,
just south of Old Tappan Road. Open Tuesday through
Saturday* 5 P.M. *to* 11 P.M., *Sunday* 1 P.M. *to* 9 P.M.
Built in the early 1750s by Cornelius Meyers, this struc-
ture has always served as a public tavern. It was sold to
Casparus Mabie in 1755.

On July 4, 1774, the local Committee of Correspondence met here to draft and sign the Orangetown Resolutions, a formal protest against the oppressive policies
of the Crown and a call for a boycott of British goods.

Major André was imprisoned in one of the rooms here
on September 28, 1780, and guarded by six soldiers.
General Nathanael Greene established his headquarters
in the taproom during André's trial.

On the morning of André's execution, everyone in the
tavern was visibly moved by the prisoner's fate, but he
himself remained calm. When one servant entered the
room in tears, André reprimanded him for being un-

Mabie's Tavern, Tappan (ALPER)

manly. Later that morning the condemned officer made a pen-and-ink self-portrait (now preserved at Yale University). At the appointed hour he departed Mabie's for the site of execution.

The stone building, with its high peaked roof, has been extensively restored. The porch is a late-nineteenth-century addition. Although the '76 House is now a restaurant, the small room where André was imprisoned is set aside as a museum. It displays items and engravings associated with this episode of Revolutionary War history.

MONUMENT TO ANDRÉ *From Main Street, travel up Old Tappan Road and watch for Central Avenue on the right side of the highway. A few hundred feet past Central Avenue, make a sharp left turn onto the narrow road which ascends André's Hill. The monument is located at the top of the hill.* Just before noon on October 2, 1780, twenty-nine-year-old Major John André left Mabie's tavern for the site of his execution.

Dressed in a scarlet coat and surrounded by guards, he was followed by a large crowd of spectators and 500 Patriot soldiers. The officers rode on horseback, followed by a wagon bearing a black coffin. Not until André turned to climb the hill and caught a glimpse of the high gibbet did he realize that his plea to General Washington for a soldier's death before a firing squad had been rejected.

The wagon was drawn up beneath the gallows. Without hesitation, André climbed onto the wagon and, standing on the coffin, grabbed the rope from the hangman and adjusted the noose around his neck. To the reading of the order of execution, he responded: "All I request of you, gentlemen, is that you bear witness to the world that I die like a brave man." He then tied his handkerchief around his head, covering his eyes. Immediately afterward, his arms were securely bound above the elbows behind his back.

At the chilling sound of the snare drums, a signal was given. The wagon was yanked away, and André's body twisted violently at the end of the rope. When at last he was pronounced dead, the silent crowd turned homeward.

André was buried in a grave dug beside the gallows. In 1821 British Consul James Buchanan, at the request of the Duke of York, petitioned for the removal of André's body to England. The request was approved, and the remains were laid to rest in the south aisle of Westminster Abbey.

In 1850 a New York City merchant, James Lee, placed a small monument here but it was soon destroyed by vandals. The present monument was erected in 1868 as a result of the efforts of Cyrus W. Field (American financier and promoter of the Atlantic Cable) and Arthur Penrhyn Stanley (Dean of Westminster). The long inscription, written by Stanley, recounts the capture and execution of André and it concludes by stating:

"This stone was placed above the spot where he lay, not to perpetuate the record of strife, but in token of those better feelings which have since united two nations, one in race, in language and in religion, in the hope that friendly understanding will never be broken."

WASHINGTON–DE WINT HOUSE *20 Livingston Street (off Oak Tree Road between Jane Street and Washington Lane). Open daily 10 A.M. to 4 P.M. Free.* The oldest house in Rockland County, this dwelling was built in 1700 by Daniel De Clark, one of the Tappan patentees who purchased large tracts of land in this area from the Indians in 1682. A merchant and a brewer, he also served as magistrate and later as captain of the local militia.

De Clark's home was built of brick brought from

Monument to André, Tappan (ALPER)

Holland and of native sandstone transported by slaves from outcroppings of the Palisades.

In 1746 the property was acquired by Johannes De Wint, a wealthy plantation owner from the West Indies, and his descendants resided here until 1818. The house then passed through many hands until it was purchased and restored by the Masons in 1931.

George Washington used this house on four occasions. From August 8 to 24, 1780, he was the guest of Johannes and Antje De Wint. The general was their guest again from September 28 to October 9, 1780—during the period of Major John André's trial and execution. According to tradition, Washington ordered the shutters of his room closed in order to avoid watching the procession leading to the gallows. From May 4 to 8, 1782, he entertained Sir Guy Carleton, newly appointed Commander-in-Chief of British forces, in the De Wint house, where they drew up plans for the evacuation of British troops from New York City. Samuel Fraunces (proprietor of the famous Fraunces Tavern in Manhattan) prepared an elaborate meal here for that occasion. As Carleton and his aides departed on a ship in the Hudson River, they ordered the firing of a seventeen-gun salute to Washington—the first time a Continental officer had been so honored by the British. From November 11 to 14, 1783, Washington took shelter at the De Wint house during a violent snowstorm while traveling from Hackensack to West Point.

Today the house is furnished with eighteenth-century pieces. The **Kitchen** contains a spinning wheel, a sturdy table, a cupboard, and utensils typical of the period. A Colonial musket hangs above the fireplace. The **Sitting Room,** which is decorated with prints of Revolutionary War subjects, has an oval table supposedly used by Washington to sign the order for André's execution. Only a few modest pieces of furniture are placed in the second-floor **Bedrooms.**

Near the house stands a pedestal with a bust of Washington—a copy of a work by French artist Jean Antoine Houdon. It was dedicated in 1932 by the Tenth Masonic District of Manhattan.

A carriage-house museum, standing behind the De Wint House, displays prints and paintings showing events from Washington's life and scenes depicting the capture of Major André.

The De Wint property is administered and maintained by the Masons of New York State. The house was registered as a National Historic Landmark in 1966.

Important Colonial Houses

The following Colonial houses, now private residences, are located within a fifteen-mile radius of downtown Tappan.

DEMAREST-DINGMAN HOUSE *20 Congers Road, New City*   This house was constructed in the 1780s by the Demarest family. It was enlarged and remodeled in 1829. The dormers are a modern addition.

HAFER HOUSE *Greenbush Road, Tappan*   The oldest section of this structure served as the first schoolhouse in Rockland County. Built in 1711, it was in use until 1855.

HARING-SMITH HOUSE *Old Tappan Road, west side of De Wolfe Road, Tappan*   Frederick Haring built the main section of this house in the mid-eighteenth century. Some of the original stonework and the pine floorboards have been preserved.

KUYPER–VAN HOUTEN HOUSE   *Blauvelt and Sickeltown Roads, Nauraushaun*   This dwelling was built in 1732 by Theunis Kuyper and purchased by Rulef C. Van Houten in 1832. Extensive remodeling has been done. The house was used in scenes in the silent film version of *The Legend of Sleepy Hollow* (1922) which starred Will Rogers.

THE MANSE   *Directly opposite the Dutch Reformed Church, Main Street, Tappan*   Built in 1724, this is believed to be the oldest parsonage in continuous use in the United States. Reverend Samuel Verbryck—a friend of George Washington's and a founder of Queens College (present-day Rutgers University)—resided here. The porch, dormers, and the north wing are nineteenth-century additions.

ONDERDONK-NOWICKI HOUSE   *149 North Middletown Road, Nanuet*   This dwelling, which was constructed in 1784, retains the original fireplaces, beamed ceilings, and floorboards. Prior to the Civil War escaped slaves are said to have been hidden in the cellar here while waiting to continue their journey to Canada.

New York City

Revolutionary War History

Henry Hudson, who was searching for a route to the Orient at the behest of the Dutch East India Company, explored the New York Bay area in 1609. The following year several Dutch agents were sent to build a fur-trading post. In 1624 thirty families arrived on Manhattan to establish a settlement, New Amsterdam. The island was purchased from the Indians in 1626 by Peter Minuit, the colony's first Director General.

In 1646 peg-legged Peter Stuyvesant was appointed Director General by the Dutch East India Company. A stern, puritanical man, after he assumed the duties of administration he instituted oppressive ordinances that aroused great public resentment. Consequently, when in the fall of 1664 British war vessels loomed menacingly in the harbor and the admiral demanded the surrender of New Amsterdam, the citizens were reluctant to rally behind Stuyvesant and he was compelled to capitulate on September 8. The British quickly took control and renamed the area New York in honor of James, Duke of York. Under the British, large numbers of immigrants settled here and the town soon became a bustling seaport.

In March 1765 the British Parliament passed the Stamp Act, the first of a series of restrictive laws which infringed upon the rights of the colonists—rights enjoyed by the citizens in England. According to the terms of the act, beginning November 1, 1765, a duty was imposed on all paper, vellum, and parchment; and any contracts or business dealings transacted on unstamped paper were

not considered valid. New York inhabitants were as enraged by this harsh act as their fellow countrymen
throughout the colonies. On October 23, 1765, a band of
angry townspeople burned in effigy Lieutenant Governor
Colden, and then began destroying the property of high
British officials. The mob had just finished ransacking the
mansion of Major James of the Royal Artillery when Isaac
Sears, a leader of the Sons of Liberty (a group of political
activists), convinced them that further violence would be
detrimental to their cause and persuaded them to return
to their homes.

On October 31, 1765, two hundred merchants crowded
into Burns' King's Arms Tavern for a meeting where they
signed a document protesting British policies. They also
agreed to harass James McEvers, the stamp officer, until
he resigned. Their persistent threats, however, were met
with equally hostile ultimatums and obdurate refusals
from McEvers. These actions were not without effect, for
when news reached London of the violent reaction
throughout the colonies, Parliament was forced to repeal
the Stamp Act (in the spring of 1766).

After Parliament passed the Tea Act of 1773, which
required American colonists to pay a heavy tax on tea,
groups of irate New Yorkers placed notices in newspapers
and circulated broadsides warning of dire consequences
to any ship laden with tea that attempted to unload its
cargo. Local Patriots—emboldened by the success of the
Boston Tea Party (December 16, 1773)—coerced many
townspeople into not buying or even drinking tea, and
compelled merchants to agree not to accept shipments.

On April 18, 1774, the British ship *Nancy*, carrying
hundreds of chests of tea, anchored off Sandy Hook, New
Jersey (some twenty miles southeast of Manhattan). When
the captain was informed of the volatile situation in New
York City, he ordered his ship to return to England rather
than risk inciting mob action.

Four days later the ship *London* docked at a Hudson

River wharf. A committee of Patriots boarded the vessel and interrogated Captain James Chambers and forced him to reveal the contents of his cargo. After discovering that tea was aboard, members of the committee hastily assembled at a wharfside tavern where, following the example of their Boston compatriots, they planned to disguise themselves as Indians and return to the harbor that night to destroy the ship's cargo. But news of the presence of a tea-laden ship had spread so rapidly that an angry mob swarmed through the streets and assembled on the wharf adjacent to the *London*. Jeers and yells reached a fever pitch, and finally the crowd clambered aboard and heaved the casks of tea into the water.

The following morning, as news of New York's "Tea Party" spread throughout the city, church bells pealed and a Liberty Pole was erected on the Common. Although the British made several arrests in an attempt to punish the ringleaders, they decided to follow a more prudent course in New York than they had in Boston and, therefore, no widespread retaliatory action was taken.

After the Battles of Lexington and Concord in April 1775, militia units thronged to Boston where they laid siege to the British garrison there. The siege ended on March 17, 1776, when the British troops evacuated by sea. Their next major objective was New York City.

But General George Washington had prepared a contingency plan in the event of an attack on Manhattan. He had dispatched Major General Charles Lee to the area in early 1776 to arrange for the building of a system of defenses and the deployment of troops. Lee had decided to quarter a large force on Long Island and had planned to place a detachment at the northern tip of Manhattan in order to guard King's Bridge. When Washington arrived in New York City on April 13, 1776, fortifications were still being constructed. Fort George (at the southern tip of the island) was strengthened and Fort Washington (overlooking the Hudson River at present-day 184th

Street) was hastily erected. Reinforcements continued to arrive, and by June the Patriot army numbered nearly 20,000. Some of the forces were positioned according to Lee's plan.

Soon afterward a plot to assassinate Washington and his generals was uncovered. Prominent Loyalist citizens and traitorous soldiers were involved. One of the leaders of the conspiracy, Thomas Hickey (a member of Washington's Life Guard), was court-martialed in June 1776, convicted of mutiny and sedition, and hanged. A key figure in the scheme, David Mathews, the mayor of New York City, is believed to have planned the destruction of Patriot powder magazines in the city. He was captured and imprisoned with thirteen other Loyalists. Many others implicated in the treachery fled and were never apprehended.

During the last week of June, 130 British ships carrying troops under the command of General William Howe anchored in New York's lower bay, and on July 2 the 9,000 soldiers were landed on Staten Island. Ten days later Admiral Richard Howe (the general's brother) arrived from England with 150 vessels laden with reinforcements and supplies.

On August 22 General Howe began moving troops from Staten Island to the Brooklyn Heights area of Long Island. Five days later, after repeated skirmishes with Patriot troops, British and German detachments (under Generals James Grant and Philip von Heister) succeeded in overpowering them. It has been claimed that Patriot casualties in the Battle of Long Island were as high as 3,200 out of the 9,000 soldiers engaged. Among the prisoners taken were Generals William Alexander (Lord Stirling) and John Sullivan. (Several months later they were returned through an exchange of prisoners.)

After this devastating defeat, Washington decided to regroup his forces in Manhattan and ordered the immediate withdrawal from Long Island of the remainder

of his exhausted, demoralized troops. General William
Heath and Hugh Hughes, Assistant Quartermaster General
in New York, devised a plan to expedite the evacuation.
By the evening of August 29 every available boat
was brought to the southern tip of Manhattan. Under the
cover of darkness, and aided by a heavy fog, thousands of
Patriot soldiers were secretly transported across the East
River. By 7 A.M. the operation was completed—the men,
horses, and supplies were safe in New York City. At dawn
the British discovered only a deserted line of entrenchments.

After the defeated soldiers had joined their comrades in
Manhattan, Washington divided his forces into three
divisions commanded by Generals Israel Putnam, Nathanael
Greene, and William Heath. Early in September
these generals decided that the American position in
Manhattan was untenable and that all territory south of
Fort Washington should be abandoned. As Washington
began making preparations to withdraw, Howe seized the
initiative.

On September 13 and 14, 1776, before the Patriot
evacuation could be completed, British warships sailed
up the East River, and 4,000 troops were landed in the
Kip's Bay area (near present-day East 34th Street) on
September 15. The Americans, who were unable to defend
their positions, quickly retreated northward. As soon as
the first British and German units came ashore, they
moved toward Inclenberg (now the Murray Hill section,
Park Avenue near 35th Street). But for a quirk of fate they
would have overwhelmed the fleeing Americans. Legend
has it that several of the British officers, confident that
victory was imminent, stopped at the farm of Mary
Lindley Murray, a middle-aged Quaker and mother of
twelve children. Loyal to the Patriot cause, she tricked
them into stopping for some refreshment. While she plied
them with cakes and wine for nearly two hours, their
troops stood idly about, and the Patriots seized the op-

portunity to flee the area. That evening Washington's men
encamped at Harlem Heights (along the Hudson River
near present-day 130th Street).

The following morning, on September 16, British and
American forces encountered each other and engaged in a
minor skirmish. Washington later arrived (from his headquarters at the house of Colonel Roger Morris) and
ordered preparations for a frontal attack while a larger
force began surrounding the enemy. The maneuver was
proceeding as planned until a Patriot officer prematurely
gave the order to fire, alerting the British, who then
withdrew.

The most intense fighting of the Harlem Heights engagement occurred just after noon (in a field near present-day
Riverside Drive and 120th Street). British cannon pounded
the Americans, but a shortage of ammunition soon forced
them again to withdraw. The Americans followed in hot
pursuit. But British reinforcements were approaching, and
Washington saw that the pursuit would develop into a
full-scale battle, from which he felt his men would be
unable to emerge without heavy losses. Therefore at 2 P.M.
he called a halt to the action and ordered his troops to
pull back.

The British reported fourteen dead; the Americans,
thirty. The battle proved that the Americans had both the
ability to stand firm in the face of the enemy and the
courage to pursue them. Howe became increasingly aware
that the Americans would not be easy to defeat, a per-
ception he had gained earlier while leading forces at
Bunker Hill. After the action at Harlem Heights he
ordered the building of a series of fortifications so that
he could consolidate his gains.

Another problem soon confronted the British command.
During the night of September 20–21, 1776, a fire raged
out of control, destroying almost 500 dwellings in the city.
Although the cause of the conflagration was never determined, Loyalists accused the Patriots of destroying New

York. The Patriot generals were certainly not unhappy to see the structures in which Howe had planned to billet his soldiers go up in smoke.

On October 18 the British marched northward, forcing Washington to abandon his positions on Harlem Heights. His army then moved toward White Plains, New York.

The next blows came swiftly: the British defeated the Patriots at White Plains (on October 28) and captured Fort Washington (on November 16), taking 3,000 prisoners and large quantities of vital materiel from this last Patriot stronghold on Manhattan.

British forces occupied New York City for the duration of the Revolutionary War. It was not until November 25, 1783—twenty-two days after the signing of the Treaty of Paris—that they relinquished control of the city.

From 1785 to 1790 New York City served as the nation's capital. The years of struggles and defeats seemed to fade away as George Washington stood on the balcony of Federal Hall on April 30, 1789, and took the oath of office as the first President of the United States.

VISITORS' CENTER Information, brochures, and maps are available from the New York Convention and Visitors' Bureau, 90 East 42nd Street (across from Grand Central Station). The Bureau is open daily from 9 A.M. to 6 P.M., phone 687–1300. Information about the city can also be obtained from the Chamber of Commerce, 65 Liberty Street, phone 766–1300. Serious students of historic buildings and local history may wish to contact the Landmarks Preservation Commission of the City of New York, 305 Broadway, phone 566–7577, or the New York Historical Society, 170 Central Park West, phone 873–3400.

GUIDED TOURS   Gray Line Tours   900 Eighth Avenue, phone 765–1600. The two-hour Lower New York and

Chinatown Tour departs hourly from 9 A.M. to 2 P.M. and again at 4 P.M. during the summer and fall. The rest of the year buses leave at 9 A.M., 11 A.M., and 2 P.M. The cost is $5.50 for adults and $3.75 for children. The two-hour Upper New York and Harlem Tour starts at 10 A.M., noon, and 2 P.M. during the summer and fall. The rest of the year the buses depart at 12 P.M. and 2 P.M. The cost is $5.50 for adults and $3.75 for children. The special eight-hour "Knickerbocker Holiday" Tour, which includes most of New York's major sites, begins at 9 A.M. and 10 A.M. Reservations are required in advance; the cost is $13.50 for adults and $10.00 for children. Guided tours of the Statue of Liberty and the United Nations are also available. Also inquire about nightclub tours.

Crossroads Sightseeing Tours   1572 Broadway, phone 581–2828. The standard tours of Downtown and Chinatown as well as Uptown and Harlem are offered at $5.50 for adults and $3.75 for children. Buses depart frequently. Also inquire about the eight-hour All-Day Tour as well as tours of the Statue of Liberty, the United Nations, and New York's nightclubs.

Short Line Tours   168 West 46th Street, phone 246–5550. Standard tours are offered.

For helicopter sightseeing tours, contact **Island Helicopters,** 34th Street and East River Drive, phone 895–5372, or **Hel-Aire Copters,** 30th Street and Twelfth Avenue, phone 695–0520. Prices range from $7.00 to $50.00.

Boat tours around Manhattan Island are offered by the **Circle Line Sightseeing Yacht Corporation,** phone 563–3200. Boats sail from Pier 83 at the foot of West 43rd Street. From April 13 through October 1 tours start at 9:45 A.M., 10:30 A.M., 12:15 P.M., 1:30 P.M., 2:30 P.M., and 3:30 P.M. In July and August the schedule changes and additional tours are available. From October through March only two cruises are offered daily. The cost is $4.50 for adults and $2.00 for children.

All the above tours, schedules, and fees are subject to change.

PUBLIC TRANSPORTATION The Metropolitan Transit Authority operates subway and bus service in the area. For information, phone 330–1234. The three subway lines that run in Manhattan are the IRT, IND, and BMT. Maps of the subway system can be obtained at most token booths.

Buses run north or south on almost every major avenue. Crosstown buses travel across 8th, 14th, 23rd, 34th, and 42nd Streets, 50th Street (eastbound), 51st Street (westbound), 65th Street (eastbound), 66th Street (westbound), and along 79th, 86th, 96th, 116th, and 125th Streets. Exact change (50¢ or a subway token) is required.

On Saturday, Sunday, and holidays the Transit Authority operates a "Culture Bus Loop" in Manhattan from 10 A.M. to 6 P.M. For $1.25 the passenger can get on and off at any of twenty-two stops. (The stops include Madison Square Garden, Radio City Music Hall, City Center, Museum of Modern Art, Columbus Circle, Lincoln Center, Hayden Planetarium, Metropolitan Museum of Art, and the United Nations.) Tickets are available at subway token booths at Grand Central Station, Penn Station, Times Square, Rockefeller Center, Columbus Circle, and at the Port Authority Bus Terminal.

TAXI SERVICE Taxis can be hailed as they travel along the streets. Yellow taxis are licensed and conform to the city's codes.

ENTERTAINMENT For listings of films, plays, concerts, museum exhibitions, dance programs, restaurants, and nightclubs, consult *Cue, The New Yorker, New York* magazine, or the Arts and Leisure section of the Sunday edition of *The New York Times.*

USEFUL TELEPHONE NUMBERS Time, 637–1212; Weather, 936–1212; Police and Ambulance Emergency,

911; Police (other than emergency), 577–7000; Fire Department, 744–1000 (or 628–2900); Emergency Physicians Service, 879–1000 (or 771–8800 at night); Emergency Dentist Service, 988–6110; Traffic and Transit Conditions, 999–1234.

SELF-GUIDED TOURS The five tours below list the major sites of New York. You can conveniently see the points of interest of Tour A by walking from Battery Park to Federal Hall, then by taking public transportation to the City Hall area. Since Greenwich Village—Tour B —is a labyrinth of narrow streets, you might wish to take taxis if you feel the distances are too far to walk. If you decide on a walking tour, purchase a map of the Village. The Mid–Manhattan Tours—C and D—may be covered easily by bus or subway. The sites of Tour E, which are scattered throughout a vast area, may best be seen by automobile.

Most of the Colonial and Revolutionary War sites are clustered in lower Manhattan. In the listing below NR signifies an important *Non-Revolutionary site*; P indicates a historic house which is now a *private residence*.

Tour A	Tour B
LOWER MANHATTAN	**GREENWICH VILLAGE**
Area bounded by Chambers Street on the north, Battery Park on the south, Pearl Street on the east, and Broadway on the west.	Area bounded by 10th Street on the north, Houston Street on the south, Second Avenue on the east, and Hudson Street on the west.
Start at Battery Park:	Start at corner of Commerce Street and Bedford Street (west of Bleecker):
Battery Park Area	Isaacs-Hendricks House (P)

Tour A (Cont.)

Statue of Liberty (NR)

Castle Clinton (NR)

James Watson House (NR)

Fraunces Tavern

Site of Dutch City Hall

Site of Colonial Print Shop

Site of Kidd House

India House (NR)

Bowling Green

U.S. Customs House/
Fort George Site

Trinity Church

New York Stock Exchange
(NR)

Federal Hall

St. Paul's Chapel

City Hall Park

City Hall (NR)

End at Chambers Street
and Broadway.

Tour B (Cont.)

Site of Paine House

Site of Greenwich House

Washington Square (NR)

St. Mark's-in-the-Bouwerie

End at Second Avenue
and 10th Street.

Tour C

MID-MANHATTAN,
EAST SIDE

Area bounded by 103rd
Street on the north, 34th
Street on the south,
Franklin D. Roosevelt

Tour D

MID-MANHATTAN,
WEST SIDE

Area bounded by 80th
Street on the north,
34th Street on the south,
Fifth Avenue on the east,

Tour C (Cont.)

Drive (along the East River) on the east, and Fifth Avenue on the west.

Start at 34th Street near the East River:

Site of British Headquarters

United Nations (NR)

Morgan Library (NR)

St. Patrick's Cathedral (NR)

Rockefeller Center (NR)

Museum of Modern Art (NR)

Frick Collection (NR)

Whitney Museum (NR)

Metropolitan Museum of Art (NR)

Guggenheim Museum (NR)

Museum of the City of New York (NR)

End at 103rd Street and Fifth Avenue.

Tour D (Cont.)

and Broadway on the west.

Start at Fifth Avenue and 34th Street:

Empire State Building (NR)

Carnegie Hall (NR)

Lincoln Center (NR)

New-York Historical Society (NR)

American Museum of Natural History (NR)

End at Central Park West and 80th Street.

Tour E

UPPER MANHATTAN

Area bounded by 204th Street on the north, 110th Street on the south, Eighth Avenue / Harlem

Colonial and Revolutionary War Sites

BOWLING GREEN   *Juncture of Whitehall Street, Broadway, and Battery Place*   Here, according to legend, Peter Minuit (1580–1638), the first Director General of the colony of New Netherland, purchased Manhattan from the Indians for trinkets worth $24. From 1638 to 1647 the Green was used as a hog and cattle market. It later served as a parade ground for the Dutch militia.

In 1732, with New York under British control, the site was converted into a recreational area where Colonial gentlemen played bowls (bowling) for the annual fee of one peppercorn. A gilded equestrian statue of King George III was erected here in the 1760s. When dissension against the Crown began to surface in the early 1770s, an elaborate fence costing £843 was built around the Green, thus providing protection for the statue. But it did not prevent a mob of irate Patriots from destroying this hated symbol of British tyranny on July 9, 1776. Legend has it that 40,000 musket balls were made from the metal pieces of the statue. During the American Revolution the replicas of the royal crown ornamenting the fence were torn off by vandals.

A bronze statue of Abraham de Peyster, mayor of New York from 1691 to 1695, was placed in Bowling Green Park in 1896. It is the work of George Bissell.

CITY HALL PARK *Broadway, Chambers Street, and Park Row* During the eighteenth century this area was a Common lined with apple trees. In the early 1770s the Sons of Liberty of New York erected five successive Liberty Poles on this site, where the Patriots would rally. On July 9, 1776, the Declaration of Independence —brought by a courier from Philadelphia—was read in public here in the presence of General George Washington, his troops, and a crowd of sympathetic townspeople. Soon afterward, when the British occupied New York City, the apple trees of the Common were used as gallows to punish rebellious citizens. On the Common also stood the Provost Jail, administered by the cruel William Cunningham, who is said to have starved prisoners to death or hanged them without trial.

Nathan Hale (1755–1776), the young Connecticut schoolteacher turned Patriot spy, is believed to have been hanged here on September 22, 1776. (Some historians, however, believe the site of his execution was present-day 46th Street near First Avenue; others place it at 63rd Street near First Avenue.) At the gallows he was said to have uttered the now-famous phrase: "I only regret that I have but one life to lose for my country." (Recently discovered first-hand reports record him as stating: "It is the duty of every good officer to obey any orders given him by his Commander-in-Chief."

The earlier phrase attributed to him, which first appeared in an 1848 biography, is strikingly similar to a quotation from Joseph Addison's play *Cato*.)

On February 13, 1837, the so-called Bread Riot took place in City Hall Park. When the price of flour had tripled as a result of speculation, 6,000 irate citizens assembled here, then streamed through the streets breaking into the flour stores and destroying property.

In 1893 a statue of Nathan Hale, by sculptor Frederick MacMonnies, was erected in the park. Another statue, a bronze figure of Horace Greeley (1811–1872), founder of the *New York Tribune*, is a reminder that this area was once the center of newspaper publishing in New York. The monument, unveiled in 1890, is attributed to J. Q. A. Ward.

DYCKMAN HOUSE *204th Street and Broadway. Open Tuesday through Sunday 11 A.M. to 5 P.M. Free.* The Dyckman House is the only surviving Colonial farmhouse in Manhattan. The first dwelling on this site— built in 1748 by William Dyckman—was pillaged and burned by British troops during the occupation of Manhattan. The British established an outpost here and built fifty huts to quarter their soldiers. Soon after the Revolutionary War Dyckman rebuilt his house.

The building, which was presented to the city in 1915, has been refurbished. It is a two-story, gambrel-roofed house with lower walls of fieldstone and an upper story of clapboard. Period furnishings include a sideboard, several rushbottom chairs, a washstand, footwarmers, and two eighteenth-century Bibles—all owned by the Dyckman family.

Behind the house is a small hut reconstructed from the remains of the British camp that had been erected on the Dyckman farm.

FEDERAL HALL NATIONAL MEMORIAL *28 Wall Street at Nassau Street. Open Monday through Friday 9 A.M. to 4:30 P.M. Closed Thanksgiving, December 25,*

and January 1. Free.   Erected in 1699, the first building
which stood on this site served as the Colonial City
Hall. It was a brick structure with three arches gracing
the entrance, a small balcony extending from the second
floor, and a cupola surmounting the roof. Chambers in
the building were used by the City Common Council,
the Governor's Council, and the Supreme Court of
Judicature. The attic on the third floor was converted
into a jail.

In 1735 John Peter Zenger (1697–1746), editor of
the *New York Weekly Journal*, was imprisoned and
tried in this building on the charge of making seditious
statements against Royal Governor William Cosby.
Zenger's acquittal represented a major precedent in the
establishment of the freedom of the press.

In October 1765 delegates from nine colonies met
here to protest the hated English Stamp Act taxes. This
Stamp Act Congress formulated a Declaration of Rights
and Grievances that challenged Parliament's authority
to impose restrictive measures and taxes on the colonies.
This action, along with violent protests throughout
America, led to the repeal of the Stamp Act in March
1766.

Following the first reading of the Declaration of Independence in New York City on July 9, 1776, a riotous
crowd of Patriots, which had assembled on the City
Common (present-day Broadway and Chambers Street),
marched south to City Hall, where they defiantly ripped
the Royal Coat of Arms off the building. They then
surged through the streets to Bowling Green and toppled
the statue of King George III.

During most of the Revolutionary War, New York
City was occupied by the British, who converted City
Hall into an arsenal. When British troops evacuated on
November 25, 1783 (two years after the American
victory at Yorktown and one year after the signing of

the Preliminary Articles of Peace), the building was used for sessions of the New York State legislature.

From 1785 to 1790 New York City served as the nation's capital. The United States Congress, under the Articles of Confederation, met here until 1788 when a devastating fire, which leveled most of the area, inflicted heavy damage on the building.

The following year the structure was rebuilt under the supervision of Major Charles Pierre L'Enfant (who later drafted the master plan of Washington, D.C.). Renamed Federal Hall, it was a two-and-a-half-story building with a Greek-style pediment, a colonnaded balcony on the second floor, and a large cupola crowning the roof. Here both houses of the United States Congress, operating under the new Federal Constitution, convened to enact legislation from 1789 to 1790. A momentous event took place on the balcony of Federal Hall on April 30, 1789—George Washington took the oath of office as the first President of the United States.

After departing from his residence at 3 Cherry Street, Washington traveled by carriage in a large procession led by Colonel Morgan Lewis (who had served as chief of staff at Fort Ticonderoga and Saratoga). At the head of the procession were units of colorfully-clad cavalry and artillery soldiers followed by detachments of grenadiers. Next came Washington's carriage flanked by members of Congress. Other dignitaries marched at the rear. To the peal of bells, the thunder of cannon, and the joyous cheers of the citizens, the procession passed through the streets. Shouts of "God Bless Our President" greeted Washington as he alighted from the carriage and briskly walked up the steps of Federal Hall.

Robert Livingston, Chancellor of New York State, administered the oath. Washington's attendants were John Adams (his Vice President), James Madison, Richard Henry Lee, Baron von Steuben, and James Madison. The President then delivered his inaugural address before a joint session of Congress. The audience was deeply moved when he declaimed: "The preservation of the sacred fire of liberty, and the destiny of the republican model of government, are justly considered as deeply, perhaps as finally staked, on the experiment entrusted to the hands of the American people." After the address he traveled to St. Paul's Chapel to attend special services.

The President occupied an office in Federal Hall, and here he deliberated on the first pieces of legislation Congress enacted and charted the course of the young nation.

After the capital was moved to Philadelphia in late 1790, Federal Hall was used for official city and state functions. By 1812 the building, which had fallen into disrepair, was sold for $425 as demolition salvage.

The present building dates from 1842. The imposing facade with its eight Ionic pillars was designed by architects I. Town and A. Davis; J. Frazee was responsible for the detail work of the interior. It served as the New York City Customs House until 1862, when it became the United States Subtreasury. After serving as the Subtreasury Building, it housed other government offices from 1920 to 1939. That year the site was designated a National Historic Landmark.

The statue of George Washington on the steps of Federal Hall was executed by J. Q. A. Ward in 1883. It weighs three tons and stands twelve feet high. The guest of honor at the dedication ceremonies was President Chester A. Arthur.

Inside Federal Hall, exhibits, dioramas, and audiovisual presentations describe the history of the buildings that have stood on this site and re-create significant events of Colonial New York.

FRAUNCES TAVERN *54 Pearl Street. Open Monday through Friday 10 A.M. to 4 P.M. Closed holidays. Free.* Now a cherished New York landmark, Fraunces Tavern

George Washington statue on the steps of Federal Hall, New York City (ALPER)

was built in 1719 as a residence for Etienne de Lancey, a wealthy Huguenot. Thirty-six years later his grandson Oliver converted the building into a store with a warehouse.

In 1762 Samuel Fraunces, a West Indian of French and Negro descent, acquired the property for £2,000 and opened the Queen's Head Tavern here.

Many historic events occurred at the tavern. In 1768 a group of prominent merchants met on the second floor to organize a committee to promote the welfare of the town's business community. These men were the founders of the association that became the New York State Chamber of Commerce.

In the spring of 1774—after Parliament had passed legislation that would close the port of Boston on June 1—irate townspeople convened here to create a Committee of Correspondence to communicate with citizen groups throughout the colonies to determine a course of action against the hated act.

During 1774 and 1775 many New England Patriots and members of the Continental Congress stopped here en route to Philadelphia. John Adams recorded in his diary that the tavern offered "the most splendid dinner I ever saw."

When the Americans reoccupied New York City after the war, Fraunces returned to his tavern. Ripping down the "Queen's Head" sign and redecorating the building, he renamed it Fraunces Tavern. On November 25, 1783, when the final British contingent evacuated Manhattan, Governor George Clinton held a dinner here to honor General Washington. After viewing a parade, a large gathering of distinguished citizens retired to the tavern, where they toasted Washington and the newly independent nation, then enjoyed a sumptuous feast.

On December 4, 1783, George Washington bade farewell to his officers at a banquet held in the tavern's

Long Room. With deep emotion, he uttered: "With a heart full of love and gratitude, I now take leave of you. . . . I most devotedly wish that your later days may be as prosperous and happy as your former ones have been glorious and honorable." His former comrades-in-arms, led by General Henry Knox, then stepped forward to embrace him. After a tearful farewell, Washington departed. Walking between the ranks of a guard of honor, he proceeded to the harbor where he boarded a boat. From New York he traveled to Philadelphia, and eventually to Annapolis, Maryland, to surrender his commission to Congress, then returned to his home at Mount Vernon.

Fraunces sold the tavern in 1785 and moved to New Jersey. Four years later, after Washington's inauguration, Fraunces became the President's steward and served at his official residence on Cherry Street.

Present-day Fraunces Tavern is a reconstruction based on the plans of buildings typical of the period. The high chimneys, hipped roof with balustrade, and interior paneling are all characteristic of Georgian architecture.

Washington's Farewell to His Officers. *Painting by Alonzo Chappel.* (CHICAGO HISTORICAL SOCIETY)

The Sons of the Revolution of the State of New York acquired the property in 1904 and commissioned architect William H. Mersereau to carry out the reconstruction. In 1969 the Long Room was authentically recreated by Gerald Watland.

A museum on the upper floor displays Revolutionary War relics and Washington memorabilia. A fine restaurant occupies the ground floor.

ISAACS-HENDRICKS HOUSE *Corner of Bedford and Commerce Streets. Not open to the public.* The central portion of this house was built in the 1790s by Joshua Isaacs, who served as Paul Revere's New York business agent. In 1801 Isaacs' son-in-law, Harmon Hendricks, acquired the property. A third floor was added in the nineteenth century.

MORRIS-JUMEL MANSION *Jumel Terrace at West 161st Street, between St. Nicholas and Edgecomb Avenues. Open Tuesday through Sunday 11 A.M. to 4:30 P.M. Closed holidays. Adults 50¢, children 25¢.* This imposing mansion was built in 1765 by Colonel Roger Morris, a retired British officer, for his wife Mary, the daughter of the influential Frederick Philipse of Yonkers. Morris and George Washington had both served in the French and Indian Wars (1750s) as aides-de-camp to General Edward Braddock, and they remained close until their opposing viewpoints in the turbulent days before the Revolutionary War caused a rift in their friendship. (Legend has it that Washington had once courted Mary Philipse.)

When the political ferment erupted into war, Morris, a Loyalist, fled to England. During his absence Mrs. Morris and her four children resided in Yonkers at the Philipse Manor. In late 1777, after the British army was firmly entrenched in Manhattan, Morris returned to carry out the duties of Inspector of the Claims of Refugees. He retained the position until 1783. After the Treaty of Paris, when the British relinquished New York

Morris–Jumel Mansion, New York City (ALPER)

City, the Morris family permanently settled in England.

From September 14 to October 18, 1776—after the disastrous Battle of Long Island—General George Washington used this house as his temporary headquarters. From here he and his officers directed the defense of Harlem Heights (September 16). After the Americans evacuated Manhattan, several British officers occupied the mansion. General Henry Clinton was invited to reside here in 1777; the following year General Knyphausen and his staff were here for a short time.

After 1783 the house passed through a succession of owners. In 1810 it was purchased by a wealthy French-American merchant, Stephen Jumel. His wife—who was an ambitious social climber—remodeled it, added the pedimented portico, and installed a new entrance doorway.

According to contemporary gossip, Mme. Jumel (née Eliza Bowen of Providence) had tricked her husband into marriage by feigning a serious illness and begging to be wed before her imminent demise. After a quick recovery, she and her husband traveled in Europe where her unrefined Yankee manners were slightly more tolerated than in New York. Years later, when Jumel discovered that she had an illegitimate son, the couple became estranged. Stephen Jumel spent his final years living in Paris, where he died in 1832.

One year after his death the sixty-one-year-old Eliza Jumel married the impoverished seventy-seven-year-old Aaron Burr, the former Vice President of the United States. The marriage was short-lived; in six months they were divorced. Mrs. Burr (who took great pride in using the name) died in 1865.

The city of New York acquired the mansion in 1903. The house was refurnished in the styles of two periods— late Georgian and Federal—to re-create the ambiance of the two important families that resided here, the Morrises and the Jumels.

To the left of the entrance hallway is the **Parlor or Tea Room** in which Eliza Jumel and Aaron Burr were married in 1833. Many of the pieces here originally belonged to the Jumels. The Empire gilded sofa and two side chairs were probably made by a New York cabinetmaker, although Mme. Jumel claimed they were sent from France. The piano, an unusually fine example, was made in 1789 by Benjamin Crehore of Milton, Massachusetts. The bronze and crystal chandelier once belonged to Napoleon.

In the **Drawing Room,** to the rear of the hall, General George Washington established his Council Room in September 1776. The Sheraton-style sofa is complemented by a handsome chest of drawers made in New York in 1770. The slant-top desk and the highboy, both mid-eighteenth-century pieces, are distinguished by their graceful form and delicate carving. Two cherished Revolutionary War relics are on display here: a Hessian drum and the dispatch box of Silas Deane, a member of the Continental Congress and later a Commissioner to France.

Mme. Jumel's Bedroom, on the second floor, contains furniture she acquired during her sojourn in France: a mahogany bed, small chairs with dolphin-shaped arms, and a pair of side chairs (thought to originally have been the property of Queen Hortense of the Netherlands, Napoleon's stepdaughter). The mannequin, which represents Eliza Jumel in the 1830s, is dressed in a costume typical of the period.

Another bedroom, designated **Aaron Burr's Room,** has a desk that originally stood in Burr's New York law office, an oval table which converts into a chair and a writing desk, an elaborately carved four-poster mahogany bed (*c.* 1820), and a portrait of Burr painted by Eric Maunsbach.

The small room above the drawing room served in 1776 as the private quarters of General Washington during the final days of the Patriot attempt to hold Manhattan.

The mansion is presently administered by the Washington Headquarters Association, founded by four chapters of the Daughters of the American Revolution.

ST. MARK'S-IN-THE-BOUWERIE *Second Avenue and 10th Street. Open Tuesday through Friday 9 A.M. to 3:30 P.M., Sunday 10:30 A.M. to 2 P.M.* A Dutch chapel was built here, on the farm of Governor Peter Stuyvesant, in 1660. The oldest section of the present building dates from 1799 and includes some stones from the original chapel. The steeple (designed by Ithiel Town) was added in 1828; the portico was constructed in 1854.

Peter Stuyvesant (1610–1672), Dutch governor of New Amsterdam (Manhattan), is buried in the churchyard near the east wall. Near the grave stands a statue of him, presented by Queen Wilhelmina of Holland in 1915.

ST. PAUL'S CHAPEL   *Broadway, Fulton, and Church Streets. Open daily 7:15 A.M. to 5:45 P.M.*   St. Paul's, the oldest extant church building in New York City, was built between 1764 and 1766. Its architect, Thomas McBean, was influenced by James Gibbs' masterpiece, St. Martin's-in-the-Fields (London). An outstanding feature of St. Paul's Chapel is its eastern portico with pediment and slender Ionic columns. Towering above the west end—which originally was the front of the structure—is a spire, added in 1794.

Much of the interior decoration was designed by Pierre Charles L'Enfant (who later created plans of Washington, D.C.). His chief work in this church is the altar, the railing, and the "Glory" representing Mount Sinai and the Ten Commandments.

The three chairs in the chancel date from 1695; the

Interior of St. Paul's Chapel, New York City (COURTESY TRINITY CHURCH, NEW YORK CITY)

elaborately carved gold-leafed pulpit is of eighteenth-century origin; the fourteen chandeliers—made in Waterford, Ireland—were installed in 1802; and the organ in the west gallery was built in 1804 by John Geib, who is buried in the churchyard here.

During the Revolutionary War, when the British occupied New York City, many officers worshipped here regularly, including General Charles Cornwallis, General William Howe, Major John André, and General Guy Carleton.

After George Washington's inauguration at Federal Hall on April 30, 1789, the President and members of Congress came to St. Paul's for a special service conducted by Bishop Samuel Provoost. Washington continued to worship here until the capital was moved to Philadelphia in late 1790.

The pew reserved for President George Washington is found off the north aisle. The Bible on the prayer desk is a replica (in reduced size) of the one used by Washington during the inaugural ceremonies. The pew of Governor George Clinton (1739–1812), the first governor of New York State (1777–1795) and later a Vice President of the United States (1805–1812), may be seen off the south aisle. The coat of arms of New York State is displayed on the wall behind Clinton's pew.

Below the large east window of the portico is the grave of Patriot General Richard Montgomery (1738–1775) who was killed in the disastrous attack on Quebec in December 1775. The monument was executed by J. J. Caffieri, a French sculptor, on orders from the Continental Congress.

Several British officers of the Revolutionary War are buried in St. Paul's churchyard: Colonel Campbell, Captains Wolfe, Walker, Bond, Talbot, Logan, and Wilcox, and Lieutenant Swords. Officers of the Continental Army interred here include Majors John Lucas, Job Sumner, and John Francis. Sieur de Rochefontaine

(1755–1814), who served under General Rochambeau and helped train American artillery units, is buried in the part of the cemetery that meets the corner of Church and Fulton Streets.

SITE OF BRITISH HEADQUARTERS *Kip's Bay, 33rd–34th Streets near the East River* The brick mansion of the Kip (Kype) family, which was built in 1641, served as one of the headquarters for British officers during the occupation of New York. Major John André dined here with General Henry Clinton and his staff the evening before he departed on his ill-fated mission (September 1780) to negotiate with Benedict Arnold for the betrayal of West Point. The Kip House was demolished in 1850.

SITE OF COLONIAL PRINT SHOP *81 Pearl Street* This is the site of the print shop of William Bradford (1663–1752), who in 1693 settled in Manhattan where he established the first printing press in the colony of New York. (In 1685, in Philadelphia, Bradford had established the first printing press of the Middle Colonies, but he was arrested in 1692 for publishing seditious material. After his acquittal he left Pennsylvania.)

Bradford published the first American Book of Common Prayer (1710) and many almanacs and political pamphlets. In 1725 he founded the city's first newspaper, the *New York Gazette*.

SITE OF COLONIAL TAVERN *1 Broadway near Battery Park* The first structure on this site was a tavern built in the mid-seventeenth century and operated by Pieter Koch. Dutch soldiers from the nearby fort, which was erected close to the tip of the island in 1653, congregated here to exchange stories and to drink. According to local tradition, this tavern was the first in New York to serve "mixed" drinks in the late eighteenth century.

SITE OF DUTCH CITY HALL *71–73 Pearl Street* The New Amsterdam Stadt Huys, seat of the Dutch Colonial government, stood here. Originally an inn, the brick building was purchased by the city in 1653. The arches above the first- and second-story windows provided the only ornamental architectural features. In 1826 the structure was renovated and converted into a restaurant. It was demolished in the early twentieth century.

SITE OF FORT WASHINGTON *Fort Washington Avenue between 183rd and 185th Streets* A flagpole on this site marks the former location of Fort Washington, the Patriot fortification that was surrendered to the British on November 16, 1776. After heavy fighting, the 230 officers and 2,600 foot soldiers were taken prisoner, and an enormous amount of materiel was captured. It was one of the most serious Patriot defeats of the Revolutionary War. The fall of Fort Washington ensured British control of New York City.

SITE OF GREENWICH HOUSE *West 4th Street near Charles Street* On this site stood the Greenwich House (built 1740), the residence of British Admiral Sir Peter Warren, who was commander of the fleet in New York. The property was later acquired by the Earl of Abingdon, who was married to Warren's daughter Charlotte. After the Revolutionary War the property passed through many hands until 1821, when it was purchased by Abraham Van Nest, owner of a large saddlery business. After his death in 1864 the land was divided into parcels and sold.

SITE OF KIDD HOUSE *119–121 Pearl Street* Across Hanover Square from the India House is the site of the house occupied from 1691 to 1695 by Captain William Kidd.

In 1696 his ship was commissioned as a privateer by the Earl of Bellomont, royal governor of New York, to defend English vessels from enemy attack and pirate aggression. But Kidd himself turned pirate the following year and became notorious for his daring exploits.

Trinity Church, New York City (COURTESY TRINITY CHURCH,
NEW YORK CITY)

Captured in 1699, he was taken to London for trial, where he was convicted and hanged.

SITE OF PAINE HOUSE *59 Grove Street* From 1806 until his death in 1809 Thomas Paine (1737–1809), Patriot pamphleteer and author of *Common Sense* (1776), resided in a frame cottage that once stood here.

TRINITY CHURCH *Broadway at the head of Wall Street. Open Monday through Friday 7 A.M. to 6 P.M.; Saturday, Sunday, and holidays 7 A.M. to 4 P.M. Organ recitals on Tuesday and Thursday at 12:45 P.M. Free.* Present-day Trinity Church is the third building on this site. The first church, which was completed in 1698, faced the Hudson River. During the long tenure (1698–1746) of the first rector, William Vesey, the size of the congregation significantly increased.

During the summer of 1776 General George Washington worshipped at Trinity Church and enjoyed the services conducted by the Reverend Samuel Auchmuty. Soon afterward, when Auchmuty fell ill, his associate Charles Inglis assumed his pastoral duties. Inglis stubbornly refused to eliminate the traditional prayer for the king and royal family despite protests from members of the congregation. The precariousness of his position was relieved with the British occupation of the city in the fall. Late in 1776 the church was reduced to rubble by a fire.

The second church building—larger and more elaborate than its predecessor—was constructed in 1790. Seven years later the first bells were installed in Trinity's graceful spire. They were cast by the Whitechapel Foundry of London, England, the same company that cast Philadelphia's Liberty Bell. (Three of the eight original bells are still in use here today.) Considered structurally unsound, the building was demolished in 1839.

The present church, erected in 1846, was designed

by the prominent architect Richard Upjohn in the style of the Perpendicular English Gothic. The rectangular tower—surmounted by an octagonal spire of brownstone ashlar—soars above the well-proportioned buttressed walls.

The interior is equally as handsome as the exterior. The stained-glass windows were designed by Upjohn and executed by Abner Stephenson in a workshop on the church grounds. The reredos (screen behind the altar) portrays figures of the Apostles; the marble panels above the high altar show scenes from the life of Christ; and the rows of carved columns support groined vaulting to form an impressive nave.

Designed by Richard Morris Hunt, the bronze entrance doors depicting biblical scenes were a gift from William Waldorf Astor as a memorial to his father, John Jacob Astor III.

Many notable parishioners are buried in the churchyard: William Bradford (1663–1752), who established the first printing press in the Middle Colonies and in New York; Alexander Hamilton (1755–1804), officer in the Continental Army and later the first Secretary of the Treasury, who was killed by Aaron Burr, then Vice President, in a duel; Albert Gallatin (1761–1849), Secretary of the Treasury under Thomas Jefferson and Minister to France; and Robert Fulton (1765–1815), the inventor who designed the steamboat *Clermont*.

Near Broadway is the grave of Charlotte Temple, whose tale was chronicled by novelist Sarah Haswell Rowsan in *The History of Charlotte Temple* (1790). According to the book, the young, aristocratic Charlotte eloped with a handsome British officer who persuaded her to sail to America with him. After bearing his child, she was deserted, left alone to face poverty and starvation.

A Soldiers Monument (north side of the church)

honors the Patriots who sacrificed their lives fighting in
the American Revolution. A bronze statue (south side
of the church) has been erected to the memory of John
Watts (1749–1836), the first Speaker of the New York
State Assembly.

**UNITED STATES CUSTOMS HOUSE / FORT GEORGE
SITE** *Opposite Bowling Green. Open Monday through
Friday 9 A.M. to 5 P.M.* The Customs House stands on
the site of Fort Amsterdam, which was built in the late
seventeenth century by Dutch settlers. Within the stockade walls stood the governor's residence, a church, bar-
racks, and a supply depot. The fortification was renamed
Fort George in 1702 to honor Queen Anne's consort,
Prince George of Denmark. In the early phases of the
Revolutionary War the British strengthened the defenses here by adding six cannon mounted on the fort's
walls. Adjacent to it stood a battery (called the Grand
Battery) which consisted of twenty-two artillery pieces.
During the British occupation this battery was expanded
to include ninety-four guns. From here British and
German troops under Baron Wilhelm von Knyphausen
launched raids into New Jersey.

When the British evacuated New York City on November 25, 1783, General Henry Knox led a detachment
of American soldiers into lower Manhattan to take
formal possession of Fort George. Thousands of jubilant
citizens cheered these soldiers as they marched through
the streets to the site of the ceremony that marked the
end of the British presence in New York.

The fort was demolished in 1789 and on its site was
built an elegant mansion (under the supervision of John
McComb, Jr.) intended for occupancy by President
George Washington. However, the nation's capital
moved from New York City to Philadelphia before the
house was completed. Later the building became the
official Governor's Mansion. It was the residence of both

Governors George Clinton and John Jay. In the first decade of the nineteenth century the mansion was converted into a residence hotel.

In 1907 the massive United States Customs House was erected here at a cost of $7 million, and it is still in use today. Designed by Cass Gilbert, this building is noted for its extraordinary decoration. On projecting pedestals stand four sculptural groups representing Asia, America, Africa, and Europe. These were executed by Daniel Chester French, the sculptor of the Minuteman statue standing at the North Bridge in Concord, Massachusetts. Extending across the sixth-story level are a series of statues symbolizing the historical commercial centers of the world: England and France (by Charles Grafly), Germany (by Albert Jaegers), Denmark (by Johannes Gellert), Holland and Portugal (by Augustus Saint-Gaudens), Venice and Spain (by F. M. L. Tonetti), Genoa (by Augustus Lukeman), Phoenicia (by F. W. Ruckstull), and Greece and Rome (by F. E. Elwell). Nautical motifs—such as tridents, masts, and dolphins—also embellish the facade.

Non-Revolutionary Sites of Interest

AMERICAN MUSEUM OF NATURAL HISTORY *Central Park West between 77th and 80th Streets. Open Monday through Saturday 10 A.M. to 4:45 P.M., Sunday and holidays 11 A.M. to 5 P.M. Closed Thanksgiving and December 25. Contributions accepted.* The museum was opened in 1877 at ceremonies presided over by President Rutherford B. Hayes. The earliest section of the museum, the building in the Romanesque style

(77th Street), was designed by J. C. Cady. The structure with the classical facade (Central Park West) was erected in 1936 to the specifications of architect John Russell Pope. Its Ionic columns support statues of explorers and naturalists such as Audubon, Boone, and Lewis and Clark.

The museum features exhibits on the origin of man, skeletal reconstructions of prehistoric animals, displays of plant life of various regions of the world, as well as dioramas presenting various species of mammals and galleries showing minerals and gems. Especially memorable is the ninety-four-foot whale suspended from the ceiling of the Hall of Ocean Life.

The adjacent **Hayden Planetarium** (built during the 1930s) has one-hour shows at 2 P.M. and 3:30 P.M. on weekdays; at 11 A.M. and hourly from 1 P.M. to 5 P.M. on Saturday; hourly from 1 P.M. to 4 P.M. on Sunday. Hours are extended during the summer months. Adults $1.75, children and students $1.00. Here visitors can see the stars and planets revealed as the Zeiss projector transforms the planetarium dome into a breathtaking view of the night sky. Exhibits of related astronomical phenomena are of special interest.

CARNEGIE HALL *57th Street at Seventh Avenue. Box office usually opens about 10* A.M. This building—which houses a 2,760-seat auditorium—was designed by architect William B. Tuthill with the assistance of several consultants (including W. M. Hunt and D. Adler). It was built under the auspices of Andrew Carnegie, the steel tycoon.

The hall opened on May 9, 1891, with a five-day music festival at which Tchaikovsky conducted several of his own compositions. Ignace Jan Paderewski made his American debut here that same season. Since that time every major musician has performed in this revered hall.

Castle Clinton National Monument, New York City (ALPER)

CASTLE CLINTON NATIONAL MONUMENT *Battery Park* This massive, circular structure was built as a fortress by the federal government between 1807 and 1811 on a cluster of offshore rocks (called the Capske by the early Dutch settlers). It was connected to the shore by a 200-foot causeway. Fort Clinton guarded New York Harbor until 1822 when it was ceded to New York City. The building, which was then converted into an open-air garden and renamed Castle Garden, became a recreation area for concerts and public ceremonies. In 1845 the structure was roofed.

Among the distinguished guests officially welcomed here were: in 1824, Lafayette; in 1851, Lajos Kossuth, the former ruler of Hungary; and in 1860, the Prince of Wales, later King Edward VII of England. In September 1850, 6,000 spectators crowded into Castle Garden to hear B. T. Barnum's discovery, the soprano Jenny Lind. The publicity for the "Swedish Nightingale's" concert was so effective that some people paid as much as $225 for a pair of tickets.

From 1855 to 1890 the old fort became New York's Immigration Station. Through these walls passed almost 8 million foreign-born people who desired a new life in America.

In 1870 the island on which Castle Garden was standing was connected to the mainland as part of the landfill of the Battery Park area.

After the immigration facilities were transferred to Ellis Island, Castle Garden was transformed into an aquarium. The distinguished architectural firm of Mc-Kim, Mead and White drafted the plans for renovation of the interior. In 1941 the aquarium was relocated and this building fell into disrepair. Five years later Congress declared it a National Historic Monument. Now known as Castle Clinton, the structure is undergoing restoration.

CATHEDRAL OF ST. JOHN THE DIVINE *112th Street and Amsterdam Avenue. Open daily 7 A.M. to 6 P.M. Tours Monday through Saturday at 11 A.M., noon, and 2 P.M.* The cornerstone of St. John the Divine was laid on December 27, 1892. The original plans for the cathedral were drafted by George Lewis Heins and Christopher Grant La Farge, but the design was altered by architect Ralph Adams Cram. The choir was completed in 1911, and the central nave was finished in the early 1930s.

The bronze doors, each weighing 12 tons, portray scenes from the Old and New Testaments. The central figure of the reredos (screen behind the high altar) is a seven-foot representation of Christ. The choir is enclosed by eight granite columns, each fifty-five feet high. The baptistry, which has niches with figures from early New York history, is covered by a vaulted dome. The beautifully decorated chapels of St. Columba and St. Saviour were designed by Heins and La Farge.

When completed, St. John the Divine will be the largest Gothic church in the world. Work was halted as a symbol of the charitable obligation to divert funds to the needs of the poor, and no date has been set for the resumption of construction. The cathedral serves the Episcopal Diocese of New York.

CITY HALL   *At City Hall Park between Broadway and Park Row. Open to the public Monday through Friday 10 A.M. to 4 P.M.*   City Hall, which houses the office of the mayor of New York City and the chambers of the City Council, was built between 1803 and 1812 at a cost of $500,000. A competition held for the design of the building was won by Joseph F. Mangin, a Frenchman. Construction was supervised by John McComb, Jr. The facade, reminiscent of Louis XVI architecture, is embellished with details such as pilasters between arched windows. The roof is surmounted by a cupola.

The **Governor's Suite**—originally reserved for use by the state's chief executive when visiting the city—is now open to the public as museum rooms. They contain some of the original furnishings as well as John Trumbull's portraits of John Jay, Alexander Hamilton, and George Washington. Especially cherished is the writing table used by George Washington when New York City was the nation's capital (1785–1790).

One of the solemn moments in the history of City Hall occurred in April 1865. The body of the assassinated President Abraham Lincoln, which had been transported here from Washington, D.C., lay in state in the City Hall rotunda while thousands of grief-stricken citizens filed by the catafalque.

City Hall, as the center of local government, is the place where legislation is deliberated upon and enacted, affecting the lives of eight million New Yorkers.

EMPIRE STATE BUILDING   *Fifth Avenue and 34th Street. Observation tower is open 9:30 A.M. to midnight. Adults $1.70, youngsters (5–11) 85¢, children (under 5) free.*   Soaring 1,472 feet, the Empire State Building has 102 stories with an aggregate of 2 million square feet of office space. This great tower—built on the site of the old Waldorf Astoria Hotel—was designed by Shreve, Lamb, and Harmon in 1929. Construction progressed swiftly and the building opened two and a half years later.

FRICK COLLECTION *1 East 70th Street, at Fifth Avenue. Open June through August, Thursday, Friday, and Saturday* 10 A.M. *to* 6 P.M.; *Wednesday and Sunday* 1 P.M. *to* 6 P.M. *During the rest of the year the museum is open Tuesday through Saturday* 10 A.M. *to* 6 P.M., *Sunday* 1 P.M. *to* 6 P.M. *Closed major holidays. Children under* 10 *not admitted. Free.* Completed in 1914, the Frick mansion was designed by Carrère and Hastings in the formal Renaissance style. This dwelling was formerly the residence of industrialist Henry Clay Frick (1849–1919), one of America's steel barons who headed the Carnegie Steel Company and later became director of the United States Steel Corporation. After Mrs. Frick's death in 1931 the building was transformed (by architect John Russell Pope) into a museum to display the family's extraordinary art collection.

The distinguished collection includes works by Jacob van Ruisdael, Giovanni Tiepolo, Jean-Baptiste Greuze, Jean Chardin, Claude Lorrain, Thomas Gainsborough, Rembrandt, El Greco, and Francisco Goya.

Of particular interest are the rooms devoted to the works of Jean-Honoré Fragonard and François Boucher. Carefully chosen period pieces create a magnificent setting for their paintings.

GRANT NATIONAL MEMORIAL (GRANT'S TOMB) *Riverside Drive and 122nd Street. Open daily* 9 A.M. *to* 5 P.M. *Free.* This 150-foot-high granite mausoleum was dedicated on April 27, 1897—the seventy-fifth anniversary of the birth of President Ulysses S. Grant (1822–1885). Designed by J. H. Duncan, the tomb cost $600,000 which was raised through contributions from American citizens. Inside lie the sarcophagi of the Ohio-born President and his wife, Julia Dent Grant. Beyond the crypt are rooms containing memorabilia of Grant and the Civil War.

GUGGENHEIM MUSEUM   *89th Street and Fifth Avenue. Open Wednesday through Sunday, and holidays, 11 A.M. to 5 P.M., Tuesday 11 A.M. to 8 P.M. Closed July 4 and December 25. Free on Tuesday nights. Adults $1.00, students 50¢, children (under 7) free.*   This imposing four-tiered spiral concrete structure was designed by Frank Lloyd Wright in 1959 to house the art collection of industrialist Solomon R. Guggenheim (1861–1949). The permanent collection of twentieth-century art includes works by Wassily Kandinsky, Fernand Léger, Henri Rousseau, Pablo Picasso, Constantin Brancusi, Mark Rothko, Adolph Gottlieb, Jackson Pollock, David Smith, and Alexander Calder.

INDIA HOUSE   *1 Hanover Square. Not open to the public.*   In 1673 Nicholas Bayard, a prosperous merchant, built a mansion on this site. A devastating fire destroyed the house in 1835. Two years later this Italianate building was erected. Designed by Richard J. Carman, it is distinguished by pediments above the windows, an elaborate cornice, and fine architectural details surrounding the entrance.

In the past India House has served as headquarters for a group of foreign traders, the home of the New York Cotton Exchange, and the corporate offices of W. R. Grace and Company. Today it is a private club for businessmen and houses a small maritime museum room.

LINCOLN CENTER   *Between West 62nd and 66th Streets, Columbus Avenue, and Broadway. Guided tours daily 10 A.M. to 5 P.M. Adults $2.50, students $1.75, children $1.25.*   A committee of architects headed by Wallace K. Harrison met in the spring of 1958 to begin planning a cultural complex for New York City.

In 1962 the first building was completed—**Phil-**

harmonic Hall, designed by Max Abramovitz. The structure, which has a peristyle of forty-four columns, displays various works of sculpture in the lobby: a statue
of Gustave Mahler (by Rodin), a bust of Beethoven (by
Bourdelle), and two huge figures representing Orpheus
and Apollo (by Richard Lippold).

In 1964 the **New York State Theater,** located on the
south of the plaza, was completed. This 2,800-seat
theater with a vast four-story foyer was designed by
architect Philip Johnson.

Two years later the **Metropolitan Opera House** was
erected, replacing the auditorium at Broadway and 34th
Street. The new opera house, which cost $46 million,
was designed by Wallace K. Harrison (the architect
involved with the design and construction of the United
Nations and Rockefeller Center). Huge murals by Marc
Chagall hang above the promenade. On the lower level
is a gallery with portraits and busts of celebrated artists
who have performed with the Metropolitan Opera
Company. The first season opened in September 1966
with the world premiere of Samuel Barber's *Antony and
Cleopatra.*

To the rear of the "Met" stands the **Library and
Museum of the Performing Arts.** Designed by Skidmore,
Owings, and Merrill, the building houses more than
50,000 volumes devoted to theater, music, and dance.
It also has an extensive research library on the third
floor and a small art gallery on the ground level (Amsterdam Avenue side).

The **Vivian Beaumont Theater,** located to the north
of the library, was designed by Eero Saarinen and
opened in 1965. It has two theaters—the larger, seating 1,140, has a modified proscenium/thrust stage; the
smaller, known as "The Forum," is a theater-in-the-round
with 290 seats. The theater is the home of Joseph Papp's
New York Shakespeare Company.

The **Julliard School of Music,** designed by Bellusci,

Catalano, and Westermann, is located at 66th Street. It contains several auditoriums, including Alice Tully Hall, one of New York's major recital halls.

METROPOLITAN MUSEUM OF ART *82nd Street and Fifth Avenue. Open Tuesday 10 A.M. to 8:45 P.M., Wednesday through Saturday 10:45 A.M. to 5 P.M., Sunday and holidays 11 A.M. to 4:45 P.M. Admission by contribution.* The museum first opened in temporary quarters in 1870 with a small collection of antiquities and Dutch paintings which were a gift of General Louis Palma de Cesnola, a former consul of Cyprus. The collection grew rapidly, and in 1880 a larger building, designed by Calvert Vaux and J. Wrey Mould, was erected in Central Park along Fifth Avenue. This structure was incorporated in the monumental edifice presently occupying the site. Completed in 1902, the Renaissance-style building was designed by Richard Morris Hunt and his son, Richard Howland Hunt. Subsequent additions were designed by the well-known architectural firm of McKim, Mead and White.

Covering twenty acres of floor space, the Metropolitan Museum's 240 galleries include:

GROUND FLOOR	Costumes, ceramics, metalwork
MAIN FLOOR	Egyptian and Near Eastern art, Greek and Roman antiquities, medieval art, European furniture
SECOND FLOOR	American paintings and sculpture, Far Eastern art, prints and drawings, European paintings
AMERICAN WING	Three stories of American furnishings, decoration, and crafts

MORGAN LIBRARY *29 East 36th Street. Open Tuesday through Saturday 10:30 A.M. to 5 P.M. Closed August, holidays, and Saturdays during June and July. Free.* Erected in 1913, the main building of the Morgan Library—reflecting the architectural style of sixteenth-century Italy—was designed by the prestigious firm of McKim, Mead and White. The annex, completed in 1928, was based on the plans of architect Benjamin W. Morris.

The library contains the superb collection of industrialist J. Pierpont Morgan (1837–1913). Paintings, prints, sculpture, rare books, and manuscripts are on display. Masterpieces include *Portrait of a Moor* by Tintoretto, *Virgin and Saints Adoring the Child* by Perugino, *Martin Luther* by Lucas Cranach the Elder, and master drawings from the fourteenth to eighteenth centuries. Among the important books are the *Book of the Hours of Catherine of Cleves* and a Gutenberg Bible on vellum.

MUSEUM OF THE CITY OF NEW YORK *103rd Street and Fifth Avenue. Open Tuesday through Saturday 10 A.M. to 5 P.M., Sunday and holidays 1 P.M. to 5 P.M. Free.* The Museum of the City of New York, a Colonial-style brick building, was completed in 1932. Exhibits and dioramas trace the history of Manhattan from the time of the Indians to the present. Of special interest is the large model of Fort Amsterdam, from which visitors may view a circular panorama portraying New Amsterdam and its harbor in 1660.

MUSEUM OF MODERN ART *11 West 53rd Street. Open Monday through Saturday 11 A.M. to 6 P.M., Sunday noon to 6 P.M. Extended hours on Thursday to 9 P.M. Closed December 25. Adults $2.00, students $1.25, children 75¢.* This museum was founded in 1929 by several New Yorkers under the direction of Alfred H. Barr. The collection was temporarily located in an office building, but in 1939 this structure was erected as a permanent home for the masterpieces. Designed by Philip Goodwin and Edward Durrell Stone, it houses a distinguished collection of paintings and sculpture by twentieth-century artists. The various movements represented include Cubism, Expressionism, Abstractionism, Fauvism, and Futurism. Prints and photographs are displayed in galleries on the third floor. The sculpture garden, designed by Philip Johnson in 1951, exhibits works by Auguste Rodin, Henry Moore, David Smith, and Elie Nadelman.

The museum also owns one of the finest cinema libraries in the world. Selections of films are shown daily as part of several film series offered to the public.

NEW-YORK HISTORICAL SOCIETY   *170 Central Park West at 77 Street. Open Tuesday through Friday and Sunday from 1 P.M. to 5 P.M., Saturday 10 A.M. to 5 P.M. Closed major holidays. Free. Concerts November through May on Sunday at 2:30 P.M.*   Organized by John Pintard in the early nineteenth century, the New-York Historical Society has been housed in this building since 1908. The original section was designed by the architectural firm of York and Sawyer; the north and south wings were added in 1938 by Walker and Gillette.

The museum possesses a large collection of watercolors by naturalist John James Audubon, prints of eighteenth- and nineteenth-century New York, American-made silver, and a gallery (on the third floor) of American paintings of the Hudson River School.

The research library contains important documents relating to the history of New York.

NEW YORK STOCK EXCHANGE   *8 Broad Street between Wall Street and Exchange Place. Visitors' Gallery Tours are offered Monday through Friday 10 A.M. to 3:30 P.M. Closed holidays. Free.*   In 1792 a group of New York merchants and brokers formally established an organization to handle trading of securities. They transacted business under a tree located on Wall Street, and during inclement weather they gathered at a nearby coffeehouse. With the increase of business and the growth in the number of brokers, it was necessary to establish control over the burgeoning operations of the

Exchange. In 1817 a group of brokers, the New York Stock and Exchange Board, drafted a constitution that regulated procedures governing the buying and selling of stocks and bonds. A room was then rented at 400 Wall Street—the first quarters of the Exchange.

Today, the New York Stock Exchange is housed in an impressive structure with Corinthian columns and decorated pediment. The building, completed in 1903, was designed by George B. Post; the twenty-two-story addition was erected in 1923 under the supervision of the architectural firm of Trowbridge and Livingston.

The American Stock Exchange (formerly called the New York Curb Exchange) is located nearby at 86 Trinity Place. Designed by Starrett and Van Vleck, the building opened in 1921.

ROCKEFELLER CENTER *Between Fifth and Sixth Avenues and 48th and 52nd Streets. Tours leave at frequent intervals from 30 Rockefeller Plaza 9:30 A.M. to 5:30 P.M. Adults $2.15, youngsters (5–11) $1.35, and children (under 5) free.* Rockefeller Center is a complex of twenty-one buildings covering twenty-four acres. In 1928 John D. Rockefeller, Jr., leased the land here from Columbia University, which holds the renewal option until the year 2069. The main section of the complex was completed by the early 1940s. Architect Wallace K. Harrison supervised construction of the project.

The two most popular tourist attractions of Rockefeller Center are the RCA Building and the Radio City Music Hall. The 850-foot **RCA Building** houses the studios and offices of the National Broadcasting Company; the Rainbow Room, a nightclub on the sixty-fifth floor; and an observatory promenade on the seventieth floor. The lobby is decorated with large murals portraying the *Progress of Man* by Spanish artist José Maria Sert and sculptured panels by Gaston Lachaise.

The **Radio City Music Hall** (entrance at 50th Street and Sixth Avenue), which contains 6,200 seats, was opened in December 1932 under the direction of Samuel "Roxy" Rothafel. The foyer, fifty feet high, sweeps to a grand staircase leading to three mezzanines. Films and live entertainment are presented in the theater.

ST. PATRICK'S CATHEDRAL   *50th Street and Fifth Avenue. Open daily 6 A.M. to 8:30 P.M.*   Construction of St. Patrick's, which began in 1858, was not completed until 1886. This famous Gothic structure was designed by James Renwick (who also designed buildings for the Smithsonian complex in Washington, D.C.). The plan is in the shape of a Latin cross more than 300 feet long. The twin spires soar 330 feet.

The interior is awe-inspiring. Thirty-three pillars support the cross-ribbed arches, which rise 110 feet above the nave. Almost half the stained-glass windows are from the studios of Nicholas Lorin at Chartres and Henri Ely at Nantes. The reredos (screen behind the altar) is adorned with statues of the saints; the white marble pulpit was designed by Renwick; the fourteen Stations of the Cross—around the transept walls—are the work of Peter J. H. Cuypers.

The Lady Chapel and the adjoining smaller chapels, located behind the apse, were added by architect Charles T. Mathews in 1906.

STATUE OF LIBERTY   *Liberty Island. Open daily May through October 9 A.M. to 6 P.M.; the rest of the year, 9 A.M. to 5 P.M. Boats leave hourly, 9 A.M. to 4 P.M., from the Battery. Adults $1.25, children 50¢.*   A gift from the people of France, the Statue of Liberty commemorates the alliance of France and America during the Revolutionary War. In 1874 sculptor Frédéric-Auguste Bartholdi (1834–1904) began working on various designs for the statue. Eventually, the 152-foot-high figure was built of 300 copper plates applied to a framework designed by Gustav Eiffel (designer of the Eiffel Tower). The work was then dismantled and shipped to the United States in 1885. Through a campaign directed by Joseph Pulitzer of the *New York World*, funds were raised to build a pedestal on Bedloe's Island, the site chosen for the monument.

The dedication ceremonies took place on October 28, 1886. President Grover Cleveland delivered the principal address before a large crowd of enthusiastic citizens.

A bronze plaque at the entrance to the pedestal bears the lines written by the Jewish poet Emma Lazarus in 1883. Its stirring message speaks the promise of America: "Give me your tired, your poor, your huddled masses yearning to breathe free. . . ."

The **American Museum of Immigration,** which opened in 1966, is located at the base of the statue. It contains photographs, dioramas, and audio narratives describing the experiences of immigrants.

UNITED NATIONS HEADQUARTERS *First Avenue between 42nd and 48th Streets. Open daily 9 A.M. to 4:45 P.M. Closed Christmas and January 1. One-hour guided tours are conducted daily every 10 minutes from 9:15 A.M. to 4:45 P.M. Adults $2.00, students $1.50, children $1.00.* At a conference in San Francisco in 1945 delegates from fifty nations founded a world organization devoted to the preservation of peace—the United Nations. The charter adopted at the conference set forth their mutual goals and ideals: "To practice tolerance and live together in peace . . . , to unite our strength to maintain international peace and security, and to ensure . . . that armed force shall not be used, save in the common interest, and to employ international machinery for the promotion of the economic and social advancement of all peoples." Today 135 nations are members of the United Nations.

In 1946 John D. Rockefeller, Jr. offered $8 million

United Nations complex, New York City (NEW YORK CONVENTION AND VISITORS BUREAU)

for property along the East River to be used as a site for the organization's headquarters. The complex was designed by an international team of architects, headed by Wallace K. Harrison of the United States, and including Le Corbusier of France, Oscar Niemeyer of Brazil, and Sven Markelius of Sweden.

The 554-foot-high Secretariat Building dominates the group. (This office building is not usually open to the public.) The General Assembly Building—which is easily recognized by its low curved roof and central dome—includes the oval Assembly Hall in which the annual three-month sessions are held beginning in September.

The three-story Conference Building houses the meeting chambers of the Security Council, the Economic and Social Council, and the Trusteeship Council. An impressive stained-glass window by Marc Chagall, unveiled in 1964, was dedicated to Dag Hammarskjöld

(1905–1961), the Swedish-born Secretary-General of the United Nations from 1953 to 1961.

WASHINGTON SQUARE *West 4th Street at the foot of Fifth Avenue* Many buildings of **New York University** (founded in 1830) face Washington Square.

Judson Memorial Baptist Church, on the south side of the square, was designed by Stanford White in 1892. Its twelve stained-glass windows were executed by John La Farge. Washington Square North retains its row of early-nineteenth-century brick townhouses.

The marble **Washington Arch,** at the foot of Fifth Avenue, was designed by McKim, Mead and White. It was constructed in 1892 to replace a temporary wooden arch which had been erected near here in 1889 to commemorate the centennial of George Washington's inauguration as the first President of the United States. The sculpture on the right pier of the arch, *Washington in Peace*, was executed by Alexander Stirling Calder (the father of the contemporary artist Alexander Calder). The sculpture on the left, *Washington in War*, is the work of Herman A. MacNeil.

WATSON HOUSE *7 State Street. Now a Catholic shrine, the building is open daily 8 A.M. to 6 P.M.* When James Watson built his house here in 1793, State Street was one of the city's most fashionable residential areas. The house was enlarged in 1806, when the west wing was added. It is distinguished by oval windows in the side wall, Ionic columns, and a curved porch attributed to John McComb, Jr.

The building is now the Roman Catholic Shrine of St. Elizabeth Seton. Born in New York City, Mother Seton (1774–1821) was a champion of parochial education and founded the Daughters of Charity of St. Vincent de Paul. The first American-born saint of the Roman Catholic Church, she was canonized in 1975.

Watson House,
New York City
(ALPER)

WHITNEY MUSEUM *945 Madison Avenue, at 75th Street. Open Monday through Saturday 11 A.M. to 6 P.M. Sunday noon to 6 P.M. Extended hours on Tuesday until 10 P.M. Adults $1.00, children free if accompanied by an adult.* Designed by Marcel Breuer and Hamilton Smith in 1966, the Whitney Museum is devoted primarily to twentieth-century American art. Founded and endowed in 1929 by Gertrude Vanderbilt Whitney, the collection was first housed in a building on East 8th Street.

Important Colonial Houses in Adjacent Boroughs

Bronx

VAN CORTLANDT HOUSE *In Van Cortlandt Park, Broadway and 246th Street. Open Tuesday through Saturday 10 A.M. to 5 P.M., Sunday 2 P.M. to 5 P.M. Closed Thanksgiving, Christmas, January 1, and the month of February. Fee 50¢.* This fine house was built in 1748 by Frederick Van Cortlandt, son of Jacobus Van Cortlandt, mayor of New York from 1710 to 1719. General George Washington used this dwelling as his headquarters for several days in 1776 when his army was withdrawing from New York. Fine examples of eighteenth-century furniture, many once in the possession of the Van Cortlandt family, are on display here.

Brooklyn

LEFFERTS HOMESTEAD *In Prospect Park, Flatbush Avenue, just north of Empire Boulevard. Open Wednesday, Friday, Saturday, and Sunday 1 P.M. to 5 P.M. Closed holidays and the second Saturday of each month during the winter. Free.* This house was built in 1777 by Peter Lefferts to replace his previous home which had been burned by the British. Restored and converted into a museum in 1918, the building now houses a collection of Colonial furniture and Revolutionary War relics.

Richmond (Staten Island)

CONFERENCE HOUSE   *Foot of Hylan Boulevard, Tottenville. Open Tuesday through Sunday 1 P.M. to 5 P.M. in the summer; open Tuesday through Sunday 1 P.M. to 4 P.M. in the winter. Adults 25¢, children free.* This house was built in 1688 by Christopher Billopp. Here, on September 11, 1776, a peace conference was held between representatives of the Continental Congress —Benjamin Franklin, Edward Rutledge, and John Adams—and the commander of British naval forces, Admiral Richard Howe. (General William Howe, his brother, did not attend because of pressing military matters.) The conference failed to produce any tangible results.

RICHMONDTOWN RESTORATION   *302 Center Street, Richmondtown. Open July and August, Tuesday through Friday 10 A.M. to 5 P.M., Saturday 10 A.M. to 5 P.M., Sunday 2 P.M. to 5 P.M. Fee $1.00.* Once Staten Island's major Colonial settlement, Richmondtown now contains several seventeenth- and eighteenth-century houses that have been restored and opened to the public. Two houses are of particular interest: the **Voorlezer's House** (*c.* 1696), originally built by the local Dutch congregation for use as a meeting house and school; and the **Lake-Tysen House** (*c.* 1740), a fine example of a Colonial farmhouse.

White Plains

Revolutionary War History

On October 21, 1776—seven weeks after the start of their retreat from Manhattan—Patriot troops began arriving in White Plains. General Washington immediately ordered construction of a series of defenses. Although the army was large (nearly 20,000 men), it was composed of ill-equipped, poorly-trained raw recruits.

British and German forces (approximately 13,000), under the command of General William Howe, arrived in the area on the morning of October 28. They clashed first with several New England regiments under General Joseph Spencer and drove them back to Chatterton's Hill, located about a half-mile from the main American lines positioned in White Plains village. Washington then ordered additional units to reinforce Chatterton's Hill, and General Alexander McDougall took command. Meanwhile, British artillery fiercely pounded the site as their attack force assembled on the opposite side of the Bronx River. After the British and Hessians crossed the river, they marched to the foot of Chatterton's Hill, assumed battle formation, and began the charge. Twice they were repulsed, but a third attack by Colonel Johann Gottlieb Rall and his Hessians was successful. While some Patriot militiamen withdrew in good order, others fled in hysterical retreat. Several Massachusetts militia units fled northeast (along present-day Battle Avenue) to Purdy Hill, where Washington had been observing the action.

Once the strategic terrain of Chatterton's Hill was in

British hands, Howe decided not to pursue his victory that day, and the fighting was curtailed about 5 P.M.

That night Washington withdrew his troops northward to two hills (Miller Hill and Mount Misery) and reinforced defenses on nearby Hatfield Hill. When the British attempted to capture Hatfield Hill the next day, General William Heath's men drove them back. Afterward, the Redcoats marched toward Miller Hill, where Colonel John Glover's Patriot regiment overpowered them.

VISITORS' CENTER   Information about historical sites in White Plains may be obtained from the Chamber of Commerce, 170 East Post Road, phone 948–2110, or from the Westchester County Historical Society, 43 Read Avenue in Crestwood, phone 337–1753.

PUBLIC TRANSPORTATION   The White Plains Bus Company provides bus service throughout the area. For information and schedules, phone 949–2085.

TAXI SERVICE   Broadway Taxi, phone 948–3100; Red Top Cab, phone 949–0137; Bell Taxi, phone 949–4545; Airway Yellow Cab, phone 948–3341.

DRIVING TOUR

Start at Whitney Street and Wayne Avenue:

Chatterton's Hill

Purdy Homestead

Miller House

Miller Hill

Mount Misery

Site of Colonial Courthouse

End at South Broadway and Mitchell Place.

Howe decided to wait for additional troops before launching a final assault, which he planned for October 31, but a violent storm delayed the action and gave Washington time to withdraw his army to North Castle. Consequently, the British returned to New York City.

During the Battle of White Plains the Americans suffered approximately 200 casualties. (The reports vary widely.) British and Hessian casualties totaled nearly 300. Although the battle represented no success for Washington, he was able to prevent Howe from dealing a decisive blow to his army and bought time in which to increase his troops' effectiveness.

Colonial and Revolutionary War Sites

CHATTERTON'S HILL   *Follow Battle Avenue, then turn left onto Whitney Street. Proceed to Wayne Avenue.* This is the site of the major military action that occurred on October 28, 1776, when Patriot troops defending this hill were forced to retreat. A monument and an artillery piece (of the Spanish-American War) were placed here to honor the combatants.

MILLER HILL AND MOUNT MISERY   *To Miller Hill —follow Virginia Road to Heath Avenue. To Mount Misery—from Virginia Road turn onto Reservoir Road, then proceed to Rockledge Road, where you should turn left. Continue and turn right onto Grove Road and travel to Nethermont Avenue.* Both these areas have restored earthworks and narrative plaques detailing the battles that occurred here in October 1776. At Miller Hill the last shots in the campaign at White Plains were fired by the Patriots under Colonel John Glover. Although troops positioned at Mount Misery saw no action, they suffered from the cold fall weather (hence the name of the hill).

MILLER HOUSE   *Virginia Road (between Route 22 and the Bronx River Parkway) in North White Plains. Open Wednesday, Thursday, and Friday 10 A.M. to 4 P.M., Saturday and Sunday 1 P.M. to 4 P.M. Closed Christmas season, January, and February. Free.*   This one-and-a half-story frame house was built by the Miller family in 1738. At the time of the Battle of White Plains, when the widow of Elijah Miller was residing here, George Washington commandeered the building for use as his headquarters (after he left the Purdy house). From here he and General Charles Lee directed the strategy of the battle.

Today the restored house is sparsely furnished. The table and chairs used by Washington and his officers are on display in the **Council Room.** The **Kitchen** contains pots and utensils typical of the eighteenth century. Mannequins in Colonial costume are placed in various rooms throughout the house.

PURDY HOMESTEAD   *Follow Rockledge Avenue to the intersection of Spring Street. Open by appointment; phone 949–9530.*   Samuel Horton, a local farmer, built this house in 1721. Along with 132 acres of land, this dwelling was purchased by Jacob Purdy in the late 1730s. In 1776 George Washington used the Purdy house as his headquarters for several days prior to the arrival of the British into the area. (He then moved to the Miller house, from which he directed his troops in the Battle of White Plains.) It is believed that Washington again occupied this house for a short time during the summer of 1778.

Descendants of the Purdys resided here until 1866. A hundred years later the White Plains Monument Committee acquired and restored the property.

SITE OF COLONIAL COURTHOUSE   *South Broadway and Mitchell Place*   The Colonial courthouse of the village of White Plains once stood on the site now occupied by the Armory. It was here that the Provincial Congress of New York received the Declaration of Independence on July 9, 1776. Two days later the document was read in public from the courthouse steps by Judge John Thomas of Purchase. The building was burned by the British in late 1776.

A monument topped by an eagle commemorates the first public reading of the Declaration of Independence in Westchester County.

Important Colonial Houses

HATFIELD HOUSE   *Hall Avenue. Not open to the public.*   This dwelling appears almost as it did in Colonial times. During the Battle of White Plains General William Heath used it as his headquarters.

LYON HOUSE   *28 Colonial Road. Not open to the public.* This structure was built in the mid-eighteenth century and was the home of Revolutionary War Patriot, Captain Benjamin Lyon. In the twentieth century it was moved here from its original location opposite St. Agnes Hospital.

MILLER HOUSE   *379 Church Street. Not open to the public.*   This was the residence of Anthony Miller, who operated a mill on the Bronx River. Built in 1724, the structure was moved here from its original site on North Broadway.

New Jersey

Elizabeth

Revolutionary War History

Settled in 1664, Elizabeth (then called Elizabethtown) is the oldest English town in New Jersey. Philip Carteret was appointed royal governor of the colony in 1665 and established the capital here (where it remained until 1686). The first New Jersey Assembly convened at Elizabethtown on May 26, 1668, when representatives from the major settlements considered legislation for their mutual welfare and protection. Elizabethtown quickly grew into a bustling community and by the time of the American Revolution was a thriving commercial center.

In the early 1770s, before the formal break between the colonies and England, Elizabethtown Patriots prepared for the fighting which they knew was inevitable by organizing a Committee of Safety and by accumulating stores and materiel.

In January 1776 a British ship, the *Blue Mountain Valley*, was driven by a violent storm into Princess Bay near Sandy Hook, New Jersey, and Patriot General William Alexander (Lord Stirling) determined to seize the vessel and capture the supplies it carried. Meanwhile, the British prepared to send a ship from New York Harbor to aid the floundering *Blue Mountain Valley*. The Elizabethtown Committee of Safety called upon the local Patriots to join General Alexander's raiding party. Within three hours more than 100 young men of Elizabethtown rallied to the call, and under the command of Colonel Elias Dayton marched south to Amboy (near present-day Perth Amboy). Under the cover of night they joined Alexander's men and silently sailed toward the *Blue Mountain Valley*. Boarding the ship, they surprised the sailors and, meeting little resistance, took control. They brought their prize—with its supplies of gunpowder, coal, and food—back to Elizabethtown Point.

At the beginning of the Revolutionary War (four months after the adoption of the Declaration of Independence) the British took control of New York City. They then moved north, capturing Fort Washington (November 16, 1776), and crossed to the New Jersey side of the Hudson River, where they·drove the Americans out of Fort Lee (November 20, 1776). On November 29, 1776, the British entered Elizabethtown and seized large quantities of military supplies. The citizens were promised amnesty in return for an oath of allegiance to the Crown but most refused the offer. The town remained under British control until January 8, 1777, when the New Jersey Continentals under General William Maxwell—buoyed by Washington's recent victories at Trenton and Princeton—drove out the enemy.

In September 1777 General John Campbell led a force of British soldiers from Staten Island to Elizabethtown, where he initiated a large-scale foraging operation throughout the area. The troops commandeered more than 400 head of cattle and 300 sheep from the surrounding farms before they returned to their New York garrison.

In June 1780 the British began a last massive attempt to maintain control of northern New Jersey. On June 7 a large expedition disembarked at De Hart's Point near Elizabethtown. They advanced through the town to Connecticut Farms (present-day Union) where they confronted a Patriot force under Colonel Elias Dayton. The Patriots took the British by surprise and sent them back to New York City in retreat.

Six thousand British troops under General Wilhelm von Knyphausen made another attempt to subdue the area on June 23. They confronted 3,000 of Washington's Continental soldiers—who had just left the Morristown encampment—on a field of battle that extended between Elizabethtown and Springfield. The Americans skillfully delayed the advance of the enemy columns until the regiments of Generals Greene and Lee could concentrate their attack on the main force. After hours of fighting the British were forced to retreat, their ranks thinned by heavy casualties. Despite the Patriot success, Springfield, Connecticut Farms, and Elizabethtown were heavily pillaged.

After this campaign relative peace settled over Elizabethtown.

VISITORS' CENTER Information about Elizabeth may be obtained from the Chamber of Commerce, 135 Jefferson Avenue, phone 352–0900, or from the Elizabeth Historical Foundation, c/o Belcher-Ogden House, 1046 East Jersey Street, phone 232–7817. Serious students of history may wish to contact the Union County Cultural and Heritage Commission in Cranford, phone 272–3140.

PUBLIC TRANSPORTATION Local bus service is provided by Transport of New Jersey. For information and schedules, phone 353–6700.

TAXI SERVICE Elizabeth Taxi, phone 351–1245; Yellow Cab, phone 354–0350.

Colonial and Revolutionary War Sites

BELCHER-OGDEN HOUSE *1046 East Jersey Street. Open Wednesday 9:30 A.M. to noon from September through May, or by appointment. Free.* This dwelling was built in the late 1720s by stonemason John Ogden, the son of one of the founders of Elizabethtown.

From 1751 to 1757 Jonathan Belcher (1682–1757), royal governor of New Jersey, resided here. While royal governor of Massachusetts and New Hampshire (1730–1741), Belcher's sanctimonious manner and inefficiency had caused controversies that had led to his dismissal. By 1746, however, he had vindicated himself and was appointed to the governorship of New Jersey. The period of his administration was one of relative tranquility, for he had become more sensitive to the needs of the colonists. One of the milestones of his administration was the granting of a charter to the College of New Jersey (Princeton University). His library of 400 volumes bequeathed to the college formed the core of its collection.

During Belcher's occupancy of this house, the small western portion was added and the second floor of the eastern section was extended.

After Belcher's death in 1757, William Peartree Smith, the son of a former governor of Jamaica, moved into the house. In October 1778 his daughter Kate was married to Elisha Boudinot (brother of the distinguished Patriot Elias Boudinot) at a ceremony attended by George Washington, Alexander Hamilton, and the Marquis de Lafayette. On February 10, 1780, the house was ransacked by British soldiers who were searching for Smith's son-in-law.

From 1788 to 1797 this house was the residence of the Reverend David Austin, rector of the First Presbyterian Church. He gained notoriety by prophesying that the world would come to an end on May 15, 1796. His oratory was so persuasive that widespread panic ensued in northern New Jersey. After his prophecy failed to come true, the First Presbyterian Church decided that another pastor would better serve the needs of the congregation.

In 1797 Colonel Aaron Ogden (1756–1839), a successful lawyer and a direct descendant of John Ogden, became the owner of this house. During the Revolutionary War he had distinguished himself in combat at Brandywine and Monmouth and was wounded at Yorktown. He was elected governor of New Jersey in 1812. When Lafayette visited Elizabethtown in 1824, Ogden entertained his former comrade-in-arms here.

The Elizabeth Historical Foundation has restored the house and furnished it with eighteenth-century pieces similar to those described in the inventory of Royal Governor Belcher. The Ogden Room, however, contains furnishings of the early nineteenth century, including a Duncan Phyfe sofa and chairs.

BONNELL-BARBER HOUSE *1045 East Jersey Street. Since no consistent schedule of visiting hours is maintained, phone 355–1776 for information.* The oldest extant house in Elizabeth, this structure was built in the 1670s by Nathaniel Bonnell, one of the town's original associates (the early colonists who secured a patent from the royal governor to purchase land in the area).

The property passed to the Barber family in the mid-eighteenth century. Colonel Francis Barber drew up plans for the fortifications at the Battle of Saratoga and served valiantly at Yorktown. After the war Lafayette, as a token of his esteem, presented his sword to the New Jersey Patriot. Another member of the Barber family headed a school in old Elizabethtown (at present-day Caldwell Place and Broad Street). Alexander Hamilton and Aaron Burr were students at this academy.

The house is presently the headquarters of the state Society of the Sons of the American Revolution.

BOUDINOT MANSION (BOXWOOD HALL) *1073 Jersey Street. Open Tuesday through Saturday 10 A.M. to noon and 1 P.M. to 5 P.M., Sunday 2 P.M. to 5 P.M. Adults 25¢, children free.* This imposing Georgian mansion was built in 1750 by the mayor of Elizabethtown, Samuel Woodruff. It originally consisted of a central section with a gabled roof and two lateral wings.

In 1772 the property was purchased by Elias Boudinot (1740–1821), an important Revolutionary War Patriot. During the period leading to the independence of the American colonies, Boudinot served as a member of the New Jersey Committee of Correspondence (1774), as Commissary General of Prisoners (1777), and as a delegate to the Congress (1778–1784). Serving as president of Congress in 1782–1783, he signed the Treaty of Paris which concluded the hostilities with Great Britain and gave recognition to the new nation.

In 1772 fifteen-year-old Alexander Hamilton, who was attending school in Elizabethtown, resided with the Boudinot family.

When, on January 27, 1781, the Reverend James Caldwell, the town's fiercely outspoken Patriot preacher, was killed by a sentry of the Continental Army, his body was placed for viewing on the steps of this mansion. On that occasion Boudinot delivered a moving eulogy, proclaiming Caldwell a martyr for the cause of liberty. Boudinot and his wife Hannah (sister of Richard Stockton, a signer of the Declaration of Independence) legally adopted one of Parson Caldwell's sons.

On April 23, 1789, the Boudinots were hosts to President-elect George Washington. Boudinot and other distinguished Americans had been selected to accompany Washington from Philadelphia to New York City, where he was to take his oath of office as first President of the United States under the Constitution. The traveling party stopped here to rest and have lunch.

After Boudinot's appointment in 1795 as Superintendent of the U.S. Mint (in Philadelphia), he sold this house to Jonathan Dayton (1760–1824), a New Jersey legislator, a signer of the Federal Constitution, and a United States Senator. In 1824 Lafayette, who was touring the area, stayed overnight as Dayton's guest.

After Dayton's death the property passed through several hands until the late 1930s, when the Boxwood Hall

Memorial Association was organized to preserve and restore this historic site. Today it is administered by the New Jersey Bureau of Parks, Department of Environmental Protection.

The Boudinot Mansion is furnished with elegant pieces of the Colonial and Federal periods.

FIRST PRESBYTERIAN CHURCH *Broad Street and Caldwell Place* A wooden meeting house, a modest structure built in the 1660s, originally stood on this site. The congregation's first pastor was the Reverend Jeremiah Peck. In May 1668 the first New Jersey Assembly convened here.

In 1724, under the pastorate of Jonathan Dickinson (1688–1747), the meeting house was replaced by a large building with interior galleries and a steeple. The Reverend Dickinson, a man of extraordinary energy and intellect, instructed students for the ministry and later became the first president of the College of New Jersey (now Princeton). In November 1739 Dickinson's pulpit was shared by the eminent English evangelist George Whitefield, who attracted large crowds to the church.

The Reverend James Caldwell, who served as pastor here during the Revolutionary War, was such an ardent Patriot that armed sentries had to be stationed at the door during Sunday services to prevent disturbances by partisans of the British cause. In an attempt to silence him, a mob of Loyalists burned the church on the night of January 25, 1780.

During the Springfield and Elizabeth raids of June 1780 the Reverend Caldwell, Chaplain to the New Jersey Brigade, accompanied the troops. When a Rhode Island detachment exhausted their supply of cannon wadding (soft fibrous material used to retain the charge of powder), Caldwell ran into a nearby church and grabbed the Watts hymnals (a collection of hymns by the early-eighteenth-century clergyman Isaac Watts).

The Reverend James Caldwell shouting, "Give 'em Watts, boys!"
The Battle of Springfield, New Jersey, 1780. *Painting by John
Ward Dunsmore.* (SONS OF THE REVOLUTION—FRAUNCES TAVERN
MUSEUM, NEW YORK CITY)

As the soldiers stuffed pages of the books down the
muzzle of their cannon, Caldwell shrieked: "Give 'em
Watts, boys!"

Mysterious circumstances surrounded Caldwell's
death. On November 24, 1781, he was shot in Elizabethtown by a Patriot soldier, James Morgan, who was later
hanged for his heinous act. During Morgan's trial evidence was presented to indicate that he had been paid
secretly to kill the reverend, though he steadfastly denied
it to the end.

In 1789 a third church was erected to replace the
building which had been burned during the Revolutionary War. The structure remained essentially unchanged
until the mid-twentieth century, except for the rear
addition. A devastating fire ravaged the church in 1946;
it soon was restored following the plans of the 1789
design.

A chandelier presented by Elias Boudinot in 1800

still hangs inside this graceful, dignified church. The bell, cast in England in 1822, still calls the parishioners to worship.

Among the distinguished citizens buried in the churchyard are Aaron Ogden, governor of New Jersey in 1812 and 1813; Elias Dayton, a member of the New Jersey Committee of Safety and later a general in the Continental Army; and the Reverend Jonathan Dickinson, minister here from 1709 to 1747 and first president of the College of New Jersey.

MILITIAMAN STATUE *Union Square (Elizabeth and First Avenues)* This statue, representing a Patriot militiaman with his musket and powder horn, was sculpted after a model by Carl Conrads. It was erected by the state and unveiled in June 1905 to commemorate the 125th anniversary of the Battle of Elizabethtown. The monument honors the twelve heroic militiamen who, taking cover in the thicket on this site, turned back a column of British and Hessian soldiers. The first Patriot volley took the enemy by surprise, killing the commanding officer and causing the column to withdraw in confusion.

ST. JOHN'S EPISCOPAL CHURCH *Broad Street near Caldwell Place* In 1703 this congregation began to meet at the home of Richard Townley. Funds were soon raised to build a church, which was completed in 1706, and the spiritual leadership of the congregation was assumed by the Reverend John Brooke. In 1762 St. John's was incorporated under a royal charter from King George III.

Although some of the parishioners held Loyalist sympathies during the Revolutionary War, most of the members supported the Patriot fight for independence, causing the pro-British minister, the Reverend Thomas Bradbury Chandler, to flee to England.

In June 1780, when British units occupied the town, foot soldiers were quartered in St. John's. They destroyed the pews and defaced the interior. They also tore out the organ's metal pipes, melting them for bullets. Subsequently, the church was repaired and enlarged.

In 1859 the building, which had fallen into disrepair, was demolished and a new structure of Victorian Gothic design was erected on the site.

Recommended Side Trip

Wayne

Approaching Wayne from the south on the Garden State Parkway, take Exit 153B. (To get to the Parkway from Elizabeth, follow Route 1/9 North, then Route 22 West.) Travel along Route 46, exit at Preakness, and pass the Totowa Airport. When you come to a fork, bear right and proceed about ½ mile on Totowa Road to the Dey Mansion.

DEY MANSION   *199 Totowa Road in Preakness Valley Park. Open Tuesday, Wednesday, and Friday 1 P.M. to 5 P.M., Saturday and Sunday 10 A.M. to noon and 1 P.M. to 5 P.M. Adults 50¢, children free.*   In the 1740s Dirk Jansen Dey, a Dutch émigré, purchased 600 acres of land here for £120 and erected on the property an eight-room Georgian house. His son Theunis inherited the estate, which he named "Bloomsbury." Theunis Dey, his wife Hester Schuyler (of the influential Albany family), and various of their ten children lived in the house for nearly five decades.

Theunis Dey served as a member of the county Board of Chosen Freeholders and later as a commissioner for the Assembly and Council of New Jersey. During the Revolutionary War he became colonel of the County Militia and was given by General Washington the responsibility of organizing the defense of the territory on the western side of the Hudson River.

In July 1780 Washington decided to establish an encampment in this strategic area and selected the Dey Mansion as his headquarters. He and his staff occupied four rooms on the eastern side of the house. Here he held strategy sessions with military figures such as Generals Arthur St. Clair, William Alexander (Lord Stirling), Lafayette, Nathanael Greene, and Anthony Wayne. A committee of Congress visited the Commander-in-Chief here to discuss the disposition of units of the Continental Army.

After an inconclusive campaign in the Hudson Highlands (in New York State) in the fall of 1780, Washington again encamped his troops in the lower Preakness area of New Jersey, and he returned to the Dey Mansion during October and November 1780. The Marquis de Chastellux, French army commander and cousin of Lafayette, who visited here recorded in a diary his respect for the general and his appreciation of the warm hospitality afforded him.

The Dey Mansion was restored in 1934. Some of the original floors, paneling, and fireplaces have been preserved. **Washington's Office,** the southeast room on the first floor, is furnished with an eighteenth-century tall-case clock, a round table, and rare Windsor chairs upholstered in leather. The **Living Room** is distinguished by a handsome William and Mary highboy, a Dutch-back armchair, an unusually fine gate-leg table, and porcelain garniture. In **Washington's Bedroom** on the

second floor the four-poster canopied bed is compli-
mented by a mahogany chest of drawers with ogee
bracket feet and a mirror with high fretwork crest. A
locally crafted side chair in the Queen Anne style that
belonged to the Dey family and a goblet believed to have
been used by Lafayette are on display in the **Guest
Room.**

VAN RIPER–HOPPER HOUSE   *533 Berdan Avenue.
Open Tuesday, Friday, Saturday, and Sunday 1 P.M.
to 5 P.M. Closed two weeks in July; also closed Thanksgiving, Christmas, and January 1. Free.*   This one-and-
a-half-story Dutch farmhouse was built by Uriah Richard
Van Riper at the time of his marriage to Maria ("Polly")
Berdan in 1786. The Van Ripers, who owned 145 acres,
were prosperous farmers. In 1872 the property passed to
Andrew Hopper, who was active in local political affairs.
It was probably during Hopper's occupancy that the
front porch and dormers were added.

The restoration and furnishing of the dwelling were
carried out under the direction of Wayne Township. The
Van Riper–Hopper House now serves as the headquarters of the Wayne Historical Commission.

Morristown

Revolutionary War History

After Washington's victories at Trenton (December 26, 1776) and at Princeton (January 3, 1777), the Commander-in-Chief marched his army to Morristown. Here, during the winter months, future strategies would be planned and the preparedness and strength of the troops would be increased.

The Morristown area was ideally suited for Washington's purposes. It provided a good strategic position from which to send men forth to counter any British movements; several iron mines and foundries were located in the vicinity and could supply necessary materiel; and the terrain provided natural protection—the Watchung Mountains offering a buffer to the west and the swamps acting as a barrier to the east.

The soldiers who arrived here on January 6, 1777, were a sorry lot. Their clothes were threadbare, they were weak and wounded from battle, and their provisions were low. Through the bitter winter their suffering increased; as supplies dwindled, the men were close to starvation. Finally in March a French ship arrived bearing provisions, clothing, and munitions which sustained the Patriots until spring.

But the worst was still to be endured: an outbreak of smallpox raged through the camp. The only hope of avoiding a high death rate was to immunize the troops by inducing a mild form of the disease. Washington ordered Dr. Nathaniel Bond to oversee the inoculation of the soldiers and inhabitants in northern New Jersey. The massive project was carried out, but not before the disease had afflicted many soldiers and citizens, who were placed in isolation hospitals in the Presbyterian and Baptist churches at Morristown and in the Presbyterian church in nearby Hanover. The death toll was great and even those who survived the milder forms of the disease were scarred for life.

Military activity during the winter of 1777 was limited to driving back British patrols that ventured from their garrison in New Brunswick to forage in the area. From his headquarters in the Arnold Tavern in Morristown, General Washington held strategy sessions with his officers and laid plans for attracting and training additional infantry. By the end of the encampment in May approximately 5,000 Patriots had journeyed here to enlist. News of British troop movements preparing for a possible attack on Philadelphia provided the impetus for Washington to break camp on May 28, 1777.

Two and a half years later, in December 1779, the Continental Army again established winter quarters at Morristown. The soldiers built a city of more than 1,000 log cabins at Jockey Hollow, four miles from the center of town.

Soon the weather turned bitter cold and blizzards blanketed the campsite with four to six feet of snow. James Thacher, a surgeon in the army, reported that many soldiers were "buried in the snow like sheep." Others, he wrote, were "destitute of blankets and some of them . . . actually barefooted and almost naked."

Washington, from his headquarters at the Ford Mansion, issued an appeal to the magistrates of local communities to urge civilians to send provisions for his desperate, starving men. The citizens failed to respond and it became necessary to confiscate stores with a promise of payment at some indefinite future time.

Only one major military action occurred during the second Morristown encampment. On January 14–15, 1780, General William Alexander (Lord Stirling) organized

2,500 men in a surprise attack on Staten Island. Five hundred sleighs carried the soldiers across the frozen Hudson River from Elizabethtown Point to Staten Island. The British, who had learned from informants of the attack, had withdrawn into the protection of their garrison. Seventeen prisoners were captured with a small amount of supplies, but the major objective of surprising the British had proved a failure.

When British troops began raiding the Elizabeth-Springfield area in June 1780, Washington ordered his troops to leave the Morristown encampment to counter the growing threat.

The following winter—while a large part of Washington's army was garrisoned in upper New York State—the Pennsylvania Line (consisting of ten infantry regiments and one of artillery) occupied the log huts at Jockey Hollow. The bitter winter and the long duration of the war demoralized the soldiers. They grumbled about the poor quality of their food and the lack of sufficient clothing, and they began to resent the terms of their enlistment. The men contended that their enlistments should have expired after three years but that they were forced to remain in service.

On the evening of January 1, 1781, the Pennsylvania Line seized the artillery and ammunition and started to march to Philadelphia to press their claims on Congress. Their commander, General Anthony Wayne, vainly attempted to persuade the soldiers to lay down their arms and turn back.

Two days later, on January 3, the mutineers reached Princeton and sent a list of their grievances to the Congress. Fearing that unrest might spread, the delegates sent a committee from Philadelphia to negotiate with the soldiers. While the negotiations were in progress, the British sent agents to induce the mutineers to join their side, but these overtures were rebuffed.

An agreement between Congress and the soldiers was concluded on January 7 with a promise that new uniforms would be issued and enlistments would be terminated at the end of three years. This permitted many of the men to return to their homes in time for the spring planting.

VISITORS' CENTER Information, pamphlets, and books are available from the Morristown Historical Museum, 230 Morris Street, phone 539–2016. Also contact the Morris County Historical Society, 68 Morris Street, phone 267–3465, or the Chamber of Commerce, 330 South Street, phone 539–3882.

PUBLIC TRANSPORTATION Local bus service is provided by Transport of New Jersey. For information and schedules, phone 277–0180.

TAXI SERVICE Morristown Taxi, phone 539–2555; Downey Taxi, phone 539–2573; Patsy Taxi, phone 538–2492.

WALKING AND DRIVING TOURS Visitors should first stop at the Ford Mansion and see the sights in the vicinity. Afterward, a drive through Morristown may prove interesting before continuing to Fort Nonsense. Then proceed southwest along Western Avenue or Mt. Kemble Avenue to the Jockey Hollow area. (P indicates a historic Colonial house which is now a *private residence*.)

Walking **Tour A**	**Driving** **Tour B**
Ford Mansion Area, Morris Street:	Downtown Morristown:
Ford Mansion	Schuyler-Hamilton House
Morristown Historical Museum	Condict House (P)
	Mills House (P)
Washington Statue	Wood House (P)
Washington's Life Guard Camp	Stiles House (P)

**Driving
Tour C**

Jockey Hollow Route:

Fort Nonsense

Kemble Estate (P)

Van Doren Barn (P)

Wick House

Jockey Hollow Area

Colonial and Revolutionary War Sites

**FORD MANSION (WASHINGTON'S HEADQUAR-
TERS)** *230 Morris Street. If you enter Morristown on
Route 202 South, continue along Speedwell Avenue
until you come to a fork in the road. Bear left onto Spring
Street and travel three blocks to Morris Street. Turn left
and proceed several blocks on Morris Street until you see
the Ford Mansion (on the left-hand side of the road).
Open daily 10 A.M. to 5 P.M. Closed Thanksgiving, De-
cember 25, and January 1. Adults 50¢, children free.*
This mansion was the residence of Colonel Jacob Ford,
Jr. (1738–1777), a wealthy iron manufacturer and
powder mill owner. At his iron works, located on the
Wippany River near Morristown, munitions were manu-
factured for the Continental Army. While serving as
area commander of the Eastern Battalion, Morris County
Militia, in the fall of 1776, Ford contracted pneumonia.
He was returned to his home, where he died on January

11, 1777. His wife Theodosia (daughter of Dr. Timothy Johnes, pastor of the local Presbyterian church) and their five children continued to reside here. One of the sons, Timothy, was wounded in battle on June 7, 1780.

The exterior of this Georgian structure (built between 1772 and 1774) is characterized by fine ornamental detail: a denticulated cornice, a second-story Palladian window, and small rectangular windows (near the entrance) flanked by pilasters. It is no surprise, then, that George Washington chose this imposing dwelling for his headquarters during the winter encampment of 1779–1780. In addition to the Commander-in-Chief and his wife Martha, several servants and aides-de-camp took up residence here. At that time Mrs. Ford and her children occupied the two rooms east of the first-floor hallway.

Many of the period pieces displayed in this mansion belonged to the Ford family. Several items in the **Living Room/Dining Room**—the mahogany Chippendale secretary, the Queen Anne side chair, and the dropleaf table—may have been used by Washington. He entertained many distinguished guests here, including the Minister of France, Chevalier de la Luzerne, and a representative of the Spanish government, Don Juan de Miralles.

Washington's Office—now furnished with a desk and Windsor chairs—served as the center for local military operations. Here reports were drawn up and battle strategies were discussed. Later Washington ordered a separate office built for him on the estate grounds, and this room was then used as an office by his aides.

The **Kitchen** contains furniture and utensils typical of the period. In the adjoining **Pantry** dairy products were prepared and provisions were stored. Washington, finding the kitchen area inadequate for the large number of people who had taken up residence here, had a kitchen outbuilding constructed to the east of the house.

In one corner of the **Aides' Room** stands a Revolutionary War field bed; it is original except for the center underbrace and the tester. This long, narrow room also contains chests of drawers, chairs, and a desk—pieces similar to those used by Washington's aides-de-camp during the winter of 1779–1780. Three of the general's highly respected staff assistants were Robert Hansen Harrison, Tench Tilghman, and Alexander Hamilton. Hamilton, a lieutenant colonel, held a position of great responsibility, drafting secret military documents and preparing reports to the Congress. He met his future wife, Elizabeth Schuyler (daughter of the powerful General Philip Schuyler), at the Ford Mansion when she came to pay her respects to Washington while visiting her relatives, Dr. and Mrs. John Cochran, who were living nearby.

The second-floor **Guest Bedroom** is designated the "Lafayette Room," honoring the young Frenchman who fought with the Patriot armies. On May 10, 1780, Lafayette returned to General Washington from France bearing a message from King Louis XVI that the French government had agreed to send additional military assistance to the Americans. Lafayette remained here several

Ford Mansion, Morristown (ALPER)

weeks, except for a brief journey to deliver important documents to the Congress. The room contains simple but dignified furnishings: a four-poster canopied bed, a highboy, and a chest of drawers.

The other two **Bedrooms** on this floor were used by George and Martha Washington. Items believed to have been here during the 1779–1780 occupancy include the Windsor chairs, the campaign chest, the Chippendale-style dressing table, and the mahogany highboy.

During the late nineteenth century the Ford Mansion was restored through the efforts of the Washington Association of New Jersey. Since 1933 the property has been administered by the United States National Park Service.

"**FORT NONSENSE**"   *From downtown Morristown follow Western Avenue, turn left onto Ann Street, then make a right turn onto the road leading to the hill.*   The origin of the fort's name has never been officially determined. According to tradition, it is derived from the fact that Washington, in order to keep his troops occupied, initiated the project as "nonsense" work. Historians, however, have pointed out the strategic value of the fort as a stronghold where a small detachment of soldiers could guard supplies while the main army was engaged in military maneuvers.

Plans are under way to reconstruct the original fortification.

JOCKEY HOLLOW NATIONAL MILITARY PARK *From the Morristown Green (the town square) you can take either of two routes to Jockey Hollow: follow Route 202 South (Mt. Kemble Avenue) to Tempe Wick Road, then turn right; or proceed on Washington Street for a short distance, then turn left onto Western Avenue (which becomes Jockey Hollow Road) and continue for about 3 miles until you arrive at the parking lot near Grand Parade Road in Jockey Hollow. Open daily until 6 P.M. during the winter and until 8 P.M. during* *the summer. Closed Thanksgiving, December 25, and January 1. Free.* This National Historical Park, established by an Act of Congress in 1933, is administered by the federal government. The main points of interest are described below.

Army Hospital This log structure with flanking wings is a replica of the Colonial military hospital that was located on Basking Ridge about eight miles away. The reconstruction was based on the original architectural plans of Dr. James Tilton, hospital physician in 1779–1780.

Cots were arranged in rows on the dirt floor so that the patients could lie with their feet toward the large, central fireplace. The treatment of the wounded was primitive by today's standards. Amputations were performed without anesthesia; only laudanum (a tincture of opium) or gin were used to ease the pain.

Soldiers' Huts On the west slope of Sugarloaf Hill (overlooking the army hospital) stand five reconstructed huts similar to those used by the soldiers encamped here in 1779–1780. Each of these crude log structures, with double- and triple-tiered bunks, could hold approximately twelve men. The standard floor plan of a soldier's hut was fourteen feet by fifteen feet with a fireplace at one end.

Officers' cabins were larger. Construction was of notched logs with clay to seal the chinks in the walls. Boards or hand-split shingles were used to cover the peaked roofs. When spring arrived, openings were cut in the walls to serve as windows.

Parade Ground The level ground below Sugarloaf Hill was used as a parade ground where Continental soldiers assembled for inspection and executed military drills.

MORRISTOWN HISTORICAL MUSEUM *Behind the Ford Mansion, 230 Morris Street. Open daily 10 A.M. to 5 P.M. Closed Thanksgiving, December 25, and Janu-*

Soldiers' huts, Jockey Hollow National Military Park (ALPER)

ary 1. Free when admission fee is paid at the Ford Mansion. Built in 1935, this museum displays a fine collection of relics of the Revolutionary War period. In the **American Revolution Room** (to the right at the end of the first floor hall) visitors can view swords, powder horns, wood canteens, and several types of muskets (including the French Charleville Musket and the British "Brown Bess"). Rooms on the second floor exhibit Colonial costumes, pewter objects, and early maps of America. One case is filled with articles owned by George and Martha Washington—a tea caddy, silver spoons, wine glasses, porcelain bowls, a Masonic scarf, and a satin slipper.

SCHUYLER-HAMILTON HOUSE *5 Olyphant Place. Open Tuesday and Saturday 2 P.M. to 5 P.M., or by appointment. Free.* During the Revolutionary War this two-story dwelling was owned by Jabez Campfield, a prominent Morristown physician. At the time of the 1779–1780 encampment he made the house available as a residence for Dr. John Cochran, Chief Physician and Surgeon General of the Continental Army, and his wife (the sister of General Philip Schuyler). During the winter encampment Mrs. Cochran was visited by her niece Elizabeth Schuyler, who attracted the attention of one of Washington's aides-de-camp, Alexander Hamilton. That spring, when General Schuyler came to Morristown to confer with George Washington, he gave his permission for the betrothal of his daughter to Hamilton, and the couple married soon afterward.

The house—administered by the Daughters of the American Revolution since 1923—has been refurbished and furnished with typical Colonial pieces. The **Parlor** contains a painting of Dr. Jabez Campfield, the Campfield Bible, a New Jersey tall-case clock, and an eighteenth-century desk. The **Master Bedroom,** which is dominated by a Sheraton-style field bed, displays mementos of Elizabeth Schuyler Hamilton.

SITE OF WASHINGTON'S LIFE GUARD CAMP. *Opposite the Ford Mansion, 230 Morris Street*   On this site fourteen large cabins were built to house the 250 men who served as Washington's private guard. The soldiers, under the command of Major Caleb Gibbs, were distinguished by their blue coats, red vests, and black tricorn hats. They were under orders to protect Washington's headquarters from any disturbances or enemy fire by surrounding the house and barricading the doors.

One evening Martha Washington, who had retired to bed early, was jolted out of her sleep by a burst of gunfire, and a moment later she was astonished to see a detail of guards rushing into her bedroom to assume positions of readiness at the windows. The alert was suspended shortly afterward when it was discovered that the disturbance had been caused by the overzealous reaction of a sentinel to one of Washington's aides who had returned from courting a local maiden and had forgotten that evening's password.

WASHINGTON STATUE   *Opposite the Ford Mansion, 230 Morris Street*   This bronze equestrian statue of George Washington was unveiled on July 16, 1931. After New Jersey Supreme Court Justice Charles W. Parker addressed the large crowd that had assembled for the occasion, Miss E. Mabel Clark presented the statue to Mayor Clyde Potts, who accepted on behalf of the citizens of Morristown. As the American Legion Drum Corps played the "Call to the Colors," the bunting which draped the statue was pulled away, revealing the impressive work of sculptor Frederick Roth.

WICK HOUSE   *Near the southwestern edge of Jockey Hollow, just west of Tempe Wick Road and Jockey Hollow Road. Open daily 1 P.M. to 5 P.M. Closed Thanksgiving, December 25, and January 1. Free.*   This small, shingled house was built in the early 1750s by Henry Wick, a farmer who had settled in the area in 1748 after acquiring a tract of 1,100 acres.

When the Pennsylvania Division encamped at Jockey Hollow during 1779–1780, the commander, Major General Arthur St. Clair, selected this house as his temporary headquarters. (At that time Wick was away from home serving with a company of Morris County cavalry.) Washington, Wayne, Stark, and Greene frequently consulted here with St. Clair.

The dwelling has been restored and furnished with period pieces based on the inventory of Henry and Mary Wick. The wicker-seat chairs and corner cupboard in the **Dining Room,** the small bed and wooden trunk in one of the **Bedrooms,** and the wooden bowls and utensils in the **Kitchen** all reflect a modest but comfortable lifestyle. The desk in the **Dining Room** is believed to have been here during the Revolution. The rooms have wood-sheathed walls, exposed ceiling beams, and fireplaces with flues entering a central chimney.

During the mutiny of the Pennsylvania Line (January 1781), Wick's daughter Tempe (Temperance) is said to have hidden her favorite horse in a bedroom for several days to prevent the animal's being seized by marauding soldiers.

Important Colonial Houses

BLACHLEY HOUSE *Hardscrabble Road and Corey Lane. Not open to the public.* Although structurally altered, this fine house retains its original paneling and woodwork. Constructed in the 1750s, it was the residence of Ebenezer Blachley, a physician. He was the uncle of Tempe Wick, remembered locally for hiding her horse from scavenging soldiers during the mutiny of the Pennsylvania Line.

CONDICT HOUSE *Cutler Street near Speedwell Avenue. Not open to the public.* The original section of this house was built in 1799 by Silas Condict, a framer of New Jersey's first constitution (1776) and a member of Congress (1781–1783).

DRAKE HOUSE *Mendham Road near Cold Hill Road. Not open to the public.* This structure (*c.* 1750) was the residence and workshop of Jacob Drake, who is said to have built the coffins for the soldiers who died during the terrible winter at Jockey Hollow.

KEMBLE ESTATE *Tempe Wick Road near Route 202. Not open to the public.* Loyalist Peter Kemble, president of the Royal Council of New Jersey, built this mansion in the mid-eighteenth century. General William Smallwood, commander of the Maryland regiments, commandeered it for his headquarters during the Jockey Hollow encampment of 1779–1780. The following year the house was occupied by General Anthony Wayne, who unsuccessfully attempted to disband the mutinous soldiers of the Pennsylvania Line.

MILLS HOUSE   *27 Mills Street. Not open to the public.* This dwelling was constructed in the early 1740s by the two Mills brothers—Timothy, a surveyor, and Samuel, a tax collector.

STILES HOUSE   *77 Glenbrook Road. Not open to the public.*   The earliest section of this house is believed to have been built in the 1750s. The property was owned by Ebenezer Stiles, who operated an iron forge in the area.

VAN DOREN BARN AND MILL   *Childs Road and Route 202. Not open to the public.*   The barn (built about 1768) that once stood on this site has been moved across the road. The stone gristmill still standing here ground the grain used by the troops at Jockey Hollow.

WOOD HOUSE   *83 South Street. Not open to the public.* The original dwelling dates from 1763 and served as the farmhouse of Christopher Wood. The first floor is presently occupied by a bookstore.

Non-Revolutionary Sites of Interest

SPEEDWELL HISTORIC VILLAGE   *333 Speedwell Avenue (Route 202), several miles outside Morristown. Open April 1 to November 1 Tuesday and Thursday 10 A.M. to 4 P.M., Sunday 2 P.M. to 5 P.M. Adults 50¢, youngsters (12–18) 25¢, children free.*   The buildings of this restoration are associated with the Vail family, owners from 1814 to 1873 of the Speedwell Iron Works, once located near this site. Here were cast the boilers and engines for the *Savannah*, the first steamship to cross the Atlantic (1819).

Speedwell Village was organized in 1966 as a non-profit educational corporation to preserve the historic structures described below. They have been renovated and are now open to the public. The site is listed in the National Registry of Historic Sites.

Carriage House   Gears and patterns from the Iron Works are on display here.

Estey House   Dating from 1786, this house was built by Moses Estey at the corner of Water and Spring Streets in Morristown to replace an earlier structure destroyed by fire. The building is now undergoing restoration.

Factory and Gristmill   This mill formerly served the Vail family and their neighbors. In a room on the second floor of the adjoining factory Samuel F. B. Morse (1791–1872) developed the telegraph (January 1838). Alfred Vail (1807–1859), the son of Judge Stephen Vail, provided financial assistance and helped in the formulation of Morse's dot-and-dash code. Replicas of early telegraphic equipment are on exhibit.

Vail Homestead   Built in the late eighteenth century, this house was the residence of Judge Stephen Vail and his family. Their personal belongings are among the interesting mementos here.

Recommended Side Trip

Stanhope

WATERLOO VILLAGE RESTORATION   *Follow Route 202 North out of Morristown, then pick up Route 53 North to Interstate 80. Travel west along Route 80 until* *you come to the Stanhope/Route 206 Exit. Take the exit and proceed north, watching for the Waterloo Village signs. Approaching the Restoration, you will have to turn off Route 206 onto a narrow road, then proceed 2.3 miles to the site. Open Tuesday through Sunday 10 A.M. to 6 P.M. Adults $2.50, children $1.50.* Settled by the English in the 1740s, this quiet community began to prosper in 1763 when an iron forge (Andover Forge) was built here. Since the owners, Allen and Turner, were Loyalists, the Colonial government confiscated their property during the Revolutionary War. Weapons and ammunition for the Continental troops were then produced here in large quantities. During the New Jersey campaign of 1776–1777 many wounded Continental soldiers were left in this village to recuperate.

During the war James Moody, a Loyalist living in the area, attempted to recruit men for the British army, but few from Waterloo Village volunteered. Not only do legends damn him for being a Loyalist, but they attribute to him the suicide of a local maiden with whose affections he toyed. It is said that Moody's ghost still roams the countryside in search of fresh recruits and comely maidens!

When the Morris Canal became operational in the 1830s, Waterloo became an important depot along the waterway and the village enjoyed increased prosperity. In the early twentieth century, when the canal closed, most of the townspeople moved away and the abandoned buildings fell into disrepair.

Recently Waterloo Village was purchased by Percival Leach and Louis Gualandi, who have restored the structures and furnished them with appropriate antiques.

The cluster of buildings here includes an inn, church, gristmill, general store, blacksmith shop, and several large houses. Three eighteenth-century dwellings are of special interest: the **Canal House** (*c.* 1760), which provided quarters for workmen of the Andover Forge and later was used by operators of the canal locks; the **Homestead** (original section 1750), a barn that was converted into a two-story house; and the **Old Stagecoach Inn** (*c.* 1740, with additions in the 1830s), which served as a stage-coach stop and inn.

On weekends Colonial crafts are demonstrated, and in the summer a concert series is scheduled.

Somerville

Revolutionary War History

In the spring of 1777 New York City was occupied by the British troops of General William Howe (who had taken control of the city in the fall of 1776). The capture of Philadelphia, seat of the Continental Congress, was a major objective in the suppression of the colonies. In late May 1777 George Washington moved his army from Morristown to the Somerville area in readiness to intercept Howe's forces, should they begin to advance across New Jersey toward Philadelphia. The Continental Army encamped at Middlebrook, on the north edge of Bound Brook, just east of Somerville.

By mid-June Howe had transported 18,000 men into New Jersey and had deployed them between New Brunswick and Somerset. On June 24 Washington sent General Nathanael Greene to attack the British rear guard and ordered the units under General William Alexander (Lord Stirling) to take up positions near Metuchen. Two days later Howe, organizing his soldiers into two columns, attempted to encircle Alexander's men and to seize the passes leading to the Middlebrook encampment, thereby cutting off Washington's path of return. But the gunfire between Alexander's soldiers and the British served as a warning to Washington, who quickly retreated to safety. Realizing that Washington held the strategic advantage, Howe abandoned his campaign and marched his troops to Amboy (present-day Perth Amboy), from which point they sailed to Staten Island.

From November 1778 to June 1779 the Continental

Army again took up quarters at the Middlebrook encampment. Almost 8,000 soldiers set to work building a city of log huts surrounded by redoubts. Included in the garrison were a powder magazine, a horse corral, and a hospital. General Washington established his headquarters at the Wallace house in Somerville.

To provide speedy warning of a threat to the encampment, Washington ordered beacons built on the highest hills of the area. These log beacons—which were constructed in the form of pyramids, each sixteen feet square at the base and twenty feet high—were filled with brush that could quickly be set afire.

The winter encampment was established not only for the purpose of defending a strategic position, but also for training and refitting the soldiers for future campaigns. During the winter of 1778–1779, under the direction of Baron von Steuben, Washington's volunteer army of farmers and tradesmen was transformed into an effective fighting force.

VISITORS' CENTER Information about Somerville may be obtained from the Historic Sites Center, c/o the Wallace House, 38 Washington Place, phone 725–1015, or from the Chamber of Commerce, 31 North Bridge Street, phone 725–1552.

PUBLIC TRANSPORTATION Bus service in the area is provided by Transport of New Jersey. For information and schedules, phone 725–2737.

TAXI SERVICE Allstate Skyview Taxi, phone 725–2233; Jim's Taxi, phone 722–7422.

Colonial and Revolutionary War Sites

OLD DUTCH PARSONAGE 65 *Washington Place. From Route 22 take Bridge Street (or a parallel street) into Somerville. Turn right onto Main Street and proceed until you come to a fork in the road. Bear left at this fork, and travel about one block. Just after going under a railroad bridge, make a sharp left onto Middagh Street, go one block, then turn left onto Washington Place. The Old Dutch Parsonage is on the right side of the street; the Wallace House is half a block farther down on Washington Place. Open Tuesday through Saturday 10 A.M. to noon and 1 P.M. to 5 P.M., Sunday 2 P.M. to 5 P.M. Closed Thanksgiving, December 25, and January 1. Adults 25¢, children free.* This dwelling was built in 1751 by the Reverend John Frelinghuysen, who came to northern New Jersey from Amsterdam, Holland, to serve as minister to a group of citizens of the Dutch Reformed faith. He and his wife (Dinah Van Bergh) and their son (Frederick) resided here. In the large room on the second floor Frelinghuysen tutored divinity students. The school he established in the parsonage evolved into Rutgers Theological Seminary.

After his death in 1754 his widow married one of the theological students, Jacob Rutzen Hardenbergh. Hardenbergh became minister to the congregation (the first one licensed to preach without studying in Holland) and held classes at the parsonage. In 1785 he was chosen to serve as president of the newly founded Queen's College (Rutgers University).

Frederick Frelinghuysen (1753–1804) was educated

Old Dutch Parsonage, Somerville (ALPER)

at Princeton and admitted to the New Jersey Bar in 1774. Early in the Revolutionary War he organized an artillery company which was active in the New Jersey campaign. Frelinghuysen served in the Continental Congress from 1777 to 1779 but resigned to become a colonel in command of the First Somerset Regiment. After the war he was elected to the United States Senate (1793–1796).

During the winter of 1778–1779 General and Mrs. Washington—who were occupying the Wallace house across the street—were frequent guests of the Hardenberghs at the Dutch Parsonage. Young Frederick Frelinghuysen often visited his mother and stepfather at the same time as the Washingtons.

The house was removed 100 yards from the original site by the Frelinghuysen family in 1907 when the Central Railroad condemned the property for right-of-way. The local chapter of the Daughters of the American Revolution was instrumental in restoring the structure. Now administered by the state of New Jersey, the Old Dutch Parsonage is furnished with pieces of the eighteenth and nineteenth centuries.

SITE OF TUNISON'S TAVERN   *Hotel Somerset, corner of Main and Grove Streets.*   In 1769 Cornelius Tunison built a tavern on this site which soon became a popular hostelry and stagecoach stop. Tunison was an ardent supporter of the Patriot cause, and his son Garrett served as chief surgeon of Colonel John Lamb's regiment.

When the British destroyed the Dutch Reformed Church of Raritan the congregation was permitted to hold services in the tavern's sitting room. According to tradition, several of Washington's staff officers were quartered here during the winter of 1778–1779 and Washington sometimes exchanged toasts with innkeeper Tunison to "the American victory."

WALLACE HOUSE   *38 Washington Place. Open Tuesday through Saturday 10 A.M. to noon and 1 P.M. to 5 P.M., Sunday 2 P.M. to 5 P.M. Closed July 4, Thanksgiving, December 25, and January 1. Adults 25¢, children free.*   John Wallace, a retired Philadelphia merchant, purchased land here in December 1775 and soon afterward began constructing a house on the site. The structure was nearly completed in 1778 when General George Washington selected it as his headquarters while the Continental Army was located at the nearby Middlebrook encampment (from November 1778 to June 1779). Washington and his wife paid a rent equivalent to $1,000. Among the many officers who stopped here on military business and to partake of Martha Washington's hospitality were William Alexander (Lord Stirling), Nathanael Greene, Henry ("Light-Horse Harry") Lee, and Henry Knox.

The house is furnished with fine eighteenth-century antiques. Pieces associated with the Washingtons include a Lowestoft tea set that belonged to Martha Washington; a Queen Anne dining room table presented to the general by Frederick Frelinghuysen; a campaign chest typical of the period; and a flowered quilt sewn for Washington by local women.

In the late nineteenth century the Revolutionary Memorial Society acquired the property. Since there had been no major architectural alterations, only interior renovations were necessary. The Wallace House is now administered by the New Jersey Department of Environmental Protection.

Important Colonial Houses

VAN HORNE MANSION *Off the Calco traffic circle going into Bound Brook, Route 28. Not open to the public.* General William Alexander (Lord Stirling) and his wife, along with Henry ("Light-Horse Harry") Lee, resided here during the winter of 1778–1779.

VAN VECHTEN HOUSE *From the Wallace House (on Washington Place) drive back to the main road, proceed to the fourth traffic light, and turn right, traveling toward Finderne. Just before the Raritan River Bridge is a narrow road to the right; follow it to the house. Not open to the public.* The oldest portion of this house was built in 1715 by Michael Van Vechten, and the brick extension was added by his son Derrick (a member of the New Jersey Assembly). During the winter of 1778–1779 General Nathanael Greene and his wife occupied this dwelling. At a Christmas party held here it is said that Washington danced for two hours continuously with the charming Mrs. Greene.

Recommended Side Trip

Site of Middlebrook Encampment, Bound Brook

From Somerville follow Route 22 East until you arrive at the intersection of Routes 22 and 527 (Mountain Avenue) in Bound Brook. Continue for .1 mile past this intersection, then turn left onto Middlebrook Avenue. Travel for about ½ mile to the encampment site.

Since 1894 this tract of land, the site of the Middlebrook encampment of the winter of 1778–1779, has been maintained by the Washington Camp Ground Association. Very little is to be seen here—only a flagpole flanked by two cannon (Civil War period) and a cabin.

Washington Crossing

Revolutionary War History

The autumn of 1776 was a dark time for the Patriot cause. The British had dealt a decisive blow against the Continental Army, driving Washington's troops out of New York City and sending them into harried retreat across New Jersey and into Pennsylvania. In order to travel quickly and thereby avoid an overwhelming defeat, the Patriot soldiers were forced to abandon valuable stores and supplies. By mid-December the British had gained control of most of New Jersey and were within striking distance of Philadelphia—the largest city in the colonies and the seat of the Continental Congress.

In late December Washington determined to attack the garrison at Trenton in order to weaken the enemy stranglehold on New Jersey and to boost the morale of his poorly clad, ill-fed army. The strategy called for a three-pronged attack. George Washington with the main force was to cross the Delaware River at McKonkey's Ferry, several miles north of Trenton on the Pennsylvania side. General James Ewing was to cross at Trenton and take the bridge over Assunpink Creek, cutting off the path of any Hessian retreat. General John Cadwalader was to create a diversionary maneuver by crossing at Bristol, Pennsylvania, and distracting enemy troops near Bordentown, New Jersey.

At 6 P.M. on December 25, 1776, the attack began. In the bitter cold Washington assembled a force of 2,400 soldiers and eighteen cannon along the banks of the Delaware River. A freezing rain began as the soldiers huddled together waiting for the boats that would ferry them to the opposite side. These men were dressed in tattered uniforms; many who were without shoes had their feet wrapped in rags.

Into the howling wind General Henry Knox shouted directions to the troops, ordering them into the Durham boats (fifty feet long, eight feet wide, and twelve feet deep), which were manned by the stalwart Massachusetts sailors of General John Glover's Marblehead Regiment.

The crossing was led by the Commander-in-Chief himself. Along with him in the first boats were General Adam Stephen's brigade of artillerymen. The oarsmen's task was a difficult one, for the river was clogged with ice floes and they were forced to pull against the strong northern wind, which by now was heavy with snow. Upon reaching the New Jersey shore, the infantry was stationed around the landing site to provide safety for those who would follow.

Meanwhile, Generals Ewing and Cadwalader had marched their units to the sites on the river chosen for their crossings. By the time the troops had assembled at their appointed locations, the rain had been transformed into a brutal snowstorm, making the officers believe it would be foolhardy to attempt a crossing.

By 11 P.M. the snow and sleet were so intense that Washington's men were nearly blinded, but still the intrepid oarsmen continued to ferry the Patriot troops across the river. When General Washington received a message from General Sullivan that the men's powder and muskets were drenched, he swiftly replied, "Tell General Sullivan to use the bayonet; I am resolved to take Trenton."

Finally, at 3 A.M., the last boat had reached the New Jersey shore. As the storm continued to rage around them, the commanding officers—Greene, Sullivan, and Washington—regrouped their exhausted, half-frozen regiments and at 4 A.M. began the nine-mile march to Trenton.

State Park Sites

The park is located approximately 9 miles northwest of Trenton on Route 29. New Jersey Route 546 West also leads to the site. Washington Crossing State Park, which has facilities for picnicking, is open from dawn to dusk.

FLAG MUSEUM   *Open May 1 to Labor Day, Tuesday through Sunday 1 P.M. to 5 P.M. Free.*   This museum is housed in a fieldstone barn on the property of the McKonkey Ferry House. Displayed here is a fine collection of flags associated with American history. Revolutionary War buffs will enjoy seeing the following: the Pine Tree Flag (sometimes called the Massachusetts Colony Flag) used by the Patriots at the Battle of Bunker Hill (June 17, 1775); the Gadsden Flag—designed by Colonel Christopher Gadsden of South Carolina—portraying a rattlesnake on a yellow background (first hoisted on the Continental Navy ship *Alfred* in December 1775); the Grand Union Flag, used by many units of the Continental Army (adopted January 1776); and the Stars and Stripes, authorized by the Continental Congress (June 14, 1777).

A twenty-five-foot diorama (with audio narrative) portrays the Continental Army's crossing of the Delaware River and the march to Trenton.

McKONKEY FERRY HOUSE (JOHNSON'S FERRY HOUSE)   *Open Tuesday through Saturday 10 A.M. to noon and 1 P.M. to 5 P.M. Closed Thanksgiving, December 25, and January 1. Fee 25¢.*   At the time of the

Revolutionary War this inn (built 1740) was operated by Rut Johnson. It was at Johnson's Ferry Inn that Washington and his officers sought momentary refuge from the storm while the remaining troops were crossing the river. According to tradition, Washington relaxed for an hour in one of the upstairs bedrooms.

William McKonkey—son of Samuel McKonkey, ferry master for many years on the Pennsylvania side of the river—moved to this dwelling in New Jersey after the Revolutionary War, and the house has since been known by his name.

Three rooms are presently open to the public: the taproom, the public room, and a bedroom. The furnishings are of the Colonial period. Among the items of special interest are a Hessian sword, a blanket chest of apple wood (c. 1690), and pewter utensils.

The state of New Jersey acquired the property and restored it in the 1920s.

Sightseers may wish to cross to the Pennsylvania side of the river to visit the Crossing sites there.

Trenton

On the morning of December 26, 1776, Washington's 2,400 soldiers completed their crossing of the Delaware River and began to march on Trenton, where 1,400 Hessians were quartered.

At Birmingham, about four miles from the town, the troops divided into two columns. General Nathanael Greene's brigade (with the regiments of Stephen, Mercer, and Alexander) marched down Pennington Road to approach Trenton from the north. General John Sullivan (with the regiments of St. Clair, Sargent, and Glover) continued on the road parallel to the river to approach the town from the west.

Three regiments of Hessians (called the Rall, Knyphausen, and Lossberg) and twenty light dragoons of the 16th British Regiment were quartered in Trenton. Their commander, Colonel Johann Gottlieb Rall, arrogantly assumed that the Americans, whom he called *Pöbel* ("rabble"), could never defeat his well-trained soldiers. (Rall was disparagingly characterized by one of his English comrades "as noisy, unacquainted with the language, and a drunkard.")

On the evening of December 25, while Rall sat washing down his heavy Christmas dinner with tankards of ale at the house of Abraham Hunt, the Continental troops began their stealthy crossing of the Delaware River. An informer interrupted the revelry with a message warning of Patriot troop movements, but the drunken Rall stuffed the paper into his pocket unread.

At eight o'clock the next morning he was awakened out of a stupor by the frantic yells of Lieutenant Jacob Piel. He reported a skirmish between the Hessians stationed at the Pennington Road outpost and the advance guard of General Stephen's troops, an encounter that had sent the Hessians retreating.

In Trenton the Hessian soldiers quickly organized. The Rall Regiment formed in the lower part of King Street (now Warren Street); the Lossberg Regiment occupied Queen Street (now Broad Street); the Knyphausen Regiment was held in reserve near Second Street. A heavy rain began to fall as the men ran through the streets to take up their battle stations.

Meanwhile, General Alexander's units had arrived at the junction of King and Queen Streets—a strategic location which commanded the entire town. Orders were given for four artillery pieces under Captain Thomas Forrest to be aimed down Queen Street, and two cannon under Captain Alexander Hamilton were positioned to be trained down King Street. A burst of fire from the Patriot guns swept through the streets, cutting a path down which the infantry charged. The panicked retreat of the Hessian soldiers resulted in the capture of their batteries.

At the same time Sullivan's troops launched an assault on the Knyphausen Regiment and drove them back. The driving rain had made many of the muskets ineffective, forcing the men to fight hand-to-hand with bayonets and swords.

By 9 A.M. the Patriots had gained strategic control of the city and Rall had no alternative but to order a general retreat. No sooner had he told his subordinates to regroup at the orchard at the southeast corner of town than a musket shot from the Patriot ranks cut him down. (He died the following day.)

In the pandemonium that ensued the enemy was forced to surrender. Twenty-two Hessians were killed and 92 wounded; 948 prisoners were captured (including 32

Surrender of Colonel Rall at the Battle of Trenton. *Painting by Alonzo Chappel.* (CHICAGO HISTORICAL SOCIETY)

officers); and 6 cannon and 1,000 muskets were seized. Only four Americans were wounded, including Lieutenant James Monroe (the future president) and Captain William Washington (the cousin of the Commander-in-Chief).

Although the battle had been won, Washington knew his men were too exhausted to confront any British reinforcements that might be sent into the Trenton area. At noon, trudging through the slush and mud, the weary men returned to their boats down the road they had traveled earlier that morning.

Thirteen years later, on April 21, 1789, Washington returned to Trenton—this time as President-elect of the new nation en route to his inauguration in New York City. With a salute of cannon and a military escort, he entered Trenton, stopping at the bridge at Assunpink Creek (where on January 2, 1777, the Americans encamped before the Battle of Princeton) to be honored with a choral ode composed for the occasion. He then proceeded to the City Tavern at Second and Queen Streets, where he lunched with leading citizens of the city before departing for Princeton, the next stop of his journey.

On September 25, 1824, Trenton (now the state capital) played host to a beloved Revolutionary War hero, the Marquis de Lafayette. He was escorted into the city accompanied by the governor of New Jersey, a group of prominent citizens, and a corps of cavalry. After viewing a parade in his honor, he went to the Assembly Room of the State House and was greeted by members of the city and state governments. Later an elaborate dinner was given for him at the Trenton House on North Warren Street. During the evening, speeches and toasts were exchanged, and the present days of peace were contrasted with the bleak hours of December 1776.

VISITORS' CENTER Information and brochures about Trenton may be obtained from the Chamber of Commerce, 104 North Broad Street, phone 393–4143. Serious students of history may wish to consult the staff of the New Jersey State Education Department Library, Division of Archives and History, phone 292–6209.

PUBLIC TRANSPORTATION Bus service throughout the metropolitan Trenton area is provided by the Mercer Metro Bus Line, phone 396–9171.

TAXI SERVICE ABC Radio Cab, phone 394–5082; Yellow Cab, phone 396–8181; Penn Station Cab, phone 396–8700.

DRIVING AND WALKING TOURS Sightseers will need to drive or take public transportation to the Trent House (located on the south edge of the downtown area) and the Trenton Battle Monument (on the north edge of the business district). The other major Colonial sites—such as the Old Barracks and Old Masonic Lodge—are clustered in the vicinity of the State Capitol on West State Street. From here proceed east to visit the First Presbyterian Church and the Friends Meeting House.

Colonial and Revolutionary War Sites

FIRST PRESBYTERIAN CHURCH *120 East State Street. Open Monday through Friday 8:30 A.M. to 4:30 P.M. and Sunday morning.* The first building on this site, a modest stone structure, was erected in 1726 as a place of worship for Trenton's Presbyterians. In 1762 the congregation purchased land on Third Street (present-day Hanover Street) where a parsonage was constructed. Both the parsonage and the church were commandeered by Hessians during the winter of 1776. As the soldiers departed, they ransacked the buildings, which were not fully repaired until after the war.

In 1806 a new church was built here. It had interior galleries supported by columns and an elaborately decorated pulpit. A graceful spire towered above the town. President James Monroe, who as a young man had fought in the Battle of Trenton, attended services here in 1817; and the Marquis de Lafayette worshipped with the congregation when he visited Trenton in 1824.

The present church was erected in 1840 to create enlarged facilities for the growing congregation. Its Greek Revival facade, with Ionic columns supporting an unadorned pediment, has become a city landmark. In 1949 the First Presbyterian Church was designated as the Capital Church of the Synod of New Jersey.

Many distinguished citizens are interred in the church's cemetery, including Colonel Isaac Smith, commander of the local militia during the Revolutionary War and later a United States Congressman; Abraham Hunt, wealthy merchant who entertained the Hessian commander, Colonel Johann Gottlieb Rall, while Washington's troops crossed the Delaware; and Moore Furman, Aaron Woodruff, and James Ewing, Trenton's first three mayors.

FRIENDS MEETING HOUSE   *East Hanover and Montgomery Streets. Not open to the public.*   The original meeting house on this site—completed in November 1739—was a one-story, hipped-roof brick structure that faced Montgomery Street (then known as Quaker Lane). Designed by William Plaskett, the building consisted of one large room (thirty feet by forty feet) furnished with plain benches. During the Revolutionary War Continental troops passing through the area were invited to make their quarters here, and in 1776 British dragoons were billeted here for a short time.

The original building was enlarged and remodeled in the mid-nineteenth century.

In the adjoining cemetery many prominent citizens are buried, including Dr. Thomas Cadwalader, the first

Old Barracks, Trenton (ALPER)

burgess of the Free Borough of Trenton; Colonel Lambert Cadwalader (his son), a member of the United States Congress from 1784 to 1787; General Philemon Dickinson, head of the New Jersey Militia during the Revolution; and George Clymer, a Pennsylvania signer of the Declaration of Independence.

OLD BARRACKS *South Willow and West Front Streets. Open Monday through Saturday 10 A.M. to 4:30 P.M. Closed Thanksgiving, Christmas, January 1, February 22. Adults 75¢, students 50¢, children 25¢.* This stone building was constructed in 1758 to quarter British troops during the French and Indian Wars. In March 1759 Joseph Yard and John Allen were appointed commissioners of the Trenton Barracks to oversee maintenance of the building and the supplies.

The two-story Barracks consisted of a 130-foot central section with two 58-foot wings. An officers' residence later was added onto the north wing. The kitchens were originally located in the basement of the south wing. The Barracks—which was large enough to accommodate 300 men—had plastered walls and open fireplaces. Furnishings were simple: bunk beds, roughly hewn tables, and plain chairs and benches.

During the Revolutionary War the Trenton Barracks was occupied at various times by British, Hessian, and Patriot troops. When the war erupted, the British were the first to be billeted here. In December 1776, at the time of the Battle of Trenton, a detachment of Hessians was stationed here. Later, when the Patriots controlled the area, units of the Continental Army occupied the building. After the Battle of Yorktown (October 1781), when hostilities had largely ceased, the Barracks was converted into a hospital for American soldiers.

In 1782 the structure was remodeled into a series of small apartments for use as private dwellings. Through the efforts, in the first two decades of the twentieth century, of the Oliphant Chapter of the Daughters of the American Revolution and the state of New Jersey, the Old Barracks has been preserved and restored.

Today, visitors may view fine examples of eighteenth-century furniture, Revolutionary War relics and mementos of Patriot leaders. Among the noteworthy pieces are a writing table designed and built for Aaron Burr, third Vice President of the United States; a maple field bed made in Maryland in the 1790s; and a cherrywood tall-case clock made by a Philadelphia craftsman in 1780.

Items associated with New Jersey leaders are a chess set which once belonged to Philemon Dickerson, a governor of the state; side chairs originally owned by Francis Hopkinson, a New Jersey signer of the Declaration of Independence; and china once in the possession of the family of Richard Stockton, a signer of the Declaration of Independence.

Of particular historic interest is a section of the arch erected over the bridge at Assunpink Creek in April 1789 when President-elect Washington journeyed to Trenton on his way to New York City. The twenty-foot-high arch was covered with masses of evergreens, wreaths of laurel, and garlands of flowers. On September 25, 1824, the same arch was erected in front of the Trenton State House in honor of Lafayette's visit to the city.

OLD MASONIC LODGE BUILDING *South Willow and Lafayette Streets. Open Monday through Friday 10 A.M. to noon and 2 P.M. to 4 P.M. Free.* Built in 1793, this structure served for sixty-two years as the meeting hall of the Trenton Masonic Lodge Number 5. George Washington—traveling from Philadelphia to New York City for his inauguration as the first President—stopped only briefly in Trenton on April 21, 1789, but it is believed he took time to visit with his Masonic brothers in this building.

The first floor is a museum displaying Masonic mementos. The second-floor lodge room still contains the original chairs used by the Master and the Warden.

SITE OF DOUGLASS HOUSE *191 South Board Street. Not open to the public.* The house that originally stood on this site—built in the early 1760s by Jacob Bright—was owned at the time of the Revolutionary War by Alexander Douglass, Quartermaster of the Continental Army. It was here, on January 2, 1777, that General Washington called a council of war with Generals Greene, Mercer, Knox, St. Clair, and Cadwalader to refine the strategy for an attack on enemy troops positioned at Princeton.

In the 1860s, when the Lutheran Church of the Redeemer was built on this site, the Douglass House was moved to the rear of the lot. For many years it was used as a parsonage. At the beginning of the twentieth century it was moved to another site, and today, a private residence, it stands in Mill Hill Park (near Front and Montgomery Streets).

SITE OF HUNT HOUSE *Northwest corner of State Street and Warren Street* During the Revolutionary War the general store and residence of Abraham Hunt stood on this site.

On Christmas night, December 25, 1776, Hunt's guest, Colonel Johann Gottlieb Rall (the commander of the Hessian troops at Trenton), received a note warning of the imminent attack by the Patriot troops— a note which in his drunken state he grievously ignored. (Historians disagree as to whether Hunt was a Loyalist obsequious to the town's occupiers or a Patriot secretly serving Washington's cause.)

The house was demolished in 1884.

SITE OF POTTS-LEE HOUSE *Warren Street near Perry Street* The house that stood on this site at the time of the Revolutionary War was owned by Stacy Potts, a prominent Quaker. When the Hessians occupied Trenton in 1776, their commander, Colonel Rall, seized this dwelling for his headquarters. During the Battle of Trenton he was mortally wounded and carried back to the house, where he died the following day.

From November 1 to December 24, 1784, the Congress (under the Articles of Confederation) convened in Trenton. Richard Henry Lee of Virginia, president of the Congress, leased the house and resided here during this period.

In 1853 the structure was demolished. The rectory of St. Mary's Church is now located on this site.

TRENT HOUSE   539 *South Warren Street. Open Monday through Saturday 10 A.M. to 4 P.M., Sunday 1 P.M. to 4 P.M. Closed Thanksgiving, December 25, and January 1. Adults 25¢, children 10¢.*   William Trent (1655–1724), a Scotsman who had settled in Philadelphia in 1682, purchased 800 acres in this area in 1714 with plans to build a summer home. By 1719 an imposing red brick mansion with white cupola was erected here. Two years later Trent and his family decided to settle in this house permanently. When a community sprang up nearby, it was named in his honor—Trenton (Trent's Town).

A wealthy merchant and a shipowner in partnership with William Penn, Trent also served in the Pennsylvania Assembly (1710, 1715) and was later elected Speaker of the House (1717–1718). After he moved to New Jersey, Governor Burnet appointed him judge of the Court of Common Pleas in Hunterdon County (1719) and then Chief Justice of New Jersey (1723).

After William Trent's death in 1724, the property passed through many hands. The house was occupied by numerous distinguished citizens, including three New Jersey governors: Lewis Morris (resident from 1742 to 1746); Philemon Dickerson (resident from 1835 to 1838); and Rodman McCamley Prince (resident from 1854 to 1859). During the Revolutionary War Colonel John Cox, Assistant Quartermaster General of the Con-

tinental Army, owned the estate. The last owner of
the property, Edward A. Stokes, presented it to the city
of Trenton in 1929.

The mansion—the oldest private residence in Trenton—is furnished with elegant pieces dating from 1640
to 1760. The only piece original to the house is the
eighteenth-century tall-case clock (made by John Wood
of Philadelphia), which belonged to Trent's youngest
son.

The paneled **Drawing Room** is noted for its handsome
sofa and draperies of matching golden brocatelle. Hanging above the rare japanned card table (which converts
into a writing table) is a japanned corner cupboard
dating from 1675. The firescreen and stand near the
fireplace retain their original tapestries.

Dominating the **Dining Room** is the handsome oak
gate-leg table and chairs bearing the Stuart crest. The
chandelier, one of the oldest in the house, is of Flemish
brass.

Mrs. Trent's **Sitting Room** and **Bedroom** are furnished
with a maple William and Mary day bed, a chest-desk
and a ladder-back chair, a chest of drawers with inlay
decoration, a four-poster canopied bed, and blue-and-
white Chinese porcelain garniture.

The two outstanding pieces in the **Southeast Bedroom**
are the Dutch kas made of three kinds of wood (poplar,
pine, and cherry) and the small Queen Anne tea table
(made in Philadelphia).

The **Kitchen,** which is located in the basement, is representative of the period and displays utensils com-
monly used in the northern colonies.

TRENTON BATTLE MONUMENT   *Intersection of
North Warren and North Broad Streets (and Brunswick,
Princeton, and Pennington Avenues). The observation
platform at the top of the monument, reached by elevator, is open weekdays 10 A.M. to 5 P.M. Adults 25¢,
children 10¢.*   Located on the highest point overlooking

Trenton Battle Monument, Trenton (ALPER)

the town, this monument marks the site of the Patriot artillery positions during the Battle of Trenton. The 137-foot-high granite column is topped by a 13-foot bronze statue of George Washington. He is represented in his uniform as a Continental general—an exact reproduction, according to some sources, of the one worn by him at Trenton.

The bronze reliefs on the south, west, and east sides of the pedestal depict respectively *The Opening of the Battle, The Continental Army Crossing the Delaware River,* and *The Surrender of the Hessians.* These plaques are attributed to Thomas Eakins. On the north side of the pedestal is a bronze tablet presented by the Society of the Cincinnati of New Jersey.

Guarding the entrance to the monument stand two bronze figures representing soldiers who fought courageously at the Battle of Trenton and in other New Jersey campaigns. One is the statue of Private Blair McClenachan of the Philadelphia Light-Horse Troop; the other is of Colonel John Glover of the Marblehead (Massachusetts) Regiment.

In the late 1880s, after the United States Congress appropriated $30,000 and the New Jersey legislature contributed $15,000, the monument was commissioned. The cornerstone was laid on December 26, 1891, before a crowd of distinguished guests including Daniel J. Bechtel, mayor of Trenton, and Leon Abbett, governor of New Jersey. The erection of the pedestal and column was completed on August 31, 1893, and one week later the statue of George Washington—executed by John H. Duncan of New York City—was hoisted to the top of the shaft.

On October 19, 1893, the Trenton Battle Monument was dedicated at a gala ceremony commemorating the 112th anniversary of the British surrender at Yorktown.

WATSON HOUSE   *151 Westcott Street. By appointment only. The building may be open to the general public*

during the Bicentennial. Free.   This two-and-a-half-
story stone dwelling is a fine example of an early Quaker
farmhouse of the region. It was built in 1708 by Isaac
Watson, who emigrated to this country from England in
1679. He acquired large tracts of land in central New
Jersey around the bluffs leading toward the Delaware
River. Here Watson set aside a parcel of ground to be
used as a Quaker cemetery. (It is near present-day
Riverview Cemetery.)

This house is remarkably well preserved. Several of
the fireplaces are original and the window casements
are little altered. The window sashes were originally of
lead, and it is claimed that during the American Revolution the metal was melted into bullets for the Continental Army.

The house is furnished with late-seventeenth-century
and early-eighteenth-century furniture. Of particular
interest are the Pennsylvania painted cupboard, the
linen press, and the William and Mary chairs.

Descendants of Isaac Watson lived here until 1837.
The property is now administered by the Daughters of
the American Revolution.

Non-Revolutionary Sites of Interest

NEW JERSEY STATE CAPITOL   *121 West State Street.*
*Open daily 9 A.M. to 5 P.M.; in the summer 9 A.M. to
4:30 P.M. Free.*   Trenton was selected as New Jersey's
capital in 1790. Two years later the first Trenton State
House was constructed; it was a small roughcast building with a belfry. An adjoining structure was erected in
the late 1790s to provide offices for the secretary of

state and storage space for public records. In 1848 two additional buildings were constructed contiguous to the main structure and a rotunda was added.

A devastating fire on March 21, 1885, reduced the Capitol building to rubble. Soon afterward the legislature appropriated $275,000 for a new structure. Work was completed on the domed Renaissance-style edifice by 1889. Throughout the twentieth century additions and modifications were made.

Among many leaders who made speeches at the first State House were the Marquis de Lafayette, Daniel Webster, and Abraham Lincoln.

NEW JERSEY STATE MUSEUM *205 West State Street. The main building is open Monday through Saturday 9 A.M. to 5 P.M., Sunday 2 P.M. to 5 P.M. Closed holidays. Planetarium shows on weekends at 2, 3, and 4 P.M. Free.* This museum is noted for its outstanding exhibits in the fields of geology, archaeology, and biology. The planetarium offers weekend programs on varied astronomical themes.

Recommended Side Trip

Batsto

From Trenton and points north take Route 206 South to Hammonton, then proceed along Route 30 East for about a mile before turning onto Route 542 East (a two-lane paved county road) toward Batsto.

The first furnace of the Batsto Iron Works was built in

1766 by Charles Read, a lawyer and later Justice of the New Jersey Supreme Court. During the Revolutionary War the Works were operated by Colonel John Cox, Assistant Quartermaster General of the Continental Army, who supervised the manufacture of cannon and munitions for Washington's troops.

The only threat to Batsto occurred in the autumn of 1778, when General Henry Clinton dispatched to this area Captain Patrick Ferguson and a brigade of British soldiers to destroy Patriot strongholds and supplies. On their march to seize the Batsto Iron Works, the troops burned the village of Chestnut Neck. News of the approach of Pariot units under the command of Count Casimir Pulaski forced the British to flee the area, discontinuing their search-and-destroy mission.

In 1779 the Iron Works were sold to Joseph Ball, who had served as manager here under Colonel Cox. The management was subsequently assumed by other businessmen until 1848, when the furnace fires were permanently extinguished. Ten years later the furnace was dismantled. The state of New Jersey acquired the property in the early twentieth century, and it is now administered by the Department of Environmental Protection.

HISTORIC BATSTO IRON WORKS *Open weekdays 11 A.M. to 5 P.M., weekends 11 A.M. to 6 P.M. During the summer the hours are 10 A.M. to 6 P.M. daily. Adults $1.00, youngsters (12–18) 25¢, children (under 12) 10¢.*

VISITORS' CENTER Books, pamphlets, and souvenirs may be purchased here. Inquire at the desk about guided tours.

BLACKSMITH SHOP   This is a reconstruction of a typical blacksmith shop in which metal objects were repaired and small tools were made for use by local citizens.

CARRIAGE SHED   Various styles of horse-drawn vehicles are displayed here: sleighs, surreys, and sulkies.

GENERAL STORE   Although the General Store was enlarged and renovated in the mid-nineteenth century, its oldest section is pre-Revolutionary. The structure houses New Jersey's oldest working post office in addition to a museum exhibiting glass objects—a reminder of the time (1848 to 1867) when a glass factory was located at Batsto.

GRISTMILL   In this building (*c*. 1828) corn and wheat were ground into grain for the workmen of the village.

MANSION   This mansion was built about 1780 as a residence for the ironmaster who supervised the operation of the Works. In 1876 Joseph Wharton, then owner of the Batsto Iron Works, remodeled the interior and enlarged this house. He also added the porches and the eighty-five-foot tower. Although the tower was ostensibly built as a fire lookout, the workmen whispered that it was used to spy on them.

The rambling mansion has thirty-six rooms, but only twelve are open to the public. They are furnished with eighteenth- and nineteenth-century antiques.

WORKMAN'S COTTAGES   *After leaving the Mansion, walk down the hill and cross the bridge to the area of the cottages.* These two-story wooden dwellings, built in the 1820s, served as the workmen's living quarters. Several of the buildings are presently being restored.

Princeton

To capitalize on his victory at Trenton (December 26, 1776) and to reestablish American control of New Jersey, Washington planned to have his troops cross the Delaware River again and strike at the British garrisoned in Princeton and New Brunswick. On December 29, 1776, the Patriot soldiers—many debilitated from the marches to and from Trenton several days earlier—began to prepare for the assault. It took two days to reach the Trenton area, where they encamped and built earthwork defenses along a ridge near Assunpink Creek.

Meanwhile, Cornwallis' army of 8,000 men had reached Princeton and then had marched to Trenton. In the late afternoon of January 2, 1777, these British forces attacked the American positions but, with the coming of darkness, withdrew. Observing the wretched condition of Washington's troops, the British settled down for the night confident of the next day's victory.

Faced with the certainty of annihilation, General Washington hit upon an audacious stratagem. Under the cover of night the men would leave camp, slip past the enemy's left flank, and attack the British rear guard ten miles north at Princeton.

The plan was put into operation at once. To deceive the British, Washington ordered the soldiers to build up their campfires. He then sent a detachment of men to work with picks and shovels at the earthworks so that the enemy, hearing the noise, would assume that the Patriots were preparing for the coming battle.

At 1 A.M. on January 3 the troops began to stealthily withdraw from the camp. Wagon wheels were wrapped in rags to muffle the sound; the men were given strict orders not to speak; and all commands were whispered.

As the first rays of light penetrated the dark gray sky, the army arrived at Stony Brook (about two miles from Princeton). There the troops were divided. Three brigades under General Sullivan continued the advance toward Princeton, while Mercer's and Cadwalader's units remained to secure the Stony Brook Bridge and thereby prevent the arrival of any British or Hessian reinforcements from Trenton.

As Mercer's troops neared the bridge they encountered two British regiments, under Colonel Charles Mawhood, which were on their way from Princeton to join Cornwallis' army at Trenton. The opposing forces met in an adjacent orchard and exchanged a volley of fire. Before the Patriots could reload, the British—with bayonets ready— charged their line, sending the Americans in disorderly flight. General Mercer fell to the ground bleeding from seven bayonet wounds. As Mawhood's men pursued the fleeing remnants of Mercer's unit, Cadwalader's forces arrived. But they, too, were driven back.

At the height of the pandemonium, George Washington and a detachment rode into the fray—just at the moment when the bewildered Patriots were on the verge of surrender. Urging the soldiers to hold their ground and fight, he galloped his white stallion to the front of the lines and inspired the men by his heroic example. While Captain Joseph Moulder's two-gun battery fired on the enemy, the Americans rallied to the general's exhortations. They regrouped and, with yells and jeers, advanced on the British. As the fighting became more intense, the Patriots gained the advantage and forced Mawhood's men to withdraw in defeat.

The victorious Continental troops then marched toward Princeton. They encountered detachments of British soldiers who were planning to join Mawhood's units and quickly overpowered them. The majority of these Redcoats scrambled in retreat to New Brunswick, but a small contingent barricaded itself in Nassau Hall (of the College of New Jersey) in downtown Princeton. When Captain Alexander Hamilton's troops fired on the building, the men surrendered, and the town was securely in Patriot hands.

The Continental soldiers then pursued the British as far as Kingston, but there Washington and his staff agreed that the men were too exhausted to continue. The officers' original plan of chasing the British from their stronghold, New Brunswick, was abandoned. Instead it was decided to march the troops to an encampment at Morristown.

During the campaign in the Princeton area forty Americans were killed or wounded while twenty-eight British were killed and fifty-eight wounded. In a short period of time—from December 26, 1776, to January 6, 1777—George Washington had reversed the inexorable thrust of the British army and had raised the morale of the Patriots, who once again believed that freedom from England was possible.

In the autumn of 1777 General Israel Putnam, leading a detachment of Patriot soldiers, was given charge of protecting the Princeton area from the possibility of British incursions. At that time the New Jersey legislature moved to Princeton, where it remained until 1788. Among its first official acts was consideration of a bill authorizing the procurement of clothing for the state's regiments. The following year Governor William Livingston issued a proclamation setting aside December 18, 1778, as a day of solemn thanksgiving in gratitude for the recognition and aid given to the Patriot cause by the French government. During 1778 the New Jersey Council of Safety (the successor to the Committee of Safety) also held sessions in Princeton.

From June 30 to November 4, 1783, the United States Congress (under the Articles of Confederation) convened in Princeton. It was here that the British government's agreement to the terms of the Treaty of Paris—the treaty that formally ended the war and acknowledged the independence of the new nation—was officially announced to the American people.

VISITORS' CENTER Information about Princeton and brochures describing historic sites may be obtained from the Princeton Chamber of Commerce, 44 Nassau Street, phone 921–7676. Also contact the Historical Society of Princeton, c/o Bainbridge House, 158 Nassau Street, phone 921–6748.

PUBLIC TRANSPORTATION Limited bus transportation is provided in Princeton by the Mercer Metro Bus Line, phone Trenton 396–9171.

TAXI SERVICE Princeton Taxi, phone 921–6748; A-1 Able, phone 924–9766.

WALKING AND DRIVING TOURS Most of Princeton's major points of interest can be seen in two walking tours and a drive south along Mercer Street. NR signifies an important *Non-Revolutionary site*; P indicates a historic house which is now a *private residence*.

Walking Tour A	Walking Tour B
Area along Nassau Street between Vandeventer Street and John Street. Also the Princeton University campus.	Area along Stockton Street, Edgehill Street, and Mercer Street.
Start at Nassau Street near Vandeventer:	Start at Stockton Street near Bayard Lane:
Bainbridge House	Princeton Battle Monument

Walking
Tour A (Cont.)

First Presbyterian
Church

Nassau Hall

Cannon Green

Princeton University
Chapel (NR)

Princeton University Art
Museum (NR)

Geological and Natural
History Museum (NR)

End on the Princeton
campus.

Walking
Tour B (Cont.)

Morven

Einstein House (NR/P)
Westland (NR/P)

End on Mercer Street
near Hibben Road.

Driving
Tour C

Area southwest of the downtown
district. From Nassau Street, drive
south along Mercer Street.

Princeton Battlefield Park

Olden House (P)

Friends Meeting House

End on Quaker Road, off Mercer Street.

Colonial and Revolutionary War Sites

BAINBRIDGE HOUSE *158 Nassau Street. Open Monday through Friday 10* A.M. *to 4* P.M., *Saturday 1* P.M. *to 3* P.M., *Sunday 2* P.M. *to 4* P.M. *During the summer open weekends from 10* A.M. *to 1* P.M. *Free.* Robert Stockton, of the distinguished Princeton family, built this Georgian structure in the mid-1760s. It was rented to Absalom Bainbridge, a physician, who, remaining loyal to England during the American Revolution, was forced to flee the colony. (His wife and family remained here, and his son William achieved fame as a naval hero during the War of 1812 when he commanded the U.S.S. *Constitution.*) In 1783, when the Continental Congress convened in Nassau Hall, several delegates were provided with accommodations in this house.

The interior was remodeled about 1815 during the occupancy of Dr. Ebenezer Stockton. Today, visitors may see a **Doctor's Office** with furnishings and equipment typical of the Federal period. There are **Period Rooms** on the ground floor, and a small research library is located on the second floor. The building now serves as the headquarters of the Historical Society of Princeton.

FIRST PRESBYTERIAN CHURCH *61 Nassau Street, opposite Palmer Square. Open daily 9* A.M. *to 5* P.M. The first church building on this site was completed in 1766 on land donated by the College of New Jersey (present-day Princeton). Samuel Finley, minister of the church and president of the college, delivered the first sermon. (The early presidents of the college were all

*Bainbridge House,
Princeton* (ALPER)

Presbyterian clergymen and pastors of this congregation.)

In 1776 Cornwallis quartered troops here; they wantonly damaged the interior by ripping out the wooden pews for use as firewood. After the Battle of Princeton wounded Patriot troops were cared for in this building. While the Congress was convening in Princeton in 1783, George Washington and distinguished Congressmen attended the college's commencement exercises, which were held in this church.

The structure was burned to the ground in 1813 through the carelessness of the sexton. A second building stood on this site from 1814 until 1835, when it, too, was destroyed by fire. The present church, designed by Charles Steadman, dates from 1836. Taber Sears, a New York architect, was commissioned to refurbish and modernize the interior in 1922.

FRIENDS MEETING HOUSE   *Quaker Road. Proceed on the Mercer Street Extension, turn left onto Quaker Road.*   A community of Quakers settled in the Princeton area in 1696. Their first meeting house on this site was erected in 1709 and was used until 1724, when a larger building was constructed. After a fire destroyed it in 1758, the present two-story meeting house was built. The masonry was the work of William Worth, a local artisan. The stone fireplaces at each end and the interior work has been preserved. The front porch is a later addition.

In January 1777 the meeting house served as a makeshift hospital for the soldiers wounded during the Battle of Princeton. It is believed that many of the unidentified dead were buried nearby in unmarked graves.

In the autumn of 1777 the Princeton area was under the military jurisdiction of Patriot General Israel Putnam. The peace-loving Quakers' refusal to bear arms aroused his anger and he had several Quaker leaders imprisoned. Governor Livingston was appealed to and, respecting their religious convictions, he ordered the men released. His humane decision met with the approval of General George Washington.

Near the gate of the Friends Cemetery is a memorial stone to Richard Stockton (1730–1781) who, as a member of the Continental Congress, was a signer of the Declaration of Independence. Since the exact location of Stockton's grave is unknown, the New Jersey Sons of the American Revolution erected this marker in 1913.

MORVEN   *55 Stockton Street. Open Tuesday 2 P.M. to 4 P.M. from January through June; also by appointment. Free.*   Richard Stockton purchased land here in 1701 and completed the main portion of this house about 1709. Upon his death, the property passed to his son John and then to his grandson Richard, a signer of the Declaration of Independence, who moved into the mansion in 1757 with his wife Annis. They named their home "Morven" after the mythical kingdom (in central Scotland) of Fingal, which is described in Macpherson's Ossian poems (1760–1761). The two large wings and the porch of the mansion were added at a later date.

Lord Cornwallis commandeered Morven as his headquarters for a short time in 1776 during the British occupation of Princeton. Stockton was taken prisoner and incarcerated in Amboy and later in New York City. The wretched conditions of the British prison destroyed his health, and when he returned to his home he was an invalid. He never fully recovered and died in 1781.

When the Congress convened at Nassau Hall in 1783, Elias Boudinot, president of Congress (and brother of Annis Stockton), was invited to stay at Morven. On July 4, 1783, an important state celebration was held here for dignitaries. George Washington (who resided at nearby Rockingham from August 23 to November 10) was a frequent dinner guest at the house and delighted in listening to Mrs. Stockton's recitations of her verse.

In 1944 the property was purchased by Walter E. Edge, governor of New Jersey, who bequeathed it to the state for use as the official governor's residence.

Several rooms are open to the public. Among the important furnishings on view are a highboy owned by Richard Stockton (the signer of the Declaration of Independence), chairs sent to the Stocktons from France after the American Revolution, and portraits of members of the Stockton family.

NASSAU HALL *Princeton University Campus. Open Monday through Saturday 9 A.M. to 5 P.M. The Faculty Room (formerly the Prayer Hall) is open Monday through Saturday 2 P.M. to 4 P.M. Free. Free tours are arranged through the Orange Key Society; phone 452-3603.* Nassau Hall (named in honor of King William III of

*Nassau Hall,
Princeton* (ALPER)

the House of Nassau) was erected in 1754 to contain
the lecture halls, students' chambers, and Prayer Hall
of the College of New Jersey (present-day Princeton
University). The building, which was designed by
William Shippen and Robert Smith, had three entrances
in the front and a chimney at each end. A kitchen was
located in the basement until 1762 when a kitchen outbuilding was constructed.

The list of illustrious students who attended classes
here in the period before the Revolutionary War includes Benjamin Rush (graduated 1760), James Madison (1771), Philip Freneau (1771), Aaron Burr (1772),
and Henry Lee (1773). Students paid £25 a year for
accommodations and were required to bring their own
furniture and servants.

Several important political events occurred on the
lawn of Nassau Hall. In early January 1774—several
weeks after the Boston Tea Party—students burned the
college's supply of tea in a bonfire and placed an effigy
of the hated Governor Hutchinson of Massachusetts in

the center of the blaze. On July 9, 1776, a large crowd of students and local citizens gathered to hear for the first time the document that formally severed the ties of the colonies to England—the Declaration of Independence.

Soon after the state constitution was adopted in late 1776, the New Jersey legislature assembled in Nassau Hall to inaugurate the first governor, William Livingston. At these sessions the state seal, the first of its kind in the new nation, was adopted.

When Princeton was occupied by the British in November 1776, they converted Nassau Hall into a barracks. During the Battle of Princeton American guns under the command of Alexander Hamilton fired on the building, tearing through the walls and forcing the British to surrender. (On the walls of the Prayer Hall hung a portrait of King George II, who was "beheaded" by a cannonball!)

When, in June 1783, Continental Soldiers in Philadelphia revolted over a pay dispute, the Congress moved to the safety of Princeton. From June 30 to November 4 the members convened in Nassau Hall (in the Prayer Hall and in the library room above the main entrance). Among the notable occurrences during this session were the ceremonies honoring George Washington for his service to the nation as Commander-in-Chief of the Continental Army; the signing of the Treaty of Paris (by which England officially ended the hostilities and recognized America as a sovereign nation); and the welcoming of the first foreign ambassador to the new nation—Peter van Berckel of the Netherlands.

In 1802 a fire swept through the building. Shortly afterward it was restored under the supervision of architect Benjamin Henry Latrobe. But in 1855 another, more devastating, conflagration struck, gutting the structure. John Notman, a Philadelphia architect, redesigned the hall, placing turrets at each end, raising the roof, adding a high cupola, and altering the arrangement of rooms in the east end.

On display in the **Faculty Room** (formerly the Prayer Hall; redesigned and enlarged by Notman in 1855) is the dramatic canvas *George Washington at the Battle of Princeton* (1783–1784) by Charles Willson Peale, who fought in the campaign. Several fine portraits of signers of the Declaration of Independence—Richard Stockton, Benjamin Rush, and John Witherspoon—may also be seen here. An orrery (an astronomical instrument) built by David Rittenhouse (an eighteenth-century American astronomer) is an object of great interest to visitors.

The two bronze tigers on the entrance steps of Nassau Hall, executed by A. P. Proctor, were presented to the university in 1911 by the class of 1879.

Located behind the building on **"Cannon Green"** is an artillery piece used by the British in December 1776–January 1777 and seized by the Patriots. It was intended for the fortifications at New Brunswick during the War of 1812 but, after being transported there, was abandoned because of a malfunction in the firing mechanism. In 1838 it was returned to Princeton and installed as a permanent reminder of the college's role in the events of the Revolution.

Nassau Hall was declared a National Historic Landmark in 1961.

PRINCETON BATTLE MONUMENT *Stockton Street near Bayard Lane* The four figures on this monument portray George Washington on horseback; an allegorical representation of Liberty urging Continental soldiers forward; General Hugh Mercer, who was wounded during the Battle of Princeton; and a Patriot drummer boy. The limestone sculpture group, twenty-six feet high, is placed in front of a fifty-foot-high architectural screen. The other side of the screen is inscribed with a quotation by Andrew Fleming West (first dean of the

Graduate College of Princeton); on the narrow ends are carved the coats of arms of Princeton and New Jersey. Inspired by the Bellona relief on the Arc de Triomphe in Paris, this monument was designed by Thomas Hastings and was sculpted by Frederick Mac-Monnies.

Federal and state appropriations, as well as private contributions, were the sources of funds for the creation of this monument. It was unveiled on June 9, 1922, with President Warren G. Harding and other officials in attendance at the festive ceremonies.

PRINCETON BATTLEFIELD PARK *Off Mercer Street between Maxwell Lane and Quaker Road. (Changes in the battlefield site may be made for the Bicentennial.)* Here, on January 3, 1777, the Battle of Princeton was fought. At that time the terrain was studded with trees.

Battle Memorial This four-pillared Greek colonnade was originally part of the facade of the Matthew Newkirk Mansion, later headquarters of the St. George's Society (located at Arch and 13th Streets in Philadelphia). When the structure was torn down in the late nineteenth century, the columns were purchased to adorn Mercer Manor, a house that stood near the Princeton battlefield. After the house was demolished in 1957, the columns were removed to the battlefield site to stand as a memorial to the soldiers who had fought at the Battle of Princeton. The official dedication took place in 1959.

Marker This circular stone marker, located near the Battle Memorial, was erected in 1918. Alfred Noyes (1880–1958), the popular British poet, composed the lines engraved on the bronze plaque.

Mercer Oak According to tradition, Patriot General Hugh Mercer (1725–1777) crawled to safety under this white oak after receiving the brunt of a British bayonet thrust during the Battle of Princeton. He was carried to a nearby dwelling (the Thomas Clarke house) to receive medical attention. After nine days of efforts to save his life, he died.

Important Colonial Houses

BOUDINOT-BEEKMAN PROPERTY *68–70 Nassau Street. Not open to the public.* This property was originally owned by Elias Boudinot, a president of the Congress and brother-in-law of Richard Stockton. After the Revolutionary War the structure was converted into a tavern by Christopher Beekman, who named it the Washington Arms. Since its renovation in the nineteenth century, the building has been used for apartments and shops.

HYER-BEATTY HOUSE *Vandeventer Street near Park Place. Not open to the public.* Built in 1780 by Jacob Hyer (owner of the Hudibras Tavern), this house was sold to Colonel Erkuries Beatty. During the Revolutionary War Beatty had served as General Lafayette's aide-de-camp. When Lafayette toured the Princeton area in 1824, he visited with the Beatty family here.

OLDEN HOUSE *South side of Stockton Street, approximately ¼ mile east of Stony Brook Bridge. Not open to the public.* In December 1776, when Patriot troops were being driven across New Jersey by the British, Washington stopped to refresh himself at this modest eighteenth-century frame house, the home of Thomas Olden. It is said that Washington observed and directed troop movements from the front porch. In early January 1777, after the Battle of Princeton, wounded British soldiers who had been left behind by their retreating comrades were carried here by the Patriots. According to tradition, Washington visited the house to issue stern orders that prisoners should be treated humanely. (The structure now stands 300 yards to the north of its original location.)

STOCKTON HOMESTEAD—"THE OLD BARRACKS" *32 Edgehill Street. Not open to the public.* This field-stone structure incorporates part of Princeton's oldest building, which was erected by the grandfather of Richard Stockton in the late seventeenth century as his family's first home. (In 1709 he built a larger residence near the center of town.) During the Revolutionary War British troops were quartered here.

TUSCULUM *Cherry Hill Road west of Route 206. Not open to the public.* This mansion was built in 1773 by John Witherspoon (1723–1794), a Scotch-born Presbyterian clergyman, while he was serving as the president of the College of New Jersey (Princeton). During the American Revolution Witherspoon was an outspoken Patriot. He served on the Committee of Correspondence and, as a member of the Continental Congress, signed the Declaration of Independence. In 1787 he was a delegate to the New Jersey convention that ratified the Federal Constitution.

Tusculum (named after the ancient Roman summer resort) was occupied briefly in 1776 by the 40th British Foot Regiment. When Congress convened in Princeton in 1783, Witherspoon acted as host to the many distinguished guests in the area.

Non-Revolutionary Sites of Interest

EINSTEIN HOUSE *112 Mercer Street. Not open to the public.* Albert Einstein (1879–1955) resided in this house from 1933 to 1955, when he was a member of the Princeton Institute for Advanced Study.

GEOLOGICAL AND NATURAL HISTORY MUSEUM *Guyot Hall, Princeton University. Open Monday through Saturday 10 A.M. to 4 P.M., Sunday 2 P.M. to 4 P.M. Free.* This fine collection includes specimens of meteorites, rocks, and fossils. Rotating exhibitions highlight geological discoveries and trace the evolution of animals.

PRINCETON UNIVERSITY ART MUSEUM *McCormick Hall. Open Tuesday through Saturday 10 A.M. to 4 P.M., Sunday 2 P.M. to 4 P.M. Closed holidays. Free.* This museum houses an impressive collection of paintings and sculpture of varied periods from ancient to modern. Outstanding examples of pre-Columbian, African, and Far Eastern art are on display as well as traditional European works, including paintings by Veronese, Cranach, and Bosch.

PRINCETON UNIVERSITY CHAPEL *Near Nassau Hall on the campus.* Designed by Ralph Adams Cram and dedicated in 1928, this chapel was built at a cost of almost $3 million. The Gothic structure contains some of the finest stained-glass windows in the United States. Its 1,800 seats are regularly filled for concerts on the magnificent organ which has 10,000 pipes and 125 stops.

WESTLAND *Hodge Road and Cleveland Lane. Not open to the public.* President Grover Cleveland owned this mansion (built 1854) from 1896 until his death in 1908.

WILSON HOUSE   *25 Cleveland Lane. Not open to the public.*   This dwelling was the residence of Woodrow Wilson while he was governor of New Jersey (1910–1912). While president of Princeton (1902–1910) Wilson lived in "The Prospect," then the official residence of the university president.

Recommended Side Trip

Rocky Hill

ROCKINGHAM   (BERRIEN   HOUSE)   *Route   518, Rocky Hill. From Nassau Street in Princeton, turn right onto Route 206 North (Bayard Lane) and travel 8½ miles to Route 518 East. Proceed along 518 (toward the town of Rocky Hill) for approximately 2 miles. The house is located on the left side of the road. Open Tuesday through Saturday 10 A.M. to noon and 1 P.M. to 5 P.M., Sunday 2 P.M. to 5 P.M. Closed Thanksgiving, December 25, January 1. Fee 25¢*   This two-story house— moved here from its original location along the Millstone River about a mile away—was built in 1734–1735. In 1764 Judge John Berrien purchased the dwelling and soon afterward enlarged it to accommodate his growing family. After his suicide in 1772, his wife and six children continued to reside here for eleven years.

In 1783, while the Congress was holding sessions in Princeton, Mrs. Berrien was seeking a purchaser for the property. When news arrived that George Washington was coming to Princeton to formulate plans for a peacetime army, Mrs. Berrien was persuaded to rent her house to the general. He arrived on August 23, 1783, from the encampment at Newburgh, New York.

Washington was soon joined by his wife. Although Martha was recovering from an illness, she immediately began receiving guests and entertaining dignitaries. On September 5 the Washingtons invited members of Congress to an elaborate dinner served under a captured British marquee which was erected on the Rockingham lawn. At a later dinner party Peter van Berckel, the Minister from the Netherlands, was the honored guest.

At Rockingham Washington wrote his "Farewell Orders to the Armies of the United States." He delievered the deeply moving speech on November 2, 1783, from the second-story porch of the Berrien house to a small gathering of his former comrades-in-arms. Washington departed eight days later.

Today, the house is furnished with fine antiques of the eighteenth century. The **Dining Room** contains a handsome Queen Anne drop-leaf table, Chippendale chairs, and a graceful highboy made in Philadelphia. Among the guests entertained here were James Madison, John Paul Jones, Thomas Jefferson, Alexander Hamilton, and Thomas Paine. The small **Bedroom** on the first floor, used by Martha Washington, is well appointed with representative furnishings and historical engravings. The second-floor **Study**—with its large writing table and aide's desk—is the room in which General Washington wrote his farewell speech to the army. Items of interest in the **Dressing Room** and **Bedroom** include a Chippendale washstand, a commode chair, and a campaign bed. The **Kitchen** outbuilding is a replica of the original.

The property became an official historic site of the state of New Jersey in 1963. The Daughters of the American Revolution contributed furniture to the house, and the Stony Brook Garden Club planted the herb and flower gardens.

Freehold

Revolutionary War History

In the late spring of 1778, while Washington's forces were in their winter encampment at Valley Forge, Philadelphia was occupied by British troops under the command of General Henry Clinton. The occupation had begun on September 26, 1777, but the capture of the city—the seat of the Continental Congress—had not paralyzed the American government as the British had expected.

By June 1778 members of the Parliament had begun to despair of winning the war. In October 1777 the British had suffered a significant loss of troops when General John Burgoyne had surrendered at Saratoga, New York, and the growing Franco-American alliance had placed the British in the position of having to wage a war at sea while continuing the campaign on the American continent. Prepared to sue for peace, the Crown sent a commission under the Earl of Carlisle to offer the colonies redress for their grievances and certain concessions—short of independence.

Faced with these conditions, Clinton (who had only recently assumed from General William Howe command of the British forces) determined to remove his army from Philadelphia and consolidate with the forces in New York City. On June 18, 1778, he began the withdrawal—the march that would take his soldiers across New Jersey.

The Patriot army of 12,000 departed from its quarters at Valley Forge to pursue the British. On June 23 Washington established his headquarters at Hopewell (seven miles northwest of Princeton) and the next day called a council of war to settle on a course of action. General Charles Lee argued that the Continental forces, despite their winter of drilling under Baron von Steuben, were no match for the experienced, well-equipped British army, whereas Generals Greene, Wayne, and Lafayette insisted that by avoiding a confrontation they would be losing an opportunity to strike at the foe. A compromise was reached: they would send detachments to harass the enemy's left flank and rear but they would refrain from engaging in a major battle. At 4 A.M. the next morning, after a report describing British troop movements was received from Philemon Dickinson, commander of the New Jersey militia, Washington modified his plans and decided to adopt a more aggressive strategy.

On June 26 Clinton reached Monmouth Courthouse (near present-day Freehold). The preceding days had exacted a brutal toll on his soldiers; the men had been forced to carry heavy backpacks and wear stiff, uncomfortable uniforms in the 90° heat. The next day Washington sent 5,000 troops under the command of General Charles Lee to close in on the enemy.

Early on the 28th the advance guard under Colonel William Grayson came into contact and repelled units of British cavalry and infantry. Later, near Monmouth Courthouse, detachments of Lee's column engaged the enemy's rear guard, but British reinforcements arrived, causing the Patriots to temporarily fall back. The fighting that followed was an uncoordinated series of inconclusive skirmishes.

Then Lafayette, under orders from General Lee, led several regiments in an attack on the British left flank. As he encountered the enemy, Lafayette found it necessary to move to another position which offered a greater strategic advantage. To the other Continental generals, this maneuver appeared to be a retreat, which would leave them without the support of the main army. Generals Scott and Maxwell therefore began to withdraw, an action resulting in a panic that General Lee was unable to stop.

As the soldiers were fleeing, General Washington approached with additional troops. Angrily confronting Lee, the Commander-in-Chief rebuked him for not controlling the flight. Afterward, Washington galloped through the ranks, rallying the men and inspiring them to renewed action.

The Americans took up positions near the West Ravine and Wemrock Brook: Alexander's (Stirling's) men marched to the left; Greene's division was posted to the right; and Wayne's forces occupied the center ground. Six cannon were positioned on nearby Comb's Hill.

When a detachment of the 42nd British Regiment ("Black Watch") attempted to surround Alexander's men, their attack was brought to a bloody halt. A battalion of British Guards and the 37th and 44th Regiments then advanced against Greene's troops but were driven back by the heavy artillery fire. Soon afterward a large force of light infantry, grenadiers, and dragoons charged Wayne's positions, but they were met by a barrage of fire forcing them to withdraw. After three other unsuccessful attempts, they finally penetrated the American lines.

The Continental troops began to regroup in preparation for a counterattack, but the officers were concerned that the heat was too oppressive to push the men to further exertion. Both sides held their positions without any forays, although the artillery fire continued until about 5 P.M.

During the night Clinton's troops quietly slipped away, and the following morning they reached Middletown. By July 5 they had safely arrived in New York City.

Neither army could claim victory. The Americans reported 69 killed and 142 wounded; the British tallied 65 killed and 170 wounded. Almost 100 soldiers of both armies died of heat exhaustion. Clinton had made his journey from Philadelphia to New York City with little loss of personnel and equipment, and Washington had gained the knowledge that his formerly ill-prepared army could function as a cohesive fighting unit.

(In the summer of 1778 General Charles Lee wrote an abusive letter to Washington accusing him of having insulted his honor at Monmouth. The Commander-in-Chief convened a court of inquiry, which found Lee guilty of breach of orders and misbehavior. Lee was suspended from his command for the period of one year. He later sent a vitriolic letter to Congress which so enraged the legislators that he was dismissed from the military in January 1780).

The Battle of Monmouth, fought near Freehold, has been called the last important engagement in the North.

VISITORS' CENTER   Books and pamphlets describing the Freehold area are available from the Monmouth County Historical Association, 70 Court Street, phone 462–1466.

PUBLIC TRANSPORTATION   Bus service throughout the region is provided by Transport of New Jersey. For information and schedules, phone 462–0717.

TAXI SERVICE   Freehold Taxi, phone 431–4343; Warren Taxi, phone 462–1781.

Colonial and Revolutionary War Sites

CLINTON'S HEADQUARTERS   *150 West Main Street. This house is being restored. It may be open to the public for the Bicentennial. Phone 462–1466 for information.*

Benjamin Cook, a local farmer, purchased land here in 1706 and soon afterward built a modest house. Cook, a high-spirited lad, was indicted by a grand jury on August 27, 1700, for "riotously assembling" and assaulting the sheriff. The following year he was indicted again for participating in a violent disturbance in Middletown against government officials. Because of great public sympathy for the rioters' grievances, the charges were dismissed.

In the mid-eighteenth century the property was acquired by the wealthy Covenhoven family, who enlarged and remodeled the house and added a kitchen wing. On June 26, 1778, William Albertse Covenhoven and his wife Elizabeth were residing here when General Henry Clinton commandeered the house for his headquarters. When the general and his aides discovered that most of the furniture had just been removed for safe-keeping, he persuasively insisted that such an act was unnecessary and an affront to his honor as a general. Assuring the Covenhovens that their possessions, if brought back, would be unharmed, Clinton sent several horsemen to have the wagons returned. The next morning Mrs. Covenhoven discovered that her belongings had been plundered and stolen; in addition, the horses and cattle had been driven away. But Elizabeth's greatest suffering was caused by the Redcoats' forcing her (then seventy-four years old) to sleep in the damp milk room. The British officers departed on June 28, after the Battle of Monmouth.

Upon William Covenhoven's death in 1790, his oldest son inherited the property. In the nineteenth century the house had many owners. It was acquired in 1966 by the Monmouth County Historical Association, which undertook the restoration and furnished it according to a Covenhoven inventory.

MONMOUTH BATTLE MONUMENT *Opposite the Monmouth County Historical Association, 70 Court*

Street   The cornerstone of this monument was laid in 1878, the centennial of the Battle of Monmouth. Designed by Emelin T. Little and Douglas Smythe, the granite monument consists of a triangular base on which rests a cylindrical block supporting a three-part eighty-five-foot-high shaft topped by a statue. The statue represents an allegorical figure, "Liberty Triumphant." The statue was destroyed by lightning in 1913 and was replaced by another figure for which Mary Anderson, a celebrated actress of the time, modeled.

The monument's five bronze tablets, designed by J. E. Kelly, depict bas-relief scenes of the Battle of Monmouth: *Colonel Nathaniel Ramsey Defending His Guns, Washington Rallying His Troops, Molly Pitcher at the Cannon, The Council of War at Hopewell,* and *The Charge of Anthony Wayne.*

The monument, which cost $40,000 to complete, was unveiled on November 13, 1884. A parade of New Jersey regiments marching through the town preceded the dedication ceremony at which Theodore M. Morris, president of the Monument Association, delivered the chief oration, followed by an address by Governor Leon Abbett. After a thirteen-gun salute, the monument was unveiled before a crowd of 25,000 who had gathered to mark the occasion.

MONMOUTH BATTLEFIELD SITE   *To reach the battlefield site from Freehold, travel northwest for about 3 miles along Route 522 (toward Englishtown).*   Visitors to the area can see the following points of interest: the Craig House, Molly Pitcher's Well, and Old Tennent Church.

CRAIG HOUSE   *Located on Schibanoff Road, west of Route 9. Presently closed for restoration.*   This two-story frame dwelling (built about 1715) was the home of John Craig, a paymaster in the Continental Army. During the Battle of Monmouth members of his family fled for safety, but before leaving they hid their valuable pieces of silver in the well. British soldiers, espying metallic glints under the water, ordered the well drained and recovered the silver. Afterward, they ransacked the house hoping to find other treasures.

MOLLY PITCHER'S WELL *On Route 522* A marker along the highway indicates the location of "Molly Pitcher's Well."

Molly Pitcher is the name given to Mary Ludwig Hays, wife of Private William Hays (of the 4th Continental Artillery Regiment), whom she followed to war. An energetic, earthy woman, she is reported to have smoked and chewed tobacco. During battles Molly is said to have assisted her husband at the cannon, and several legends have arisen from her actions.

One report of the Battle of Monmouth relates that as she stood, her feet spread apart, handing ammunition to her gunner husband, enemy cannon shot passed between her outstretched legs and tore away her petticoat. She laughingly observed that little damage had been done and continued passing the gun powder.

Another report relates that during the heat of the battle Molly was kept busy drawing water to relieve the thirst of the soldiers. As she was passing around her bucket to the men, enemy fire wounded her husband. Molly immediately stepped into his place, reloaded the cannon, and continued to fire at the British.

One explanation for the existence of several stories concerning Molly Pitcher is that many women accompanied their husbands or lovers to the war and actively aided the soldiers in carrying water, nursing the wounded, and even occasionally manning the guns. Each of the incidents described above is likely to have occurred during the Battle of Monmouth, but probably to different women. Legend, however, has ascribed them all to Mary Hays. Furthermore, the name "Molly Pitcher" may have been a good-natured term used by the soldiers to describe those women who carried water to them.

The well now found on this site was dug in 1860, but it is believed that the spring here was the one from which Molly filled her buckets.

OLD TENNENT CHURCH   *Main Street, Tennent. Open Sunday morning or by appointment; phone 446–6299.* Emigrants from Scotland who began settling in the Freehold area in the late seventeenth century built their first meeting house in the nearby town of Marlboro in 1705. Twenty-six years later they completed on White Hill a second and larger church, now known as Tennent Church. Originally called the Old Scots Church, the building was renamed in honor of two of the beloved pastors who served here, John Tennent (1730–1733) and his brother William (1734–1777). William Tennent passionately supported the Patriot cause, and when he died in 1777 he was buried beneath the middle of the church floor so that his grave could not be defaced by Loyalist sympathizers.

The shingled church, which is forty feet by sixty feet, was constructed by members of the parish. Messrs. Crawford, Baird, McKnight, and Rhea were among those who helped build the structure; William Redford Craig, a local cabinetmaker, made the pulpit; Benjamin Van Cleve fashioned the iron finishings (including the door latches and hinges) as well as the weather vane on the steeple. Near the pulpit was the "Elders Square" where respected leaders of the church were seated. The wide gallery was once partitioned off to separate Negro servants from other members of the congregation. In the nineteenth century the old pews were replaced and the pipe organ, still in use today, was installed.

During the Battle of Monmouth the wounded Patriots were brought here for medical attention. According to local tradition, cannonballs pierced the side walls of the church. (As late as 1916 cannonballs were dug up on the grounds.) Several days after the battle Samuel Craig and his brother discovered a uniformed Hessian peering out from behind a tree. When they called out to him, there was no response. As they cautiously approached, they discovered their foe was, in reality, the corpse of a wounded soldier who had apparently taken refuge in the forest.

On the church grounds are buried Lieutenant Colonel Henry Monckton, a British officer killed in the Battle of Monmouth; the Reverend John Woodhull, pastor of Tennent after the Revolutionary War; and men (many in unmarked graves) who fought for the American cause during the Revolutionary War and the War of 1812.

MONMOUTH COUNTY HISTORICAL ASSOCIATION MUSEUM *70 Court Street. Open Tuesday through Saturday* 11 A.M. *to* 5 P.M., *Sunday* 2 P.M. *to* 5 P.M. *Closed during December and the last two weeks of July. Free.* This three-story brick house was built in 1931 in the Georgian style. Although not a period house, the dwelling contains an outstanding collection of furniture, silver, and porcelain of the seventeenth and eighteenth centuries. Revolutionary War mementos are also displayed.

Of particular interest are: a desk which belonged to a cousin of George Washington; crewel bedhangings dating from about 1700; a secretary-desk made for James Wilson (a Pennsylvania signer of the Declaration of Independence); and Staffordshire china depicting the landing of Lafayette in America. Two New Jersey pieces on display are an eighteenth-century kas by Matthew Egerton, Jr., of New Brunswick and a late-seventeenth-century chair by Robert Rhea of Monmouth County. History buffs will admire a flag that was captured from the British during the Battle of Monmouth; maps of the battle; and the well-known painting, *Wash-*

ington at Monmouth (1857), by Emanuel Leutze (the artist renowned for the canvas, *Washington Crossing the Delaware* [1851]). Other important paintings are by Gilbert Stuart, Benjamin West, and Thomas Sully.

ST. PETER'S EPISCOPAL CHURCH   *33 Throckmorton Street. Open 9 A.M. to 5 P.M.* The first Episcopal church in the area, a crude timber structure, was built in the 1690s. In 1736, after King George II granted a charter to the parish, work was begun on a second church building. Because materials were difficult to obtain, the structure was not completed for many years.

During the American Revolution the Reverend William Ayres, rector of St. Peter's, so infuriated members of his congregation by praying for the royal family that he was removed from his position by force. During the Battle of Monmouth the British commandeered the church for use as a makeshift hospital for their wounded soldiers. In 1781 and 1782 the building was used as a storehouse by New Jersey units of the Continental Army.

In 1878 the church was enlarged and renovated: the ceiling was raised; the chancel was enlarged; and new lighting fixtures, pews, and windows were installed. The interior was completely remodeled in 1950.

Salem

Revolutionary War History

In 1675 John Fenwick and a group of Quakers settled in this region and founded Salem and nearby Greenwich, the first permanent English-speaking settlements on the Delaware River.

Salem took its first stand in the quarrel between the colonies and England shortly after the British Parliament passed the Boston Port Bill which, on June 1, 1774, prohibited all commercial vessels from sailing into Boston Harbor. Irate citizens of Salem assembled at the courthouse and adopted a resolution stating that "we conceive the Boston Port Bill . . . to be the most arbitrary exertion of tyranny over a free and loyal people, and of the most dangerous and alarming tendency."

Despite similar expressions of outrage throughout the colonies, the British maintained their oppressive restrictions against the citizens of Boston. On October 13, 1774, Salem Patriots met and organized a committee to raise funds to alleviate the difficulties suffered by the Bostonians.

Hostilities were brought closer to home in May 1776: a confrontation between British naval ships and local Patriot crafts shocked inhabitants of the area. After pursuing the American brig *Lexington* off Cape May, the British vessels *Roebuck* and *Liverpool* sailed up the Delaware River, where they opened fire on a dozen row galleys that had set out from Philadelphia. Outraged, the local Patriots organized into the Salem County Militia under the leadership of Colonel John Holme.

In the winter of 1777–1778—when Howe's army was

occupying Philadelphia and Washington's troops were quartered at Valley Forge—the war came to Salem. In mid-February 1778 General Anthony Wayne led a detachment out of Valley Forge to seek provisions for the starving soldiers. On the 19th they arrived in Salem. One hundred fifty cattle were rounded up and herded north to Haddonfield, where they were ferried across the Delaware River en route to Valley Forge.

Hugh Cowperthwaite, a Loyalist who lived in Salem, furtively observed the Patriot soldiers' movements and galloped to Philadelphia to inform the British of Wayne's activities. General Howe immediately sent troops (under Lieutenant Colonel Abercrombie) down the Delaware River with orders to disembark near Salem and dispatched The Queen's Rangers (under Major Simcoe) and the 42nd British Regiment (under Colonel Sterling) to patrol the land route. But Wayne's men had outmaneuvered them and were able to return safely to Valley Forge. As the British returned to Philadelphia, they left behind a trail of pillage and destruction.

In March 1778 Howe, discovering that his supplies of food were dwindling, dispatched troops under Colonel Charles Mawhood and Major John Simcoe to Salem on a foraging operation. Meeting no opposition, they entered the town and took control, establishing headquarters at the house of Samuel Dick. Then, acting on reports of Loyalist informants, the British ambushed several small detachments of Patriot militiamen.

On the evening of March 21 Colonel Mawhood ordered an attack on Hancock's Bridge (approximately five miles from Salem), where 200 militiamen had gathered. Simcoe's men sailed down the Delaware River and up Alloway Creek to within striking distance of the objective. The 27th Regiment of Foot followed a land route and approached from the northwest.

But fate favored the Patriots that evening, for by the time the British had arrived, all but twenty militiamen had withdrawn. Infuriated, the British slaughtered the militiamen and attacked the nearby Hancock house where thirty Quakers, who had supported the Patriots, had taken refuge. The Redcoats surrounded the house and without warning burst in, awakening the sleeping men and mercilessly bayoneting them to death. The infamous deeds of that night are spoken of locally as the "Massacre at Hancock's Bridge."

VISITORS' CENTER Pamphlets and books about Salem may be obtained from the Salem County Historical Society, 79–83 Market Street, phone 935–5004 .

PUBLIC TRANSPORTATION Limited bus service in the area is provided by Transport of New Jersey. For information and schedules, phone Camden 365–7000.

TAXI SERVICE Edward Aaron Taxi, phone 935–0259; Lum's Taxi, phone 935–2555.

Colonial and Revolutionary War Sites

FRIENDS MEETING HOUSE *At the head of Walnut Street. Not open to the public.* Built in 1772, this modest structure is still in use today. During the Revolutionary War local Loyalists who had borne arms for the British were brought here for trial. Some of these British sympathizers were permitted to leave the colony and their property was confiscated; others were thrown into prison.

In the Friends Burying Ground (on West Broadway) a 500-year-old oak tree marks the spot where John Fenwick, the founder of Salem, concluded a peace pact with the Indians in 1675.

HANCOCK HOUSE   *Hancock House is located about 5 miles from downtown Salem. From Salem follow the main street, East Broadway, east to a fork in the road, where you should bear right at the sign for Hancock's Bridge. Travel along this narrow road for several miles to the site. The house is temporarily closed. It is usually open Tuesday through Saturday 10 A.M. to noon and 1 P.M. to 5 P.M., Sunday 2 P.M. to 5 P.M. Fee 25¢*
Judge William Hancock, who for many years was a member of the New Jersey Assembly, built this house in 1734.

In March 1778, when British raiding parties were roving through the countryside, the Quaker Patriots—who had offered food and shelter to Continental soldiers—were given refuge here by Judge Hancock. Early on the morning of March 21 a detachment of almost 300 Redcoats and Loyalists attacked a militia patrol along the nearby creek and then stormed the Hancock house. The rudely-awakened captives were herded to the attic where they were brutally bayoneted to death.

This fine Georgian house has Flemish bond brickwork, a peaked roof with dormers, and an overhang between the first and second stories. The original mantels and fireplaces have been preserved, and the furnishings are mostly of the eighteenth century. Visitors may view memorabilia and relics of the period.

The cabin (*c.* 1645) near the Hancock House served as the home of an early Swedish settler. It is built of hand-hewn white cedar planks four inches thick and was brought to this site from a nearby location in Salem County.

SALEM COUNTY HISTORICAL SOCIETY MUSEUMS
79–83 Market Street. Open Tuesday through Friday

1 P.M. *to* 3 P.M., *and by appointment. Adults 75¢, children 25¢.*   These "row" houses, built in the 1720s, are
now museums administered by the Salem County Historical Society. The collections consist of eighteenth-
and nineteenth-century furniture, paintings, china, and
dolls. Noteworthy are the rare Sheraton sideboard made
by cabinetmaker George Whitlock of Delaware, Chippendale-style chairs, pieces of Wistarburg glassware,
and Colonial farm implements. Of special interest is the
tall-case clock formerly owned by Colonel Benjamin
Holme, a resident of Salem. Made by Thomas Wagstaff
of London, it plays six tunes prior to the striking of the
hour. Redcoats confiscated the clock in 1778; five years
later Holme recovered it from British headquarters in
New York City and returned it to his house.

Behind the Salem County Historical Society Building
stands a small brick octagonal structure built in 1736
by John Jones as his law office. During the American
Revolution it was used by Dr. Ebenezer Howell; it was
pillaged in the British raid on Salem in February 1778.

Recommended Side Trip

Greenwich

From Salem, travel southeast along Route 49. At
Shiloh, take the southern route (leading past Roadstown)
toward Greenwich.

At the time of the American Revolution the population
of Greenwich—then the largest and most prosperous town

in Cumberland County—was strongly aligned with the Patriot cause. On December 22, 1774, Greenwich citizens staged a "Tea Party" to defy British authority.

On December 12, 1774, the British brig *Greyhound* was bound for Philadelphia with a cargo of tea. The captain, J. Allen, was warned that a group of Philadelphia citizens was planning to seize the tea. He therefore sailed up the Cohansey Creek to Greenwich, where his cargo was secretly unloaded and stored in the cellar of Dan Bowen's house on Market Square.

Residents of the area were still outraged over the oppressive legislation passed by Parliament several months earlier—the Boston Port Bill (which closed Boston to commerce) and the Administration of Justice Act (which protected officials of the Crown accused of capital offenses). When news leaked out that East India tea was being stored in the town, thirty-five Patriots representing Greenwich and neighboring communities hastily convened to decide a course of action.

On Thursday evening, December 22, 1774, forty young Patriots gathered at the house of the Reverend Philip Vickers Fithian, where (in emulation of the Boston Tea Party held the year before) they disguised themselves as Indians. They then marched swiftly to Market Square, seized the chests of tea, and dragged them to a nearby field. There they heaped the chests and destroyed them in a hugh bonfire. The blaze illumined the night and attracted many sympathetic spectators who, through their refusal to interfere, gave silent approval to the Patriot cause.

During the Revolutionary War Greenwich was spared the devastation of military action, except for the occasional pillaging of foraging parties.

HISTORIC GREENWICH

Information about the town's historic sites may be obtained from the Cumberland County Historical Society, c/o the Gibbon House, Ye Greate Street, phone 455–4055.

All the houses discussed below—except for the Philip Vickers Fithian House—may be seen by walking down the main street, Ye Greate Street.

GUIDED TOURS Many of the private residences are open during special tours sponsored by the Cumberland County Historical Society. For information, contact the Society by writing to their headquarters, P.O. Box 16, Greenwich, New Jersey 08323.

BOND HOUSE   *Ye Greate Street. Not open to the public.*   The original section of this house, constructed in 1725, served as a rectory for St. Stephen's Episcopal Church, which stood a short distance to the south. In the nineteenth century the rectory was converted into a private home, and it later came into the possession of Dr. Levi Bond.

BOWEN-WILLIAMS HOUSE   *Ye Greate Street. Not open to the public.*   This house was built by the Bowen family in the early 1770s. The lower section is a later addition.

FITHIAN HOUSE   *Approximately ¾ of a mile east of Ye Greate Street toward Bridgeton. Not open to the public.*   The Reverend Philip Vickers Fithian, an ardent anti-Loyalist, was born in this house in 1747. It was here that the men of the area gathered on December 22, 1774, to disguise themselves as Indians before seizing and burning the cargo of tea.

FRIENDS MEETING HOUSE   *Ye Greate Street. Open Sunday 2 P.M. to 5 P.M. April through October.*   The first meeting house on this site was a crude log structure built in 1690 for the "use, service and purpose . . . for those people in scorn called Quakers." The first session of the Cumberland County Court was held there in May 1748. In 1771 the present brick building was erected after the original meeting house had been destroyed by fire.

GIBBON HOUSE *Ye Greate Street. Open Saturday and Sunday 2 P.M. to 5 P.M. April through October. Fee 25¢.* Built by merchant Nicholas Gibbon in 1730, this house is noted for its fine Flemish brickwork. Now the headquarters of the Cumberland County Historical Society, the building contains a collection of artifacts, silver, clothing, and memorabilia of the eighteenth and nineteenth centuries.

HARDING HOUSE *Ye Greate Street. Not open to the public.* The interior of this house (*c.* 1734) still reflects its Colonial origins. The low ceilings show hand-hewn beams, and some of the doors still retain their original locks and hinges.

OLD STONE TAVERN *Ye Greate Street. Not open to the public.* Built in 1728 by Jacob Ware, this tavern provided accommodations for travelers and served as a meeting place for the townspeople. In 1748 citizens of the county met here to vote on the location of the county seat. When the decision was read aloud that Cohansey Bridge (Bridgeton) was chosen as the seat of government, angry residents of Greenwich started to riot, damaging the interior of the tavern. Today, the building is furnished with fine antiques of the period.

PIRATE HOUSE *Ye Greate Street. Open to the public. Contact the Cumberland County Historical Society for the schedule.* Although this structure was built in 1734, many alterations have changed the exterior. According to local legend, a pirate named John (his full name is unknown) once lived here. Accused of treacherous dealings by his partners, he was chained by them in the attic and left to die. Legend has it that at night ghostly chains can be heard rattling as John struggles to free himself from his lingering punishment.

REEVE-SHEPPARD HOUSE   *Ye Greate Street. Not open to the public.*   The earliest section of this dwelling was built in 1686, making it the oldest house still standing in Greenwich.

WOOD MANSION   *Ye Greate Street. Not open to the public.*   Richard Wood, a prominent merchant in Greenwich, built this fine residence in 1765. The store which he operated is still standing nearby.

Pennsylvania

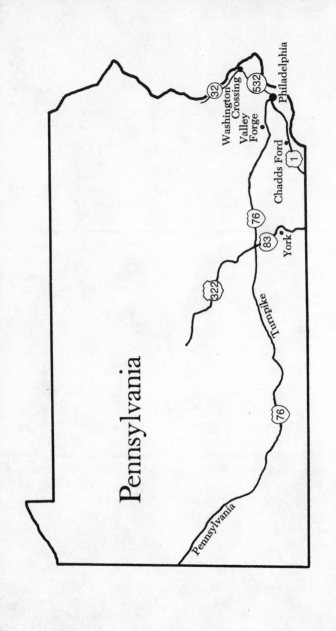

Washington Crossing

Revolutionary War History

The autumn of 1776 was a dark time for the Patriot cause. The British had dealt a decisive blow against the Continental Army, driving Washington's troops out of New York City and sending them into harried retreat across New Jersey and into Pennsylvania. In order to travel quickly and thereby avoid an overwhelming defeat, the Patriot soldiers were forced to abandon valuable stores and supplies. By mid-December the British had gained control of most of New Jersey and were within striking distance of Philadelphia—the largest city in the colonies and the seat of the Continental Congress.

In late December Washington determined to attack the garrison at Trenton in order to weaken the enemy stranglehold on New Jersey and to boost the morale of his poorly-clad, ill-fed army. The strategy called for a three-pronged attack. George Washington with the main force was to cross the Delaware River at McKonkey's Ferry, several miles north of Trenton on the Pennsylvania side. General James Ewing was to cross at Trenton and take the bridge over Assunpink Creek, cutting off the path of any Hessian retreat. General John Cadwalader was to create a diversionary maneuver by crossing at Bristol, Pennsylvania, and distracting enemy troops near Bordentown, New Jersey.

At 6 P.M. on December 25, 1776, the attack began. In the bitter cold Washington assembled a force of 2,400 soldiers and eighteen cannon along the banks of the Delaware River. A freezing rain began as the soldiers huddled together waiting for the boats that would ferry them to the opposite side. These men were dressed in tattered uniforms; many who were without shoes had their feet wrapped in rags.

Into the howling wind General Henry Knox shouted directions to the troops, ordering them into the Durham boats (fifty feet long, eight feet wide, and twelve feet deep), which were manned by the stalwart Massachusetts sailors of General John Glover's Marblehead Regiment.

The crossing was led by the Commander-in-Chief himself. Along with him in the first boats were General Adam Stephen's brigade of artillerymen. The oarsmen's task was a difficult one, for the river was clogged with ice floes and they were forced to pull against the strong northern wind, which by now was heavy with snow. Upon reaching the New Jersey shore, the infantry was stationed around the landing site to provide safety for those who would follow.

Meanwhile, Generals Ewing and Cadwalader had marched their units to the sites on the river chosen for their crossings. By the time the troops had assembled at their appointed locations, the rain had been transformed into a brutal snowstorm, making the officers believe a crossing would be foolhardy to attempt.

By 11 P.M. the snow and sleet were so intense that Washington's men were nearly blinded, but still the intrepid oarsmen continued to ferry the Patriot troops across the river. When General Washington received a message from General Sullivan that the men's powder and muskets were drenched, he swiftly replied, "Tell General Sullivan to use the bayonet; I am resolved to take Trenton."

Finally, at 3 A.M., the last boat had reached the New Jersey shore. As the storm continued to rage around them, the commanding officers—Greene, Sullivan, and Washington—regrouped their exhausted, half-frozen regiments and at 4 A.M. began the nine-mile march to Trenton.

Washington Crossing State Park was created in 1917 by an Act of the Pennsylvania Assembly. The 500-acre park,

Washington Crossing the Delaware. *Painting by Emanuel Leutze.* (METROPOLITAN MUSEUM OF ART, NEW YORK CITY. GIFT OF JOHN STEWART KENNEDY)

administered by a commission appointed by the governor, is divided into two sections—the Washington Crossing/Lower Park area and the Bowman's Hill/Upper Park area, located five miles to the northwest along Route 32.

Located seven miles south of New Hope on Route 32, the park is open daily from dawn to dusk and is free.

VISITORS' CENTER Information about the park's historical sites may be obtained in the lobby of the Memorial Building.

State Park Sites

BOWMAN'S HILL TOWER *Upper Park. Turn off Route 32. Open 8 A.M. to sunset. Free.* This hill was named for Doctor Jonathan Bowman who, according to tradition, was the surgeon aboard Captain William Kidd's pirate ship. After Kidd was hanged in 1700, Doctor Bowman, wishing to live in seclusion, traveled here and built a cabin on this site.

During the encampment of Patriot troops in the vicinity, Washington's sentries used this hill as a lookout. In 1930 the Commonwealth of Pennsylvania erected an observation tower at the top of Bowman's Hill to mark the spot of the Patriot outpost. The stone tower is 110 feet high and has a 121-step circular staircase.

MEMORIAL BUILDING *Lower Park. Open daily 9 A.M. to 5 P.M. Free.* Near the Patriot troops' point of embarkation now stands the Memorial Building, erected by the Commonwealth of Pennsylvania in 1959. Inside may be seen a copy of Emanuel Leutze's famous painting, *Washington Crossing the Delaware* (1851). The original work was displayed here from 1952 until 1969, when it was returned to the Metropolitan Museum of Art in New York. The copy is by Robert B. Williams of Washington, D.C. A library in the east wing contains original manuscripts and letters of the Revolutionary War period.

In front of the Memorial Building is a reflecting pool surrounded by flags of the thirteen original colonies and the so-called Betsy Ross flag. Standing at the head of the pool is a twenty-five-foot shaft topped by a

Memorial building, Washington Crossing State Park (ALPER)

statue of George Washington; it was erected in 1916
by the Patriotic Order Sons of America.

OLD FERRY INN   *Lower Park. Near the river, off Route
532. Open 9 A.M. to 5 P.M. Free.*   In 1776 Samuel
McKonkey, who operated a ferry across the Delaware
River, owned an inn (*c.* 1757) on this site. According
to tradition, General Washington ate a meal here in the
late afternoon of December 25, just before the crossing
began. The property was purchased by Mahlon K.
Taylor in 1777.

Little remains of the inn of Revolutionary days. The
oldest section of the present building was erected between 1780 and 1790. The eastern wing was added in
1810, and the northern room was built about 1850.
Much of the original paneling and woodwork have been
preserved. The antiques throughout the first floor were
donated by the Bucks County Federation of Women's
Clubs.

OLD GRISTMILL   *Upper Park. A short distance south of the Thompson-Neely House, off Route 32. The structure is undergoing restoration.*   During the last half of the eighteenth century this mill was operated by Robert Thompson and his son-in-law William Neely. Here, in December 1776, they ground grain for the Patriot soldiers encamped in the area.

POINT OF EMBARKATION MONUMENT   *Lower Park. At the foot of the steps near the Memorial Building.*   Today, a monument stands near the river's edge where Washington's troops boarded their boats on Christmas night 1776. The brownstone monument was erected in 1895 by the Bucks County Historical Society.

SOLDIERS' GRAVES   *Upper Park. Follow the road leaving the Thompson-Neely House over the Delaware Canal and past the picnic area.*   Soldiers of the Continental Army were buried in this field. Many of the

Point of Embarkation Monument, Washington Crossing State Park (ALPER)

forgotten warriors lie in unmarked graves. The base of the memorial flagstaff is composed of thirteen triangular sections set with native stones brought here from the thirteen original colonies.

THOMPSON-NEELY HOUSE *Upper Park. Open daily 10 A.M. to 5 P.M., Sunday 1 P.M. to 5 P.M. Free.* In 1702 John Pidcock purchased land here on which he constructed a small one-story farmhouse. The property was acquired in 1753 by Robert Thompson, who built the west wing onto the house four years later. In 1766, when his daughter married William Neely, Thompson enlarged the structure by adding a second floor, where the young couple resided. The eastern wing dates from 1788.

From December 9–25, before the army's crossing of the Delaware River, this house served as headquarters for General William Alexander (Lord Stirling), Captain James Moore, and Lieutenant James Monroe (later the fifth United States President). Known as the "House of Decision," it was the meeting place for General George Washington and his officers to discuss strategy. Here they made plans for the crossing of the river and the subsequent attack on Trenton.

The rooms, furnished with appropriate eighteenth-century pieces, have been given various names—for example, the **Hospital Room,** a downstairs bedroom that was used for wounded officers; and the **Council Room,** the kitchen in which Washington and his aides are reputed to have made their momentous decisions.

Sightseers may wish to cross to the New Jersey side of the river to visit the Crossing sites there.

Philadelphia Area

Revolutionary War History

The earliest permanent settlers in the Philadelphia area were the Swedes, who established a community here, New Sweden, in the 1640s. In 1655 New Sweden surrendered to a Dutch military force from New Amsterdam (now New York), but the Dutch control was short-lived, ending in 1664 when New Amsterdam surrendered to the English.

In 1681 William Penn (1644–1718) received from King Charles II a charter for the colony north of Maryland and west of the Delaware River. (This grant was in payment of a debt owed by the king to Penn's father.) A Quaker, Penn had a vision of a "Holy Experiment"—a community in which people would be free to worship openly as they pleased. He sent surveyors and agents to the colony—named Pennsylvania ("Penn's Woods")—and shortly afterward Thomas Holme began to draft street plans for the colony's major city and capital, Philadelphia (Greek for "brotherly love").

English Quakers arrived here in great numbers. Others attracted by the principle of religious freedom also settled here, including Welsh Nonconformists and German Pietists. Penn resided in the colony from 1682 to 1684 and again from 1699 to 1701. By the time of his death in 1718, Philadelphia had developed into a thriving community.

During the first half of the eighteenth century Philadelphia established itself as America's leading port, exporting produce from the fertile Pennsylvania farmlands, iron from the furnaces along the Schuylkill River, and products manufactured in Pennsylvania and nearby colonies. By the time of the American Revolution, Philadelphia, with a population of 40,000, had become America's largest city.

After the British Parliament passed the Stamp Act in March 1765, violent protests erupted throughout the American colonies. In Philadelphia a mob of irate citizens burned an effigy of stamp master John Hughes and attempted to compel him to resign his post, but he refused and firmly maintained his authority. Bands of dissidents that roamed the streets so alarmed the royal governor and the mayor that they temporarily fled the city. The unruly crowds even hurled taunts and threats at Benjamin Franklin's wife because her husband, then in England, had not been able to prevent the British government from passing the oppressive act. In desperation, Mrs. Franklin purchased arms and ammunition to protect herself and her property against the anger of the mob. But fortunately she was forced to suffer only verbal abuse. Franklin defended American rights during the debates leading to the repeal of the Stamp Act and consequently regained favor from the freedom-loving Philadelphians.

With the passage of the Tea Act in mid-1773 Philadelphia was once again rocked by turmoil. On October 13 a scathing attack on the policies of the Crown appeared in the *Pennsylvania Journal*. The anonymous author—probably Thomas Mifflin—asserted that the Tea Act constituted taxation without representation and demanded the resignation of Philadelphia consignees of the East India Company. Within the next several days numerous broadsides were circulated calling on Americans to boycott tea. On the afternoon of Saturday, October 16, more than 700 local citizens gathered at the State House (now called Independence Hall) where they adopted a resolution condemning Parliament and appointed a committee to persuade the city's consignees to support their cause.

The two major firms acting as consignees for the East India Company were the Wharton Company and James & Drinker. The Wharton family immediately pledged that they would "do nothing . . . to enslave America" but James & Drinker issued a noncommittal statement that "if the Tea should ever arrive and we should be so appointed or have any concern in it, our Conduct will be open to our Fellow Citizens." In late November, even though antagonism continued to grow toward the managers of James & Drinker, they still intended to unload and store the cargo of the tea ship *Polly*, which was nearing the port of Philadelphia.

On November 27, 1773, broadsides were circulated warning that the owner of any pilot boat leading the *Polly* up the Delaware River would be tarred and feathered. Rumors abounded that if the captain of the tea ship attempted to moor at one of the piers, he would be seized and tarred and feathered. Terrified that the rumors might prove to be true and that more serious violence might erupt, the managers of James & Drinker expediently tendered their resignation as consignees of the East India Company. Reluctantly the company recalled its ship.

Additional legislation passed by Parliament in 1774 once again outraged the colonists. A series of acts—referred to as the Coercive or Intolerable Acts—protected officials of the Crown accused of capital offenses, modified the government of Massachusetts, closed the port of Boston to commerce, and provided for the continuance of the quartering of British troops in America. Protests and riots became widespread, and in their wake came a call for an assembly of Patriot representatives from all the colonies—the First Continental Congress.

Philadelphia's central location between the northern and southern colonies led to its selection as the meeting place for the Continental Congress. Fifty-six delegates from every American colony except pro-British Georgia gathered at Carpenters' Hall from September 5 to October 26, 1774. Peyton Randolph of Virginia was unanimously elected president and Charles Thomson was chosen secretary. One of the early debates focused on voting procedures, and it was decided that each colony would be given one vote. During the October sessions the members adopted a declaration defining the personal rights of the American colonists, denounced the taxation policies of the British government, and protested the quartering of British soldiers without the consent of the Colonial governments. They also called for the formation of a Continental Association to enforce economic sanctions against the mother country. As a final action the Congress prepared a petition to the king demanding redress of their grievances. On October 26 the delegates adjourned with the understanding that a second Congress would be called in May of 1775 if the British government had not begun to act upon their demands.

The Second Continental Congress was inevitable, and on May 10, 1775, the delegates returned to Philadelphia to hold their sessions in the State House. They reelected Peyton Randolph as president, but he withdrew and John Hancock succeeded him on May 24. One of the first acts of the Congress was the appointment of George Washington as Commander-in-Chief of the Continental Army and the voting of $2 million in bills of credit to finance the Revolution.

In a final attempt to seek reconciliation with England, a committee of members, led by John Dickinson, drafted the so-called Olive Branch Petition on July 5. It expressed a desire for the restoration of harmonious relations and professed a willingness to accept the authority of King George III if the colonists' grievances were redressed. Loyalist Richard Penn (a descendant of William Penn) was sent to London, but the king refused to grant him an audience.

The Crown was unyielding. Faced with such an intractable position, the delegates determined to sever America's ties with England. On June 7, 1776, Richard Henry Lee introduced a resolution "that these United Colonies are, and of right ought to be, free and independent States." The motion was immediately seconded by John Adams. Four

Declaration of Independence. *Painting by John Trumbull.*
(OFFICE OF THE ARCHITECT OF THE CAPITOL, WASHINGTON, D.C.)

days later Congress appointed a committee—Thomas Jefferson, John Adams, Benjamin Franklin, Roger Sherman, and Robert R. Livingston—to draft an official document stating its position. Jefferson was largely responsible for the initial draft, after which the other members of the committee made minor alterations of the text. The Declaration of Independence was formally adopted on July 4, 1776.

The introductory statement of the Declaration promulgated the theory of natural rights—that "all men are created equal, that they are endowed by their Creator with certain unalienable Rights; that among these are Life, Liberty, and the Pursuit of Happiness." The main section of the document enumerated some twenty-eight specific grievances, indicting King George III for creating the conditions that forced the colonies to declare their independence.

The Congress ordered the document engrossed on July 19, and it was accordingly put on parchment, probably by Timothy Matlock of Philadelphia. On August 2 the members of the Continental Congress signed the Declaration of Independence. (The signatures of six absent members were affixed later.)

As the seat of the Continental Congress and America's largest city, Philadelphia became a prime military objective of the British army. In the fall of 1777 General William Howe removed 13,000 soldiers from the British garrison in New York City to the head of the Chesapeake Bay, where the troops began a fifty-mile march to Philadelphia. After defeating Washington's army at Brandywine Creek on September 11, the British proceeded with little opposition to Philadelphia, which they occupied on September 26. (The Continental Congress had already fled to Lancaster, then to York, Pennsylvania.) There they remained during the winter of 1777–1778 while Washington's forces endured the bitter winter at Valley Forge.

In January 1778 a group of Patriots at Bordentown, New Jersey, floated a number of crudely built incendiary devices downstream in the rapid current of the Delaware River. They were intended to explode upon hitting the British ships anchored in the river opposite Philadelphia. At dusk, however, the vessels were ordered to the piers to avoid the ice floes which were posing a threat to their safety. Later that evening, when one of the kegs ignited near the city, it sent the British troops rushing to their batteries, and for hours afterward the roar of guns could be heard echoing across the river as the soldiers futilely fired at any object moving in the water. The Patriots ridiculed the enemy by referring to the events of the evening as the "Battle of the Kegs."

During the British occupation General Howe, distressed by what he felt to be lack of support from his government, resigned his post as Commander-in-Chief of British forces in America. He was replaced by General Henry Clinton, who assumed command in Philadelphia on May 18, 1778. To mark the occasion, two British officers, John André and Oliver De Lancey, organized a celebration called the "Mischianza" (Italian for "mixture" or "medley"). The festivities began with a regatta of brightly decorated barges on the Schuylkill River. Later, a mock tournament was staged in which the Knights of the Blended Roses and the Knights of the Burning Mountain, all dressed in medieval costume, confronted each other. After jousting with lances, they fought furiously with swords until the marshal of the field rushed in and declared their valor had been proved and the games were ended. In the evening hundreds of officers and prominent Loyalists escorted their ladies to a ball held in a ballroom decorated with festoons of flowers and eighty-five mirrors. The blast of fireworks illuminated the night sky before the midnight supper, which ended with toasts to the king and the royal family. The guests then danced until dawn. The Mischianza was not only a farewell celebration for Howe; it also proved to be a farewell for the British army in Philadelphia.

When General Clinton realized that the capture of the city had not produced the results hoped for, he decided to consolidate his troops with those in New York City. On June 18, 1778, after thousands of Loyalists had boarded transport ships, the British troops evacuated Philadelphia.

The Congress soon returned. While the delegates had been holding sessions at the courthouse in York, they had formally adopted the Articles of Confederation (November 15, 1777), which united the independent states for joint action and defined their powers in relationship to those of the national government. The Articles were then sent to the thirteen states for ratification, which was not accomplished until March 1, 1781. After the cessation of hostilities and the signing of the Treaty of Paris (1783), the inherent weaknesses of the Articles of Confederation became apparent as the Congress encountered difficulties enforcing its legislation and levying taxes. Many prominent leaders advocated strengthening the centralized government, and a general convention was called to revise the Articles.

During the Philadelphia Convention—held in the State

House from May 25 to September 17, 1787—the delegates, with George Washington presiding as president, reached the decision to create a federated government. The powers and limits of this new government were codified in the document that still guides our nation—the United States Constitution. The Constitution provides for three independent branches: a bicameral Congress with a Senate and House of Representatives; an executive branch headed by the President and Vice President (whose duties include presiding over the Senate); and a judiciary system. The Convention adopted the Constitution in September 1789, then sent it to the states for ratification. Eleven states ratified it by July 1788; North Carolina and Rhode Island (the only state which had not sent a delegate to the Convention) withheld endorsement until the spring of 1789.

The first session of Congress operating under the Constitution was held in New York City in 1789. From December 6, 1790, to May 14, 1800, Philadelphia served as the United States capital. The Senate and House of Representatives convened in Congress Hall, and the United States Supreme Court occupied chambers in the City Hall

Signing of the Constitution. *Painting by Howard Chandler Christy.* (OFFICE OF THE ARCHITECT OF THE CAPITOL, WASHINGTON, D.C.)

building. President George Washington resided in the Executive Mansion on Market Street (between 5th and 6th Streets). With the city crowded with legislators and prominent citizens from all the states, Philadelphia enjoyed a dazzling social and cultural life. When the seat of government moved to Washington, D.C., in 1800, Philadelphia's golden age began to fade.

VISITORS' CENTER   Information, maps, and brochures are available from 9 A.M. to 5 P.M. at the Philadelphia Convention and Tourist Bureau, 1525 John F. Kennedy Boulevard (at 16th Street), phone 864–1976. By the time of the Bicentennial, a Visitors' Center will be constructed at the corner of Chestnut and 3rd Streets in the Independence Hall area. Serious students of historic buildings and local history may wish to contact the Independence National Historical Park Headquarters, 313 Walnut Street, phone 627–1776, or the Historical Society of Pennsylvania, 1300 Locust Street, phone 732–6200.

GUIDED TOURS   **Gray Line Tours**   Phone 569–3666. The two-and-one-half hour Historic Philadelphia Tour departs at 9:30 A.M., 11 A.M., 1:30 P.M. and 2:30 P.M. from March 30 to October 25. The rest of the year the buses leave at 9:30 A.M., 11 A.M., and 1:30 P.M. The cost is $6.75 for adults, $3.75 for children. The two-and-one-half-hour Modern Philadelphia Tour starts at 10 A.M. daily (year-round) and costs $6.75 for adults, $3.75 for children. Tours of Valley Forge, which are scheduled only from March 30 to October 25, are offered at 1:15 P.M. daily and cost $10.00 for adults, $6.00 for children. Inquire about other tours. Buses depart from 16th Street and John F. Kennedy Boulevard.

   Harbor Tours, Inc.   Phone 925–7640. Boat tours are offered which sail down the Delaware River on the

Pennsylvania side as far as the mouth of the Schuylkill and return along the New Jersey shore. From July 1 to Labor Day tours start at 11 A.M. and 2 P.M. from Monday through Saturday, 1 P.M. and 3 P.M. on Sunday. The fall and spring schedules are erratic, so telephone. Adults $2.50, children $1.25. Boats depart from Pier 11, Delaware Avenue and Race Street.

All the above tours, schedules, and fees are subject to change.

PUBLIC TRANSPORTATION The city's buses, trolleys, and subways are operated by SEPTA, the Southeastern Pennsylvania Transportation Authority. An inexpensive map of public transportation routes may be purchased at most newsstands.

From May through November SEPTA operates a "Cultural Loop Bus" in the area from 9:30 A.M. to 5:30 P.M. For 50¢ the passenger can get on and off at any of twenty stops. (The stops include Independence Hall, Betsy Ross House, Christ Church, City Hall, and the Philadelphia Museum of Art.)

TAXI SERVICE Several taxi companies, including Yellow Cab and United Cab, service the metropolitan Philadelphia area. Taxis can be hailed as they travel along the streets. You can telephone for taxi pickup by calling Yellow Cab, 922–8400.

ENTERTAINMENT For listings of films, plays, concerts, museum exhibitions, and dance programs, consult *Philadelphia Magazine* and local newspapers, especially the Friday and Sunday editions.

USEFUL TELEPHONE NUMBERS Time, 846–1212; Weather, 937–1212; Police, 231–3131; Fire or Rescue Squad, 563–6700; Physicians Service, 563–5343; Dental Emergencies, 922–5100 or 563–9650.

SELF-GUIDED TOURS Most of Philadelphia's major sites—listed in Tours A, B, and C below—may be seen by walking or by taking public transportation. To reach the historic houses of Germantown (Tour D), take the Reading Railroad (from 11th and Market) to Wayne Junction or SEPTA Route 23 trolley on Germantown Avenue. Traveling to Germantown by car, follow North Broad Street (away from City Hall) to the 3700 block, where Germantown Avenue will be off to the left. (Since you cannot make a left turn here, proceed two blocks to Pike Street, then turn left, and come around to Germantown Avenue.) If you have time, try also to visit the Colonial mansions in Fairmount Park. Tours are offered by the Park House Office of the Philadelphia Museum of Art, 26th Street and the Franklin Parkway, phone 763–8100. In the listing below NR signifies an important *Non-Revolutionary site.*

Tour A

Area bounded by Chestnut Street on the north, Walnut Street on south, 2nd Street on the east, and 7th Street on the west.

Start at Walnut and 7th Streets:

Washington Square

Atwater Kent Museum (NR)

Independence Hall

Congress Hall

Old City Hall

Second Bank of the United States (NR)

Tour B

Area bounded by Race Street on the north, Market Street on the south, Front Street on the east, and 5th Street on the west.

Start at Market Street near 3rd Street:

Franklin Court

Christ Church

Elfreth's Alley

Betsy Ross House

Friends Meeting House

Benjamin Franklin Bust

Christ Church Cemetery

United States Mint (NR)

Tour A (Cont.)

Carpenters' Hall

Pemberton House

First Bank of the United States

City Tavern

Bishop White House

Todd House

St. Joseph's Church

End at Willings Alley, near 4th and Walnut Streets.

Tour B (Cont.)

End at 5th and Arch Streets.

Tour C

Area along the Benjamin Franklin Parkway from Logan Circle (off 19th Street) to 26th Street.

Start at Logan Circle:

Franklin Institute (NR)

Rodin Museum (NR)

Philadelphia Museum of Art (NR)

End at 26th Street and the Parkway.

Tour D

Area in Germantown along Germantown Avenue from 15th Street to Upsal Street.

Start at Courtland and 18th Streets:

Stenton Mansion

Germantown Historical Society

Grumblethorpe

Clarkson-Watson House

Deshler-Morris House

Clivedon (Chew House)

End at Germantown Avenue, just past Johnson Street.

Colonial and Revolutionary War Sites

CARPENTERS' HALL   *320 Chestnut Street below 4th Street. Open daily 10 A.M. to 4 P.M.; 9 A.M. to 8 P.M. during the Bicentennial. Closed holidays. Free. In summer short plays based on Colonial events are performed on the grounds.*   The Carpenters' Company of Philadelphia—organized by local master carpenters in 1724 for their mutual welfare and for the further study of their craft—voted to erect a guild hall in 1770. They commissioned Robert Smith (who had designed Princeton University's Nassau Hall) to supervise the planning and construction of the building. Carpenters' Hall, a two-story cross-shaped structure with a cupola, was completed in January 1774. The first floor was utilized for meetings and for the transaction of the Carpenters' Company business; the second floor was used by the Library Company of Philadelphia, which set up a reading room and a meeting chamber for the directors of the company.

When the British Parliament—in retaliation for the Boston Tea Party (December 16, 1773)—passed the Boston Port Bill closing Boston Harbor to all commerce beginning June 1, 1774, outraged Philadelphians organized a Committee of Correspondence which included Robert Smith and several men from the Carpenters' Company. Throughout the summer outspoken Pennsylvania Patriots assembled here, urging decisive action against the British government. As tension increased, similar groups in other colonies called for an intercolonial congress.

The First Continental Congress, composed of fifty-six

Carpenters' Hall, Philadelphia (ALPER)

delegates from twelve colonies, met at Carpenters' Hall
on September 5, 1774. (Georgia was the only colony
that did not send an official representative.) The members elected Peyton Randolph, a distinguished Virginia
lawyer, to serve as president. During the following weeks
these Patriots enumerated their grievances against the
Crown: they denounced oppressive legislation (such as
the Coercive Acts of 1774) and declared thirteen Acts
of Parliament to be without legal authority. To seek redress for these grievances, they drafted resolutions setting forth the rights of the colonists, agreed on an
embargo of British goods, and prepared a document to
be sent to King George III. Adjournment came on
October 26.

Refusal by the Crown officials to eradicate the in-
justices, followed by news of the eruption of open
hostilities at Lexington and Concord (April 1775),

precipitated another meeting of the delegates. From May 10 to August 2, 1775, while the Second Continental Congress convened at the State House (now called Independence Hall), several of its committees occasionally met here at Carpenters' Hall. In early May 1776 a group of prominent Pennsylvania citizens gathered here for preliminary meetings leading to the drafting of the Pennsylvania constitution.

During the Revolutionary War members of the Carpenters' Company participated in the building of American defenses on the Pennsylvania and New Jersey sides of the Delaware River. In early 1777 the first floor of the Carpenters' Hall was converted into a hospital for wounded Patriots, and during the British occupation it was used for the care of disabled British soldiers. When the city was once again in Patriot hands, military supplies were stored in the cellar here.

From 1791 to 1797 the building was rented to the

Actors presenting a play based on Revolutionary War events, courtyard of Carpenters' Hall (ALPER)

First Bank of the United States and the Carpenters' Company moved into quarters in the nearby "New Hall." During the first two decades of the nineteenth century, Carpenters' Hall was used as a United States Customs House.

In 1859 the building was refurbished and opened as an historic shrine. On display are original chairs used by members of the First Continental Congress and a collection of tools and equipment used by Colonial carpenters.

CHRIST CHURCH AND CEMETERY *2nd Street, above Market Street. Open daily* 9 A.M. *to* 5 P.M. The Anglican parish of Christ Church, which was organized in 1695, first worshipped in a modest wooden meeting house near this site. By the 1720s, the congregation had grown so large that a committee was formed to make plans for a new building. John Kearsley, a parishioner, designed the structure and supervised construction, which began in 1727. The north and south exterior walls of Christ Church have a series of bays separated by pilasters, and an imposing Palladian window dominates the east wall.

The 200-foot spire was added in 1754, financed by a subscription organized by several prominent Philadelphians, including Benjamin Franklin. The church bells were brought to the city from England by Captain Richard Budden.

When the First and Second Continental Congresses met in Philadelphia, many of the delegates attended services at Christ Church—much to the dismay of Loyalist parishioners. The delegates were so impressed by the sermons of the Reverend Jacob Duché that they invited him to serve as chaplain to the Congress. Upon the adoption of the Declaration of Independence on July 4, 1776, Duché directed that the bells of Christ Church peal forth the tidings of freedom. Soon after the British occupation of the city in 1777, he was imprisoned, and his period of confinement convinced him to become a supporter of the Crown.

After the Revolutionary War, the Reverend William White became pastor at Christ Church. In 1789 a convention of the Episcopal Church of America assembled here, drafted a constitution, and adopted new books of prayer. This convention formally severed the church's ties with the ecclesiastical establishment in England.

When, from 1790 through 1796, President George Washington and his wife resided in Philadelphia—then the United States capital—they worshipped frequently at Christ Church, in pew 58. Pew 70 was reserved for Benjamin Franklin.

The interior of the church is simple, yet elegant. The original eighteenth-century "wineglass" pulpit is quite rare. The silver communion pieces presented to the parish by Queen Anne and the original 1744 brass chandeliers may still be seen. The magnificent stained-glass windows were made in the early twentieth century by Heaton, Butler, and Bayne of London. The "Liberty Window," in the west end of the north wall, depicts two scenes: the granting of the Magna Carta by King John in 1215 and the convening of the First Continental Congress in 1774.

Behind the church are buried James Wilson (1742–1798) and Robert Morris (1734–1806), both signers of the Declaration of Independence. Also interred here is General Charles Lee (1731–1782), a general in the Continental Army who was suspended from command because of his insubordination at the Battle of Monmouth.

In the Christ Church Cemetery, located at Arch and 5th Streets, are buried Benjamin Franklin (1706–1790) and his wife Deborah. (It is a local tradition—some think a disrespectful one—to throw a penny on the grave of the creator of "Poor Richard" for luck.) Four other signers of the Declaration of Independence are laid to rest here: Joseph Hewes (1730–1779), George Ross (1730–1779), Francis Hopkinson (1737–1791), and Benjamin Rush (1745–1813).

CITY TAVERN *2nd Street between Chestnut and Walnut Streets. Reconstruction in progress.* In 1772 a group of prominent Philadelphians—including Governor John Penn and attorney Benjamin Chew—formulated plans for a city tavern. Funds were raised through a subscription, and construction began soon afterward. Completed in late 1773, the tavern not only provided accommodations for travelers but also became a social center for the townspeople. Food and drink were served in the public rooms on the ground floor; rooms—including a long, narrow banquet hall (called the "Long Room")—reserved for meetings and private dinners were found on the second floor; and rooms for overnight guests were located on the third floor.

When hostilities began to intensify between the colonies and England, City Tavern was destined to be the scene of many important moments in the struggle for independence. In the summer of 1774, after Paul Revere arrived in Philadelphia with news that Britain had closed Boston Harbor to commerce, a protest meeting was held in the Long Room. One of the leaders of the group, John Dickinson (a member of the Pennsylvania Assembly), denounced the oppressive act but would not approve rebellion against the mother country. Charles Thomas (a local Patriot), while vehemently challenging Dickinson's conservative view, became so excited that he fainted. The only action the opposing sides could agree upon was the formation of a committee to convey an expression of sympathy to the Bostonians.

During the first week of September 1774, when representatives to the First Continental Congress began arriving in Philadelphia, several rented rooms in the City Tavern. The delegates held a preliminary meeting here in which they decided to hold their sessions in

Carpenters' Hall. During the Second Continental Congress of 1775–1776 the delegates dined together every Saturday evening at the tavern.

City Tavern was also the scene of many festive occasions celebrating both British and American victories during the Revolutionary War. In 1777–1778, when the British were occupying Philadelphia, a series of elegant balls was given here by Loyalists in honor of the British officers. In 1781, when Philadelphia was once again under American control, news of Washington's victory at Yorktown was cause for a gala celebration by jubilant citizens.

George Washington frequently dined here in 1787 while serving as president of the Constitutional Convention. Over the dinner table the merits of the Constitution being drafted were hotly contrasted with the weaknesses of the Articles of Confederation.

In the 1790s the building—then primarily a coffee-house—began to fall into disrepair and patronage declined. A fire damaged the structure in 1834, but after repairs the business continued to operate until 1854. At that time the dilapidated building was demolished.

Independence National Historical Park is reconstructing City Tavern, which it hopes to open as a restaurant for the Bicentennial.

CONGRESS HALL   *6th and Chestnut Streets (Independence Hall Complex). Open daily 9 A.M. to 5 P.M.; 9 A.M. to 8 P.M. during the Bicentennial. Free.*   Completed in 1789, this brick structure was designed by Henry Hill for use as the county courthouse. In December 1790, however, the United States Congress moved to Philadelphia from New York City, and it held its sessions in this building. (The nation's seat of government remained here for ten years, until 1800 when the capital was moved to the District of Columbia.)

The House of Representatives, with Frederick A. Muhlenberg as Speaker, convened in the chamber on

Senate Chamber, Congress Hall, Philadelphia (INDEPENDENCE NATIONAL HISTORICAL PARK, PHILADELPHIA)

the first floor. The delegates sat in leather seats behind mahogany desks arranged in semicircular rows. The Senate, with Vice President John Adams presiding, met in the main room on the second floor. The elaborately decorated Senate Chamber was flanked by committee and conference rooms, including an office for the secretary, Samuel Alleyn Otis, who supervised a small staff which copied documents, distributed reports, and handled mail.

Many historic events took place in this building. President George Washington, reelected to a second term of office, made his inaugural address here in 1792, and four years later he delivered an emotional farewell speech before retiring to Mount Vernon. That same year John Adams was elected the second President of the United States, and on March 4, 1797, Chief Justice Oliver Ellsworth administered the oath of office here to

Adams and to Thomas Jefferson, his Vice President. Upon the death of George Washington in December 1799, Chief Justice John Marshall delivered a eulogy that included the now famous phrase (of Henry Lee): "First in war, first in peace, first in the hearts of his countrymen."

Here, in Congress Hall, legislators of the Federal and Republican parties debated issues and enacted laws that directed the course of the young nation. It was in Congress Hall in 1791 that the Bill of Rights—the first ten amendments—was formally appended to the Constitution.

During the decade Congress convened in this building it ruled on Indian affairs; ratified the Jay Treaty of 1794 with Great Britain, which regulated commerce and navigation; considered action against the government of France, which had ignored the seizure of American ships by French privateers; and in 1798 passed the Alien and Sedition Acts, which imposed strict supervision over immigrants and permitted the arrest of any alien considered dangerous.

After Congress moved to Washington, D.C., this building was once again occupied by officials of the county and municipal governments. In 1913 the Pennsylvania Society of Colonial Dames undertook restoration of Congress Hall. Further improvements were made by the National Park Service when it assumed administrative responsibility in 1950.

ELFRETH'S ALLEY *Between Front and 2nd Streets, north of Arch Street. Private residences open only the first Saturday of June.* Elfreth's Alley, dating back to the early eighteenth century, is the oldest continuously occupied street in the United States. The modest row houses lining this street were the residences of Colonial cabinetmakers, blacksmiths, and tailors. The two oldest surviving structures, numbers 120 and 122, were constructed in the mid-1720s. A small museum, located at number 126, is open on a limited schedule during the summer (phone 925–0934).

FIRST BANK OF THE UNITED STATES *120 South 3rd Street. Open daily* 9 A.M. *to* 5 P.M. *Free.* In 1791, on the recommendation of Secretary of the Treasury Alexander Hamilton, Congress passed legislation creating a national bank—the First Bank of the United States. Granted a twenty-year charter, it established its main office in Philadelphia, with branches in eight other cities. The bank not only acted as a fiscal agent for the government but also conducted a general commercial business.

The bank's twenty-five directors set up temporary offices in Carpenters' Hall until headquarters could be moved into the new bank building in 1797. Designed by

First Bank of the United States, Philadelphia (ALPER)

Samuel Blodget, Jr., the handsome structure had a marble facade with a colonnade of six Corinthian columns supporting an elaborately decorated pediment.

When the charter expired in 1811, the Congress refused to renew it—despite the fact that the bank was well managed and very successful. Stephen Girard (1750–1831), a powerful Philadelphia shipowner and merchant of French descent, purchased the building, took control of the remaining assets, and received a state charter. The Girard Bank helped finance government debt during the War of 1812.

Offices of the Girard Bank and its successor, the Girard National Bank of Philadelphia, were located here until 1926. The American Legion and the Board of City Trusts subsequently used the building. In the mid-1950s a Philadelphia information center was established in the rotunda. Recently, exhibits describing American government of the eighteenth century were installed.

BENJAMIN FRANKLIN BUST *Arch Street below 4th Street* This huge bust of Benjamin Franklin—located one block from his grave in Christ Church Cemetery— was designed and executed over a ten-year period by Reginald E. Beauchamp, assistant to the president of the *Philadelphia Bulletin* and director of the Poor Richard Club.

The sixteen-foot fiberglass bust is covered with 80,000 copper pennies donated by Philadelphia schoolchildren, sons and daughters of employees of the *Philadelphia Bulletin*, and members of the city's firefighting companies. The design scheme of the bust was suggested by a maxim by Benjamin Franklin: "A penny saved is a penny earned."

The bust was dedicated on June 10, 1971, by Mary T. Brooks, then the director of the United States Mint.

FRANKLIN COURT *Between 3rd and 4th Streets, off Market Street, on an alley called Orianna Street* This is the site of the house that Benjamin Franklin (1706–

*Benjamin Franklin
bust, Philadelphia*
(ALPER)

1790) built in 1764. Because of extensive traveling during his diplomatic career, he spent little time here. However, he did reside in the dwelling while attending the Continental Congress (1775–1776) and during the last five years of his life. The building was torn down in 1812.

FRIENDS MEETING HOUSE *Arch Street between 3rd and 4th Streets. Open daily 10 A.M. to 4 P.M. Closed Thanksgiving, December 25, and January 1. Free.* Throughout the eighteenth century the Quakers of the Philadelphia area held meetings in a modest wooden structure located at the corner of 2nd and Market Streets. By 1804 it had become so dilapidated that it was demolished and a new brick building was erected on this site. The west wing was added in 1811. The largest Friends' meeting house in the world, it is the setting of the Philadelphia Yearly Meeting, held every spring, of Friends residing on the East Coast.

Inside the meeting house are dioramas depicting events in the life of William Penn, including Penn writing his "Frame of Government," negotiating a treaty with the Indians, and perusing a map of Philadelphia by surveyor Thomas Holme.

The land surrounding the meeting house was originally used as a burial ground under a patent issued by William Penn in 1701. James Logan, Penn's secretary and later a mayor of Philadelphia, is interred here in an unmarked grave.

GLORIA DEI (OLD SWEDES') CHURCH *Delaware Avenue and Swanson Street. Open daily 9 A.M. to 5 P.M.* Gloria Dei Church stands in Southwark, an area settled by Swedes in the mid-seventeenth century. Here they constructed modest homes and erected a log blockhouse to provide protection. Religious services were held in the blockhouse by a lay preacher of the Swedish Church. In 1691 the Reverend Andress Rudman arrived to guide the spiritual life of the community. He immediately ordered the building of a church, and a rectangular brick structure was completed in 1700 on the site of the old blockhouse.

At the time of the Revolutionary War the Reverend Nickolas Collin was rector of the church, and he urged the young men of his congregation to fight for the Patriot cause. When British soldiers occupied Philadelphia in 1777, they destroyed the vacated houses of those residents of the Southwark area who had left to join the Continental Army. During the occupation the Reverend Collin remained an outspoken Patriot, and he supervised the removal of the church's organ pipes so that the metal could be melted for musket shot. He also continued to hold special memorial services for those parishioners who were killed in the war, many of whom were buried in the churchyard.

By 1845 the descendants of the original Swedish settlers who now comprised the congregation had been so completely assimilated into the American mainstream that they voted to join the Diocese of the Episcopal Church.

Today, the church still retains objects from its Colonial past. Located near the altar is a handsome baptismal font. The vestry contains rare Bibles and historic documents. A wood carving of two cherubs, which was brought here from Sweden by the seventeenth-century settlers, graces the front of the organ gallery. Gloria Dei was designated a National Historic Site in 1942.

SITE OF GRAFF-JEFFERSON HOUSE *700 Market Street, at 7th Street. Reconstruction in process.* On this site once stood the home (built in 1775) of Jacob Graff, Jr., a bricklayer. When Thomas Jefferson came to Philadelphia to attend the Second Continental Congress in 1775–1776, he rented rooms on the second floor of this house. There he drafted the Declaration of Independence.

In 1777 Graff sold the house. Afterward, it was occupied by a succession of tenants, including John Dunlap, publisher of the *Pennsylvania Gazette* and printer of the first copies of the Declaration of Independence. During the nineteenth century members of the distinguished Gratz family lived here. The structure was demolished in 1884. Plans are under way to reconstruct the building in which one of the most important documents of American liberty was conceived.

INDEPENDENCE HALL *Chestnut Street between 5th and 6th Streets. Open daily 9 A.M. to 8 P.M. July through Labor Day, and 9 A.M. to 5 P.M. the rest of the year. Hours may be extended during the Bicentennial. Free. A sound and light show, "A Nation is Born," is presented on the grounds Tuesday through Saturday at 9 P.M. in July and August. Free.* Eighteenth-century Philadelphia, capital of Pennsylvania, was a center of political and commercial activity. In 1729 it became apparent that a suitable building was needed to house the governing bodies of the colony—the Pennsylvania Assembly, the state Supreme Court, and the Governor's Council. Andrew Hamilton, a prominent lawyer and architect, was commissioned to create the designs for the structure. The construction, which began in 1732, was supervised by master carpenter Edmund Woolley. Labor problems delayed construction, and the two-story brick State House was not completed until 1748. (Later, it was renamed Independence Hall.) The tower and belfry were added in 1753.

Courtroom To the right of the entrance is the chamber once used by the Pennsylvania Supreme Court. Citizens accused of major crimes (such as burglary and murder) were confined to the prison at Walnut and 6th Streets and were brought here for trial. During the trial the courtroom was arranged in the traditional English style, with the defendant standing enclosed in the prisoner's dock, the jury seated in the box near the wall, and both lawyers placed together behind the table in front of the judges' bench. Townspeople observed the proceedings from behind the railing near the back of the room.

Assembly Chamber (Chamber of the Continental Congress and the Constitutional Convention) To the left of the entrance is the room that was used by the Pennsylvania Assembly until May 1775, when the Second Continental Congress began holding sessions here. One of the first major decisions made was the appointment of George Washington of Virginia as Commander-in-Chief of the Continental Army. It was here on July 4, 1776, that the Declaration of Independence was adopted. On August 2, after John Hancock (president of Congress) reminded the delegates of the gravity of openly breaking with the Crown, the document was

Independence Hall, Philadelphia (NATIONAL PARK SERVICE, WASHINGTON, D.C.)

Assembly Chamber, Independence Hall (INDEPENDENCE
NATIONAL HISTORICAL PARK, PHILADELPHIA)

signed by all the men present. The signatures of six
absent delegates were added later. (Visitors can still
see the original silver inkstand—made in 1756 by Philip
Syng—used by the signers.)

When the British occupied Philadelphia in September
1777, the Congress was forced to flee to Lancaster, then
farther west to York, Pennsylvania. Redcoats occupied
the building, and because of the scarcity of firewood
during the bitter winter of 1778, they ripped apart the
furniture here and burned it in the fireplaces. Congress
returned to Philadelphia in the summer of 1778 and
held sessions in this room for the next five years.

On June 21, 1783, a group of 300 soldiers stationed
in the city mutinied over a dispute with Congress concerning pay, clothing accounts, and pensions. (Similar
acts of defiance had occurred only four months earlier

at the Continental Army encampment near Newburgh, New York.) After seizing the local arsenals, the rebellious soldiers marched to the State House where Congress was meeting, surrounded the building, and demanded that the delegates take decisive action to resolve their grievances. Some of the soldiers, drunk on whiskey, shouted abuses and threats. The alarmed Congressmen met for three hours, until almost 3 P.M., then, marching en masse, they passed through the ranks of the mutineers without molestation. Within the next few days, as troops sent by General Washington were entering the city to quell the disturbances, the members of Congress were resettling in Princeton, New Jersey, where they convened from June 30 until November 4, 1783.

It was in this room in the State House, from May 25 to September 17, 1787, that delegates from twelve states (Rhode Island refused to participate) gathered to draft the Constitution, which replaced the Articles of Confederation. After long and vigorous debates, a compromise was reached and a committee—James Madison, Alexander Hamilton, William Samuel Johnson, Rufus King, and Gouverneur Morris—was appointed to draft the document. It was approved and signed by the delegations on September 17, then sent to the state conventions for ratification.

During the stormy sessions here the eighty-one-year-old Benjamin Franklin often alluded to the chair from which George Washington presided over the Convention by cynically questioning whether the rayed sun carved on the back was rising or setting. When the Convention finally concluded its debates by adopting the Constitution, Franklin leaned over to one of his fellow delegates and triumphantly asserted that now he knew it was a rising sun.

Liberty Bell (To be moved in 1976 to a pavilion erected on Independence Hall Mall) In 1752 Pennsylvania was planning a fiftieth anniversary celebration of William Penn's Charter of Privileges, which granted religious freedom to the colony. In commemoration of the event the Pennsylvania Assembly voted that a bell be purchased for the State House. The Whitechapel Foundry of London, England, was commissioned to cast the bell. When it arrived in Philadelphia on September 1, 1752, it was hung on a tripod in back of the State House to be tested. As soon as the clapper struck the barrel of the bell, the side cracked. Two local artisans, John Pass and John Stow, offered to recast it. But after the process had been completed, the tone was so unsatisfactory that the bell once again had to be melted and recast. When large quantities of copper were added to the metal, an alloy was produced which provided an acceptable tone. The new bell was then hung in the recently constructed belfry of the State House on June 7, 1753.

On July 8, 1776, after Colonel John Nixon read the Declaration of Independence to a jubilant crowd that had assembled on the grounds of the State House, the bell was rung, tolling the message of liberty.

As British troops approached Philadelphia in the fall of 1777, the Patriots, fearing that the bell would be melted for enemy cannon, removed it and sent it for safekeeping to Allentown, Pennsylvania. There it was hidden in the basement of the Zion High German Reformed Church. After the British occupation of Philadelphia ended, the bell was returned to the State House.

On July 6, 1835, the bell was tolled throughout the funeral procession of John Marshall, Chief Justice of the United States Supreme Court. By the end of the day, a crack had developed. From that time forth, except for the marking of very special occasions, the bell has remained silent.

The name "Liberty Bell" did not become popular until 1839, when a group of Abolitionists known as the

Friends of Freedom, or the Liberty Party, chose the bell as a symbol for its cause because of the bell's inscription: "Proclaim Liberty throughout all the Land and to all the Inhabitants Thereof" (Leviticus xxv, 10). The image of the bell appeared on all the party's publications, gaining for the bell the sobriquet which has lasted through the decades.

Second Floor Chambers   Three rooms are located on the second floor—the Governor's Council Chamber, the Committee Room, and the Long Gallery.

In the Governor's Council Chamber, the governor of Pennsylvania and his Provincial Council met to transact official business. Here they conferred with foreign officials and prominent citizens of the various colonies.

The Committee Room, located to the southeast, was originally used for committee meetings and as a library for the Pennsylvania Assembly. While the Continental Congress and the Constitutional Convention met in the first-floor Assembly Chamber, the Pennsylvania legislators held their sessions in this room.

The Long Gallery (100 feet long by 20 feet wide) was used for state banquets and official receptions. A lavish reception was held here to honor the members of the Second Continental Congress and, according to tradition, thirty-two toasts were exchanged.

Today, the room is graced by a painting of James Harrison by Benjamin West. Harrison, a lieutenant governor of the colony before the Revolutionary War, has the distinction of being the only man to break both his legs by falling down the State House stairs!

The Pennsylvania government continued to occupy this building until the state capital was moved to Lancaster in 1799. (In 1812 the seat of government was moved to Harrisburg.) From 1802 to 1828 artist Charles Willson Peale opened a museum here on the second floor, where he displayed not only portraits of prominent

Americans but also a collection of stuffed animals, minerals, and machines.

For the Centennial Celebration held in 1876, Independence Hall was renovated and a new bell, donated by Henry Seybert, was hung in the tower. In 1896 the Daughters of the American Revolution restored the historic structure to its original eighteenth-century appearance and refurnished it with fine period pieces. The building came under the jurisdiction of the National Park Service of the United States Department of the Interior in 1950 as part of the newly established Independence National Historical Park.

"MAN FULL OF TROUBLE" TAVERN AND PASCHALL HOUSE   *127–129 Spruce Street. Open April through November, Tuesday through Saturday 1 P.M. to 4 P.M.; during the rest of the year open only on Saturday and Sunday 1 P.M. to 4 P.M. Adults 50¢, youngsters (10–16) 25¢, children (under 10) free.*   Built in 1759, the "Man Full of Trouble" tavern was a popular stopping place for travelers seeking refreshment and overnight accommodations. Sailors from ships docking in the nearby Delaware River also came here for rum and conversation. The property was purchased in 1829 by Nicholas Stafford and was renamed Stafford's Inn. The tavern ceased operating in the 1880s. The adjacent Paschall House was built in 1760 by merchant Benjamin Paschall.

The tavern and house have been restored by the Knauer Foundation. The paneling and fireplaces on the second floor are original. The basement kitchen is equipped with traditional Colonial implements. In the tavern's taproom/dining room, the bar is lined with old pewter mugs and the dresser displays eighteenth-century china. The rooms are graced with fine period pieces, including a set of Windsor chairs that belonged to Chief Justice John Jay.

MIKVEH ISRAEL BURIAL GROUND *Spruce Street, west of 8th Street. By appointment only.* In 1740 the congregation of Mikveh Israel began to hold services in a small house in Sterling Alley. A synagogue was built on Third and Cherry Streets in 1784 under the supervision of Rabbi Gershom Seixas. This cemetery, the oldest Jewish cemetery in Philadelphia, has been used by the congregation since 1757.

Haym Salomon (1740–1785), who gave his personal fortune to support the Patriot cause during the American Revolution, is buried here. He was twice imprisoned by the British authorities for his views. Later, he arranged the escape of captured Patriot soldiers. When Robert Morris became Superintendent of Finance in 1781, he called on his friend Haym Salomon to help raise money for the government, and once again Salomon contributed his own wealth to support the fledgling nation.

Here also is found the grave of Michael Gratz (1740–1811), who signed the Nonimportation Resolutions against the Stamp Act and during the war aided the Patriots by running supplies on his ships through the British blockade. His daughter Rebecca Gratz (1781–1869), noted for her beauty, wit, and philanthropic acts, is believed to have served as the model for the character Rebecca in Sir Walter Scott's *Ivanhoe* (1819).

Twenty-one Patriot soldiers of the Jewish faith—including Benjamin Nones, a member of General Washington's staff—are also interred here.

OLD CITY HALL *Chestnut and 5th Streets (Independence Hall Complex). Open daily 9 A.M. to 5 P.M.; 9 A.M. to 8 P.M. during the Bicentennial. Free.* When construction of City Hall was completed in 1791, the United States capital had moved to Philadelphia and the city government made chambers in this building available to the United States Supreme Court. In August 1791 the

Court—which had held its first session in New York City on February 2, 1790—moved into its new quarters in the large courtroom at the end of the first floor here. (City and district courtrooms were located in the other rooms.)

The Judiciary Act of 1789 had provided for five Associate Justices and one Chief Justice. (In 1869 the number was fixed at eight Associate Justices and a Chief Justice.) Here, in 1791, assembled the first members of the Supreme Court—John Rutledge, William Cushing, James Wilson, John Blair, and James Iredell. John Jay served as the first Chief Justice from 1789 to 1795; John Rutledge was appointed in 1795; and Oliver Ellsworth held the position from 1796 to 1800. The decisions of these courts helped to codify the laws of the land under the Constitution.

The Supreme Court—and Congress—moved to the District of Columbia in 1800. The chambers occupied by the high court then reverted to agencies of the city of Philadelphia.

Old City Hall was restored in 1916. In the early 1970s the interior was returned to its original eighteenth-century appearance.

PEMBERTON HOUSE (ARMY-NAVY MUSEUM) *Chestnut and 3rd Streets. Open daily 9 A.M. to 5 P.M. Closed Christmas and January 1. Free.* This house was built in 1775 by Joseph Pemberton, a prosperous Quaker merchant. The interior was gutted and renovated for the installation of exhibits of eighteenth-century American military history. Dioramas of battles, uniforms, and weapons are displayed. Of special interest is a diorama of the Battle of Saratoga (October 1777) and a map with lights pinpointing major campaigns of the Revolutionary War.

POWEL HOUSE *244 South 3rd Street. Open Tuesday through Saturday 10 A.M. to 4 P.M., Sunday 1 P.M. to 4 P.M. Closed major holidays. Adults $1.00, youngsters (12–16) 50¢, children (under 12) 25¢.* This handsome three-story dwelling was built and designed by Charles Stedman in 1765. Three years later, the property was purchased by Samuel Powel for £3,150 after business failures caused Stedman to offer it for sale. Powel served two terms as mayor of Philadelphia—in 1775–1776 and again in 1789–1790. During the British occupation of the city the Earl of Carlisle made his residence here, and Powel and his family returned to the house after the British departed. In the 1790s, when President George Washington resided in Philadelphia, he was a frequent guest at elaborate receptions given here by the Powels.

After Samuel Powel's death in 1793, his wife continued to reside here. When she moved to her country estate (across the Schuylkill River) in 1805, she sold this townhouse. The building was restored in 1931 by the Society for the Preservation of Landmarks. The elegant second-floor drawing room is distinguished by remarkable carving above the mantelpiece, ornate doorway frames with pediments, and elaborate plaster ceiling decorations.

The house is furnished mainly with eighteenth-century Philadelphia pieces. The furnishings and appointments original to the house include the dining room Chippendale chairs, a tea table, all the china, and most of the paintings. Of special interest is a sewing table presented to Mrs. Powel by Martha Washington.

BETSY ROSS HOUSE *239 Arch Street. Open daily 9:30 A.M. to 5:15 P.M. Closed Christmas. Free.* On June 14, 1777, Congress adopted the resolution that "the flag of the United States shall be thirteen stripes, alternate red and white, with a union of thirteen stars of white on a blue field." Although it is known that Betsy Ross (1752–1836) made flags for the government during the Revolutionary War, historical research has failed to prove conclusively that she sewed the first American flag. Yet the legend persists that a committee of Congress—including George Washington, Robert Morris, and George Ross (a relative of Betsy Ross' husband)—came to the

*Betsy Ross House,
Philadelphia*
(ALPER)

house of the Philadelphia seamstress to ask her to make the "Stars and Stripes."

John Ross, son of an Anglican clergyman, and Elizabeth ("Betsy") Griscom served simultaneous apprenticeships at Webster's Shop on 2nd Street (below Chestnut). They married in 1773, moved into this house, and opened an upholstery shop here. John fought for the Patriot cause, and after he lost his life in 1776 while guarding military supplies, his wife continued to reside here. She married Captain Joseph Ashbourn in June 1777.

The house was built about 1704 by Thomas Marle, a carpenter. At the time of the Rosses' occupancy, it was owned by Hannah Lythgow, who rented it to the couple. In the nineteenth century the building had a succession of owners. In 1937, with funds donated by A.

Atwater Kent, the dwelling was restored to its Colonial appearance by architect Brognard Okie and opened to the public.

The **Betsy Ross Room** is believed to have the original flooring, window sashes, fireplace, and corner cupboard. Today, the house is furnished with modest pieces of eighteenth-century furniture.

ST. JOSEPH'S CHURCH *Willings Alley, near 4th and Walnut Streets. Open daily 6:30 A.M. to 5 P.M.* St. Joseph's is the church of the oldest Roman Catholic parish in Philadelphia. The first house of worship on this site was built in 1734. In 1757, to accommodate the growing congregation, the church was razed and a larger building was erected here during the pastorate of Father Robert Harding. The present structure dates from 1839.

During the Revolutionary War Lafayette, the Comte de Rochambeau, and Admiral de Grasse all worshipped at St. Joseph's when participating in campaigns near Philadelphia. An illustrious parishioner here was Joseph Bonaparte, the older brother of Napoleon I. After having been forced to abdicate his throne as King of Spain (1813) and following the final defeat of Napoleon (1815), Joseph Bonaparte fled to the United States and resided for a short time in Philadelphia.

ST. PETER'S CHURCH *3rd and Pine Streets. Open daily 9 A.M. to 5 P.M.* St. Peter's parish was established in 1753 as a "South End" chapel of Christ Church. This handsome brick church was designed by Robert Smith (architect of Carpenters' Hall) and John Kearsley (a designer of Christ Church). On September 4, 1761, after a procession from Christ Church to the new St. Peter's, the first service was held here. Dr. William Smith, Provost of the University of Pennsylvania, delivered the sermon. The present tower and spire date from 1842.

Many of the original pews have been preserved.

Among the church's treasured possessions are rare Bibles and prayer books, eighteenth-century silver pieces, and portraits by Charles Willson Peale. Samuel Powel, twice mayor of Philadelphia (in 1775–1776 and 1789–1790) worshipped in pew number 41. George Washington occasionally worshipped here in the early 1790s.

In the cemetery are buried Benjamin Chew (1722–1810), Chief Justice of the Pennsylvania Supreme Court; Charles Willson Peale (1741–1827), a noted artist; Nicholas Biddle (1786–1844), president of the Second Bank of the United States; and Stephen Decatur (1779–1820), a naval hero of the War of 1812.

TODD HOUSE *4th and Walnut Streets. Open Tuesday through Saturday 11 A.M. to 3 P.M., Sunday 1 P.M. to 4 P.M. Free. Tickets must be obtained in advance at the Pemberton House, Chestnut and 3rd Streets.* This three-story brick house was built in 1775 by Jonathan Dilworth, a land speculator. In 1791 John Todd, a young lawyer, and his wife of two years, Dolley (née Payne), made their residence here. Todd, with his law clerk Isaac Heston, established an office in the front room on the first floor.

Through her husband's clients, Dolley soon gained the reputation of a charming, intelligent woman. In this house she gave birth to two sons.

The tranquility of her life was shattered in September 1793, when a yellow fever epidemic struck Philadelphia. Todd sent his wife and children away from the city, but he remained to tend to his law practice. He contracted the disease, and after weeks of suffering, died on October 24, 1793. Two weeks later, one of the infant sons, also afflicted, died. Although Dolley contracted a mild form of the disease, she recovered.

Upon returning to Philadelphia in the spring, the bereaved widow remained here in seclusion. But soon Aaron Burr, the Senator from New York, came to convey his condolences and brought with him James Madison, the Congressman from Virginia. (Both men were attending sessions of Congress, which was convening in Philadelphia.) The forty-two-year-old Madison became so enchanted by the twenty-three-year-old Dolley that he soon proposed marriage. The couple were married on September 15, 1794, and the Madisons changed their residence to a house on Spruce Street. The house here was held in trust for the son, John Payne Todd, who inherited it in 1826 and sold it soon afterward.

During Madison's term of office as fourth President of the United States (1809–1817), Dolley was praised for her wit and gracious entertaining.

Between 1796 and 1807 Colonel Stephen Moylan, who had served under General George Washington in various capacities during the Revolutionary War, resided in this townhouse. Subsequently, tenants occupied it. In the early 1950s the building was restored and opened to the public. The property is now part of the Independence National Historical Park.

Today, the house is furnished with fine antiques of the eighteenth century. Among the important pieces are a handsome secretary-desk, a graceful English sideboard, an unusual ladder-back settee, and an impressive four-poster bed. Especially cherished is a wine glass once owned by John Hanson (1715–1783) of Maryland, the first president (1781–1782) to serve under the Articles of Confederation.

WASHINGTON SQUARE *Walnut Street, between 6th and 7th Streets* This square was one of five laid out in 1681 by William Penn's surveyor, Thomas Holme. In the first decade of the eighteenth century it was enclosed by a fence and set aside as a "potter's field," a place for the burial of the indigent and unknown. When the British occupied Philadelphia in 1777, Continental soldiers who died at the nearby military prison were unceremoniously buried here. Many of the men had been captured at Brandywine and Germantown. Throughout the remaining years of the war, the bodies of soldiers who had died of camp diseases were piled on top of each other in deep pits dug in the square, then covered with earth. Hundreds of victims of the 1793 yellow fever epidemic were also laid to rest here.

Today, a monument honoring George Washington and his Continental soldiers dominates the square. The statue of George Washington is a copy of the work (begun in 1785) by Jean Antoine Houdon. (The original statue now stands in the Capitol Building in Richmond, Virginia.) On the architectural screen behind Washington are inscribed words from his Farewell Address (September 17, 1796): "The independence and liberty you possess are the work of joint counsels and joint efforts— and common dangers, sufferings, and success."

At the foot of the statue is the grave of the Unknown Soldier of the Revolutionary War. The inscription is a reminder that this forgotten warrior died "to give you liberty."

Each of the flagpoles surrounding the monument bears a flag representing one of the thirteen original colonies.

BISHOP WHITE HOUSE 309 *Walnut Street. Open Monday through Friday at 11 A.M., 1 P.M., and 2 P.M. Free. Tickets must be obtained in advance at the Pemberton House, Chestnut and 3rd Streets.*   The Reverend William White (1748–1836), who had served as chaplain to the Continental Congress from 1777 to 1781 (after Jacob Duché), became rector of the united congregations of Christ Church and St. Peter's Church after the Revolutionary War. He was an ardent reformer of American Anglicanism who fought successfully to free it from the control of the English ecclesiastical hierarchy. When he was consecrated Bishop of the Diocese of Pennsylvania in 1787, he was permitted to dispense with the traditional oath of allegiance to England. He helped organize a national church with a native episcopacy. In 1789 a convention of high American church officials meeting at Christ Church adopted a constitution, revised the Book of Common Prayer, and approved the name to be used for the church body in the United States: the Protestant Episcopal Church.

This fine house was built for Bishop White in 1786–1787 by his friend Samuel Powel (who had served as mayor of Philadelphia). White, with his wife and children, took up residence here in 1787, and he remained until his death. It was in this house that he wrote his treatise, *The Case of the Episcopal Church Considered,* and received news that he was to be elevated in 1795 to the powerful position of Bishop of the Protestant Episcopal Church of the United States.

Upon the death of his wife Mary two years later, he immersed himself in his work. He also organized groups to provide aid and services to the poor, the orphaned, and the ill. In the first decade of the nineteenth century he invited his son Thomas and his family to reside with him in this house. Bishop White died in his bedroom on July 17, 1836, surrounded by the beloved members of his family.

Soon after White's death the property was sold. In 1858 the building was converted into suites of offices. In the early 1960s the house was renovated and refurnished under the auspices of the Independence National Historical Park.

Visitors to the dwelling can see furniture and possessions that would have been found in the home of an affluent eighteenth-century family. Among the important pieces are a pianoforte made by the Kneller Company of Philadelphia, a Hepplewhite sideboard, a table crafted by one of the vestrymen of Christ Church, a sofa which belonged to Robert Morris (Bishop White's brother-in-law), a silver bread plate that was presented to the Whites as a wedding gift, a set of dishes purchased by the bishop as a present for one of his granddaughters, and Bishop White's portable writing table.

Non-Revolutionary Sites of Interest

ATWATER KENT MUSEUM   *15 South 7th Street between Market and Chestnut Streets. Open daily 8:30 A.M. to 4:30 P.M. Closed holidays. Free.*   This museum specializes in exhibits relating to Pennsylvania history. Students of Colonial history and culture will enjoy viewing re-creations of Indian life along the Schuylkill River, models of eighteenth-century houses and ships, and Colonial artifacts. Several dioramas depict events of the Revolutionary War, such as Paul Revere's ride to Philadelphia to bring news of the closing of Boston Harbor by the British (1774) and the Battle of Germantown (1777). Founded in 1938 by industrialist A. Atwater Kent, the museum is housed in the original building of the Franklin Institute which was erected in 1826.

CITY HALL   *Broad and Market Streets. Open Monday through Friday 9 A.M. to 5 P.M. Closed holidays. The tower's observation platform is open daily 9:30 A.M. to 4 P.M. Guided tours, starting from Room 202, are available Monday through Friday at 10 A.M. If you plan to tour the building by yourself, phone 686–1776 to verify the hours the City Council Chamber and the courtrooms are open to the public.*   In 1871 John Rice, president of Philadelphia's Commission for the Erection of Public Buildings, broke ground on Penn Square for a new City Hall. The next year hundreds of workmen began the construction of the edifice, which was designed by John J. McArthur, Jr. It took two decades to erect, and another decade to complete the decoration. The cost was a staggering $24 million. When City Hall (which covers five acres) was completed, it was the highest building in America.

Numerous pieces of sculpture by Alexander Milne Calder (grandfather of the twentieth-century artist Alexander Calder) adorn the exterior and interior. The twenty-four-foot, ten-ton bronze statues on each of the tower's four upper cornices represent an Indian brave, his squaw, a Swedish settler, and his wife.

Crowning City Hall, at a height of 548 feet, is a 26-ton bronze statue of William Penn which was assembled in twenty-six sections. It is also the work of Calder. A

City Hall, Philadelphia (PHILADELPHIA CONVENTION AND VISITORS BUREAU)

long-existing Philadelphia tradition holds that no building in the city may be higher than Penn's head, but no such ordinance has ever been passed.

The spacious interior is decorated with friezes, frescoes, reliefs, mosaics, and statuary.

The marble-and-gold City Council Chamber and several courtrooms are open to the public on a limited schedule.

FRANKLIN INSTITUTE   *Benjamin Franklin Parkway at 20th Street. Open Monday through Saturday 10 A.M. to 5 P.M., Sunday noon to 5 P.M. Closed holidays. Adults $1.50, youngsters (6–12) $1.00, children (under 6) free. Planetarium 25¢ additional charge.*   Founded in 1824 for the study of applied sciences, the Institute was named in honor of Benjamin Franklin. This imposing building, which was designed by John T. Windrim and erected in 1933, contains exhibits relating to science, technology, and industry. Scheduled demonstrations include a visual smoke chamber, computer operations, and printing. There are fascinating displays on meteors, aviation, atomic energy, and communications. In a special area youngsters gain practical knowledge of the principles of physics through exhibits that require pulling levers, pushing buttons, and sliding weights. The twenty-foot statue of Benjamin Franklin in Memorial Hall is by James Earl Fraser (who also designed the image of the Buffalo which used to appear on the American five-cent piece).

The museum also contains the **Fels Planetarium,** where shows on astronomical themes change periodically. The programs are scheduled from Monday through Friday at 3 P.M. (also at noon in the summer), Saturday at 11 A.M., 1 P.M., 2 P.M., and 3 P.M., Sunday at 2 P.M., 3 P.M., and 4 P.M.

HERITAGE HOUSE   *1346 North Broad Street. Open Monday through Friday 9 A.M. to 5 P.M. (Usually by appointment.) Closed holidays. Free.*   This museum has exhibits describing black history and culture. Emphasis is placed on contributions to music, dance, drama, and art. Of special interest is the gallery presentation, *Four Hundred Black Builders of American Heritage.*

HISTORICAL SOCIETY OF PENNSYLVANIA *1300 Locust Street. Open Tuesday through Friday* 9 A.M. *to* 5 P.M., *Monday* 1 P.M. *to* 5 P.M. *Closed holidays and the month of August. Free.* Founded in 1824, this organization was one of the earliest historical societies in the United States. The museum displays paintings of Revolutionary War leaders, Colonial furniture, Philadelphia silver pieces, and Pennsylvania clocks. Cherished items include furnishings and possessions of William Penn, Benjamin Franklin, and James Logan, as well as those of President George Washington when he was residing in Philadelphia in the 1790s. Paintings by Peale, West, Stuart, and Sully are exhibited; a popular work is *Congress Voting Independence,* started in 1788 by Robert Edge Pine and completed by Edward Savage.

OLD MARKET AND HEAD HOUSE *2nd Street from Pine to Lombard Streets* The old Second Street Market was built in 1745 and was used continuously until the late 1950s. Here, under the eaves and on the streets, vendors displayed for sale their fresh vegetables, fruit, eggs, and fish. Butchers set up stalls inside the market house. During the eighteenth and nineteenth centuries, market days were held on Tuesdays and Fridays from April through September. The Old Market House was restored to its original appearance in 1960.

The brick Head House (so called because of its location at the "head" of the market) was constructed in 1804 as a firehouse for volunteer fire companies. It was restored in 1960 as part of the redevelopment of this area. A nineteenth-century hose-reel firefighting apparatus is on display in one of the rooms.

PENNSYLVANIA ACADEMY OF FINE ARTS *Broad and Cherry Streets. The Academy building will be closed for renovations until March 1976. The usual schedule is*

Tuesday through Saturday 10 A.M. to 5 P.M., Sunday 1 P.M. to 5 P.M. Closed holidays and the month of August. Free. The Pennsylvania Academy of Fine Arts, founded in 1805, is the oldest museum and art school in the country. The collection grew from works purchased in Europe during the first decade of the nineteenth century by Nicholas Biddle (later director of the Second Bank of the United States). The present building, completed in 1876, was designed by Frank Furness. On display are works by American painters Charles Willson Peale (one of the Academy's founders), Gilbert Stuart, Thomas Sully, Thomas Eakins, George Inness, Winslow Homer, and John Sloan.

PHILADELPHIA MUSEUM OF ART *Benjamin Franklin Parkway and 26th Street. Open Tuesday through Sunday 9 A.M. to 5 P.M. Closed holidays. Adults $1.00, children 25¢. Free Sunday until 1 P.M. and all day Tuesday.* The Philadelphia Museum of Art was founded in 1876 and was first housed in Memorial Hall on the grounds of the Centennial Exposition in Fairmount Park. Because the collection had grown over the decades, larger quarters were needed and construction was begun in 1924 on a new building at the terminus of the Franklin Parkway. The architects were C. L. Borie, Jr., H. Trumbauer, and C. C. Zantzinger. On March 26, 1928, the first section of the museum, devoted to British and American art, was formally opened to the public. Several wings were added in the 1940s.

Today, the museum, one of the finest in the United States, displays paintings and sculpture from the Middle Ages to the twentieth century. It also features pre-Columbian pieces, a collection of Oriental objects, and an exhibit of silver and glass. Of special interest are a Hindu temple and a Chinese Buddhist temple hall. The Furniture Wing contains more than thirty European and American period rooms. The American Painting Gallery is noted for the representative works of Sargent, Eakins, and Peale. The outstanding permanent collections include those of Louis E. Stern, John G. Johnson, and Walter Arensberg.

PHILADELPHIA ZOOLOGICAL GARDEN *34th Street and Girard Avenue. Open daily 9:30 A.M. to 5 P.M. Adults $2.00, children 50¢.* Covering forty-two acres, the Philadelphia Zoological Gardens has 1,400 birds, mammals, and reptiles, many of which live in special areas re-creating their native habitats. Of particular interest are the African Plains Exhibit featuring giraffes, zebras, and ostriches. The Reptile House, with its naturalistic settings, includes a tropical river exhibit with an electronic thunderstorm. In the Hummingbird House birds are permitted to fly about freely amid lush tropical vegetation. Younger visitors will enjoy a two-acre children's zoo where they are permitted to feed and to pet the animals. Additional fee for the Hummingbird House, 25¢ and for the children's zoo, 25¢.

POE HOUSE *530 North 7th Street. Open Monday through Friday 10 A.M. to 5 P.M., Saturday and Sunday 2 P.M. to 5 P.M. Closed holidays. Adults $1.00, children free.* Writer Edgar Allan Poe (1809–1849) lived in Philadelphia from 1838 to 1844, where he edited *Burton's Gentleman's Magazine* and later *Graham's Magazine.* Three of those years (1842 through 1844) he resided in this house with his tubercular wife Virginia and her mother Mrs. Clemm. Here he worked on the first draft of "The Raven" (which he published in a volume of poetry in 1845).

On display are first editions of Poe's works and interesting memorabilia.

RODIN MUSEUM *Benjamin Franklin Parkway and 22nd Street. Open Tuesday through Saturday 9 A.M. to 5 P.M. Closed holidays. Adults 50¢, children 25¢. A combination ticket to the Rodin Museum and the nearby Philadelphia Museum of Art is available for $1.25.* This Renaissance-style building—erected in 1929 and designed by Paul P.

Second Bank of the United States, Philadelphia (ALPER)

Cret and Jacques Greber—was given to the city by Jules E. Mastbaum, an owner of a chain of movie theaters. The museum contains the largest collection outside France of the works of François Auguste René Rodin (1840–1917).

A bronze replica of *The Thinker* (1888) is placed near the entrance. The monumental *Burghers of Calais* (1894) dominates the main gallery. In addition to the fine collection of sculpture, drawings by Rodin are also on display.

SECOND BANK OF THE UNITED STATES *420 Chestnut between 4th and 5th Streets. Open daily 9 A.M. to 5 P.M. Closed Christmas and January 1. Free.* The Second Bank of the United States was chartered in 1816 and capitalized at $35 million. It began transacting business on January 7, 1817, in temporary headquarters at Carpenters' Hall. During its first two years of existence, under the directorship of William Jones, the bank was mismanaged; but in 1819 Langdon Cheves (a former member of the House of Representatives) was chosen director and soon the institution was placed on a sound financial basis. Cheves realized the need for a new bank building, and in early 1819 he announced a competition for an architectural design. The winner was thirty-one-year-old William Strickland, whose magnificent design for a Greek Revival building became a reality during the 1820s.

Upon Cheves' resignation in 1822, Nicholas Biddle took over the management of the Second Bank of the United States. Although it prospered, President Andrew Jackson, who believed the bank represented the elite commercial classes of the East, vetoed the bill for its recharter in 1832. Jackson, viewing Biddle's power as a threat, withdrew government deposits. Left with only modest assets, the bank subsequently operated under a state charter until 1845. After the bank ceased operations, the building was used as the United States Customs House. In 1939 the Department of the Interior acquired the property.

The building now houses the portrait gallery of Independence National Historical Park. The collection includes portraits of important Revolutionary War leaders and military heroes. A popular attraction are the works of Charles Willson Peale and those of his son Rembrandt Peale.

UNITED STATES MINT *5th and Arch Streets. Open Monday through Friday 9 A.M. to 3:30 P.M. Closed holidays. Free.* The first United States Mint, created by an Act of Congress, was established in 1792 in Philadelphia, then the nation's capital. (Today, there are also mints operating in San Francisco and Denver.) The present building, designed by Vincent G. Kling and Partners, has a special gallery with audio narrative which provides a fascinating tour for visitors. One can also see the melting, casting, and pressing operations.

U.S.S. *OLYMPIA* *Pier 11 North—Delaware Avenue and Race Street (under the Benjamin Franklin Bridge). Open Thursday to Saturday 10 A.M. to 5 P.M., Sunday 11 A.M. to 6 P.M. Closed Thanksgiving, Christmas, and January 1. Adults $1.00, children 50¢.* The U.S.S. *Olympia* was the flagship of Admiral George Dewey (1837–1917) during the Spanish-American War. Just after midnight on May 1, 1898, Dewey sailed into Manila Bay (Philippines) and engaged the enemy fleet at dawn. During the battle he destroyed eight Spanish ships while sustaining few American casualties. On August 13 Dewey aided General Wesley Merritt in capturing Manila.

In World War I the *Olympia* was in the patrol force of the Atlantic Fleet and was assigned to convoy duty. In 1921 she carried from France the body of the Unknown Soldier, which now lies in Arlington Cemetery.

Visitors may tour the ship and view exhibits of naval weaponry.

Fairmount Park

Fairmount Park was the site of the Centennial Exposition of the Revolutionary War. Eight million people attended the Exposition, which was open from May 10 through November 10, 1876. The first-day ceremonies were attended by President Ulysses S. Grant, Emperor Dom Pedro II of Brazil, the governors of Louisiana, Pennsylvania, and Massachusetts, and other important dignitaries. The largest structure on the grounds was the Main Exhibition Building, 464 feet wide by 1,880 feet long, covering 21 acres. Among the displays was a section devoted to new inventions, including the electric light, the telephone, and the typewriter. The principal exhibits of the fifty foreign countries that participated were housed in the Main Exhibition Building, although separate pavilions were erected by England, Spain, Sweden, Chile, Turkey, Germany, Brazil, France, Portugal, and Japan. Almost two-thirds of the states built small pavilions containing reception lounges and exhibition rooms. After the Exposition closed, most of the structures were disassembled and the park once again became an area for Philadelphia's cultural and recreational activities.

Covering more than 7,800 acres, Fairmount Park is the largest city park in the world. It contains a zoo, Robin Hood Dell, Playhouse in the Park, and several fine Colonial houses. (For guided tours of the Colonial houses, phone 763–8100.)

Important Colonial Houses

CEDAR GROVE *Open Tuesday through Saturday 10 A.M. to 5 P.M. Closed holidays. Adults 25¢, children 10¢.* Cedar Grove, which originally stood in Harrowgate near Frankford, was built in 1748 by Elizabeth Coates Paschall (widow of Joseph Paschall) as a summer home. The property was inherited by a great-niece, Sarah, who married Isaac Wistar Morris in 1795. The needs of their growing family prompted them to double the size of the house. By matching exterior architectural features, the structure retained its unity and balance.

By 1888 the Frankford area had become so industrialized that the owners, John and Lydia Morris, moved out of the house. In 1927 a descendant presented the dwelling to the city and arranged to have it transported, stone by stone, to this site where it was reconstructed.

The house contains many original furnishings of the

Morris family. They date mostly from the eighteenth and nineteenth centuries, and several fine pieces were made by eighteenth-century Philadelphia cabinetmakers.

The house is administered by the Philadelphia Museum of Art.

LEMON HILL   *Open Thursday 11 A.M. to 4 P.M. Also open the second and fourth Sundays in July and August. Adults 50¢, children 25¢.*   In 1770 Robert Morris purchased land here, along the banks of the Schuylkill River, on which he planned to erect a summer house. A prominent Pennsylvanian, Morris later became a signer of the Declaration of Independence, served as president of the Pennsylvania Assembly, and was appointed chairman of the Congressional Committee of Finance. Morris drew from his personal fortune to help finance the Patriot cause during the Revolutionary War. In 1798 his financial empire crumbled and he was placed in debtors' prison for three and one-half years.

Henry Pratt, a prosperous merchant, then purchased the property and built an elegant mansion here. Because of the lemon groves he planted on the grounds, the estate came to be known as "Lemon Hill."

The house and twenty-five acres were acquired by the city in 1844 and during the following decades served as a public recreational area. In 1925 the house was purchased and renovated by Fiske Kimball, director of the Philadelphia Museum of Art, for use as his residence. After his death in 1955, the Colonial Dames of America assumed administrative responsibility for Lemon Hill.

MOUNT PLEASANT   *Open Tuesday through Sunday 10 A.M. to 5 P.M. Closed holidays. Adults 25¢, children 10¢.*   This handsome mansion was built in 1761 by John Macpherson, a Scottish sea captain who acquired his fortune through privateering. By studying books of architectural design, he gained enough knowledge to design this Georgian structure. Macpherson was a man of many interests: he lectured on astronomy, invented many gadgets and a vermin-free bed, and published a fortnightly business newspaper.

During the Revolutionary War he was an ardent Patriot. He acted as an advisor to members of the Continental Congress when they were considering organizing a navy. His son John, who served as an aide-de-camp to General Richard Montgomery, was killed in the disastrous assault on Quebec in December 1775.

During the summer of 1779 Macpherson moved to his townhouse in Philadelphia and rented this mansion to the Spanish Minister, Don Juan de Mirailles. It was still under lease to Mirailles in March 1780, when Benedict Arnold, then military governor of Philadelphia, purchased Mount Pleasant for his bride Peggy Shippen. But they never lived here. Before they could take possession of the house, Arnold was charged with official misconduct and he decided to remain in the city while the court-martial was in progress. (He was found guilty of two minor charges, but his punishment was only a light reprimand.)

A succession of tenants subsequently occupied the house until 1792 when it was purchased by General Jonathan Williams, the first superintendent of the West Point Military Academy. Descendants lived here until 1868, the year the estate was incorporated into Fairmount Park.

In 1925 Mount Pleasant was restored and refurnished by the Philadelphia Museum of Art, which still administers the property.

STRAWBERRY MANSION *Open Tuesday through Sunday 11 A.M. to 5 P.M. Closed holidays and during the month of January. Adults 50¢, children 25¢.* In 1774 Charles Thomson purchased the small farmhouse (*c.* 1768) on this site, calling it Somerton. A teacher of languages at the Franklin Academy, he was highly respected by intellectuals in Philadelphia, and members of the First Continental Congress selected him to serve as official secretary. When the British occupied Philadelphia in 1777, a detail of soldiers was sent to Somerton to search the house for important documents. Thomson and his wife fled, and the Redcoats, after ransacking the house and finding nothing, burned it to the ground.

Judge William Lewis purchased the land in 1797 and constructed a mansion here. Members of the United States Congress, then meeting in Philadelphia, were often entertained here.

In the early 1820s the wealthy Hemphill family occupied the mansion. A son, Alexander, built the south wing in 1827 for a ball which he hosted while his parents were traveling in Europe. The following year the north wing was erected by the parents to restore architectural balance to the structure. Another son, Coleman, planted hundreds of strawberries in the garden from roots imported from Chile—hence the name "Strawberry Mansion."

When Hemphill lost his fortune in 1833, he was forced to sell the property. The next owner turned the house into a restaurant that offered unusual strawberry desserts.

Strawberry Hill became part of Fairmount Park in 1867. It served as a recreational area until 1929, when the Committee of 1926 (organized for the Sesquicentennial) purchased the mansion and restored it.

SWEETBRIAR *Open Monday through Saturday 10 A.M. to 5 P.M. Closed holidays and the month of July. Adults 25¢, children 10¢.* This land was granted by William Penn, the founder of Pennsylvania, to Patrick Robinson, a member of the Town Council and clerk of the Provincial Court. In 1791 John Ross purchased the property and erected a small farmhouse here. When Samuel Breck, of a distinguished Boston family, married Ross' daughter Jean in 1795, the couple was given this land as a wedding gift. Two years later, they built this handsome two-story house as their year-round residence.

Active in Philadelphia affairs, Samuel Breck became a trustee of the University of Pennsylvania and a founder of the Savings Fund Society. He also served as a state senator and a United States Congressman. Many prominent international diplomats were guests at Sweetbriar, including Talleyrand (1794) and Lafayette (1825).

The Brecks sold the estate to William S. Torr in 1839 after the death of their only child. In 1866 an agency of the city of Philadelphia acquired Sweetbriar to be incorporated into Fairmount Park. The house was restored by the Junior League in 1927. Today, the Modern Club of Philadelphia maintains the property.

WOODFORD *Open Tuesday through Sunday 1 P.M. to 4 P.M. Closed holidays and during the month of August. Free.* A one-story house was built on this site in the 1750s by William Coleman, who held many important posts in Philadelphia, including treasurer of the Library Company, trustee of the University of Pennsylvania, city councilman, and judge of the County Court. Soon after his death in 1769, the property was acquired by Alexander Barclay, His Majesty's comptroller of customs, who used the house as a summer residence. He died in 1771, and ownership of Woodford passed to his wife's brother-in-law, David Franks. Franks, a prominent merchant and Crown agent for Philadelphia, enlarged the house, which he occupied with his wife and four children.

A staunch Loyalist, Franks entertained lavishly during the British occupation of Philadelphia in 1777–1778. Lord Howe was a frequent guest here and, according to tradition, one of his officers fell in love with Franks' younger daughter.

In late 1778, after the British had departed, Franks sent to his brother in London a letter with secret information about Patriot supplies. It was intercepted, resulting in Franks' arrest. Because of his influence, however, the charges were dropped. But in early 1779, when he attempted to smuggle a vital document to Major John André in New York City, his act was discovered and he was forced to flee Philadelphia. Woodford was then confiscated.

The next owner of the house was Isaac Wharton, who further enlarged it and added a kitchen to the rear. The property remained in the family until 1868, when it was acquired by the city. The handsome dwelling was then used as the park guard headquarters. In 1930 the building was refurbished and opened to the public.

Germantown

On October 2, 1777—six days after the British occupied Philadelphia—General Washington called a council of war to discuss strategy for an attack on the British forces encamped in Germantown. It was a propitious time for aggressive action, for 3,000 soldiers from Howe's Germantown encampment had been sent to escort supplies from Head of Elk, Maryland. Furthermore, General Cornwallis, who was in command of the forces in Philadelphia, had just dispatched several regiments across the Delaware River into New Jersey to capture the fortification at Billingsport.

The strength of the Patriot army had been increased after the Battle of Brandywine (September 11, 1777) by a steady stream of new recruits, and Washington considered his 11,000 troops sufficient to conduct a successful assault on Germantown.

The strategy called for dividing the American army into four columns and launching a surprise attack on the enemy. The first column, led by General John Sullivan, would include the brigades of Generals Anthony Wayne, William Alexander (Lord Stirling), William Maxwell, and Thomas Conway. The second column, commanded by General Nathanael Greene, would be composed of several brigades including those of Generals Adam Stephen and John Peter Muhlenberg. These troops were to deliver the main blow— a thrust at the center of the British lines positioned along both sides of Germantown's Shippack Road (present-day Germantown Avenue). Two other columns—commanded by General William Smallwood and General John Armstrong—were to act as pincers by simultaneously attacking the rear of the British line on their north and south flanks. The plan was for these attacks to begin at five o'clock on the morning of October 4, 1777.

The strategy was derived from classic military sources. Hannibal and Scipio Africanus had won victories with similar strategies, but there was one fundamental difference with Washington's plan. Hannibal and Scipio had directed their weakest soldiers to the center and had used their stronger forces for the pincers, but Washington called for the opposite deployment. This reversal in troop placement—as well as miscalculations of weather conditions and terrain—doomed the campaign to failure.

The sixteen-mile march to Germantown began as scheduled at seven o'clock on the evening of October 3. Each soldier had a piece of white paper pinned to his hat to help identify him in the darkness. At Mount Airy (approximately three miles from their objective) Conway's troops, acting as the advance guard for Sullivan's column, encountered a patrol from a small British outpost located nearby. The sound of artillery being fired served as an alarm to the British army in the area and removed the element of surprise upon which Washington was relying. Soon, Colonel Thomas Musgrave, commander of the outpost, arrived with a regiment of Redcoats and joined in the fray. To counter, Sullivan deployed his men into line and sent the British scurrying in retreat to Germantown. There Musgrave's soldiers quickly took shelter behind the solid stone walls of the house of Benjamin Chew. Upon the advice of General Henry Knox, Washington decided that Musgrave's barricaded men must be captured before Sullivan's column—the first to arrive in Germantown—could safely proceed with their role in the master battle plan. Through the heavy dawn mists Alexander's and Maxwell's brigades were sent to lay siege of the Chew house, but their fire could not penetrate the thick walls. Attempts at burning the dwelling were also futile.

Meanwhile, Greene's column, which was traveling over a longer route, began to approach Germantown. One of the brigades, led by General Adam Stephen had, without consulting Greene, left the column to reinforce the Patriots besieging the Chew house. When Greene's division finally reached the town, they successfully engaged the enemy at Luken's Mill, then attacked the troops positioned farther west near the market house. The British were routed and many prisoners were taken.

Sullivan's and Wayne's troops, meanwhile, were raiding the British center. But the fog had become so thick that the attackers were having difficulty finding their way. Hearing the artillery fire intensify at the Chew house, the Patriot line swung around to move in and reinforce the soldiers there. No sooner had they begun to grope their way through the fog than they perceived shadowy forms advancing toward them. Assuming the enemy was upon them, the Patriot soldiers under Wayne and Sullivan opened fire. Pandemonium resulted: men darted in panic through the gray-white fog. But their fire had been precipitant; the forms were not those of their foe but of their comrades, the men of General Stephen's brigade who had earlier broken away from Greene's column.

Soon afterward, as Sullivan's troops began to run out of ammunition, they were surrounded by the British and were forced to retreat. Greene's men—the next to break under the thrust of the British—were routed by the combined forces of Grey, Grant, and Agnew. Bravely, Greene's soldiers maintained a strong rear-guard action as they retreated.

The entire Patriot center was now in flight. Washington led them back to the safety of their original encampment and continued eight miles beyond. Finally, he learned of the fate of the other two columns involved in the operation—those under Smallwood and Armstrong. Smallwood's men, forced to march over rough terrain, arrived after the major action had already occurred, so withdrew. Armstrong had advanced along Manatawny Road to the junction of Wissahickon Creek, where his troops encountered a detachment of British and Hessians. Both sides exchanged fire for several hours, until the Hessians charged, driving the Patriots from the area.

Of the 9,000 British soldiers engaged in the battle, 70 were killed and 450 were wounded. The Patriots reported 152 killed, 521 wounded, and 400 captured. (Fifty-three Patriots lost their lives on the lawn of the Chew house.)

Despite the display of courage in engaging a victorious enemy so soon after a stunning defeat (Brandywine), the Patriot loss at Germantown was a serious setback to Washington's prestige and to the fortunes of the Continental Army.

CLARKSON-WATSON HOUSE *5257–77 Germantown Avenue. Open Tuesday, Thursday, and Saturday 1 P.M. to 5 P.M. Closed holidays. Fee 25¢.* The oldest section of this house dates from the mid-eighteenth century. Here, in November 1773, Thomas Jefferson, Secretary of State under President Washington, rented quarters to escape the yellow fever epidemic in Philadelphia.

The Bank of Germantown, after renovating the building, occupied it from 1825 to 1868. One of the clerks,

John Fanning Watson, wrote a history of the region, *Annals of Philadelphia* (1830).

Now the building houses the Costume Museum of the Germantown Historical Society.

CLIVEDON (THE CHEW HOUSE)   *6401 Germantown Avenue. Open daily 10 A.M. to 4 P.M. Closed Christmas. Adults $1.25, students 50¢.*   Clivedon, the most elaborate of the Colonial Germantown houses, was designed and built as a summer home by Benjamin Chew (1722–1810), a prominent attorney who later became Attorney General (1755–1769) and Chief Justice of the Pennsylvania Supreme Court (1774–1776). Construction of Clivedon took four years to complete—from 1763 to 1767—and cost £4,700. Built in the English Neo-Palladian style, it is a two-and-a-half-story rectangular structure with a central pedimented pavilion slightly breaking forward from the plane of the front facade. The extraordinary entrance doorway is flanked by fluted columns supporting a classical entablature. (The addition to the rear of the house dates from the 1850s.)

During the Revolutionary War Chew was a staunch Loyalist. In 1777, at the time of the Battle of Germantown, he was residing at his townhouse in Philadelphia. Clivedon—with its thick, seemingly impregnable, walls —was commandeered by British Colonel Thomas Musgrave. He ordered his men to shutter the first-floor windows and, after placing several guards at the entrance, instructed the remaining soldiers to take positions at the windows on the second floor. One of the earliest rounds of the Patriot cannon fire battered down the door, but the Redcoats barricaded the entrance with tables and chairs. As the Patriot soldiers advanced, taking cover behind the cherry trees, they fired into the second-story windows. Later, several unsuccessful efforts were made to set the house on fire. The besieged British soldiers held back the attack until reinforcements arrived to relieve them.

Although stonework had shattered, walls had become

The Attack upon the Chew House. *Painting by Howard Pyle.*
(DELAWARE ART MUSEUM, WILMINGTON)

pockmarked with holes, plaster had fallen, and woodwork had splintered, there was no structural damage.
Carpenters were employed the following year to make
repairs.

In 1779 Chew, fearing that he might be forced to
flee Pennsylvania, sold the property to Blair Mc-
Clenachen, a merchant and shipowner. Eighteen years
later, while Chew was serving as the president of the
High Court of Errors and Appeals, he repurchased Clivedon. His descendants resided here until 1972.

Most of the furniture now seen in the house belonged
to the Chew family. Among the rare pieces are an
arched-back sofa with scrolled arms, a set of nine side
chairs formerly owned by Lieutenant Governor John
Penn, eighteenth-century Chippendale mirrors and
matching girandoles, and a mahogany chest of drawers
made in the 1770s by Jonathan Gostalow, a Philadelphia
cabinetmaker.

The house is now administered by the National Trust
for Historic Preservation.

DESHLER–MORRIS HOUSE   *5442 Germantown Avenue. Open Tuesday through Sunday 1 P.M. to 4 P.M. Closed holidays. Fee 25¢.*   David Deshler, a wealthy Philadelphia merchant, built this dwelling as his summer home in 1772. After the Battle of Germantown, British General William Howe occupied this house for a short time. Upon Deshler's death in 1792, Colonel Isaac Franks purchased the property.

In the summer and fall of 1793, when a yellow fever epidemic struck Philadelphia, then the nation's capital, many officials of the government fled the city to the relative safety of Germantown. Consequently, President George Washington made arrangements to rent this house, and moved in on November 16, 1793. The next day he held a cabinet meeting in the parlor with Thomas Jefferson (Secretary of State), Alexander Hamilton (Secretary of the Treasury), Henry Knox (Secretary of War), and Edmund Randolph (Attorney General). The cabinet met here again on November 21. At the end of the month, the epidemic having abated, the President resumed residence in Philadelphia.

Colonel Franks sent Washington a bill for $131.56 covering the rent, the cost of repairing a chair broken by the Chief Executive, expenses for cleaning the house, payment for "three ducks, four fowls, and one bushel of potatoes," and reimbursement for a "flat iron, large fork, and four plates," all of which were missing.

To escape the oppressive city heat in the summer of 1794, Washington again rented this house. Arriving on July 30, he was accompanied by his wife Martha and her two grandchildren, Eleanor Parke Custis and George Washington Parke Custis. They remained here until September 20.

In 1804 Isaac Franks sold the house to Elliston Perot. Soon afterward, he converted the carriage house into a school for his children. Upon his death in 1834, the property passed to his son-in-law Samuel B. Morris,

*Deshler–Morris
House, German-
town* (ALPER)

captain of the Philadelphia Troop of Light Horse, who
lived here until his death in 1859. Morris' descendants
were occupants until the twentieth century. The house
ment in 1948, and today it is administered by Independence Hall National Historical Park.

The eighteenth-century furnishings include a four-
poster canopied bed believed to have been in the
possession of one of Washington's aides; a fine Chippendale mirror; andirons and a bedwarmer owned by the
Morris family; and portraits of Patriot leaders Thomas
Paine, Patrick Henry, Jonathan Trumbull, and Robert
Livingston.

GERMANTOWN HISTORICAL SOCIETY *5214 Germantown Avenue. Open Tuesday, Thursday, and Saturday 1 P.M. to 5 P.M. Closed holidays. Free.*   In this eighteenth-century building the Germantown Historical
Society operates a small museum specializing in items
reflecting Germantown's past. On display are furniture,

Bibles, tools, household implements, clocks, silver, and china.

GRUMBLETHORPE   *5267 Germantown Avenue. Open Tuesday through Saturday 2 P.M. to 5 P.M. Closed holidays. Adults 50¢, children 25¢.*   Merchant John Wister built this dwelling in 1744. The stones were quarried from a hill on the grounds and the timber for the interior came from forests he owned.

During the Battle of Germantown the Wisters were residing in their home in Philadelphia. A German servant, Justina, was working in the garden at Grumblethorpe when British General James Agnew commandeered the house for his temporary headquarters. Wounded during the fighting, he was brought back here, where he died later that evening.

Wister, an enthusiastic horticulturist, planted extensive gardens on this property, and it is claimed that some of the bushes he planted are still thriving.

After his death in 1789, descendants resided here until the early twentieth century. In 1940 the Philadelphia Society for the Preservation of Landmarks assumed administrative responsibility for Grumblethorpe.

STENTON MANSION   *18th and Courtland Streets. Open Tuesday through Saturday 1 P.M. to 5 P.M. Closed holidays. Adults 50¢, children 10¢.*   Stenton was built between 1728 and 1734 by James Logan (1674–1751), who had served as William Penn's trusted secretary and a member of the Provincial Council. In 1723 he became mayor of Philadelphia and in his later years was appointed Chief Justice of the Pennsylvania Supreme Court.

During the Battle of Germantown, General William Howe chose this house for his headquarters. From here he consulted with his staff and planned strategy.

On July 8, 1787, while attending the Constitutional Convention in Philadelphia, George Washington dined here with James Logan's son George, who had inherited the estate.

Generations of Logans lived here until the city acquired the property in 1900. The Society of the Colonial Dames of America maintains the house. Many of the original outbuildings—including the orangery, weaving shed, and kitchen—have been preserved.

The **Log House** now on the grounds of Stenton was built in 1790 and formerly served as the caretaker's home of the Friends Burying Ground. The structure was recently moved here from its original location at 16th and Race Streets.

Recommended Side Trips

Old Fort Mifflin

Follow the Schuylkill Expressway East (Interstate 76) until its end. (Follow signs directing traffic toward the airport.) Keep to the right and go around, not through, Airport Circle. Three quarters of the way around the circle, get onto Island Road South. (It will be the first road after the turnoff to the Industrial Highway.) Proceed to the end of Island Road South and make a left turn. Turn left again and then make a sharp right onto the road that takes you to the fort.

Open Memorial Day to Labor Day 10 A.M. to 4 P.M.; open during the rest of the year only on Sunday 10 A.M. to 4 P.M. Adults $1.00, children 50¢.

Soon after the British occupied Philadelphia on September 26, 1777, the Patriots attempted to obstruct the passage of ships up the Delaware River by constructing a series of chevaux-de-frise (spikes attached to logs set in weighted crates) at strategic points across the river. One of these series was constructed off Red Bank (New Jersey), where Fort Mercer was located. Directly across from Fort Mercer was Fort Mifflin, the garrison built on Port Island in the river. (Over the decades the channel separating Port Island from the shore has filled in.)

When British General William Howe learned that a detachment of 450 Patriot soldiers under the command of Lieutenant Colonel Samuel Smith had occupied Fort Mifflin, he instructed Captain John Montresor to make preparations for an attack. Before engaging troops, Montresor ordered the building of batteries on the shore and floating batteries on the river. By October 10 the British began firing on Fort Mifflin. The barrage continued intermittently for almost two weeks.

On October 22 six British men-of-war, having broken through the chevaux-de-frise, moved into the area to support a land attack on Fort Mercer by 2,000 Hessians under Colonel Carl von Donop. The attack was a spectacular failure, with the Hessians suffering nearly 400 casualties including the loss of their commander. Two of the vessels —the *Augusta* and the *Merlin*—misjudging the depth of the riverbed, ran aground and were later destroyed by Patriot fire.

Infuriated, Howe directed his wrath against Fort Mifflin by ordering a coordinated attack to begin on November 10. The British batteries began a merciless bombardment on the fort, reducing the blockhouses to rubble. But the Patriots refused to give up the fight. Five days later, ships of the British fleet were able to come within range of the fortification, letting loose an intense barrage of fire which battered down the walls and delivered the *coup de grace* to the dying fort.

That night the forty surviving Patriots escaped across the river to the safety of Fort Mercer. At dawn on November 16 the British occupied Fort Mifflin and found it strewn with hundreds of corpses.

The haven offered the survivors at Fort Mercer was short-lived, for with the fall of Fort Mifflin, the loss of Fort Mercer was inevitable. On the night of October 22, the Patriot troops abandoned it, and the Delaware River came under British control.

Fort Mifflin was rebuilt during the administration of President John Adams. Other buildings were added during the Civil War, when the fort was used as a prison for Confederate soldiers.

Today the fort is being restored by the nonprofit Shacka-maxon Society. Visitors can see earthworks, the ramparts, remains of barrack buildings, and cannon (mostly of the Civil War period). On Sundays young men clad in Colonial militia costumes muster, fire muskets, and demonstrate the skills of Revolutionary War soldiers.

Pennsbury Manor

From downtown Philadelphia take North Broad Street to Girard Avenue, which you can follow to Interstate 95 (the Delaware Expressway). Travel east on Route 95 to Bristol, where you will pick up Route 13. Continue east to Tullytown, then follow the signs to Pennsbury Manor.

Open April through October Monday through Saturday 8:30 A.M. to 5 P.M., Sunday 1 P.M. to 5 P.M. During the rest of the year the site is open Monday through Saturday 9 A.M. to 4:30 P.M. Closed holidays. Adults 50¢, children free.

In 1681, after receiving a charter from King Charles II, William Penn (1644–1718) formulated plans for the establishment of a colony called Pennsylvania where religious and political freedom could flourish. In October 1682 he arrived in Pennsylvania and shortly thereafter began construction of a dwelling on this site. Required to return to England in 1684, he appointed James Harrison overseer of this property. Political affairs kept Penn in England for fifteen years—longer than he wished—and when he and his family returned in 1699, they occupied the house that had been completed in his absence. They continued to reside here until 1701, when they returned to England.

Pennsbury Manor was occupied by his son, William Penn, Jr., from 1704 until 1707; after that time the house was rented to tenants. Descendants of Penn sold the property at the end of the eighteenth century.

When, in 1932, the Pennsylvania Historical Commission celebrated the 250th anniversary of Penn's arrival in America, only the foundation of Pennsbury Manor remained. Architect Brognard Okie was commissioned to reconstruct the mansion from archaeological evidence, historical reports, and information derived from Penn's letters. The reconstruction of Pennsbury Manor was completed in the summer of 1939; it was then furnished with appropriate period pieces and opened to the public. It is considered by many authorities to contain the finest collection of seventeenth-century antiques in the state of Pennsylvania.

Chadds Ford

On August 25, 1777—almost five weeks after departing from New York City—the British fleet transporting a force of 13,000 British and Hessian soldiers anchored near Head of Elk, Maryland, at the northern tip of the Chesapeake Bay, fifty miles from their objective: Philadelphia. Upon landing, General William Howe separated his army into two divisions, one under General Charles Cornwallis and the other under the Hessian General Wilhelm von Knyphausen. They advanced slowly, delayed by the unloading of supplies, the inclement weather, and the weakened condition of the soldiers from the long period spent at sea. By September 10 the British army had marched as far as Kennett Square, about five miles west of Chadds Ford, a crossing on Brandywine Creek.

Washington's troops, which had been preparing to confront the British to prevent them from reaching Philadelphia, had bivouacked near Chadds Ford on the preceding day. They hastily erected earthworks and redoubts. Afterward, troops under Generals Anthony Wayne, William Maxwell, Thomas Proctor, and Nathanael Greene occupied the area surrounding Chadds Ford (where General Washington remained), while the brigades of Generals William Alexander (Lord Stirling), Adam Stephen, and John Sullivan took up defensive positions along the east bank of Brandywine Creek about two miles to the north.

At four o'clock on the morning of September 11 Knyphausen began moving his division eastward from Kennett

Square toward the American positions at the Ford. Two
miles down the road they encountered a Patriot detachment under General William Maxwell which had been
sent out to reconnoiter and, if possible, delay the enemy's
approach. Although the initial volleys of Patriot fire threw
the British and Hessians into confusion, Maxwell's men
were soon repulsed and were eventually driven back to
the main camp across the Brandywine. At about 10:30
A.M. Knyphausen's men occupied the hills on the west
side of Brandywine Creek at Chadds Ford. Sporadic
artillery fire was exchanged during the next several hours,
but neither side attempted a full-scale assault.

Meanwhile, about 8,000 British troops led by Howe
and Cornwallis, after leaving Kennett Square, traveled
northeast for approximately six miles, crossed the Brandywine, then nearing Sconneltown, veered southward and
marched to Osborne Hill, where they prepared to attack
the Americans on a second front.

Near 11 A.M. Washington received a reconnaissance
report from Colonel Moses Hazen, giving an account of
the movements of the Howe-Cornwallis column. After a
second message arrived from Lieutenant Colonel James
Ross corroborating the information, Washington summoned his officers to a council of war. His generals
decided to attack the Howe-Cornwallis column (to the
north) immediately and to launch a simultaneous assault
on Knyphausen (across the Creek to the west). Greene's
advance guard was already crossing the Brandywine toward Knyphausen's forces when a third message arrived—
from General John Sullivan based on information from
Major James Spear—claiming that the enemy column was
not marching to the north and that Hazen's earlier report
was erroneous. Believing the latest report to be the most
reliable, Washington countermanded his orders and can-
celed the attacks.

Little happened until 2 P.M., when a local farmer,
Thomas Cheyney, rode into camp in a frenzy, shouting

that he must be taken to the Commander-in-Chief. When the guards refused his demands, he related information so startling that he was immediately brought to General Washington. He then repeated that he had seen the Howe-Cornwallis column on the east side of Brandywine Creek near Sconneltown heading toward the Patriot lines. As his information contradicted the dispatches from General Sullivan, Washington's aides refused to believe Cheyney, and even suggested that he was a Loyalist acting under orders to mislead them. It was not until nearly 4 P.M., when a courier from a reconnaissance unit brought corroborating information, that Washington realized the gravity of his position.

To meet the threat, he was forced to divide his troops. He ordered the brigades of Alexander, Stephen, and Sullivan to leave their entrenchments along the east bank of the Brandywine and take up positions to the northeast, on the high ground near the Birmingham Meeting House. Washington, along with the troops of Wayne, Proctor, Maxwell, and Greene, remained at Chadds Ford in order to hold back any attack that might be launched by Knyphausen.

By the time the Patriot troops had taken up positions, the British had massed on and around Osborne Hill (one and a half miles northwest of the Birmingham Meeting House), and shortly afterward they began their attack. In the ensuing battle the Americans were driven back five times and five times they furiously fought their way forward to their old position. After an hour and forty minutes of intense fighting, the Patriots could no longer hold back the well-trained British and Hessian troops, and the American lines finally broke into harried retreat.

During this time Washington, hearing the relentless gunfire from the Birmingham Meeting House area, became concerned that the men under Alexander, Stephen, and Sullivan might need support and sent General Greene's troops as reinforcements. With the Commander-in-Chief at their head, the troops rushed to the aid of their compatriots. But this action was too late, for as they approached the battle site (near 6 P.M.), they beheld a mass of Patriot soldiers scurrying in retreat. Greene opened his ranks, giving the fleeing men an opportunity to pass through and regroup, but the British juggernaut could not be stopped. Washington and his generals were able to restrain their soldiers' panic, and the retreat continued in orderly fashion.

Meanwhile, at Chadds Ford, Knyphausen had launched his assault on the Patriot ranks, which were now diminished by Washington's and Greene's redeployment. In the face of heavy Patriot artillery fire, the enemy moved across the Creek, took up formation, and steadily ascended the slopes. The American left flank was the first to fall, and four cannon were destroyed. General Wayne's men bravely stood their ground until the British Guards and Grenadiers from the Howe-Cornwallis ranks arrived to join in the fray and overpower the American center. Finally, the British seized the advantage and sent the Patriots in scattered flight. At sunset the defeated Americans straggled toward Chester. That night the victorious British pitched their tents on the recently secured battlefield.

The British reported 90 killed, 480 wounded, and 6 missing. The Patriot toll was estimated at 300 killed, 600 wounded, and 400 taken as prisoners. Among the wounded was the nineteen-year-old Lafayette who, only three months after his arrival from France, sustained a leg wound in his first battle here.

The Battle of Brandywine was a devastating defeat for the Americans. Fifteen days later, after meeting only minor opposition, the British occupied Philadelphia—the seat of the Continental Congress and America's largest city.

VISITORS' CENTER   Information about the sites of the area may be obtained from the Chadds Ford Historical Society, Route 1, phone 388–1132.

Colonial and Revolutionary War Sites

BRANDYWINE BATTLEFIELD PARK   *On Route 1, 1½ miles past the intersection with Route 202. Open 10 A.M. to 5 P.M. during the summer. The hours may be extended during the Bicentennial. Free.*

LAFAYETTE HOUSE   The oldest section of this house was built in 1745 by Joseph Gilpin, a prosperous farmer. The property was inherited by his son Gideon who, with his wife Sarah, was residing here at the time of the Revolutionary War. Although a Quaker who did not support the war, Gilpin agreed to permit Lafayette to use his house as headquarters during the Battle of Brandywine. After the British victory the Redcoats plundered the house and barn, seizing 48 sheep, 28 swine, 230 bushels of wheat, 12 tons of hay, and 100 dozen potatoes.

In 1778 Gilpin opened a tavern here, but his fellow Quakers continued to heap scorn on him until he finally closed the business.

Upon Gilpin's death in late 1825, the house and land were sold. A succession of tenants occupied the house until 1949, when it was acquired by the Commonwealth of Pennsylvania to be preserved as a historic site.

Today, visitors may also see on the grounds a Revolu-

Lafayette House, Brandywine Battlefield Park (ALPER)

tionary War cannon; a small root house (built in 1809) used for the drying and storing of roots and herbs; and a carriage house containing a carriage used by the Marquis de Lafayette in July 1825, when he toured the area and stopped here to visit with his former host.

WASHINGTON'S HEADQUARTERS The house occupied by General Washington during the Battle of Brandywine was owned by Benjamin Ring, who operated several local mills. It was a commodious structure, large enough to accommodate Ring's wife and ten children. As the headquarters of the Patriot Commander-in-Chief, the house became the focus of British wrath, and after the battle soldiers mercilessly pillaged the estate.

Throughout the first half of the nineteenth century the property was in the possession of the Harvey family. Ownership passed to others until 1931, when a fire reduced the building to rubble. Only the scorched foundation remained until an agency of the Commonwealth of

Pennsylvania commissioned architect C. Edwin Brumbaugh to undertake reconstruction of the historic site.

The present-day house is furnished with pieces typical of the eighteenth century. In one room mannequins are arranged in a tableau showing the meeting between Patriot officers and Thomas Cheyney, who reported British troop movements.

JOHN CHADD HOUSE   *Route 100. Open 10* A.M. *to 5* P.M. *during the summer. Free.*   This house was built in 1725 by John Chadd, who in 1731 began operating a ferry across Brandywine Creek. Later, he opened a tavern in the house of his deceased parents, but he eventually turned the management over to another person. Chadd died in 1760 and his widow continued to reside here until her death in 1799.

When Mrs. Chadd heard artillery fire during the Battle of Brandywine, she quickly bolted the doors and windows and hid her valuables. The building suffered only minor damage.

The Chadd House is presently undergoing restoration.

FRIENDS MEETING HOUSE (BIRMINGHAM MEETING HOUSE)   *On Birmingham Meeting Road. Not open to the public.*   This modest fieldstone structure dates from 1763. Near here the Patriots took up positions to confront the British on Osborne Hill. During the early phases of the battle the Patriots used the meeting house as a hospital. Afterward, wounded British soldiers were brought here for medical care.

Non-Revolutionary Site of Interest

BRANDYWINE RIVER MUSEUM *On Route 1, one block southwest of Route 100. Open daily May 20 to October 15, 9:30 A.M. to 5 P.M. Adults $1.00, youngsters (6–12) 75¢, children (under 6) free.* This museum is devoted primarily to the works of Howard Pyle, Newell Convers Wyeth, and Andrew Wyeth and his son James. Their paintings are in the realistic mode. The museum is administered by the Tri-County Conservancy.

Valley Forge

Revolutionary War History

The fall of 1777 was marked by a series of disasters for the Continental Army in Pennsylvania. On September 11 Washington's soldiers suffered a serious defeat at Brandywine Creek. On October 4—eight days after the British had occupied Philadelphia—the American attack on Germantown, a dismal failure, turned into a retreat. On November 16 British forces took control of the former Patriot garrison at Fort Mifflin on the Delaware River. General Washington's troops withdrew to Whitemarsh, but after several sorties by General William Howe's forces early in December, Washington decided to move his men to a safer encampment. On December 11 they began to march toward the site of their new winter encampment—Valley Forge.

Rain and snow had turned the roads into mire, and it took the ill-clad, demoralized soldiers eight days to travel the thirteen miles. Finally, on December 19, the 9,000 men began to set up their tents for the bivouac at Valley Forge.

The area provided a natural defensive position. It was protected on the north by the Schuylkill River and on the west by both the steep slope of Mount Joy and a creek. In addition, it commanded a view of the approaches from the east and south. To provide further protection, entrenchments and redoubts were built.

The men immediately started constructing huts. Soon after Christmas shelters for most of the soldiers were completed, but inadequate clothing and shortages of food

began to inflict grievous suffering. Uniforms were threadbare, exposing the men's bodies, and their shoes were
worn beyond repair. Many soldiers endured the pain of
frozen feet and legs, which turned gangrenous and had
to be amputated. Others lay half starved and emaciated.
Since foraging parties could not gather sufficient provisions, the diet was usually limited to "fire-cakes," a
mixture of flour and water baked into thin cakes. When
the water from the nearby creek became contaminated
from the poor sanitary arrangements of the camp, in-
testinal disorders became a common affliction. Hundreds
of horses starved to death, and as the weakened men
were unable to dig graves in the frozen earth, the
scattered carcasses posed a further danger to health.

The result was inevitable—an outbreak of typhus ran
rampant throughout the camp. The seriously ill were transported to hospitals at Ephrata, Bethlehem, and Yellow
Springs. For those who remained in camp the nightmare
continued. As the death toll increased, so did the number
of desertions.

The arrival in February of the Prussian Baron von
Steuben, who had come to aid the Patriot cause, was an
important moment for the Continental Army. Appointed
by Washington to train the troops, he devised a drill
manual based on European models. Since he could speak
only German and French, he wrote the manual in French.
It was translated into English by an aide, Pierre Duponceau, then copied into the regimental orderly books.
Von Steuben quickly chose a model company of 100
men. Acting as drillmaster, he gestured and pantomimed
until the trainees imitated and mastered the maneuvers.
In mid-March a drill program was initiated for all the
soldiers, who were taught to march in column, to deploy
from column into line, to effectively use muskets in a coordinated attack, and to charge with bayonets.

Washington organized a mock battle between two

divisions, one led by Von Steuben and the other by Duponceau. According to tradition, the soldiers were performing brilliantly until the near-sighted Duponceau believed he spotted a group of Redcoats about a half-mile from the encampment. He sent an officer to rush back to Valley Forge with the news, but when the soldiers returned, they reported that what he had sighted was merely a number of red petticoats hanging on the bushes to dry!

The arrival of spring brought with it an improvement in the conditions of the camp. The Commissary Department was able to send more supplies and provisions, and the men were given a daily ration of bread, beans, meat, and spirits. In addition, the soldiers were able to fish the Schuylkill River and thereby supplement their rations. Spring also brought with it an influx of volunteers who swelled the ranks of the Continental Army.

When, on May 1, 1778, news arrived of the signing of the Treaty of Alliance between France and America, the camp at Valley Forge exploded with jubilation. In celebration, a grand review was organized. Several brigades marched in precision formation before General Washington and his senior officers, then the salute of guns echoed across the hills, followed by shouts of "Long Live the King of France!" After the review Washington invited his officers to a reception, where Von Steuben was heaped with praise for the spectacular change he had effected.

During the second week in June, Washington received reports that the British troops in Philadelphia were dismantling their artillery and were preparing to remove supplies. On June 18 the British army evacuated the city, and that same day Washington issued orders for the Continental Army at Valley Forge to break camp in order to pursue and harass the enemy.

The Americans left behind a scene of misery which is a legacy of the commitment to the cherished ideal of freedom, even though the cost be suffering and sacrifice.

From Philadelphia travel west on the Schuylkill Expressway—Interstate 76—then take Route 363 North. The Visitors' Center is located at the junction of Routes 363 and 23.

VISITORS' CENTER An audio-visual presentation is given here as part of an orientation program for visitors. Items associated with the Revolutionary War are also on display.

GUIDED TOURS A self-guided **automobile tape tour** (with recorder) is available daily from April through October from 9 A.M. to 2:30 P.M. The cost is $5.00 for two hours with a 50¢ overtime charge.

A **bus tour** departs from the Visitors' Center several times daily from April through October from 9 A.M. to 3 P.M. The fee is $3.70 for adults and $1.55 for children.

If you are in Philadelphia, inquire at the **Gray Line Tours** office, phone 569-3666.

DRIVING TOUR Valley Forge State Park is crossed by labyrinth of roads, which may confuse sightseers. The following route is suggested in order to see the major points of interest. Stop at the sites that interest you. After leaving the Visitors' Center, travel along the Outer Line Drive—past "Fort" Muhlenburg, the Maine Monument, and the Massachusetts Monument—until you arrive at the National Memorial Arch. Head toward the right and follow the circle around the Arch until you come to the extension of the Outer Line Drive. Turn right and proceed past the Pennsylvania Columns, the Pennsylvania Soldiers' Huts, the Wayne Equestrian Statue, the Von Steuben Statue, and the Monument to the Unknown Dead. Turn right at the crossroads onto Baptist Road. To your right is Artillery Park; proceed to the Camp Schoolhouse area, which is off to the left. At the intersection of Baptist and Gulph Roads, make a left turn onto Gulph Road. Travel a distance, then after passing Camp Road you will come to Inner Line Drive, where you should turn left. Ascend Mount Joy to the Observation Tower, then as you come down the hill, bear right until you reach Baptist Road. Turn right, proceed to Valley Road (Route 252), then turn right again. As you travel along Valley Creek you will see the headquarters of Generals Knox, Maxwell, and Alexander. When you arrive at Route 23 at the intersection, turn left and go a short distance to Baron von Steuben's Headquarters, which is just past the Maryland Marker. Retrace your route to the intersection of Valley Road and Route 23, then turn left to the Bake House and the Potts-Washington House. Follow the road around to the right—past the site of Washington's Life Guard and the Delaware Monument—then you will come to Port Kennedy Road (Route 23). Bear to the left and follow the road to General Varnum's Headquarters and the Star Redoubt and the Rhode Island Monument, which are both directly across the road (on the Schuylkill River side). Continue to the last stop: the Washington Memorial Chapel and Valley Forge Museum. Across the road, on the edge of the Parade Ground, stands the Waterman Memorial. Follow Port Kennedy Road back to the Visitors' Center.

Valley Forge State Park Sites

Valley Forge State Park, which embraces 2,200 acres, is administered by the Valley Forge Park Commission of the Commonwealth of Pennsylvania. In addition to its numerous monuments and historic sites, the park has many recreational areas.

ARTILLERY PARK This site was occupied by the troops and artillery pieces under the command of General Henry Knox, Chief of Artillery. The guns here today are replicas, and they serve as an appropriate tribute to Knox, who organized the transporting of cannon (in December 1775/January 1776) from Fort Ticonderoga to Boston, eventually forcing the British to evacuate the city.

BAKE HOUSE This house was built in the 1750s by John Potts, owner of the Valley Creek Forge. In 1773, when William Dewees bought an interest in the business, he took possession of this property.

During the winter encampment of 1777–1778 the house served a dual purpose: it functioned as an adjunct to Washington's headquarters and the basement was used as a bakery.

Here aides to General Washington prepared dispatches and kept records of the dreadfully low supplies. Downstairs in the cellar Christopher Ludwig and his assistants kept the ovens hot and baked thousands of "fire-cakes" to feed the half-starved soldiers.

In the spring of 1778 this house was frequently used for recitations and plays. A favorite of the officers was Joseph Addison's historical tragedy *Cato* (1713). The audience heartily applauded when one of the characters declared: "My voice is still for war. Gods! can a Roman senate long debate which of the two to choose, slavery or death?"

The Bake House has been restored and furnished with eighteenth-century antiques. Visitors can see a Joseph Wills Pennsylvania clock, a fine Queen Anne drop-leaf table, delft plates and bowls, a six-legged wooden settee, a Philadelphia lowboy, and a slat-back rocking chair. Because several court-martials were held here, the Pennsylvania Society of the Sons of the American Revolution has furnished one of the rooms in the style of a Colonial military courtroom.

CAMP SCHOOLHOUSE / HOSPITAL One of the oldest schoolhouses in America, this stone structure was built in 1705 on land owned by Letitia Penn Aubrey (daughter of William Penn, founder of Pennsylvania). During the winter encampment of 1777–1778 this building was used as a hospital. After the Revolutionary War, it resumed its function as a schoolhouse and continued in service until 1840. It was restored and opened to the public in 1908.

Nearby are a blacksmith's shop and the stables that sheltered the army's artillery horses.

DELAWARE MONUMENT The state of Delaware erected this monument "in memory of her gallant sons who endured the hardships and privations of the memorable winter of 1777–1778 on the hills of Valley Forge." At the dedication ceremonies on October 31, 1914, the monument was unveiled by Helen Marian Scott, a descendant of Joshua Clayton, the last president of Delaware under the constitution of 1776 and subsequently governor of the state. The principal address was delivered by Henry C. Conrad, Associate Justice of the Delaware Supreme Court.

"FORT" HUNTINGTON The earthworks here indicate the defense positions and encampment of the Connecticut troops under General Jedediah Huntington.

"FORT" MUHLENBERG Reconstructed earthworks and several huts on this site mark the location of the defenses and encampment of General J. P. G. Muhlenberg's brigades, which were part of General Nathanael Greene's division.

HEADQUARTERS AREA The Headquarters Area more or less parallels Valley Road leading to Route 23.

Alexander's Headquarters General William Alexander (Lord Stirling) took up residence in this dwelling, the home of the Reverend William Currie, rector of St.

Peter's Church in Great Valley and St. David's in Radnor. Many additions have been made to the house since the eighteenth century.

Knox's Headquarters   General Henry Knox and his wife Lucy occupied this Georgian-style house, owned at the time by Samuel Brown.

Maxwell's Headquarters   General William Maxwell was a guest of the Brown family here during the winter of 1777–1778.

Von Steuben's Headquarters   This two-story Colonial structure served as the residence of the army's drill-master, Baron von Steuben. For a short time, ill soldiers were brought here to recuperate out of the brutal elements.

MAINE MARKER   This monument honors those soldiers at Valley Forge whose homes were in the part of New England that is now Maine. (Maine was not admitted into the Union until 1820.) Dedicated on October 17, 1908, the monument was erected by the Maine Society of the Sons of the American Revolution.

MARQUEE SITE MARKER   The Valley Forge Park Commission erected this stone in the early 1940s to mark the spot where General Washington pitched his tent during the first days of the encampment before moving into the Potts house. The linen marquee (field tent), which was made in Philadelphia, was first used by Washington at Dorchester Heights (overlooking Boston) in 1776. It served as his personal command post. Today, the marquee is displayed in the museum adjacent to the Washington Memorial Chapel at Valley Forge.

MARYLAND MARKER   This stone marker was erected in August 1963 by the Maryland Society of Pennsylvania. The plaque lists the senior officers serving under Generals John Sullivan and William Smallwood.

MASSACHUSETTS MONUMENT   At the end of the first decade of the twentieth century the Massachusetts–

Valley Forge Commission, headed by Philip Reade, made plans for the erection of a monument here to pay tribute to the Revolutionary War soldiers from Massachusetts. The Van-Amringe Granite Company of Boston was commissioned to create the monument, which consists of an exedra and a large stone bearing an inscription and the state seal. The dedication ceremonies took place on November 19, 1911.

MONUMENT TO THE UNKNOWN DEAD   This stone marker, located near the Von Steuben Statue, pays tribute to the estimated 3,000 Patriot soldiers who died from starvation and disease at Valley Forge during the bitter winter of 1777–1778. Almost all the corpses were buried in unmarked graves so that spies in the camp would not be able to determine the reduction in the army's ranks. The marker was dedicated by the Valley Forge Chapter of the Daughters of the American Revolution on June 18, 1911.

MOUNT JOY AND OBSERVATION TOWER   Legend has it that William Penn named this area Mount Joy while he was surveying here in 1683. Penn had lost his way in the dense forests on the slope across Valley Creek and was forced to spend the night there, in danger of attack by prowling wolves. At dawn he discovered a path leading down the steep hill and to the base of another hill, which he climbed. From the summit he was able to see the Schuylkill River and the route back to Philadelphia. In a moment of rejoicing he named this hill "Mount Joy" (and called the one on the opposite side of the creek "Mount Misery")!

Mount Joy was an important point in the Patriot defense line because, from an observation tower and from lookout platforms in the trees, sentinels could view the surrounding countryside and the approaches from Philadelphia—the roads by which the British could launch an attack.

Today a seventy-five-foot-high steel tower (1906) marks the spot where the log observation tower of the Continental Army once stood.

NATIONAL MEMORIAL ARCH On June 25, 1910, the United States Congress appropriated $100,000 for the erection of a memorial arch at Valley Forge. Architect Paul Philippe Cret (1877–1945) of Philadelphia—who also designed the Gettysburg Peace Memorial and the Folger Shakespeare Library in Washington, D.C.—received the commission. After a committee reviewed Cret's designs for the project, construction was begun and the arch was completed in 1913. Official dedication ceremonies were held on June 19, 1914.

Three years later, the federal government transferred the custody of the monument to the Commonwealth of Pennsylvania at a ceremony (June 19, 1917) in which Governor Martin G. Brumbaugh expressed the gratitude

Observation tower on Mount Joy, Valley Forge State Park (ALPER)

National Memorial Arch, Valley Forge State Park (ALPER)

of the citizens of the state to James B. Clark, Speaker of the United States House of Representatives.

The inscription appearing on the face of the arch is from a letter written by George Washington on February 16, 1778: "Naked and starving as they are we cannot enough admire the incomparable patience and fidelity of the soldiery."

Another inscription is from the speech delivered at Valley Forge on June 19, 1878—the 100th anniversary of the evacuation of the Continental Army from their winter encampment—by a prominent Philadelphian, Henry Armitt Brown: "And here, in this place of sacrifice, in this vale of humiliation, in this valley of the shadow of that death, out of which the life of America rose, regenerate and free, let us believe with an abiding faith, that to them union will seem as dear and liberty as sweet and progress as glorious as they were to our fathers and are to you and me. . . ."

Inside the span of the arch are bronze tablets listing the names of the officers who served under Washington here—De Kalb, Lafayette, Lee, Mifflin, Von Steuben, Alexander (Stirling), and Sullivan.

NEW JERSEY MONUMENT   The state of New Jersey erected this monument to honor the New Jersey troops encamped here under the command of General William Maxwell. The thirty-five-foot shaft is surmounted by a bronze statue of a Continental soldier. During the dedication ceremonies on June 18, 1918, New Jersey Governor James F. Fielder delivered the principal address and the monument was unveiled by Eleanor Wilson (daughter of Woodrow Wilson, then President of the United States).

PARADE GROUND   In this large open field Baron von Steuben drilled the Continental soldiers, transforming them from raw recruits into disciplined military units. The grand review (May 1778) organized to celebrate the Franco-American alliance was held on the Parade Ground before General Washington and his senior officers.

PENNSYLVANIA COLUMNS   These two columns topped by eagles were erected in 1909 by the Commonwealth of Pennsylvania at a cost of $8,000. The design for the commemorative columns was the work of sculptor Henry Kirke Bush-Brown, who was also commissioned to execute the Valley Forge statue of General Anthony Wayne.

POTTS-WASHINGTON HOUSE   Built in 1760, this dwelling was the property of Isaac Potts, owner of the forge and coal houses located near Valley Creek. In the mid-1770s the house was rented to Deborah Hewes, who at the time of the encampment offered it to General Washington. Martha Washington arrived in February 1778, and she frequently attended to the ill soldiers.

The building, which is ninety percent original, is furnished with period pieces. Among the important pieces are a walnut chest of drawers made in Pennsylvania; a handsome highboy with fine carving; several rush-seat chairs; and an oak bed, formerly owned by Charles Thomson, the first secretary to the Continental Congress.

On the lawn stands a statue of George Washington, a reproduction of the famous work (begun in 1785) by Jean Antoine Houdon (which is now in the Capitol Building at Richmond, Virginia). This replica was originally placed in 1931 near the Washington Memorial Chapel; it was moved to its present site in 1957 and was set on a new pedestal.

In the stable on the grounds General Washington kept his two stallions, Blueskin and Nelson. Early in 1778 the structure was converted into a hospital.

RHODE ISLAND MONUMENT This marker was erected by the state of Rhode Island to honor its sons who served in the Continental Army. During the dedication ceremonies on October 13, 1963, patriotic speeches were delivered by Governor John H. Chafee and Woodrow W. Tucker, the overseer of the Rhode Island State Grange.

SITE OF WASHINGTON'S LIFE GUARD A cluster of huts marks the site of Washington's Life Guard, the unit of soldiers organized to protect the Commander-in-Chief and ordered to act as a security detachment at his headquarters.

SOLDIERS' HUTS Construction requirements for the soldiers' huts were prescribed by the General Orders issued by George Washington upon arrival at Valley Forge. The huts were: "to be of the following dimensions, viz. 14 x 16 feet each; sides, ends and roofs made of logs, and the roofs made tight with split slabs, or in some other way; the sides made tight with clay. Fireplace made of wood and secured with clay on the inside 18 inches thick, this fireplace to be in the rear of the hut. The door to be in the end next to the street; the door to be made

Soldiers' huts, Valley Forge State Park (ALPER)

of split oak slabs unless boards can be produced. Side walls to be 6⅓ feet high."

STAR REDOUBT Erected on the strategic ground overlooking the Schuylkill River, this star-shaped redoubt was built by army engineers under the supervision of General John Sullivan. It was the largest of the fortifications protecting the encampment at Valley Forge. The present Star Redoubt is an early-twentieth-century reconstruction.

VALLEY FORGE MUSEUM The collection housed in this museum was begun by the Valley Forge Historical Society soon after its founding in 1918. Among the items on display are paintings and prints portraying events in the life of George Washington, Revolutionary War muskets, letters written by Washington, a collection of china, eighteenth-century silver objects (including cups made by Philadelphia silversmith Edmund Milne), and a medicine chest used by Washington at Valley Forge. Especially cherished are the Commander-in-Chief's marquee (field tent) and his battle flag. Admission fee, 25¢.

VARNUM'S HEADQUARTERS During the Valley Forge encampment this two-story stone house was the property of David Stephens. General James Mitchell Varnum, commander of the Rhode Island brigades, set up headquarters here at Stephens' invitation. In February 1778 Varnum wrote a letter lamenting that the "situation of the camp is such that in all human probability the army must soon dissolve."

Numerous court-martials were held in this house—for theft, insubordination, assaulting an officer, spying or aiding a spy, and absence without leave. The punishment for minor offenses was a lashing (sometimes with salt washings); the punishment for serious offenses was death by hanging.

VON STEUBEN STATUE This tribute to Baron von Steuben—the man who has been called "the first teacher

Von Steuben Statue, Valley Forge State Park
(ALPER)

of the American Army"—was erected by the National German-American Alliance of the United States at a cost of $10,000. The sculptor was J. Otto Schweizer of Philadelphia, and the statue was cast by the Van Amringe Company of Boston. Dedication ceremonies were held on October 9, 1915.

The relief on the base, which depicts Baron von Steuben drilling Continental soldiers at Valley Forge, is from a painting attributed to the eighteenth-century artist Ralph Earl. The relief was the gift of William M. Austin of New York, a descendant of Colonel William North, who served as aide-de-camp to von Steuben.

Friedrich Wilhelm, Baron von Steuben (1730–1794) served in the Prussian army and in 1762 became an aide to Frederick the Great. Losing royal favor and deeply in debt, he traveled to Paris where, in 1777, he met a friend of Benjamin Franklin's who suggested to von Steuben that he serve the Patriot cause in America. After meeting with members of the Continental Congress, he reported to Washington at Valley Forge. As a result of his military reforms, he was commissioned a major general and appointed Inspector General of the Continental Army in May 1778.

WASHINGTON MEMORIAL CHAPEL The cornerstone of this chapel was laid on June 19, 1903—the 125th anniversary of the evacuation of Valley Forge. Construction proceeded slowly, and the Gothic-style building (designed by architect Milton Medary, Jr.) was finally completed in 1917. The first rector here was the Reverend W. Herbert Burk, formerly pastor of All Saints Church in Norristown.

The interior of the Washington Memorial Chapel is distinguished by extraordinary stained-glass windows, the work of Nicola D'Ascenzo of Philadelphia. The George Washington Window, over the entrance, depicts thirty-six scenes from Washington's life. Perhaps the most famous panel is the one showing the Commander-in-Chief kneeling in prayer at Valley Forge.

The unusual ceiling—called the "Roof of the Republic"—is decorated with the official emblems of the fifty states, arranged in the order of their admission into the Union.

The magnificent pulpit is of carved limestone; the intricately carved choir stalls are the work of Edward Maene of Philadelphia; the handsome choir screens are decorated with figures representing Washington's Life Guard. The relief tablet to the east of the entrance commemorates the signing of the Declaration of Independence, and the tablet on the west wall honors the framers of the Federal Constitution. Both panels were executed by Martha M. Hovenden in 1926 and 1936 respectively.

Religious services are held in the Washington Memorial Chapel on Sunday mornings.

The **Valley Forge Bell Tower,** adjacent to the chapel, was built with funds donated by the National Society of the Daughters of the American Revolution. Soon after the dedication ceremonies on April 18, 1953, the fifty-eight bells of the carillon were installed and were assigned names of the states. The Illinois bell, the largest, weighs four tons and measures seventy-one inches in diameter. The music from this carillon echoes throughout the hills of Valley Forge.

WATERMAN MEMORIAL This monument stands above the only marked soldier's grave which has survived 200 years at the Valley Forge encampment site. The imposing granite shaft has replaced the original gravestone of Lieutenant John Waterman of Rhode Island, who died on April 23, 1778. Erected by the Daughters of the American Revolution, the memorial was dedicated by Pennsylvania Governor William A. Stone in October 1901.

WAYNE STATUE On May 11, 1905, the Pennsylvania legislature appropriated $30,000 for a monument to

Wayne Statue, Valley Forge State Park (ALPER)

honor Patriot General Anthony Wayne. A committee was appointed—John P. Nicholson, Richard M. Cadwalader, and John Armstrong Herman—to oversee the project. In 1906 the committee reviewed designs submitted by twelve sculptors and selected the design of Henry Kirke Bush-Brown (1858–1935). From Bush-Brown's plaster model (completed in his studio in Newburgh, New York) the Bureau Brothers of Philadelphia cast the magnificent bronze equestrian statue. The pedestal, of red granite, is the work of Captain William R. Hodges of St. Louis, Missouri.

The monument was unveiled at dedication ceremonies on Saturday, June 20, 1908. The main address was delivered by Governor Samuel W. Pennypacker who declared: "It was here that Anthony Wayne who loved action as the eagle loves the sun, in his heart fretted and suffered, but openly cheered his soldiers, inspiring in them confidence." Mr. Bush-Brown also spoke and his daughter Lydia unveiled the monument to the salute of guns of the Third United States Artillery Company.

A plaque on the pedestal recounts the career of Anthony Wayne (1745–1796). Born in Chester County, Pennsylvania, he was a deputy of the Provincial Convention (1774), a delegate to the Pennsylvania Assembly (1774, 1784–1785), a member of the Committee of Safety (1775–1776), and a representative to the Pennsylvania Convention called to ratify the Constitution (1787). He fought gallantly in many Revolutionary War battles, including those at Brandywine and Germantown (1777), Monmouth (1778), Stony Point (1779), and Yorktown (1781). In 1792 Wayne succeeded Arthur St. Clair as Commander of the American Army.

To the right of the statue, beyond the hill, is a path that leads to a replica of a brigade hospital similar to those used at Valley Forge during the winter of 1777–1778.

Approximately 100 yards down the road from the

statue are several reconstructed officers' huts to mark the camp of Wayne's Pennsylvania brigades. They were erected by the Pennsylvania Society of the Sons of the American Revolution.

York

Revolutionary War History

In 1741 the Penn family commissioned Thomas Cookson to survey and divide into lots the land which became the town of York. By 1775 a community of nearly 300 families had sprung up here.

When, in mid-June 1775, the Second Continental Congress issued a call for troops to join General George Washington during the siege of the British garrison at Boston, a recruiting station was set up in York. So many more local men volunteered than the quota required that the officer in charge hit on an idea to select the best marksmen. He hastily sketched a face in chalk on a barn door and announced: "I'll take only the men who can hit the nose at 150 yards." One hundred crack-shots hit the target and were summarily recruited. The newly formed company of York County riflemen departed on July 1 for the camp of the Continental Army in Cambridge, Massachusetts.

On the evening of July 30, five days after their arrival, a detail of the York Patriots was sent out to harass a British patrol. The attempt was unsuccessful, and Corporal Walter Cruise was captured in the fray. He was sent to England to be tried on charges of treason, but the court determined that it had no jurisdiction in the case and he was released. Before returning to America, Corporal Cruise was clandestinely contacted by an American agent in England who entrusted him with secret dispatches for General Washington warning that the British government had enlisted German mercenaries to fight in the colonies.

Throughout the course of the Revolutionary War, soldiers from the York County Company fought valiantly in many important northern campaigns.

When General William Howe's British regiments occupied Philadelphia in September 1777, the Continental Congress first fled to Lancaster, Pennsylvania, but after meeting there for only one session, sought refuge in York. The Congress remained here for nine months—from September 30, 1777, to June 27, 1778—until the British evacuated Philadelphia. Local residents opened their homes to accommodate the delegates. John Adams, Samuel Adams, Richard Henry Lee, and Edward Rutledge were guests of Daniel Roberdeau in the largest mansion in town on South George Street. John Hancock, who served as president of Congress until October 29 (when he was succeeded by Henry Laurens), took up residence at the house of Colonel Michael Swope on West Market Street.

During the sessions, which were held in the courthouse, Congress resumed debate on the Articles of Confederation—the framework for uniting the independent states for joint action and defining their powers in relationship to those of the national government. Adopted on November 15, 1777, the thirteen Articles established a centralized body of government. They created a unicameral, or single-house, Congress in which each state would have one vote and would be represented by not less than two and not more than seven delegates, selected annually by each state as its legislature determined. Congress had the sole right to issue currency, to declare war and make peace, and to negotiate treaties and alliances— with the exception of treaties of commerce, which could not be effected without the consent of a majority of the states' legislatures. The states retained the "sovereignty, freedom, and independence, and every power, jurisdiction, and right, which is not . . . expressly delegated to the United States, in Congress assembled."

One of the principal shortcomings of the Articles was

that Congress was granted no authority to tax; the power of levying taxes was reserved exclusively to the states. The absence of an independent executive branch was another weakness; instead, the Congress established "A Committee of States." Consisting of one delegate from each state, the committee—which was entrusted with the power to act during Congressional recesses—elected a presiding officer who could not serve more than one year in three. By March 1, 1781 (seven and one-half months before Yorktown, the last major battle of the Revolutionary War), all the states had formally ratified the Articles. Because of the inherent weaknesses of the Articles of Confederation, they were superseded by the Federal Constitution of 1787.

Here at York, during the winter of 1777–1778, occurred a conspiracy against George Washington known as the Conway Cabal. The principal agents of this plot were General Thomas Conway, General Horatio Gates, and General Thomas Mifflin. Capitalizing on Washington's numerous defeats (beginning in August 1776 at Long Island, New York, down to the recent disaster at Brandywine in September 1777), they wished to topple him and replace him with General Gates as Commander-in-Chief.

The first intimations of treachery were revealed when Colonel James Wilkinson, an aide to General Gates, was traveling to Congress to report Gates' victory over Burgoyne at Saratoga (October 17, 1777). Stopping at a tavern in Reading, Pennsylvania, Wilkinson gossiped to an aide of General William Alexander about the growing sentiment in high circles against Washington. Wilkinson also told of a statement written in a dispatch between Generals Conway and Gates that questioned Washington's competence. Word concerning this dispatch swiftly reached the Commander-in-Chief, and he immediately sent a terse letter (dated November 9) to Conway stating:

Sir: A letter which I received last night contained the following paragraph: In a letter from General

Conway to General Gates, he says, "Heaven has determined to save your country, or a weak general and bad counselors would have ruined it." I am, sir, Your humble servant.

Now that they knew Washington was aware of their duplicity, the conspirators became plagued with fear. Conway replied to Washington that there was nothing improper in his conduct and attempted to clarify his statement. Gates, unable to discover the means by which the news had been leaked, wrote to Washington accusing him of prying into his private papers. Gates also sent a copy of the accusation to Henry Laurens, the president of Congress at York. In the interchange of letters between Gates, Washington, and Congress that followed, General Gates extricated himself from the affair by feigning ignorance and by shifting the blame to others.

In the meantime, however, the attempts to dilute Washington's authority had achieved a measure of success. Congress, with many members displeased with Washington's recent military record, created a Board of War—with temporary headquarters at York—and named Gates president of it, made Mifflin a member, and promoted Conway to Inspector General of the Continental Army. When the new Inspector General visited Washington at Valley Forge in late December, the reception he received was marked by chilly politeness, which he promptly reported in letters to Congress.

The intrigue continued until spring, when the personal motives behind the Conway Cabal were finally perceived by the members of Congress. Gates was directed to leave York and resume the command of the Northern Army. In the summer of 1780 he was appointed commander of Patriot forces in the South, but he fell into disgrace in August because of the disastrous defeat of his troops at Camden, South Carolina. Mifflin was removed from the Board of War and in February 1779 resigned from the army. Conway sent a fiery letter to Congress threatening to resign and discovered to his chagrin that Congress gladly accepted his resignation. He later was wounded by General John Cadwalader in a duel brought on, according to tradition, by Conway's derogatory remarks about Washington.

Thirteen years later, in 1791, when George Washington visited York, the gala reception offered him was in marked contrast to the hostile greeting he would have received here during the uncertain days of the Conway Cabal. He was now President of the United States.

VISITORS' CENTER Maps and brochures are available from 9 A.M. to 5 P.M. daily at the Colonial York Visitors' and Tourist Bureau, 1455 Mt. Zion Road, phone 755–9638. Information about the area may also be obtained from the Historical Society of York County, 250 East Market Street, phone 848–1587, or from the Chamber of Commerce, 13 East Market Street, phone 854–3814.

PUBLIC TRANSPORTATION The Reliance Motor Coach Company provides bus service in York. For information and schedules, phone 843–0520.

TAXI SERVICE Yellow Cab, phone 843–8811.

Colonial and Revolutionary War Sites

GOLDEN PLOUGH TAVERN AND GATES HOUSE
Corner of West Market Street and Pershing Avenue. Open Monday through Saturday 10 A.M. to 4 P.M., Sun-

day 1 P.M. to 4 P.M. During the summer, open until 5 P.M. Closed holidays. Admission to both buildings: adults $1.00, youngsters (12–17) 35¢, children (under 12) free. The Golden Plough Tavern was built in 1741 by Martin Eichelberg, who had emigrated to Pennsylvania from Germany. The half-timber structure he erected here reflects the domestic architectural style of his native land. This tavern was not only a resting point for travelers, but was a center of activity for the men of the town. Guests were served meals in the dining room and slept in rooms on the second floor.

In 1751 the property was sold to Joseph Chambers, a minor official of the town, who, soon afterward, built the adjoining house. Both the tavern and the private residence were acquired by George Irwin, a merchant, in 1771. It was he who leased the house during the first four months of 1778 to General Horatio Gates, the newly appointed president of the Board of War.

During Gates' residence he became involved in the machinations of the Conway Cabal. When General Lafayette visited Gates in February 1778 to discuss the possibility of an invasion of Canada, Gates hosted a dinner here for the young Frenchman. According to local tradition, Lafayette embarrassed several of the guests—who were conspirators in the Conway Cabal—by proposing a toast to General Washington. Some men flushed while others reluctantly placed their wine glass to their lips. The awkward moment revealed to Lafayette the depth of hostility toward the Commander-in-Chief.

The Golden Plough Tavern and the Gates House were restored in the early 1960s. Today, visitors can see fine examples of eighteenth-century antiques, including a table with dentil-like molding, a Wills clock with unusual inlay, a Pennsylvania settle with oxhide covering, and a handsome Chippendale desk.

On the edge of the lawn behind the tavern stands a modest log cabin. Constructed in 1812 by Barnet Bobb,

Golden Plough Tavern and adjacent Gates House, York (ALPER)

it is typical of the houses built in the area by German settlers. In 1969 the cabin was moved here from its original site three blocks away.

HISTORICAL SOCIETY OF YORK COUNTY   *250 East Market Street. Open Monday through Saturday 9 A.M. to 5 P.M., Sunday 1 P.M. to 5 P.M. Closed holidays. Adults 50¢, youngsters (12–17) 25¢, children (under 12) free.*   The Historical Society operates a museum here that specializes in items reflecting York's past. On display are furniture, household implements, weapons, and costumes. Of special interest is a transportation section featuring a Conestoga wagon (named after Conestoga, Pennsylvania, where it was first made) and an engine built for the Baltimore and Ohio Railroad. Visitors will be fascinated by a full-scale model of a village square—with an apothecary shop, a print shop, a cabinetmaker's shop, and a silversmith shop.

ST. JOHN'S CHURCH   *140 North Beaver Street. Open 9 A.M. to 5 P.M.*   In 1769 a church was erected on this site to serve the spiritual needs of Anglicans residing in the area. During the early phases of the American Revolution the rector, the Reverend Daniel Batwell, alienated members of his congregation by his pro-British sentiments. One evening a group of local Patriots forcibly seized Batwell, carried him to the edge of town, and heaved him into a creek. But this harsh "baptism" did not convert him to their views!

In 1774 a bell was presented to St. John's parish by Caroline of England, the sister of King George III. Since the church had no belfry, the bell was placed in the Town Square. Two years later, when news of the adoption of the Declaration of Independence arrived in York, a group of young men hoisted the bell to the cupola of the courthouse, where it rang out the message of liberty. (The bell has been returned to St. John's and is now displayed on the ground floor.)

Two Patriot officers of the Revolutionary War— Colonel Thomas Hartley and Major John Clark—are buried on the grounds of St. John's.

A gallery was installed in the church in 1810. Extensive renovations were undertaken in 1882: the building's north and south sides were torn down and its width extended by the construction of new walls; pillars were introduced to support the roof; and a front porch was added.

The interior is distinguished by handsome stained-glass windows and a triptych dating from the thirteenth century. The original altar is still in use.

SITE OF THE COLONIAL COURTHOUSE *Town Square* On this site stood the Colonial Courthouse, erected in 1756, in which the Congress held sessions during 1777–1778. The building, which had fallen into disrepair, was torn down in 1840 and a new courthouse was constructed here. By the end of the century it had become inadequate for the expanding agencies of the local government, and a new structure—the present courthouse—was designed by J. A. Dempwolf and built in 1900 on the site of its predecessors.

YORK FRIENDS MEETING HOUSE   *135 West Phila-delphia Street. Not open to the public.*   Local Quakers built this meeting house in 1766. The Flemish bond brickwork was laid by William Willis. The western section of the building was added in 1783. A small group of York Friends still holds weekly meetings here.

Non-Revolutionary Sites of Interest

BONHAM HOUSE   *152 East Market Street. Open Mon-day through Saturday 10 A.M. to 4 P.M., Sunday 1 P.M. to 4 P.M. During the summer open until 5 P.M. Closed holidays. Adults 35¢, youngsters (12–17) 15¢, children (under 12) free.*   This was the house of the Bonham family, who resided here from 1873 until the twentieth century. Now maintained as a museum by the Historical Society of York County, the building contains furniture of various periods—ranging from the Federal dining room to the Victorian parlor. Porcelain, silver, china, and glassware are displayed in special cases on the first floor.

CURRIER AND IVES GALLERY   *43 West King Street. Open Monday through Friday 8:30 A.M. to 5 P.M. During the summer also open on Saturday from 9 A.M. to 2 P.M. Closed holidays. Adults $1.00, children free.*   Almost 300 Currier and Ives prints are exhibited in this restored 1870 mansion. The subjects include domestic scenes, historical events, hunting episodes, and views of ships.

Nathaniel Currier (1813–1888) established his business in New York City in 1835, and in 1857 he formed a partnership with the artist James Merritt Ives (1824–1895). Thereafter all lithographs published by the firm carried the imprint bearing both names. After the death of Currier and Ives, their sons continued the business until 1907.

A visit to this gallery is a visual journey into America's glorious past.

Useful Facts

State Facts

MASSACHUSETTS

DELEGATES TO THE FIRST CONTINENTAL CONGRESS (1774)	John Adams Samuel Adams Thomas Cushing Robert Treat Paine
SIGNERS OF THE DECLARATION OF INDEPENDENCE (1776)	John Adams Samuel Adams Elbridge Gerry John Hancock Robert Treat Paine
SIGNERS OF THE FEDERAL CONSTITUTION (1787)	Nathaniel Gorham Rufus King
STATEHOOD (DATE CONSTITUTION RATIFIED)	February 6, 1788 (6th)
POPULAR NAME	The Bay State
CAPITAL	Boston
LARGEST CITY (POPULATION, 1970)	Boston (641, 071)
STATE POPULATION (1970 CENSUS)	5,689,170 (10th in rank)
STATE FLOWER	Mayflower
STATE TREE	Elm
STATE BIRD	Chickadee

NEW YORK

DELEGATES TO THE FIRST CONTINENTAL CONGRESS (1774)	John Alsop Simon Boerum James Duane William Floyd John Haring John Jay Isaac Low

NEW YORK (Cont.)

SIGNERS OF THE DECLARATION OF INDEPENDENCE (1776)	William Floyd Francis Lewis Philip Livingston Lewis Morris
SIGNER OF THE FEDERAL CONSTITUTION (1787)	Alexander Hamilton
STATEHOOD (DATE CONSTITUTION RATIFIED)	July 26, 1788 (11th)
POPULAR NAME	The Empire State
CAPITAL	Albany
LARGEST CITY (POPULATION, 1970)	New York (7,867,760)
STATE POPULATION (1970 CENSUS)	18,190,740 (2nd in rank)
STATE FLOWER	Rose
STATE TREE	Sugar Maple
STATE BIRD	Bluebird

NEW JERSEY

DELEGATES TO THE FIRST CONTINENTAL CONGRESS (1774)	Stephen Crane John De Hart James Kinsey William Livingston Richard Smith
SIGNERS OF THE DECLARATION OF INDEPENDENCE (1776)	Abraham Clark John Hart Francis Hopkinson Richard Stockton John Witherspoon
SIGNERS OF THE FEDERAL CONSTITUTION (1787)	David Brearley Jonathan Dayton William Livingston William Paterson
STATEHOOD (DATE CONSTITUTION RATIFIED)	December 18, 1787 (3rd)
POPULAR NAME	The Garden State

NEW JERSEY (Cont.)

CAPITAL	Trenton
LARGEST CITY (POPULATION, 1970)	Newark (382,417)
STATE POPULATION (1970 CENSUS)	7,168,164 (8th in rank)
STATE FLOWER	Purple Violet
STATE TREE	Red Oak
STATE BIRD	Eastern Goldfinch

PENNSYLVANIA

DELEGATES TO THE FIRST CONTINENTAL CONGRESS (1774)	John Dickinson Joseph Galloway Charles Humphreys Thomas Mifflin John Morton Samuel Rhoads George Ross
SIGNERS OF THE DECLARATION OF INDEPENDENCE (1776)	George Clymer Benjamin Franklin Robert Morris John Morton George Ross Benjamin Rush James Smith George Taylor James Wilson
SIGNERS OF THE FEDERAL CONSTITUTION (1787)	George Clymer Thomas Fitzsimons Benjamin Franklin Jared Ingersoll Thomas Mifflin Gouverneur Morris Robert Morris James Wilson
STATEHOOD (DATE CONSTITUTION RATIFIED)	December 12, 1787 (2nd)
POPULAR NAME	The Keystone State

PENNSYLVANIA (Cont.)

CAPITAL	Harrisburg
LARGEST CITY (POPULATION, 1970)	Philadelphia (1,948,609)
STATE POPULATION (1970 CENSUS)	11,793,909 (3rd in rank)
STATE FLOWER	Mountain Laurel
STATE TREE	Eastern Hemlock
STATE BIRD	Ruffed Grouse

Motels and Hotels

Travelers who wish to make reservations at any of the motels and hotels listed below may use the appropriate toll-free telephone numbers. In order to guarantee reservations after 6 P.M., many establishments request a credit card number, thereby holding the prospective occupant responsible for payment. Resorts frequently demand a deposit in advance. If cancellation is necessary, always notify the reservation center or motel within the required time period.

BEST WESTERN MOTELS	800–528–1234 (In Arizona dial 800–352–1222)
HOLIDAY INNS	Contact your nearest Holiday Inn. Four major reservation centers accept toll-free calls. In most regions of the Northeast dial 800–243–2350; in most regions of the Midwest dial 800–323–9050; in most regions of the South dial 800–238–5400; in most regions of the West Coast dial 800–453–5555. If you are unable to reach these numbers, consult the Holiday Inn Directory for instructions.
HOWARD JOHNSON'S MOTOR LODGES	800–654–2000
MARRIOTT HOTELS AND MOTELS	800–228–9290

QUALITY INNS	800–323–5151 (In Hartford, Connecticut, and Philadelphia, Pennsylvania, dial 800–327–3384; in Illinois dial 800–942–8600.)
RAMADA INNS	800–238–5800
SHERATON HOTELS AND MOTOR INNS	800–325–3535
TRAVELODGES	800–255–3050
TREADWAY INNS	800–631–0134
Persons with an American Express card may use the American Express Space Bank Reservation Center.	800–528–7700 (In Tennessee dial 800–542–5115)

(*Note:* In some areas it may be necessary to dial the digit 1 before 800.)

Motel and hotel prices are calculated according to the number of persons occupying a room as well as the size and location of the room. The base prices quoted below were in effect during 1974–1975 and are expected to rise. Prices do not include state, city, or local taxes (where applicable). Travelers should verify the exact rate before registering. Only a limited number of minimum-rate units are available. A few establishments permit pets; some city hotels and motor inns charge a fee for parking.

This compilation of motels and hotels is for the convenience of travelers and should not be considered a recommendation. The listing, furthermore, does not purport to be complete. Neither the author nor the publisher can be responsible for prices, procedures, accommodations, or services.

Since most rooms have telephones, televisions, and air-conditioning, these features are not mentioned in the entries below. The abbreviations used for credit cards are:

American Express	AX
Bank Americard	BA
Carte Blanche	CB
Diners Club	DC
Exxon	E
Gulf	G
Master Charge	MC
Mobil	M
Texaco	T

Motel and Hotel Listing

MASSACHUSETTS

LEXINGTON   (*Area Code 617*)

Battle Green Motor Inn   1720 Massachusetts Avenue. 862–6100. 90 rooms. Single $15 up; Double $19 up. Pool. Restaurant 7 A.M.–9 P.M. Checkout noon. AX, BA, CB, DC, MC.

Sheraton-Lexington Motor Inn   Off Route 28, Exit 45, near Route 2A. 862–8700. 120 rooms, 2 and 3 stories. Single $20 up; Double $28 up. Pool. Restaurant 7 A.M.–10 P.M. Checkout 1 P.M. AX, BA, CB, DC, MC.

Susse Chalet   440 Bedford Street. (At junction Routes 4, 225; off Route 128, Exit 44N.) 861–0850. 124 rooms, 2 stories. Single $13 up; Double $15 up. Pool. Restaurant adjacent, 6 A.M.–11 P.M. Checkout 11 A.M. AX, BA, MC.

CONCORD   (*Area Code 617*)

Colonial Inn   48 Monument Square. (On Routes 2A, 62.) 369–9200. 57 rooms. Single $13.50 up; Double $17.50 up. Restaurant 7–10 A.M., 11:45 A.M.–2 P.M., 6–9 P.M. Checkout 2 P.M. AX, BA, CB, DC, MC.

Concordian   71 Hosmer Street, Acton. (5 miles west on Route 2.) 263–7765. 53 rooms. Single $14 up; Double $17 up. Pool. Restaurant 1½ miles, 6:30–1 A.M. Checkout 11 A.M. AX, BA, CB, DC, MC.

Howard Johnson's   Elm Street. (2 miles west on Route 2 at Junction Route 2A.) 369–6100. 106 rooms, 2 stories. Single $17 up; Double $20 up. Pool. Restaurant 7 A.M.–midnight. Checkout noon AX, BA, CB, DC, E, MC, T.

Maynard   115 Powder Mill Road, Maynard. (5 miles west on Route 62.) 897–9371. 14 rooms. Single $12 up; Double $15 up. Restaurant ½ mile, 6:30 A.M.–10 P.M. Checkout 11 A.M.

BOSTON   (*Area Code 617*)

Charles River   1800 Soldiers Field Road. (2½ miles northeast of Massachusetts Turnpike Exit 17.) 254–0200. 55 rooms, 2 stories. Single $15 up; Double $21 up. Restaurant adjacent, 7 A.M.–midnight. Checkout noon. AX, BA, CB, DC, MC.

Colonnade   120 Huntington Avenue at Prudential Center. (Massachusetts Turnpike Exit 22.) 261–2800. 300 rooms. Single $26 up; Double $33 up. Pool. Restaurant 7 A.M.–10 P.M. Checkout 1 P.M. AX, BA, CB, DC, MC.

Copley Square   47 Huntington Avenue at Exeter Street. (Massachusetts Turnpike Exit 22.) 536–9000. 165 rooms. Elevator. Single $14.50 up; Double $18.50 up. Restaurant 7 A.M.–3 P.M. Checkout 2 P.M. AX, BA, CB, DC, MC.

Fenway Boylston   1271 Boylston Street. 267–8300. 94 rooms, 2 stories. Elevator. Single $17 up; Double $23 up. Pool. Restaurant 7 A.M.–11:30 P.M. Checkout 2 P.M. AX, BA, CB, DC, MC.

Fenway Commonwealth   575 Commonwealth Avenue at Kenmore Square. 267–3100. 178 rooms, 7 stories. Elevator. Single $18.50 up; Double $24.50 up. Pool. Restaurant 7 A.M.–10 P.M. Checkout 2 P.M. AX, BA, CB, DC, MC.

Hilton Inn at Logan   At Logan International Airport. 569–9300. 327 rooms. Single $21 up; Double $26 up. Pool. Restaurant 6 A.M.–midnight. Checkout noon. AX, BA, CB, DC, MC.

Holiday Inn–Charles River   5 Blossom Street at Cambridge Street. 742–7630. 300 rooms. Single $23 up; Double $29 up. Pool. Restaurant 7 A.M.–9 P.M. Checkout noon. AX, BA, DC, G, MC.

Howard Johnson's Howard Johnson Plaza. (4 miles south at Southeast Expressway Exit 16.) 288–3030. 100 rooms, 5 stories. Elevator. Single $18 up; Double $23 up. Pool. Restaurant 7–1 A.M. Checkout noon. AX, DC, E, MC, T.

Howard Johnson's 200 Stuart Street. (Just off Park Square; Massachusetts Turnpike Exit 22.) 482–1800. 360 rooms, 24 stories. Elevator. Single $22 up; Double $26 up. Pool. Restaurant 6:30 A.M.–10 P.M. Checkout noon. AX, DC, E, MC, T.

Lenox 710 Boylston Street at Prudential Center. (Massachusetts Turnpike Exit 22.) 536–5300. 225 rooms. Single $20.50 up; Double $24.50 up. Restaurant 7 A.M.–5 P.M. Checkout 2 P.M. AX, CB, DC.

Midtown Motor Inn 220 Huntington Avenue. (On Route C-9; Massachusetts Turnpike Exit 22.) 262–1000. 161 rooms, 2 stories. Elevator. Single $17 up; Double $23 up. Pool. Restaurant 7 A.M.–5 P.M. Checkout 2 P.M. AX, BA, CB, DC, MC.

Ramada Inn 1234 Soldiers Field Road, Brighton. (Massachusetts Turnpike Exits 18E, 21W.) 254–1234. 115 rooms, 2–5 stories. Elevator. Single $20 up; Double $26 up. Pool. Restaurant 7 A.M.–11 P.M. Checkout noon. AX, BA, CB, DC, E, MC.

Ramada Inn–Airport 225 McClellan Highway, East Boston. 569–5250. 210 rooms, 12 stories. Elevator. Single $19 up; Double $23 up. Pool. Restaurant 6:30 A.M.–10 P.M. Checkout noon. AX, BA, CB, DC, E, MC.

Ritz-Carlton Arlington and Newbury Streets. 536–5700. 261 rooms. Elevator. Single $35 up; Double $41 up. Restaurant 7 A.M.–4:30 P.M., 5:30–9 P.M. Checkout 3 P.M.

Sheraton-Boston 39 Dalton Street at Prudential Center. (Massachusetts Turnpike Exit 22.) 236–2000. 1,012 rooms. Elevator. Single $21 up; Double $36 up. Pool. Restaurant 7 A.M.–midnight. Checkout 1 P.M. AX, BA, CB, DC.

Sheraton-Plaza 138 St. James Avenue at Copley Square. (Massachusetts Turnpike Exit 22.) 267–5300. 452 rooms. Single $23 up; Double $30 up. Restaurant open 24 hours. Checkout 1 P.M. AX, BA, CB, DC.

Statler Hilton Park Square at Arlington Street. 426–2000. 1,076 rooms. Elevator. Single $21 up; Double $31 up. Restaurant 7 A.M.–midnight. Checkout 2 P.M. AX, BA, CB, DC, MC.

CAMBRIDGE   (*Area Code 617*)

Fenway-Cambridge   777 Memorial Drive. 492–7777. 205 rooms, 16 stories. Elevator. Single $19 up; Double $25 up. Pool. Restaurant 7 A.M.–11 P.M. Checkout 2 P.M. AX, BA, CB, MC.

Holiday Inn   1651 Massachusetts Avenue. 491–1000. 135 rooms, 4–6 stories. Elevator. Single $18 up; Double $23 up. Pool. Restaurant 7 A.M.–11 P.M. Checkout noon. AX, BA, CB, DC, G, MC.

Sheraton-Commander   16 Garden Street. (Opposite Cambridge Common.) 547–4800. 180 rooms. Single $16 up; Double $22 up. Restaurant 7:30 A.M.–2:30 P.M., 5 P.M.–9 P.M. Checkout 1 P.M. AX, BA, CB, DC.

SALEM   (*Area Code 617*)

Coach House   284 Lafayette Street on Routes 1A, 114. 744–4092. 15 rooms. Single $15 up; Double $17 up. Restaurant 5 blocks. Checkout 11 A.M.

Hawthorne Motor Hotel   18 Washington Square. (½ mile north on Route 1A.) 744–4080. 102 rooms, 6 stories. Elevator. Single $13 up; Double $17 up. Restaurant 8 A.M.–1:30 P.M. Checkout 2 P.M.

Lincoln Hotel   117 Lafayette Street. 744–1818. 20 rooms. Single $11 up; Double $13 up. Checkout 11 A.M.

QUINCY   (*Area Code 617*)

Carlton House   29 Hancock Street. (7 miles south of Boston on Route 3A at Southeast Expressway Exit 20 S, 21 N.) 471–1500. 104 rooms, 3 stories. Elevator. Single $16 up; Double $21 up. Pool. Restaurant 7 A.M.–10 P.M. Checkout 1 P.M. AX, CB, DC.

NEW YORK

TICONDEROGA *(Area Code 518)*

Belford Court Motel Montcalm Street at Wayne Avenue. 585–7000. 10 rooms. Single $11 up; Double $13 up. Restaurant 300 feet. Checkout 11 A.M.

Burgoyne Motel ¼ mile from intersection of Routes 9N, 22, 74. 585–7353. 37 rooms. Single $13 up; Double $17 up. Closed during the winter. No restaurant. Pool. Checkout 10:30 A.M. Major credit cards accepted.

Green Acres Motel and Cabins Wicker Street. (Routes 9N, 22N.) 585–2274. 8 rooms and 6 cottages. Closed during the winter. No restaurant. Single $17 up; Double $19 up. Pool. Checkout 10 A.M. Major credit cards accepted.

Ranch Motel Baldwin Road. (2½ miles south of Route 9N.) 585–6596. 11 rooms. Single $14 up; Double $18 up. Closed during the winter. No restaurant. Checkout 10:30 A.M.

Stone House Motel 429 Montcalm Street. (On Routes 9N, 22, 73 near the traffic circle.) 585–7394. 16 rooms. Single $16 up; Double $18 up. Closed during the winter. Restaurant 10 A.M.–8 P.M. Checkout 10 A.M. Major credit cards accepted.

ALBANY *(Area Code 518)*

Albany TraveLodge 1230 Western Avenue. (4 miles west on Route 20, 1½ miles east of Dewey Thruway Exit 24.) 489–4423. 75 rooms, 2 stories. Single $13.50 up; Double $17.50 up. Pool. Restaurant adjacent, open 24 hours. Checkout noon. AX, BA, CB, DC, MC, M.

Blue Spruce 16 miles southeast on Route 9, 3 miles south of Route 90 Exit B1. 684–5371. 25 rooms. Single $11 up; Double $13 up. Pool. Breakfast available 7–11 A.M. Checkout 11 A.M. AX, BA, MC.

Empire State 1606 Central Avenue. (6 miles northwest on Route 5, 3 miles north of Dewey Thruway Exit 24; Route 87

Exit 2W.) 869–5327. 59 rooms, 2 stories. Single $13 up; Double $19 up. Restaurant ½ block, 7 A.M.–10 P.M. Checkout noon. AX, BA, CB, MC.

Hilltop   16 Wolf Road. (5 miles northwest, 2 miles north of Dewey Thruway Exit 24, just off Route 87 Exit 2E.) 459–3600. 21 rooms, 1–2 stories. Single $13 up; Double $15 up. Restaurant adjacent 7 A.M.–midnight. Checkout 11 A.M. AX.

Holiday Inn #1   1614 Central Avenue. (6 miles northwest on Route 5, 2 miles north of Dewey Thruway Exit 24, ½ mile west of Route' 87 Exit 2W.) 869–0281. 158 rooms, 2 stories. Single $16 up; Double $19 up. Pool. Restaurant 6:30 A.M.–10 P.M. Checkout noon. AX, BA, DC, G, MC.

Holiday Inn #2   575 Broadway, Menands. (On Route 32, 1 mile south of junction Route 155; Route 787 Exit Menands North.) 463–1121. 120 rooms, 2 stories. Single $16 up; Double $19 up. Pool. Restaurant 6–11:30 A.M., noon–4:30 P.M., 5–10 P.M. Checkout noon. AX, BA, DC, G, MC.

Holiday Inn #3   946 New Loudon Road, Latham. (6 miles north on Route 9; Route 87 Exits 7N, 6S.) 783–6161. 116 rooms, 2 stories. Single $19 up; Double $24 up. Pool. Restaurant 6 A.M.–10 P.M. Checkout noon. AX, BA, DC, G, MC.

Howard Johnson's   Southern Boulevard. (3 miles south on Route 9W at Dewey Thruway Exit 23.) 462–6555. 180 rooms, 1–2 stories. Single $17 up; Double $21 up. Pool. Restaurant 7 A.M.–midnight. Checkout noon. AX, BA, DC, E, MC, T.

Howard Johnson's Airport   611 Troy-Schenectady Road, Latham. (6½ miles north at junction Route 7, Route 87.) 785–5891. 149 rooms, 2 stories. Single $19 up; Double $23 up. Pool. Restaurant 7–1 A.M. Checkout noon. AX, BA, DC, E, MC, T.

Kerslake's   15 miles south on Route 9W, 7 miles south of Dewey Thruway Exit 22, 4 miles north of Exit 21B. 756–2000. 38 rooms. Double $15 up. Pool. Restaurant 300 yards, 5–9 P.M. Checkout 11 A.M. AX, BA, CB, DC, MC.

Northway Inn   1517 Central Avenue. (4 miles northwest on Route 5 at Route 87 Exit 2W; Dewey Thruway Exit 24.) 869–0277. 84 rooms, 2 stories. Single $14.50 up; Double $19 up. Pool. Restaurant 6:30 A.M.–4 P.M., 5–11 P.M. Checkout noon. AX, BA, CB, DC, MC.

Schrafft's Motor Inn   4 miles south on Route 9W, ½ mile south of Dewey Thruway Exit 23. 465–8811. 100 rooms, 2

stories. Single $18 up; Double $22 up. Pool. Restaurant 7 A.M.–
3 P.M., 5–10 P.M. Checkout noon. AX, DC, MC.

Sheraton Inn Towne Motor Inn 300 Broadway. (1 block
southeast on Routes 9, 20, Route 5, 3 miles north of Dewey
Thruway Exit 23.) 434–4111. 135 rooms, 5 stories. Elevator.
Single $17.50 up; Double $25.50 up. Pool. Restaurant 7 A.M.–
10 P.M. Checkout noon. AX, BA, CB, DC, MC.

Thruway Hyatt House 1375 Washington Avenue. (3 miles
west, ½ mile east of Dewey Thruway Exit 24; Route 87 Exit
1E.) 459–3100. 237 rooms, 2–5 stories. Elevator. Single $20 up;
Double $26 up. Pool. Restaurant open 24 hours. Checkout noon.
AX, CB, DC, MC.

Tom Sawyer Motor Inn 1444 Western Avenue. (4½ miles
west on Route 20, 1¼ miles southeast of Dewey Thruway Exit
24.) 438–3594. 88 rooms. Single $15 up; Double $18 up. Pool.
Restaurant 6:30 A.M.–9:30 P.M. Checkout noon. AX, CB, DC,
MC, M.

HOOSICK FALLS, NEW YORK–
BENNINGTON, VERMONT AREA   (*Area Code 802*)

The following motels and hotels are located in or near
Bennington, Vermont—approximately fifteen miles east of
the Bennington Battlefield Site in New York.

The Bulrushes 3½ miles west, ¼ mile south of Route 9.
442–6222. 16 rooms, 5 cottages. Double $18 up. Closed during
winter. Pool. Restaurant ¼ mile, 7:30 A.M.–8 P.M. Checkout
11 A.M.

Catamount 500 South Street. (3 blocks south on Route 7.)
442–5977. 17 rooms. Single $19 up; Double $21 up. Pool. Restaurant ½ mile. Checkout 11 A.M. MC.

Darling Kelly's 1 mile south on Route 7. 442–2322. 23
rooms. Single $21 up; Double $23 up. Pool. Restaurant adjacent,
7 A.M.–10 P.M. Checkout 11 A.M. AX, BA, CB, DC, MC, M.

Greenbrier 924 East Main Street. (On Route 9.) 442–3143.
32 rooms, 2 stories. Single $19 up; Double $21 up. Pool. Restaurant 2 blocks. Checkout 11 A.M. AX, BA, DC, MC.

Iron Kettle   5 miles north on Route 7. 442–4316. 20 rooms. Single $19 up; Double $21 up. Pool. Restaurant 7 A.M.–10 P.M. Checkout 11 A.M. AX, BA, CB, MC.

Kirkside   250 West Main Street. (1 block west on Route 9.) 447–7596. 15 rooms. Single $19 up; Double $21 up. Restaurant 1 block. Checkout 11 A.M. AX, BA, CB, DC, MC.

Monument View   207 Northside Drive. (1½ miles north on Route 7.) 442–6956. 21 rooms, 3 cottages. Single $13 up; Double $16 up. Pool. Restaurant 1 block, 7 A.M.–10 P.M. Checkout 11 A.M.

New Englander   220 Northside Drive. (2 miles north on Route 7 at junction Route 67A.) 442–6311. 51 rooms, 1–2 stories. Single $18 up; Double $21 up. Pool. Restaurant 7 A.M.– 9 P.M. Checkout 11 A.M. AX, BA, CB, DC, MC, M.

The Vermonter   4 miles west on Route 9. 442–2529. 32 rooms. Single $19 up; Double $21 up. Closed during the winter. Restaurant 7:30–11 A.M., 5:30–8 P.M. Checkout 11 A.M.

SCHUYLERVILLE   *(Area Code 518)*

Burgoyne Motor Inn   220 North Broad Street. 695–3282. 11 rooms. Single $10 up; Double $14 up. Breakfast room 8–11:30 A.M. Checkout 11 A.M.

Empress Motel   177 North Broad Street. 695–3231. 12 rooms. Single $10 up; Double $13 up. Restaurant 1 block. Checkout 10 A.M. AX, BA, DC, MC.

JOHNSTOWN   *(Area Code 518)*

Holiday Inn   ½ mile north on Route 30A, 6 miles north of Dewey Thruway Exit 28. 762–4686. 100 rooms, 2–3 stories. Single $14 up; Double $22 up. Pool. Restaurant 6:30 A.M.– 10 P.M. Checkout noon. AX, BA, DC, G, MC.

Johnstown Motor Inn   55 East Main Street. (On Routes 29, 67, 2 blocks west of Route 30A; 6 miles north of Dewey Thruway Exit 28.) 762–3121. 62 rooms. Single $10 up; Double $13.50 up. Pool. Restaurant 7 A.M.–2 P.M., 5:30–9 P.M. Checkout 1 P.M. AX, DC, MC.

NEWBURGH   (*Area Code 914*)

Holiday Inn   2 miles west on Route 17K at Dewey Thruway Exit 17. 565–2100. 121 rooms, 2 stories. Single $15 up; Double $20 up. Pool. Restaurant 6 A.M.–10 P.M. Checkout noon. AX, BA, DC, G, MC.

Howard Johnson's   2 miles west on Route 17K, ½ mile west of Dewey Thruway Exit 17. 565–4100. 74 rooms, 2 stories. Single $16 up; Double $27 up. Pool. Restaurant 7 A.M.–midnight. Checkout noon. AX, E, MC, T.

Imperial '400'   314 Broadway. (At junction Routes 9W, 17K.) 565–3400. 42 rooms, 2 stories. Single $14 up; Double $15 up. Pool. Checkout noon. AX, BA, CB, DC, MC, M.

Newburgh   2 miles north on Route 9W. 562–6170. 25 rooms. Single $18 up; Double $20 up. Pool. Restaurant 7–10 A.M., 6–8 P.M. weekdays. Checkout 11 A.M. AX, BA, CB, DC, MC.

Ramada Inn   1055 Union Avenue. (At Dewey Thruway Exit 17.) 564–4500. 115 rooms, 2 stories. Single $18 up; Double $23 up. Pool. Restaurant 7 A.M.–11 P.M. Checkout noon. AX, BA, CB, DC, E, MC.

Temple Hill   310 Windsor Highway. (2½ miles south on Route 32.) 561–6620. 40 rooms, 2 stories. Single $17 up; Double $21 up. Pool. Restaurant nearby, open 24 hours. Checkout 11 A.M. AX, BA, CB, DC, MC.

Windsor   114 Route 9W, 2 miles south on Route 9W, 3 miles southeast of Dewey Thruway Exit 17. 562–7661. 30 rooms. Single $16 up; Double $18 up. Restaurant 6 A.M.–7 P.M., Sunday to midnight. Checkout 11 A.M. AX, BA, MC.

WEST POINT   (*Area Code 914*)

Palisade Motel   On Route 218, off Route 9W. 446–9400. 20 rooms, 2 stories. Single $13 up; Double $15 up. Restaurant ½ block, 7 A.M.–10 P.M. Checkout 11 A.M. AX, BA, CB, DC, MC.

Thayer Hotel   Near Thayer (South) Gate of the West Point Military Academy. (Off Route 218.) 446–4731. 240 rooms. Elevator. Single $13 up; Double $16 up. Restaurant 7–10 A.M., noon–2 P.M., 6–8 P.M. Checkout noon. AX, BA, CB, DC, MC.

STONY POINT   (*Area Code 914*)

Beef Baron Motel   ½ miles south of Route 9W. 942–0880. 9 rooms. Single $14 up; Double $16 up. Restaurant noon–2:30 P.M., 5–10 P.M. Checkout noon. AX, BA, CB, DC, MC.

TAPPAN AREA   (*Area Code 914*)

The following motels are located near Tappan in the towns of Spring Valley and Nyack.

Howard Johnson's Motor Lodge, Spring Valley. 1½ miles east on Route 59, at Dewey Thruway Exit 14. 623–3838. 72 rooms, 2 stories. Single $17 up; Double $21 up. Pool. Restaurant 7 A.M.–11 P.M. Checkout noon. AX, BA, CB, DC, E, MC, T.

Tappan Zee Inn, Nyack. Mountain View Avenue. (At Dewey Thruway Exit 11.) 358–8400. 104 rooms. Single $21 up; Double $25 up. Pool. Restaurant 7 A.M.–10 P.M. Checkout noon. AX, CB, DC, MC.

West Gate Motor Lodge, Nyack. On Route 59, just off Dewey Thruway Exit 11. 358–8100. 82 rooms, 2 stories. Single $15 up; Double $21 up. Restaurant 7–10 A.M., noon–2:30 P.M., 5:30–10 P.M. Checkout noon. AX, DC, MC.

NEW YORK CITY   (*Area Code 212*)

Algonquin   59 West 44th Street. 687–4400. 200 rooms, 12 stories. Elevator. Single $20.75 up; Double $26 up. Restaurant 7–1 A.M. Checkout 3 P.M. AX, BA, CB, DC.

Alrae   37 East 64th Street. 744–0200. 250 rooms, 17 stories. Elevator. Single $24 up; Double $29 up. Restaurant noon–2 A.M. Checkout 2 P.M. AX.

Americana   Seventh Avenue at West 52nd Street. 581–1000. 2,000 rooms, 50 stories. Elevator. Single $26 up; Double $33 up. Restaurant 7–1:30 A.M. Checkout 1 P.M. AX, BA, CB, DC, MC.

Barbizon-Plaza   106 Central Park South at Sixth Avenue. 247–7000. 1,200 rooms, 40 stories. Elevator. Single $20 up; Double $27 up. Restaurant 7 A.M.–midnight. Checkout 3 P.M. AX.

Barclay 111 East 48th Street. 755–5900. 788 rooms, 14 stories. Elevator. Single $29 up; Double $37 up. Restaurant 7 A.M.–9 P.M. Checkout 1 P.M. AX, CB.

Belmont Plaza 541 Lexington Avenue at East 49th Street. 755–1200. 800 rooms, 17 stories. Elevator. Single $23 up; Double $29 up. Restaurant 7 A.M.–10 P.M. Checkout 1 P.M. AX, BA, CB, DC, MC.

Berkshire 21 East 52nd Street at Madison Avenue. 753–5800. 500 rooms, 20 stories. Elevator. Single $32 up; Double $37 up. Restaurant 7:30 A.M.–9 P.M. Checkout 2 P.M. AX, CB, DC.

Biltmore East 43rd Street and Madison Avenue. 687–7000. 900 rooms, 26 stories. Elevator. Single $23 up; Double $29 up. Restaurant 7:30 A.M.–midnight. Checkout 1 P.M. AX, CB.

Blackstone 50 East 58th Street. 355–4200. 200 rooms, 14 stories. Elevator. Single $26 up; Double $31 up. Restaurant 7 A.M.–midnight. Checkout 1 P.M. AX, MC.

Carlyle Madison Avenue at East 76th Street. 744–1600. 500 rooms, 34 stories. Elevator. Single $36 up; Double $45 up. Restaurant 7:30–1 A.M. Checkout 3 P.M. AX, CB, DC.

Carriage House 200 East 38th Street at Third Avenue. 661–2100. 105 rooms, 17 stories. Elevator. Single $27 up; Double $31 up. Restaurant 11–2 A.M. Checkout 2 P.M. AX, CB, DC.

Commodore Park Avenue at 42nd Street. 686–6000. 2,000 rooms, 22 stories. Elevator. Single $22 up; Double $25 up. Restaurant 7 A.M.–midnight. Checkout 1 P.M. AX, CB.

Delmonico's 502 Park Avenue at East 59th Street. 355–2500. 500 rooms, 32 stories. Elevator. Single $31 up; Double $39 up. Restaurant 7–1 A.M. Checkout 1 P.M. AX, BA, CB, DC, MC.

Dixie 250 West 43rd Street. 947–6000. 700 rooms, 24 stories. Elevator. Single $16 up; Double $20 up. Restaurant open 24 hours. Checkout 1 P.M. AX, CB, DC.

Doral Park Avenue 70 Park Avenue at East 38th Street. 687–7050. 200 rooms, 17 stories. Elevator. Single $30 up; Double $39 up. Restaurant 7 A.M.–9 P.M. Checkout 2 P.M. AX, CB, DC.

Dorset 30 West 54th Street. 247–7300. 271 rooms, 18 stories. Elevator. Single $26 up; Double $33 up. Restaurant 7 A.M.–10 P.M. Checkout 1 P.M.

Holiday Inn–Coliseum 440 West 57th Street. 581–8100. 606

rooms, 11–18 stories. Elevator. Single $26 up; Double $30 up. Pool. Restaurant 7 A.M.–10 P.M. Checkout 1 P.M. AX, BA, CB, DC, G, MC.

Howard Johnson's Eighth Avenue between West 51st and 52nd Streets. 581–4100. 300 rooms, 10 stories. Elevator. Single $23 up; Double $29 up. Restaurant 7–2 A.M. Checkout 1 P.M. AX, BA, CB, DC, E, MC, T.

Lexington Lexington Avenue and East 48th Street. 755–4400. 801 rooms, 27 Stories. Elevator. Single $25.50 up; Double $29.50 up. Restaurant 7 A.M.–11 P.M. Checkout 1 P.M. AX, BA, DC, MC.

Loew's Warwick 65 West 54th Street. 247–2700. 500 rooms, 33 stories. Elevator. Single $27 up; Double $35 up. Restaurant 7 A.M.–9:30 P.M. Checkout 1 P.M. AX, BA, CB, DC, MC.

Marriott's Essex House 160 Central Park South. 247–0300. 715 rooms, 44 stories. Elevator. Single $34 up; Double $38 up. Restaurant 7 A.M.–10 P.M. Checkout 1 P.M. AX, BA, CB, DC, MC.

McAlpin Broadway at 34th Street. 736–5700. 1,250 rooms, 24 stories. Elevator. Single $18 up; Double $22 up. Restaurant open 24 hours. Checkout 1 P.M. AX, BA, CB, DC, MC.

New York Hilton Sixth Avenue between West 53rd and West 54th Streets. 586–7000. 2,153 rooms, 46 stories. Elevator. Single $30 up; Double $40 up. Restaurant 7 A.M.–midnight. Checkout 1 P.M. AX, BA, CB, DC, MC.

New York Sheraton Seventh Avenue at West 56th Street. 247–8000. 1,600 rooms, 31 stories. Elevator. Single $25 up; Double $32 up. Restaurant 6:30–1 A.M. Checkout 1 P.M. AX, BA, CB, DC, MC.

Pierre Fifth Avenue at East 61st Street. 838–8000. 700 rooms, 40 stories. Elevator. Single $45 up; Double $47 up. Restaurant 7 A.M.–noon, 1 P.M.–1 A.M. Checkout 1 P.M. AX, DC, MC.

Plaza Fifth Avenue at West 59th Street. 759–3000. 1,000 rooms, 17 stories. Elevator. Single $29 up; Double $36 up. Restaurant 7–10:30 A.M., noon–2:30 P.M., 6 P.M.–1 A.M. Checkout 1 P.M. AX, CB, MC.

Ramada Inn 790 Eighth Avenue between West 48th and 49th Streets. 581–7000. 367 rooms, 15 stories. Elevator. Single

$22 up; Double $28 up. Pool. Restaurant 7 A.M.–11 P.M. Checkout 1 P.M. AX, BA, CB, DC, E, MC.

Regency Park Avenue at East 61st Street. 759–4100. 325 rooms, 21 stories. Elevator. Single $36 up; Double $45 up. Restaurant 7 A.M.–midnight. Checkout 1 P.M. AX, BA, CB, DC, MC.

Roosevelt East 45th Street at Madison Avenue. 686–9200. 1,100 rooms, 20 stories. Elevator. Single $23 up; Double $27 up. Restaurant 7 A.M.–11 P.M. Checkout 1 P.M. AX.

St. Moritz 50 Central Park South at Sixth Avenue and 59th Street. 755–5800. 1,000 rooms, 33 stories. Elevator. Single $23 up; Double $29 up. Restaurant 7–1 A.M. Checkout 1 P.M. AX.

St. Regis-Sheraton 2 East 55th Street at Fifth Avenue. 753–4500. 541 rooms, 20 stories. Elevator. Single $33 up; Double $40 up. Restaurant 7–2 A.M. Checkout 1 P.M. AX, BA, CB, DC, MC.

Sheraton-Russell 45 Park Avenue at East 37th Street. 685–7676. 173 rooms, 10 stories. Elevator. Single $30 up; Double $37 up. Restaurant 7 A.M.–2:30 P.M. Checkout 1 P.M. AX, BA, CB, DC, MC.

Sherry-Netherland 781 Fifth Avenue at East 59th Street. 355–2800. 375 rooms, 37 stories. Elevator. Single $42 up; Double $58 up. Restaurant 11 A.M.–6 P.M. Checkout 3 P.M.

Skyline Motor Inn 725 Tenth Avenue at 50th Street. 586–3400. 240 rooms, 5–9 stories. Elevator. Single $21 up; Double $25 up. Pool. Restaurant 7 A.M.–midnight. Checkout noon. AX, CB, DC, MC.

Statler Hilton Seventh Avenue and West 33rd Street. 736–5000. 1,700 rooms, 18 stories. Elevator. Single $23.50 up; Double $31.75 up. Restaurant open 24 hours. Checkout 1 P.M. AX, BA, CB, DC, MC.

Summit East 51st Street and Lexington Avenue. 752–7000. 800 rooms, 20 stories. Elevator. Single $26 up; Double $33 up. Restaurant 7–2 A.M. Checkout 1 P.M. AX, BA, CB, DC, MC.

Taft Seventh Avenue and West 50th Street. 247–4000. 1,500 rooms, 20 stories. Elevator. Single $16 up; Double $23 up. Restaurant open 24 hours. Checkout 1 P.M. AX, BA, CB, DC, MC.

Town House 108 East 38th Street. 532–8500. 250 rooms,

24 stories. Elevator. Single $25 up; Double $29 up. Restaurant 7 A.M.–10 P.M. Checkout 1 P.M. AX, CB, DC.

TraveLodge   515 West 42nd Street near Tenth Avenue. 695–7171. 250 rooms, 3–7 stories. Elevator. Single $19 up; Double $25 up. Pool. Restaurant 7 A.M.–10 P.M. Checkout 1 P.M. AX, BA, CB, DC, MC, M.

Tuscany   120 East 39th Street. 686–1600. 200 rooms, 17 stories. Elevator. Single $31 up; Double $40 up. Restaurant 7 A.M.–9 P.M. Checkout 3 P.M. AX, CB, DC.

Waldorf-Astoria   301 Park Avenue between East 49th and East 50th Streets. 355–3000. 1,900 rooms, 42 stories. Elevator. Single $30 up; Double $40 up. Restaurant 7 A.M.–midnight. Checkout 1 P.M. AX, BA, CB, DC, MC.

WHITE PLAINS   (*Area Code 914*)

County Center   20 County Center Road. (1 mile off Bronx River Parkway, ½ block off Routes 100, 119.) 948–2400. 22 stories. Single $17 up; Double $20 up. Restaurant 1½ blocks, 7 A.M.–10 P.M. Checkout noon. AX.

Roger Smith   123 East Post Road at Chester Avenue. (On Route 22.) 949–1000. 145 rooms. Single $12 up; Double $17 up. Restaurant 7 A.M.–8:30 P.M. Checkout 2 P.M. AX, BA, CB, DC, MC.

White Plains   South Broadway and Lyon Place. 761–8100. 306 rooms. Single $25 up; Double $30 up. Restaurant 7 A.M.–9 P.M. Checkout noon. AX, BA, DC, MC.

NEW JERSEY

ELIZABETH   (*Area Code 201*)

Cadillac Motel   835 Route 1, 9. 354–3840 or 354–4239. 125 rooms. Single $18 up; Double $20 up. Restaurant 10 A.M.–10 P.M. Checkout noon. AX, CB, DC.

In-Town Motor Lodge   405 Morris Avenue. 289–8585. 30 rooms. Single $16 up; Double $18 up. Restaurant 500 yards, open 24 hours. Checkout noon. AX, DC, MC.

Redwood Motor Hotel 400 Route 1, 9. 289–8300. 64 rooms. Single $17 up; Double $19 up. Restaurant ½ mile, 9 A.M.–11 P.M. Checkout noon. AX, CB, DC.

Swan Motel Route 1, 9 in Linden. 862–4500 or 925–5300. 102 rooms. Single $18 up; Double $20 up. Restaurant adjacent, open 24 hours. Checkout noon. AX, BA, DC.

MORRISTOWN AREA *(Area Code 201)*

The following motels are located within a twenty-mile radius of Morristown.

Fountain Motor Lodge Route 10 in East Hanover. 887–5400. 54 rooms. Single $18 up; Double $20 up. Pool. Restaurant ½ mile, 8 A.M.–10 P.M. Checkout noon.

High County Motor Inn Route 10 (2 miles west of junction with Route 202) in Morris Plains. 539–7750. 60 rooms. Single $16 up; Double $18 up. Restaurant 1½ miles, 10 A.M.–11 P.M. Checkout 11 A.M.

Holiday Inn Route 46 and Interstate 80 in Ledgewood. 347–5100. 100 rooms. Single $19 up; Double $21 up. Pool. Restaurant 8 A.M. to 11 P.M. Checkout noon. AX, BA, DC, G, MC.

Howard Johnson's Route 46 at the intersection with Routes 80, 287, 280. 335–5100. 72 rooms. Single $19 up; Double $21 up. Pool. Restaurant 11:30 A.M.–midnight. Checkout noon. AX, DC, E, MC, T.

Tamac Motor Lodge Route 10 (½ mile west of junction of Route 202). 539–7000. 71 rooms. Single $17 up; Double $20 up. Pool. Restaurant 7 A.M.–2 P.M., 5:30–8 P.M. Checkout noon.

SOMERVILLE *(Area Code 201)*

Arch 1½ miles southwest on Route 22. 722–3555. 42 rooms. Single $15 up; Double $18 up. Pool. Restaurant 1/10 mile, 7 A.M.–9 P.M. Checkout 11 A.M. AX, BA, CB, DC.

Cedarcrest 530 Highway 22. 725–7000. 20 rooms. Single $12 up; Double $14 up. Restaurant 1 mile open 24 hours. Checkout 11 A.M.

Holiday Inn On 22 East. (West of junction Interstate 287 in Bridgewater.) 526–9500. 105 rooms, 2 stories. Single $18 up; Double $20 up. Pool. Restaurant 7 A.M.–10 P.M. Checkout noon. AX, BA, CB, DC, MC.

Red Bull Inn 1261 Highway 22. (West of junction Interstate 287.) 722–4000. 111 rooms, 2 stories. Single $19 up; Double $21 up. Pool. Restaurant 7–10 A.M., noon–2:30 P.M., 5–10 P.M. Checkout noon. AX, BA, CB, DC, MC.

TRENTON   (*Area Code* 609)

Holiday Inn 240 West State Street at Calhoun Street. 989–7100. 249 rooms. Single $20 up; Double $24 up. Pool. Restaurant 7 A.M.–11 P.M. Checkout noon. AX, BA, DC, G, MC.

Howard Johnson's 2991 Brunswick Pike at Franklin Road. (5 miles north on Route 1.) 896–1100. 60 rooms, 2 stories. Single $18 up; Double $20 up. Pool. Restaurant 7 A.M.–midnight. Checkout 11 A.M. AX, BA, CB, DC, E, MC, T.

Imperial '400' 350 South Broad Street. 392–7166. 51 rooms, 3 stories. Single $13 up; Double $14 up. Pool. Restaurant ½ block, 7 A.M.–midnight. Checkout noon. AX, CB, DC, MC.

PRINCETON   (*Area Code* 609)

Holiday Inn 2 miles northeast on Route 1 at Aqueduct Road. 452–9100. 104 rooms, 2 stories. Single $17 up; Double $19 up. Pool. Restaurant 6 A.M.–10 P.M. Checkout noon. AX, BA, DC, G, MC.

Nassau Inn Palmer Square. 921–7500. 120 rooms. Single $25 up; Double $30 up. Pool. Restaurant 7 A.M.–10 P.M. Checkout 2 P.M.

Solar 4 miles northeast on Route 1. 452–9090. 18 rooms, 1–2 stories. Single $14 up; Double $17 up. Pool. Restaurant 1½ miles, 9 A.M.–9:30 P.M. Checkout 11 A.M. AX, BA, MC.

Treadway Inn 1½ miles southwest on Route 1. 452–2500. 96 rooms, 2 stories. Single $20 up; Double $22 up. Pool. Restaurant 7 A.M.–9 P.M. Checkout noon. AX, BA, CB, DC, MC.

FREEHOLD   (*Area Code 201*)

Freehold   1½ miles northwest on Route 9 at junction of Route 522. 462–3450. 50 rooms, 2 stories. Single $19 up; Double $21 up. Restaurant adjacent, open 24 hours. Checkout noon. AX, BA, CB, DC, MC.

SALEM   (*Area Code 609*)

Salem Motor Lodge   237 East Broadway on Route 49. 935–1212. 29 rooms, 2 stories. Single $12 up; Double $16 up. Restaurant opposite, 7:30 A.M.–8:30 P.M. Checkout noon. AX, CB, DC, MC.

GREENWICH-BRIDGETON AREA   (*Area Code 609*)

Hiway '77'   1040 North Pearl Street. (On Route 77, 2 miles north of Route 49.) 455–2500. 38 rooms. Single $10 up; Double $13 up. Pool. Restaurant adjacent, 6:30 A.M.–9 P.M. Checkout noon. AX, BA, CB, DC, MC.

PENNSYLVANIA

PHILADELPHIA   (*Area Code 215*)

Airport   Industrial Highway. (7¼ miles southwest on Route 291 at International Airport.) 365–7000. 300 rooms, 1–4 stories. Elevator. Single $19 up; Double $21 up. Pool. Restaurant 7 A.M.–midnight. Checkout 1 P.M. AX, BA, DC, MC.

Barclay   Rittenhouse Square East. 545–0300. 600 rooms, 21 stories. Elevator. Single $25 up; Double $29 up. Restaurant 7 A.M.–9 P.M. Checkout 3 P.M. AX, CB.

Benjamin Franklin   9th and Chestnut Streets. 922–8600. 1,200 rooms, 16 stories. Elevator. Single $27 up; Double $35 up. Restaurant 7 A.M.–midnight. Checkout 3 P.M. AX, BA, CB, MC.

Franklin Motor Inn   Franklin Parkway at 22nd Street. 568–8300. 300 rooms, 3 stories. Elevator. Single $18 up; Double $22 up. Pool. Restaurant 7 A.M.–midnight. Checkout 2 P.M. AX, BA, CB, DC, MC.

Hilton Inn   10th and Packer Streets. (½ mile west of Walt Whitman Bridge.) 755–9500. 240 rooms, 11 stories. Elevator. Single $21 up; Double $27 up. Restaurant open 24 hours. Checkout 1 P.M. AX, BA, CB, DC, MC.

Holiday Inn-Airport South   45 Industrial Highway, Essington. (7½ miles southwest on Route 291 at junction Route 420.) 521–2400. 307 rooms, 6 stories. Elevator. Single $22 up; Double $25 up. Pool. Restaurant 6 A.M.–midnight. Checkout 1 P.M. AX, BA, CB, DC, G, MC.

Holiday Inn-City Line   City Line Avenue and Monument Road. (5 miles northwest on Route 1 at Schuylkill Expressway City Line Avenue Exit.) 877–4900. 499 rooms, 22 stories. Elevator. Single $20 up; Double $25 up. Pool. Restaurant 7 A.M.–9 P.M. Checkout noon. AX, BA, CB, DC, G, MC.

Holiday Inn-Independence Mall   4th and Arch Streets. 923–8660. 364 rooms, 8 stories. Elevator. Single $22 up; Double $27 up. Pool. Restaurant 6:30 A.M.–10:30 P.M. Checkout noon. AX, BA, DC, G, MC.

Holiday Inn-Midtown   1305 Walnut Street. 735–9300. 162 rooms, 20 stories. Elevator. Single $20 up; Double $25 up. Pool. Restaurant 7–1 A.M. Checkout 1 P.M. AX, BA, CB, DC, G, MC.

Holiday Inn-Penn Center   18th and Market Streets. 561–7500. 450 rooms, 25 stories. Elevator. Single $23 up; Double $28 up. Pool. Restaurant 7 A.M.–11 P.M. Checkout 1 P.M. AX, BA, CB, DC, G, MC.

Holiday Inn-Roosevelt Boulevard   8900 Roosevelt Boulevard at Tremont Street. (14 miles northeast on Route 1, 6 miles south of Pennsylvania Turnpike Exit 28.) 671–9400. 270 rooms, 10 stories. Elevator. Single $21 up; Double $26 up. Pool. Restaurant 7 A.M.–10 P.M. Checkout 1 P.M. AX, BA, DC, G, MC.

Howard Johnson's   11580 Roosevelt Boulevard. (15 miles northeast on Route 1, 3 miles south of Pennsylvania Turnpike Exit 28.) 464–9500. 74 rooms, 2 stories. Single $18 up; Double $22 up. Pool. Restaurant 7 A.M.–11 P.M. Checkout 1 P.M. AX, BA, CB, DC, E, MC, T.

Marriott   City Line Avenue and Monument Road at Schuylkill Expressway. (6½ miles northwest on Route 1, 13 miles southeast of Pennsylvania Turnpike Exit 24.) 667–0200. 750

rooms, 4–6 stories. Elevator. Single $27 up; Double $33 up. Pool. Restaurant open 24 hours. Checkout 1 P.M. AX, BA, CB, DC, MC.

Penn Center Inn 20th and Market Streets. 569–3000. 304 rooms, 22 stories. Elevator. Single $21 up; Double $26 up. Pool. Restaurant 7 A.M.–10 P.M. Checkout 2 P.M. AX, BA, MC.

Sheraton Airport Inn At International Airport. 365–4150. 345 rooms, 9 stories. Elevator. Single $26 up; Double $31 up. Pool. Restaurant open 24 hours. Checkout noon. AX, BA, CB, DC, MC.

Sheraton Motor Inn 9461 Roosevelt Boulevard. (12 miles northeast on Route 1, 4 miles south of Pennsylvania Turnpike Exit 28.) 671–9600. 198 rooms, 6 stories. Elevator. Single $24 up; Double $31 up. Pool. Restaurant adjacent, 7 A.M.–11 P.M. Checkout noon. AX, BA, CB, DC, MC.

Treadway Roosevelt Inn 7600 Roosevelt Boulevard. (12 miles northeast on Route 1, 6 miles south of Pennsylvania Turnpike Exit 28.) 338–7600. 107 rooms, 2 stories. Single $19 up; Double $23 up. Pool. Restaurant 7 A.M.–midnight. Checkout noon. AX, BA, CB, DC, MC.

Warwick 17th and Locust Streets. 735–3800. 510 rooms, 20 stories. Elevator. Single $28 up; Double $35 up. Restaurant 7 A.M.–10 P.M. Checkout 1 P.M. AX, BA, CB, DC.

CHADDS FORD–CHESTER AREA *(Area Code 215)*

Howard Johnson's 1300 Providence Road at Edgemont Avenue, Chester. (At junction of Interstate 95 and Route 320.) 876–7211. 117 rooms, 7 stories. Elevator. Single $19 up; Double $22 up. Pool. Restaurant 7 A.M.–midnight. Checkout 1 P.M. AX, BA, CB, DC, E, MC, T.

VALLEY FORGE–KING OF PRUSSIA AREA
(Area Code 215)

Holiday Inn-Valley Forge 260 Goddard Boulevard. (1 block west of Route 202, ½ mile west of Pennsylvania Turnpike Exit 24.) 265–7500. 304 rooms, 5 stories. Elevator. Single $20 up; Double $25 up. Pool. Restaurant 7 A.M.–11 P.M. Checkout 1 P.M. AX, BA, CB, DC, G, MC.

Howard Johnson's   North on Route 202 at Gulph Road. (½ mile north of Pennsylvania Turnpike Exit 24.) 265–4500. 168 rooms, 2 stories. Single $18 up; Double $21 up. Pool. Restaurant adjacent, 6:30 A.M.–midnight. Checkout noon. AX, BA, CB, DC, E, MC, T.

Sheraton-Valley Forge   On Route 363. (Near Pennsylvania Turnpike Exit 24.) 337–2000. 250 rooms. Single $24 up; Double $30 up. Pool. Restaurant open 24 hours. Checkout noon. AX, BA, CB, DC, MC.

Stouffer's Valley Forge Inn   480 North Gulph Road. (½ mile southwest of Pennsylvania Turnpike Exit 24.) 337–1800. 300 rooms, 5 stories. Elevator. Single $22 up; Double $29 up. Pool. Restaurant 7 A.M.–10 P.M. Checkout 1 P.M. AX, BA, DC, MC.

Valley Forge Hilton   251 West DeKalb Pike. (On Route 202, 1 mile north of Pennsylvania Turnpike Exit 24.) 337–1200. 216 rooms, 8 stories. Elevator. Single $22 up; Double $27 up. Pool. Restaurant 7 A.M.–midnight. Checkout noon. AX, BA, CB, DC, MC.

YORK   *(Area Code 717)*

Billy Budd Inn   Arsenal Road at Toronita Street. (2 miles north on Route 30, ½ mile north of Interstate 83 Exit 9E.) 845–5671. 100 rooms, 2 stories. Single $16 up; Double $22 up. Pool. Restaurant 6 A.M.–10 P.M. Checkout noon. AX, BA, DC, MC.

Holiday Inn   2600 East Market Street. (3 miles east on Route 462.) 755–1966. 120 rooms, 2 stories. Single $17 up; Double $22 up. Pool. Restaurant 6 A.M.–10 P.M. Checkout noon. AX, BA, DC, G, MC.

Howard Johnson's   Arsenal Road. (1½ miles north at Interstate 83 Exit 9E.) 843–9971. 124 rooms, 2 stories. Single $16 up; Double $18 up. Pool. Restaurant 7 A.M.–midnight. Checkout noon. AX, BA, CB, DC, E, MC, T.

Modernaire   3311 East Market Street. (3½ miles east on Route 462, 2 miles east of Interstate 83 Exit 8E.) 755–9625. 21 rooms, 1–2 stories. Single $11 up; Double $14 up. Pool. Restaurant ½ mile, 7 A.M.–10 P.M. Checkout 11 A.M. BA.

York TraveLodge   132 North George Street. (1½ blocks

north on Interstate 83.) 843–8974. 58 rooms, 3 stories. Elevator. Single $12 up; Double $14 up. Restaurant opposite, 5:30 A.M.– 2 P.M. Checkout noon. AX, BA, CB, DC, MC.

York Valley Inn   3883 East Market Street. (4½ miles east on Route 462.) 755–2881. 166 rooms, 1–2 stories. Single $15 up; Double $18.50 up. Pool. Restaurant 11 A.M.–10 P.M. Checkout noon. AX, BA, DC, MC.

Thanks are due to the many regional Visitors' Centers and Chambers of Commerce for the motel and hotel information in this section.

Car Rentals

Rates vary from area to area and depend on the size of the car you require. Besides the standard daily rates—which range from approximately $11 to $24 plus a mileage charge—most companies have special weekly and weekend rates. Modest insurance fees are sometimes charged. Customers usually pay for the gasoline. Major credit cards are honored by the companies listed below.

Travelers who wish further information or need reservations for automobile rentals may use the following toll-free numbers:

AMERICAN INTERNATIONAL RENT-A-CAR	800–527–6346
AVIS RENT-A-CAR	800–231–6000
BUDGET RENT-A-CAR	800–228–9650
ECONO-CAR RENTAL	800–874–5000
HERTZ RENT-A-CAR	800–654–3131
NATIONAL RENT-A-CAR	800–328–4567
THRIFTY RENT-A-CAR	800–331–4200

(*Note:* In some areas it may be necessary to dial the digit 1 before 800.)

If you wish to contact a local office of any of the above car rental agencies, consult an appropriate telephone directory of the region.

Information for International Visitors

"Visit U.S.A." Program

Under the "Visit U.S.A." Program international travelers are entitled to transportation discounts. Visitors are advised to contact travel agents abroad, preferably in their country of residence. Completing arrangements before arriving in the United States will simplify procedures. An international traveler is one who lives more than 100 miles from the United States border and who arrives by commercial ship or airplane. All the information discussed below is subject to change. The prices quoted were in effect during 1974–1975 and are expected to rise.

Airplanes Several domestic airlines (including American, Braniff, Continental, Delta, Eastern, National, Northwest, TWA, and United) offer 25 percent discount on first-class and standard air fares within the forty-eight contiguous states providing the traveler remains in the U.S. thirteen to forty-five days. A twenty-one-day unlimited air travel ticket permits international visitors to take an unlimited number of flights on the combined routes of nine regional airlines. (Fare applies only when two or more transportation carriers are participating in this special program.) The cost for the twenty-one-day ticket is $200 plus $16 tax. For passengers two through twenty-one years old who are accompanied by parents or guardians, the price is $100 plus $8 tax.

The baggage allowance is usually sixty-six pounds. If a discount ticket is purchased in the United States, strict time requirements govern the period of purchase and use.

Trains An Amerail Discount of 25 percent is offered

to international travelers (except those from Canada and Mexico) who purchase train tickets from Amtrak-appointed travel agents overseas or from Amtrak representatives in the United States. Tickets are limited to sixty days from date of sale. This program does not apply to Metro-Liner service (a special commuter train) between Boston–New Haven–New York–Washington, although discount tickets are accepted on other trains along this route. Discounts are not granted for sleeper or parlor car accommodations.

Buses A "See the U.S.A." bus fare is offered by the Greyhound Bus Company and the Continental Trailways Bus Company. (Buses are equipped with small rest rooms and air conditioning.) International visitors are permitted unlimited travel and stopover privileges. The price is $99 for fifteen days (only when ticket is purchased overseas), $165 for one month, and $220 for two months.

Car Rentals Several automobile rental companies have special "packages" for persons from other countries who are over twenty-one years old and present appropriate credentials (including a certified driver's license).

Hertz Rent-A-Car offers several plans. A one-day rental for a Ford Pinto (or similar car) costs $8.59 plus a mileage charge. Customers must pay for the gasoline and must return the car to the city of origination. The Weekend or Holiday Plans cost $11.47 per day plus a mileage charge and gasoline. Discount rates on the Weekend Plan require a minimum two-day rental; discount rates on the Holiday Plan require a minimum seven-day rental. Hertz has other discount programs available and also extends a 10 percent discount to visitors from countries outside the Western Hemisphere (which does not apply to the special rates listed above).

National Rent-A-Car has a "See the U.S.A." discount for persons who make reservations prior to arrival in America. The "Circle Tour" Plan, which costs $108, permits a seven- or eight-day rental of a Chevrolet Vega (or similar car) with 1,000 free miles. For each day extra there is an added charge of $16. Customers wishing a larger car, such as a Chevrolet Impala, may take advantage of the "Vacation Special" Discount—$118 for a seven- or eight-day rental with 1,000 free miles. These discount prices are available only in the following cities: Atlanta, Boston, Chicago, Dallas, Miami, Minneapolis, New York, Orlando, Los Angeles, Philadelphia, Portland, San Francisco, Seattle, and Washington, D.C.

Budget Rent-A-Car has Chevrolet Vegas (or similar cars) at $11.95 a day and no mileage charge. Customers are expected to pay for gasoline. Larger automobiles are also available at special rates.

Travelers are advised to verify all rates and requirements before signing any agreements. The author and the publisher cannot be responsible for changes in programs or errors in information—nor for prices, procedures, accommodations, or services.

Aid for Travelers

The United States Travel Service (Washington, D.C., 202–967–3195) has instituted a program of placing multilingual receptionists at major United States airports. These receptionists are presently on duty in New York (Kennedy Airport), Seattle, Philadelphia, Boston, Bangor, and Washington, D.C. (Dulles International Airport). By 1976 similar services will exist in Los Angeles and San Francisco. These multilingual information specialists are usually located at Information Booths near customs desks or currency exchange centers.

Offices of the Travelers' Aid Society—an organization devoted to assisting visitors—are located throughout the United States. Listed below are offices in the Northeast.

BOSTON, MASSACHUSETTS	312 Stuart Street, (617) 542–7286.
ALBANY AREA, NEW YORK	180 Old London Road, Latham, (518) 785–1318.
UTICA, NEW YORK	167 Genesee Street, (315) 733–8794.
NEW YORK CITY, NEW YORK	204 East 39th Street, (212) 679–0200.
PITTSBURGH, PENNSYLVANIA	210 Penn Central Station, (412) 281–0482.
PHILADELPHIA, PENNSYLVANIA	1218 Chestnut Street, (215) 922–0950; Philadelphia International Airport, phone City Hall (215) 365–6525.

(*Note:* Dial the area code, the number in parentheses, only when you are located outside the region or state.)

The National Council for Community Services to International Visitors (referred to as COSERV) operates a program for the benefit of businessmen and persons in government service who are traveling in America. COSERV staffs help schedule appointments, conferences, and consultations as well as arrange sightseeing tours. International visitors requesting assistance must notify COSERV at least forty-eight hours in advance, carry health and accident insurance during travel, be short-term visitors in the community, and require no financial aid. Travelers with the appropriate credentials may contact the following offices located in the Northeast.

BOSTON, MASSACHUSETTS	Boston Council for International Visitors, 55 Mt. Vernon Street, (617) 742–0460.
ALBANY, NEW YORK	Albany International Center, 22 Willett Street, (518) 436–9741.
SYRACUSE, NEW YORK	International Center of Syracuse, 500 South Warren Street, (315) 471–0252 or 471–1222.
NEW YORK CITY, NEW YORK	International Center in New York, 745 Seventh Avenue, (212) 245–4131.
PHILADELPHIA, PENNSYLVANIA	Philadelphia Council for International Visitors, 34th Street and Civic Center Boulevard, (215) 686–1776.

More information may be obtained by writing the National Council for Community Services to International Visitors, 1630 Crescent Place N.W., Washington, D.C. 20009.

Another excellent program for overseas travelers has been established by the International Visitors Service Council (referred to as IVIS), which provides general information and arranges home hospitality for visitors to the Washington, D.C. area. Anyone who wishes to meet Americans in their homes (the "Americans at Home" Program) must file an application and appear for a personal meeting at the International Visitors Service Council, 801 19th Street N.W., Washington, D.C. IVIS also has bilingual volunteers available for assistance at international conferences. To learn more about these programs, telephone (202) 872–8747.

Home hospitality is also arranged by the U.S. SERVAS Committee, P.O. Box 790, Old Chelsea Station, New York, New York 10011. Persons wishing to meet Americans in their homes must submit an application and appear for an interview. SERVAS suggests a $25 donation for their services.

Travelers under the age of thirty may wish to take advantage of the series of newly created Vacation Accommodations Centers sponsored by the British Student Travel Center. Approximately twenty centers are operational in New York, Chicago, San Francisco, and Washington, D.C. Several affiliate hotels across the United States are also participating in the program. The rates for rooms are quite reasonable. For information and an application for a VAC Card contact Vacation Accommodations Centers, 700 Eighth Avenue, New York, New York 10036, or phone (212) 354-1210. Since this program is still in its infancy, accommodations are limited.

International travelers who need general information or assistance may also phone from 7 A.M. to 11 P.M. a toll-free number, 800-255-3050. Ask to speak to one of the multilingual receptionists (French, German, Spanish, and Japanese) at the U.S.A. Desk. This service is provided by TraveLodge.

Visitors from abroad may find the staffs of local American Express offices very helpful. Government tourist agencies, of course, also specialize in aiding travelers. The following offices are all located in New York City.

AUSTRIAN NATIONAL TOURIST OFFICE	545 Fifth Avenue (212) 697-0651.
BRITISH TOURIST AUTHORITY	680 Fifth Avenue (212) 581-4700.
CANADIAN GOVERNMENT TRAVEL BUREAU	680 Fifth Avenue (212) 757-4917.
FINNISH NATIONAL TRAVEL OFFICE	505 Fifth Avenue (212) 524-0763.
FRENCH GOVERNMENT TOURIST OFFICE	610 Fifth Avenue (212) 757-1125.

GERMAN NATIONAL TOURIST OFFICE	630 Fifth Avenue (212) 757–8570.
GREEK NATIONAL TOURIST OFFICE	601 Fifth Avenue (212) 421–5777.
INDIA GOVERNMENT TOURIST OFFICE	19 East 49th Street (212) 688–2245.
IRAN NATIONAL TOURIST OFFICE	630 Fifth Avenue (212) 757–1945.
IRISH TOURIST BOARD	590 Fifth Avenue (212) 246–7400.
ISRAEL GOVERNMENT TOURIST OFFICE	488 Madison Avenue (212) 593–1685.
ITALIAN GOVERNMENT TRAVEL OFFICE	630 Fifth Avenue (212) 245–4822.
JAPAN NATIONAL TOURIST ORGANIZATION	45 Rockefeller Plaza (212) 757–5640.
NETHERLANDS NATIONAL TOURIST OFFICE	576 Fifth Avenue (212) 245–5320.
PUERTO RICO GOVERNMENT TOURIST CENTER	8 West 51st Street (212) 245–8512.
SCANDINAVIA NATIONAL TOURIST OFFICE	505 Fifth Avenue (212) 687–5605.
SPANISH NATIONAL TOURIST OFFICE	589 Fifth Avenue (212) 759–3842.
SWISS NATIONAL TOURIST OFFICE	608 Fifth Avenue (212) 757–5944.

(*Note:* When calling from New York City, do not dial the area code 212.)

Anyone encountering serious difficulties should contact a nearby consulate or an embassy in Washington, D.C.

Miscellaneous Information

To find the telephone number of a person or an institution in a distant region of the United States, dial the area code, then 555–1212. Ask the operator for the information you need, then dial the call directly. Area codes of major cities are listed below.

ATLANTA	404	MILWAUKEE	414
BOSTON	617	MINNEAPOLIS	612
CHARLESTON	803	NEW ORLEANS	504
CHICAGO	312	NEW YORK	212
CLEVELAND	216	OMAHA	402
DALLAS	214	PHILADELPHIA	215
DETROIT	313	ST. LOUIS	314
HOUSTON	713	SAN FRANCISCO	415
LOS ANGELES	213	SEATTLE	206
MIAMI	305	WASHINGTON, D.C.	202

Shoppers who plan to purchase clothing in the United States should be aware of the differences in designating sizes.

WOMEN'S SWEATERS AND BLOUSES

Continent	U.S. / England
38	32
40	34
42	36
44	38
46	40
48	42

WOMEN'S DRESSES AND SUITS

Continent	U.S.	England
42	12	34
44	14	36
46	16	38
48	18	40
50	20	42

WOMEN'S SHOES

Continent	U.S. / England
36	4
37	5
38	6
39	7
40	8

MEN'S SHIRTS

Continent	U.S. / England
36	14
37	14½
38	15
39	15½
41	16
42	16½

MEN'S SUITS

Continent	U.S. / England
44	34
46	36
48	38
50	40
52	42
54	44

MEN'S SHOES

Continent	U.S. / England
39	7
40	8
41	9
42	10
43	11
44	12

Anyone driving an automobile in the United States should be familiar with the following measurement equivalents.

DISTANCE

Kilometers	Miles
1	⅝
2	1¼
3	1⅞
4	2½
5	3⅛
10	6¼

GASOLINE

Liters	Imperial (Brit.) Gallons	U.S. Gallons
1	0.22	0.26
5	1.10	1.32
10	2.20	2.64
20	4.40	5.28

Enjoy your visit here and return soon!

Index